# Emissary of the Doomed

# Ronald Florence

# Emissary
## of the
# Doomed

*Bargaining for Lives
in the Holocaust*

VIKING

VIKING

Published by the Penguin Group

Penguin Group (USA) Inc., 375 Hudson Street, New York, New York 10014, U.S.A. • Penguin Group (Canada), 90 Eglinton Avenue East, Suite 700, Toronto, Ontario, Canada M4P 2Y3 (a division of Pearson Penguin Canada Inc.) • Penguin Books Ltd, 80 Strand, London WC2R 0RL, England • Penguin Ireland, 25 St. Stephen's Green, Dublin 2, Ireland (a division of Penguin Books Ltd) • Penguin Books Australia Ltd, 250 Camberwell Road, Camberwell, Victoria 3124, Australia (a division of Pearson Australia Group Pty Ltd) • Penguin Books India Pvt Ltd, 11 Community Centre, Panchsheel Park, New Delhi – 110 017, India • Penguin Group (NZ), 67 Apollo Drive, Rosedale, North Shore 0632, New Zealand (a division of Pearson New Zealand Ltd) • Penguin Books (South Africa) (Pty) Ltd, 24 Sturdee Avenue, Rosebank, Johannesburg 2196, South Africa

Penguin Books Ltd, Registered Offices: 80 Strand, London WC2R 0RL, England

First published in 2010 by Viking Penguin, a member of Penguin Group (USA) Inc.

10  9  8  7  6  5  4  3  2  1

LIBRARY OF CONGRESS CATALOGING IN PUBLICAION DATA
Florence, Ronald.
    Emissary of the doomed : bargaining for lives in the Holocaust / Ronald Florence.
        p. cm.
    Includes bibliographical references and index.
    ISBN 978-0-670-02072-0
    1. Jews—Persecutions—Hungary.   2. Holocaust, Jewish (1939–1945)—Hungary.   3. World War, 1939–1945—Jews—Rescue—Hungary.  4. Brand, Joel, 1906–1964.  5. Hungary—Ethnic relations.  I. Title.
    DS135.H9F66 2010
    940.53'183509439—dc22        2009035922

Printed in the United States of America
Set in Granjon  •  Designed by Carla Bolte

*To the memory of the hundreds of thousands*
*who might have been saved*

*What a misery to be a minority: Hungarian & Jew.*
—Arthur Koestler


*Whoever has caused a single soul to perish from mankind*
   *Scripture imputes it to him*
   *as though he had caused a whole world to perish.*
*And whoever saves alive a single soul from mankind*
   *Scripture imputes it to him*
   *as though he had saved alive a whole world.*
—Mishna Sanhedrin 4:5

# CONTENTS

# Emissary of the Doomed

# I

## Budapest, April 1944

*At that time we knew nothing of Auschwitz.*
—Philip von Freudiger[1]

*God has sent me ahead of you to ensure your survival on earth, and to save your lives in an extraordinary deliverance.*
—Genesis 45:7

O n the morning of April 25, 1944, his thirty-eighth birthday, Joel Brand waited outside the Café Opera, across from the Budapest opera house on Andrássy Avenue. Normally, the early hour wouldn't have bothered him: the view of the grand Renaissance-style opera house through the leafy trees was restful, the café usually had a lively crowd, and it was never too early to find good conversation. But that morning Joel Brand was nervous and uneasy.[2]

By 1944, café life in most of central Europe had been reduced to ersatz coffee and cautious whispers. Wall posters listed *verboten* activities punishable by death. It was forbidden to walk on the streets between nine at night and five in the morning; forbidden to keep firearms; forbidden to aid, abet, or shelter escaped prisoners, enemy soldiers, or citizens of countries considered enemies of Germany; forbidden to listen to foreign radio broadcasts; forbidden to refuse German currency; forbidden to be in possession of newspapers other than Nazi-approved official rags. In Prague, Vienna, Bratislava, or Krakow, the cafés were quiet: years of German occupation had made fear too palpable for talk. But Budapest was different. In Budapest, the cafés were still lively. Musicians played, including an occasional fiddler or guitarist who knew something other than the traditional gypsy tunes. You could order Colombian coffee, sweet Tokay wine, fruit brandies, even real pastry if you knew where to look. Women came to the cafés, servant girls in embroidered blouses and full skirts, stylish women in Paris fashions, and the beckoning women who worked the cafés and nightclubs in the evenings. Country gentry showed up in tall boots with pheasant feathers in their hats. And there was conversation—business deals, furtive romances, and the relentless cynicism and wit of the wags.

In April 1944, only a month after German troops occupied Hungary, the Jews of Budapest found themselves living under unwelcome new restrictions, but they had not been confined to ghettos. They could still spend time with friends, meet for prayers, attend makeshift concerts, carry on love affairs, try to pursue their professions and businesses—and they were welcome in at least some of the cafés. Joel Brand was at home in that demimonde, a devotee of the pastry and brandy, the women, the card games, and especially the conversations. Officially, he was in the knitwear business with his wife Hansi, an attractive woman, dark, voluptuous, long-legged, and buxom. Hansi managed their workshop on Rozsa Street, not far from Andrássy Avenue and the Opera, where ten or twelve weavers picked up leather, patterns, and yarn and brought back stylish leather and knit gloves and fancy stockings. While Hansi ran the workshop, Joel was supposed to sell the gloves and stockings. He was gregarious, effective at selling, and adept at ferreting out black market goods that weren't readily available in the shops, like silk stockings, filtered cigarettes, French fragrances, and fine cake flour. But he wasn't happy as a salesman. He preferred meeting women, drinking, playing cards, and café talk. On a good night at poker he could win what he earned in a week of selling gloves. And he had discovered a pursuit even more exciting than poker.

Working with other Zionists in a secret organization called Vaada, the Hungarian rescue and aid committee,[3] Brand aided Jews in occupied Slovakia and Poland, and Polish Jews living underground in Vienna (they were called *U-boats*), who were desperate for help from outside, eager to escape Nazi ghettos and deportations to the relative safety of

Hungary, and willing to pay handsome commissions for false papers, escape routes, and help bringing their funds and goods with them. The German and Hungarian counterintelligence agents enjoyed the Budapest cafés as much as Brand did, and they would provide information about the Jews in Slovakia and Poland in exchange for bribes in cash or goods. Paid enough, the agents would overlook forged papers, suggest safe routes to smuggle refugees to the relative safety of Hungary, or look the other way at illegal border crossings and questionable identity papers. Brand's colleagues arranged the false papers, raised money for the bribes, and coordinated with other organizations in the Jewish communities. Brand's role was to meet the agents at coffeehouses like Ujpo or the Café Opera where he would negotiate and handle the clandestine payments. He learned when to lose at cards, and to ignore the blatant anti-Semitic comments of the Nazi counterespionage agents like Dr. Schmidt, who when he first met Brand at the Moulin Rouge, a Budapest nightclub off Andrássy Avenue, sent the half-naked women out of the room and said, "So you are Herr Brand, are you? You want to help the 'children' and I am ready to work with you in this. But we'll always refer to them as 'children' and nothing else. You understand?"[4]

Brand and his colleagues in Vaada could only rescue a few individuals at a time, but in late 1943, Oskar Schindler, a factory owner in Silesia, had come to Budapest and dined at the fancy Gellért Hotel, on the Buda bank of the Danube, with Joel Brand and Dr. Schmidt. Brand found Schindler fascinating. Schindler had owned a series of profitable businesses, and from the stories he and others told, he was adept at dealing with the Nazi authorities. By getting his businesses declared essential to the German war effort he succeeded in manipulating his way through the Nazi bureaucracies so he could employ and harbor Jewish workers even while the Jewish populations of the area were being systematically ghettoized and deported. Schindler was aware that Jews from Poland and Slovakia were being smuggled to safety in Hungary. He had contacts with Vaada and had carried funds to Europe from Istanbul for the Jewish Agency. He also knew how to cultivate the German agents and quickly picked up Dr. Schmidt's habit of referring to Jews as children.

3

Schindler's businesses had prospered. He was tall and handsome and lived well. Even in the midst of German requisitions and wartime shortages he managed to drive fancy cars like an Adler limousine, wore fine double-breasted suits, an expensive overcoat, custom-made shirts, and a gold-on-black-enamel *Hakenkreuz* on his lapel. He ordered the best food and drinks, hinted openly about his mistresses, and smoked cigarettes from a beautiful silver case.[5]

Joel Brand didn't flaunt fine clothes or jewelry, didn't have Schindler's panache with women and magnetism for the Germans who fawned over him, and had never experienced excitement and adventure like Schindler's dangerous flirtations with passport officials. Brand was short and chunky, with a broad face and nose, protruding ears, and unruly red hair. He had never been one of those dandies that the Hungarian cartoonists relentlessly lampooned, but he wasn't a *Luftmensch* either, those singular characters who survived on no visible source of income, always finding someone from whom they could finagle a cup of coffee, a glass of wine, or a bowl of soup. He was determined to make the best of a bad situation, enough that he was willing to wait outside the Café Opera for what a German counterespionage agent named Josef Winniger had told him would be an important meeting with a German official.

At 9:00 AM, exactly when Josef Winniger had said to be ready, a Mercedes sedan pulled up on Andrássy Avenue. From the shiny condition, the color, and the license plates Brand knew it was an official German car. A voice from inside the car said, "You are Herr Brand?"

He answered, "I am."

"Please get into the car."[6]

The Mercedes sped off. It would not have surprised Brand if they had driven to the Astoria Hotel, where the Gestapo had established their headquarters in Budapest. After the Gestapo turned the basement into a center for interrogations and torture, Hungarians who were used to dancing in the Astoria ballroom had learned to avoid the sidewalks outside, where the shrieks from the basement could be heard. But the Mercedes avoided the hotel and drove over the famed cable bridge across the Danube, around Castle Hill, and then steadily up the steep grades of the Swabenberg hills in Buda. The sweet fragrance of wisteria and lilac wafted from the woods where the oak trees were just coming into leaf. Purple jacaranda blossoms and the tiny magenta buds of Judas trees framed tantalizing peeks at the villas nestled into the hillsides. Swabenberg, or as the Hungarians called it, Svábhegy, was a forested resort of villas and hotels, far enough from the hurly-burly of the city below to be quiet and restful. Joel Brand knew the area well. Just two months before, Hansi and the children had moved out of their apartment on Buljovsky Street in the working-class suburbs to the east of downtown Pest while their apartment was fumigated, and took temporary rooms at the Majestic Hotel in Swabenberg.[7] They had stayed there on earlier occasions when their apartment was overcrowded with refugees or when their youngest son's asthma flared up.

Just past the village of Svábhegy, with its station for the cog railway that led up from the city below, the Mercedes turned into a familiar side road and pulled up across from the Majestic Hotel at a twenty-four-room guesthouse called the Little Majestic. It was smaller and more luxurious than the Majestic, and nestled into the hillside, secluded by dense stands of pine and oak and surrounded by a well-tended park and a hanging-garden.[8] SS guards saluted when Brand and the plainclothesmen from the car entered the ground floor. Brand was told to wait there under the guns of the guards before he was escorted to a large office. The door was marked SONDEREINSATZKOMMANDO, IVB, JEWISH DEPARTMENT.[9] Inside, a man of medium height and build, with thinning fair hair, stood in front of a table, legs astride, with his hands on his hips. He had large ears, thin lips, and blue eyes that seemed small for his face. He wore the uniform of an SS *Untersturmbannführer*, the equivalent of a lieutenant colonel.

"Do you know who I am?" the man behind the desk shouted.

Before Joel Brand could respond, the *Untersturmbannführer* answered his own question: "I am Eichmann."

A day before, and two hundred kilometers north of Budapest, a young man dressed in a Dutch tweed jacket, white sweater, woolen riding breeches, and riding boots—expensive-looking clothing that would have been difficult to come by in wartime—showed up at the office of a Dr. Pollack in Cadca, a market town in northern Slovakia. He explained to the nurse that he had to see the doctor privately to discuss a "gentleman's disease."[10]

The young man did not have a gentleman's disease, but on close examination his clothes were filthy and his feet were badly swollen. While Dr. Pollack cut off the young man's riding boots, bandaged his feet, and gave him carpet slippers to wear, the young man explained that he had crossed the border from occupied Poland "on his stomach." A Slovak farmer had given him Dr. Pollack's name, explaining that because of the shortage of physicians, Jewish doctors had been exempted from the deportations. The young man then told the astonished doctor that he and his friend, who was waiting outside, had escaped from the Nazi camp at Oswiecim, Poland, known in the West by its German name, Auschwitz.

Dr. Pollack gave the young man an address where he and his friend could hide, and quietly notified a member of the local Jewish Committee. A day later, the two young men were told to wait in a park in the provincial town of Zilina. Dressed in peasant shirts, with their almost shaved heads and a bottle of slivovitz they were told to carry, they looked like newly recruited soldiers on leave before they were sent to the front. Erwin Steiner, a member of the Slovakian Jewish Committee, met them at the park and arranged for them to come to a clandestine meeting in a home for the aged.

The members of the Jewish Committee—Dr. Oskar Neumann, recognized by the authorities as the official spokesman for Slovakia's Jews, and his colleagues the engineer Oskar Krasnansky and Steiner—were well known and respected in the Slovakian Jewish community. When Czechoslovakia was dismembered after the 1938 Munich agreement between Hitler and Chamberlain, the premier, Monsignor Josef Tiso, found himself the head of state of a new rump Slovakia. Jewish community leaders in Slovakia, aware of the Nuremberg Laws and other measures against the Jews in Germany, organized themselves and established an office in Bratislava. As Nazi-inspired anti-Jewish measures were introduced into Slovakia by the compliant Tiso, the Jewish Committee tried to intervene by petitioning officials, offering quasi-legal payments and bribes, and applying whatever pressure they could exert through contacts abroad. In 1942, when they heard about what the German and Slovakian officials were calling a "resettlement" program for Slovakian Jews—rounding up the entire Jewish populations of villages and towns for deportation to what were called "labor camps"—the committee tried to mitigate the disruptions to families and the hardships of the journeys. They brought food and water to the railroad stations where Jews were loaded onto the trains of cattle cars that would take them to the camps in Poland. The committee provided soothing words and prayers, reassurances to those who were about to be torn from the only homes they had ever known. They took down names and addresses of deportees, so they could notify relatives and try to keep families who had been separated in touch with one another. Although they were powerless to halt the deportations, they kept detailed ledgers with the names, addresses, and ages of those who had been sent off for resettlement.[11] The information was important, a record for the families, for legal authorities, and for history. They planned to use the records to someday bring families back together. The members of the Jewish Committee considered themselves responsible for the Jewish community.

Over a period of months, they had watched helplessly as sixty thousand Slovakian Jews, from shtetls, villages, and cities, boarded the cattle cars, seventy-five to each car, with a single bucket of water and another bucket that would serve as the only toilet. When the trains left, everyone aboard seemed to disappear. No one came back from the labor camps. There were never reports that anyone had been released because of health or age, or sent home for family or other reasons. No one had sent as much as a postcard back from the camps. No one escaped. Some of the Slovak guards who had been on the trains until they reached the Polish border talked about what awaited the Jews, but the Slovak police and soldiers had been known to taunt Jews, and their remarks could be dismissed as idle threats and scare tactics. Occasional postcards from relatives in Poland told stories of terrible atrocities in the camps in Poland and Silesia, but the writers were Poles, not Slovaks. Later, scattered propaganda broadcasts from the West reported atrocities in the German-run concentration camps—stories of terrible conditions, starvation, typhus, and dysentery, and rumors of arbitrary executions, killing squads, and mass burials. But the stories were always second- or third- or fourth-hand. A reporter in the West had heard from someone with connections inside occupied Europe, who had heard stories from someone who mysteriously had heard from one of the German-run labor camps. No firsthand witness ever came forward.

The members of the Jewish Committee tried to make sense of the rumors. Some argued that the worst of the rumors about the deportations from Poland and Slovakia must be true, that those who had been sent away had been murdered, annihilated.[12] It was a logical conclusion from the fact that so many had been deported and never heard from again. But for many who knew they too were at risk for a future deportation, it was a difficult mental journey from the terrifying rumors, stories of what *might* have happened, to the acceptance or internalization of the possibilities.[13] Those who lived in constant peril, who had seen their families and friends shipped off in cattle cars, did what they could, *whatever it took,* to fend off hopelessness. Hope and the determination to survive justified ignoring or denying scraps of evidence and apparent logic that in different circumstances might have been compelling. Without indisputable facts, with no firsthand evidence, the terrible stories remained only rumors. What might seem a denial of the truth to some was a blessing for others: those with relatives and friends who had been deported could still hope, could carefully put away the clothing and possessions of those who had left on the trains, keep a place clear at the table, and look forward to the day when the missing would finally return.

The Jewish Committee had nowhere to turn for help in Slovakia. They had tried to get immigration permits to Palestine for Jews trapped by the new regulations, but there were limited permits available, and the Turkish authorities would allow only eight Jews per week to transit through Turkey. In desperation the committee appealed to the local Catholic hierarchy for compassion. In March 1943 the bishops of the Roman Catholic

Church in Slovakia met, declared their sympathy for the plight of the Jews, and ordered a pastoral letter decrying the deportations read from the pulpits in parish churches. Their letter was written in Latin, a language few in Slovakia understood.[14]

The Jewish Committee had been in sporadic contact with rescue organizations in neutral Switzerland and Turkey. Through connections in Geneva and Istanbul they had exchanged information with the International Red Cross, the American Joint Distribution Committee (JDC), and the Jewish Agency in Jerusalem. They encouraged and followed efforts by the Red Cross and the JDC to send supplies to those who had been deported. They had gotten reports of the visits of delegations from the International Red Cross that had inspected the concentration camp at Theresienstadt in northern Bohemia, the only Nazi camp that allowed visitors. From the reports it certainly was no spa, but the Red Cross described the camp as clean and orderly, with decent food, health services, and cultural activities like orchestras, chamber groups, painting classes, and dramatic presentations. Excerpts of the reports circulated among the remaining Jews in Slovakia. The committee could only hope the reports were reassuring to those families who had seen relatives and friends deported to camps in Poland.

The two young men—their names were Walter Rosenberg and Alfred Wetzler—met the Jewish Committee members in the comfortable living room of a home for the elderly in Zilina. Rosenberg explained that the distinctive clothes they had initially worn had been "organized"—a camp euphemism for stolen—from the part of Auschwitz they called Kanada, where goods taken from the arriving Jews were sorted and inventoried. They showed the committee members the numbers tattooed on their forearms: Rosenberg was 44070, his companion Fred Wetzler was 29192. To the astonishment and disbelief of the committee members, they recounted their harrowing escape from the newer Birkenau camp at Auschwitz. They had prepared for months: a Russian in the camp taught them to not trust their legs but to become invisible, to carry no money so they would not be tempted to buy anything, to use strong Russian tobacco soaked in water to fool the tracking dogs, to take a knife for hunting, a razor in case they were captured, and a watch to time their journeys and make sure they were never caught out of hiding during daylight. They were forbidden to carry papers in the camp, and had to memorize everything, including a map of Silesia from a child's atlas they had studied in a camp latrine. Learning from the failed escape attempts of others, they hid for three days in a woodpile at a construction site inside the camp perimeter, using Russian tobacco to ward off the search dogs. Already past a water-filled moat six yards wide and five yards deep, and a barbed-wire high-voltage fence five yards high, they waited until the Germans called off the three thousand men and two hundred dogs that were on call to patrol the no-man's-land, and only then escaped over the outer fence. To avoid the roads from southern Poland into Slovakia, they forded streams and walked in the woods. As they snuck along the Sola River at night, peasant girls dropped off half-kilo loaves of bread "by accident."[15]

Rosenberg and Wetzler were offered sherry, then led into a dining room laid out with a clean white tablecloth and sparkling cutlery. They ate heartily and spoke in a rush, describing the facilities at the camp and the precise and unvarying procedures by which Jewish deportees were received from the trains. Rosenberg explained the methodical rigidity of the protocols the Germans followed as they separated a few who were strong and young enough to work from each arriving train and sent the rest to gas chambers, and from there to huge crematoria. As a laborer in the camp, he had counted the arriving cattle cars, taken an informal census of those who were spared to work in the camp, and counted the trucks that left the unloading ramp area after the arrival of each train, each truck carrying exactly one hundred Jews. He had also gotten reports of the "goods" taken from those sent to the gas chambers and counts from those who dealt with the bodies at the crematoria. He had used the information to estimate the number of Jews murdered at the camp, calculating in his head because it was forbidden to have pencil and paper. He had gone over the figures and his methods carefully and was sure of his numbers. By his calculations, at least 1,760,000 Jews had already been murdered at Auschwitz.[16]

The members of the committee listened politely. What Walter Rosenberg and Fred Wetzler reported was horrifying, but the committee members had heard shocking stories before. They had long steeled themselves against rumors that might prove unfounded and that would only further depress an already suffering Jewish population.

When the meal was finished, the table was cleared and liqueurs and cigars were brought out. At that moment, Walter Rosenberg looked around the table at his hospitable hosts and suddenly had the horrible feeling "that they did not believe a word we were saying."[17] He caught himself and realized that *of course no one would believe what he had said.* "How could they? Human minds had yet to be trained to absorb the thought of mass-murder on an Auschwitz scale." He and Fred Wetzler were the first people ever to escape from Auschwitz, the first to bring out the unbelievable facts of what went on in the camp at the end of the railroad spur where trainload after trainload of Jews from the cities and towns of Europe arrived daily.

After the liqueurs, Rosenberg and Wetzler were led into another room, where members of the committee produced some of the ledger books in which they had carefully recorded the names of deported Jews. The committee members were cordial and polite, but did not conceal their skepticism.

"When, for instance, did you leave, Mr. Rosenberg?" one of the men asked.

"June 14th, 1942," Rosenberg said. He knew the date as well as he knew his own birthday.

The man flipped pages in the ledger until he found the page he wanted. Heads around the room nodded. "Where did you leave from?" the man asked.

Rosenberg answered, "Novasky."

There were more nods. "Can you name any of the people on the transport with you?"

Rosenberg prided himself on his memory. From the day he boarded that train, crushed into a cattle car, he had determined to remember what he saw. He reeled off the names of thirty people who had been on the train with him. He saw the man's finger trace up and down the page of the ledger at each name. Around the room everyone watched the same finger, their suspicious glances turning slowly to masks of horror as they realized that Rosenberg had indeed gone to Auschwitz with a transport of Slovakian Jews, which meant that he must have escaped from the camp, that he had in fact been a witness to the horrors he and Wetzler had described.

"They realized, I think, at that moment," Rosenberg wrote later, "that the heavy covers of their books held nothing but obituaries. . . . The myth of the resettlement areas was melting in their minds and the shock was terrible."[18]

But even as he named those on the deportation train with him, Rosenberg could still see skepticism in the eyes staring at him. The gap between what he had seen and recounted and what the members of the Jewish Committee had long allowed themselves to believe was too great to bridge in a moment. The committee members had hoped and almost convinced themselves that the rumors they had heard about places like Auschwitz were *bobemayses,* old wives' tales. Only that belief had allowed them to continue pretending that their records and efforts to engage the Red Cross and provide food and water at the stations when Jews were deported mattered. As soon as they allowed themselves to believe that the resettlement journeys to Poland were one-way trips, that the tens of thousands from Slovakia and the hundreds of thousands from Poland who had taken those cattle trains would never come back, that they had gone not to labor camps but to their annihilation—if the rumors of mass executions, gas chambers, and crematoria were actually true—all that the committee members had done was for naught. The careful records they had kept had been a charade. The notifications they had so diligently provided to families were nothing but false hopes.

Earlier in the war, there had been different stories of atrocities. After the first battles of the German blitzkrieg campaign against the Soviet Union, tales came back of Jews given shovels, told to dig trenches, then lined up at the edges of the graves they had dug and shot by SS machine gunners. There were stories of trucks specially fitted to inject carbon monoxide exhaust from the engine into a sealed compartment at the rear where Jews were confined in a space too tight for movement. For many, those stories were also too horrible to believe.

Slovakia was close enough to Austria and Germany to have long felt the pull and pressure of German *Kultur*. Although Slovakian was the official language, with smatterings of Polish in the north, Hungarian in the south, and Ukrainian in the east, educated people, especially in the cities, learned German. They read German literature, listened to German-language broadcasts from Vienna, and used German as their lingua franca for travel. They had long listened to German music, viewed and purchased German art, celebrated German technology and crafts. For anyone steeped in the composers and authors and dramatists of the German enlightenment, the rumors from the Ukraine and Poland, stories of unparalleled cruelties and barbarism, were too fantastic to believe. For Slovakians, used to looking toward the west for *Kultur* and civilization, it was easier to believe stories of Soviet than German atrocities.

The Jews in Slovakia had seen Nazi excesses and outrages. They had seen goods and homes appropriated by the Germans. They had watched the ghettoization of Jews, families forced into cramped spaces in confined quarters, fenced off with barbed wire and electric fencing. They had seen the relentless expropriations, the stripping away of the right to work, the loss of the freedoms to meet or pray or shop, the imposition of humiliations like the yellow Star of David that Jews had to wear on their outer clothing. The application of the once-shocking Nuremberg Laws had become so common in central Europe that once-unthinkable anti-Jewish measures had become a new baseline, a bizarre new norm for Jewish life. And yet as horrible as the outrages were, they were still hard to believe as something other than a temporary aberration. People who had looked to Germany as the nation of enlightenment, the land of Beethoven and Mendelssohn and Goethe and Lessing, could not easily accept the extremes of the new Nazi Germany. An upstart like Hitler, with his outrageous rhetoric and ugly tirades, might have become the head of state and government of Germany, and exerted authority over proud institutions like the German army, the Reichstag, the universities, and the cultural institutions. But few wanted to believe that the German people, ordinary Germans from city and town and farm, could become cold-blooded killers. It took a total collapse of faith in what had long been the admired and respected *Kultur* of central Europe to believe that ordinary Germans would operate gas chambers and crematoria as if they were a factory, that they would participate willingly in a massive enterprise that had as its sole products the ill-gotten gains of expropriation and the deaths of millions. The few who recognized that Hitler and Himmler had "concocted a radical new way of withdrawing them [the Jews] from Europe" were prophets out of their time, and mostly ignored.[19]

And so, even after Walter Rosenberg's precise recollections of his own deportation and his exact recall of names of others on the train, the committee members were hesitant to believe him. No one had come back from Auschwitz before. How could they suddenly trust these two young men?

The committee members decided to take Rosenberg and Wetzler into separate rooms for further questioning. Stenographers were brought into the two rooms, and Rosenberg and Wetzler were independently asked to dictate detailed statements about their experiences, from their initial journey to Auschwitz through their escape.

Walter Rosenberg had been preparing for that opportunity from the moment, almost two years before, when he realized that he was on a journey from which there was little hope of returning. He had always had a good memory in school, and he invented mnemonic tricks to help him remember details. With the members of the Jewish committee listening, and the secretary writing as fast as she could to take down his words, he described what he had seen from the moment he arrived at the train siding in the camp and found himself selected for work. He described how he estimated the numbers of people who arrived on the cattle trains that came to the spur at Auschwitz, and how many of them then disappeared. One of his jobs at Auschwitz was as a *Blockschreiber*, a term the Germans loosely translated as "pen pusher." He described how the Germans kept detailed records of how many people arrived and what happened to them. He explained the machinery of the extermination factory and its commercial side, the vast profits that the Nazis reaped from the gold, jewelry, money, clothing, shoes, artificial limbs, spectacles, prams, and human hair that were systematically taken from the arriving Jews, cataloged, and packaged for resale or reshipment to "deserving" parties in Germany. He explained how even the ashes from the crematoria were used as fertilizer. Everything he said was news: the selection procedure at the railroad ramp, how the young and strong were sent to work while the rest were condemned on the spot to their deaths, and the horrifying confidence trick by which 1,760,000 Jews had been lured to the gas chambers. His testimony took hours.

While Rosenberg was describing what he had seen and remembered, Fred Wetzler was in another room, with another stenographer, telling a similar story. Later that evening, the members of the committee compared the two transcripts. They differed in details. Although Rosenberg and Wetzler were from the same town in Slovakia, they had arrived at Auschwitz at different times and by different routes, were in different barracks, worked at different jobs at the camp, and were assigned to different sectors as the camp was expanded to include a second facility called Birkenau on the other side of the railroad tracks. For the first year they were at Auschwitz they never met, and it was only shortly before Rosenberg discovered the possibility of escape that they got together. But enough of their independent stories matched that the members of the committee realized the two young men were telling the truth.

The committee members agreed that if the horrifying details these two young men had described were widely known, it would surely put an end to the denials of the atrocities perpetrated on the Jews of Europe. It would almost certainly focus the attention of the United Nations, as the Allies in the West were called, on the dire situation of the Jews. And once the truth about the fate of the Jews was known, the Allies and the relief organizations would surely turn their attention to the Jews, they would do whatever had to be done to stop the murders and rescue those who had managed to survive. Beginning that night, and working feverishly, the members of the committee edited the two transcripts into a single report. By April 27 they had finished their editing, and Rosenberg and

Wetzler were given an opportunity to read through the finished report. They each found a few inaccuracies but agreed that it was more important to get the report out to the world than to lose time retyping it for minor corrections.[20]

The Slovakian Jewish Committee, aware that even possession of the report put the entire committee in danger, agreed to have the incendiary document translated from the original Slovak into German and smuggled to the western Allies. The translation and copying would have to be done in secrecy. The committee was also concerned for the personal safety of Rosenberg and Wetzler. There were no doubt fugitive warrants out for them, and May 1 was a traditional trade union holiday in Slovakia, when the police took special precautions to prevent anti-Nazi demonstrations, including unannounced searches of houses, schools, and suspicious residences. If the two refugees from Auschwitz were discovered in one of those searches, they and the Jewish community that was hiding them would be in great danger. The committee concluded that safest place for the two young men was in the High Tatra mountains in northern Slovakia. Someone suggested a town named Litovsky Svaty Mikulas where they could be hidden among an unsuspecting gentile population. The committee offered them forged identity papers with new names. Wetzler chose to keep his name; Rosenberg chose Rudolf Vrba, a not unusual Czechoslovakian name, as his new nom de guerre.

The committee entrusted the dangerous job of reproducing the report to a Jew named Josef Weiss, who worked at the Office for Prevention of Venereal Disease in Bratislava, where statistics on sexually transmitted diseases were collected. Potential embarrassments in the office files and the delicacy of the issue in a Catholic country meant that officials and the police would be reluctant to come to his office. The committee dispatched one of the copies Weiss made to the office of the Jewish Agency in Istanbul via what they had been told was a reliable courier. Another copy went to Rabbi Dov-Ber Weissmandel, the son-in-law of the respected rabbi of Nitra, the head of the Orthodox Jewish community in Slovakia. Weissmandel offered to smuggle the report to the Geneva office of Hechalutz, the Zionist youth organization in Switzerland, and his father-in-law agreed to have the report translated into Yiddish. A third copy was hand-delivered to Monsignor Giuseppe Burzio, the papal chargé d'affaires in Bratislava.[21] The committee hoped that Burzio would get his copy to the Vatican, that Hechalutz would get its copy to representatives of the American and British governments, that the copy sent to Istanbul would reach Palestine and the Jewish Agency, and that the Yiddish copy would reach other distinguished and respected Orthodox rabbis. Once the report was in the hands of the right people, they assumed, it would bring swift responses from the pope, from the governments of Britain and the United States, and from the relief agencies they had long tried to contact.

Walter Rosenberg, now known as Rudolf Vrba, had one final concern before he went into hiding in the Tatra Mountains. He explained to the committee members that while Auschwitz had been a relentlessly gray and unchanging factory of death, a monotony of sameness, there were a few moments he remembered vividly. One such moment was at exactly 10:00 AM on January 15, 1944. Rosenberg was working in Birkenau, the newer section of the complex, at a facility called the Quarantine Camp where he watched a group of Polish prisoners with theodolites and other surveying equipment begin preparations for new construction. He recognized a prisoner on the other side of the fence, a German political prisoner from Berlin named Joseph who had served as a *kapo* (a trustee assigned to administrative or specialized duties). Rosenberg and the other prisoners knew him as Kapo Yup.

Through the fence, Rosenberg asked Kapo Yup what he and the other prisoners were doing. Yup asked for some cigarettes before he explained that they were building a road that would run straight from the loading ramp alongside the rail tracks to new crematoria that had been built on the Birkenau side of the camp. Kapo Yup then told Rosenberg that he had heard from an SS man that one million Jews from Hungary would be arriving at Auschwitz soon, and the old ramp facilities, which required long lines of trucks to take the Jews to the gas chambers and crematoria, were inadequate to process such numbers.[22]

Auschwitz was built on lies. Each group of arrivals was greeted with lies. Their eagerness to believe those lies was the only way to maintain the smooth efficiency of the process by which millions were annihilated. But a few who were young and strong and resilient enough to survive at Auschwitz, like Walter Rosenberg, had been there long enough to learn how to recognize the occasional truth in what they saw and heard. Before he left for a safe house in the High Tatras with his new name, Walter Rosenberg warned the members of the Jewish Committee: "One million Hungarians are going to die. Auschwitz is ready for them. But if you tell them now, they will rebel. They will never go to the ovens. Your turn is coming. But now it is the Hungarians' hour. You must tell them immediately."

"Don't worry," the committee members assured him. In addition to translating the report into German, they had also translated a copy into Hungarian. "We are in daily contact with the Hungarian Jewish leaders. Your report will be in their hands first thing tomorrow." They made good on their promise. On April 28, 1944, three days after Joel Brand met with Adolf Eichmann, his Vaada colleague Rezső Kasztner traveled to Bratislava and was given a copy of what they were now calling the Auschwitz Protocols.[23]

While Rosenberg and Wetzler were still in Zilina, a train from Hungary passed through the town carrying Jews en route to Poland. Representatives of the local Slovakian Jewish community were on hand at the station, and passed milk and cookies to the unwitting Jews crowded into the cattle cars.[24]

Joel Brand had heard of him and knew his reputation, but Adolf Eichmann wasn't widely known in 1944.[25] Rumors and occasional travelers' reports testified to the brutal efficiency of the ghettoizations and deportations of hundreds of thousands of Jews from Poland, Holland, Slovakia, and Greece to camps in Poland and German Silesia, and Eichmann was often credited as the shadowy figure who directed those huge actions. The deportations had taken place during crucial phases of the war on the Eastern Front, when German armies were engaged in the decisive battles at Stalingrad and Kursk. That Eichmann had successfully requisitioned rolling stock to transport Jews to "resettlement" camps in Poland, fighting off challenges for freight cars from army logistics offices and other claimants who wanted to use the railcars to carry men, provisions, and equipment for the battlefront armies and the occupation forces, testified to his bureaucratic talents and dedication. Brand and his colleagues on rescue groups like Vaada also knew that there had been no significant disruptions of Eichmann's practiced and brutally efficient procedures. There were stories in the cafés about the Warsaw ghetto uprising in the spring of 1943, but they focused mostly on the brutal crushing of the revolt, when some seven thousand of the fifty-six thousand captured Jews were shot and the rest deported to camps.

After the German occupation of Hungary in mid-March 1944, they knew that Eichmann was facing his ultimate mission: Hungary, the largest intact Jewish population in Europe, and especially Budapest with its great synagogue, an opera and museums patronized by the Jews, boulevards of grand houses owned by Jews, huge industrial enterprises managed by Jews, legal and medical professions where Jews were prominent, and a vibrant culture in which Jews were visible and celebrated as both artists and patrons. For the Nazis, Budapest—the Nazis sometimes called the city "Judapest"—was the crown jewel of European Judaism, the ultimate target of the Final Solution.

Gossip in the Budapest cafés already reported on the perquisites Eichmann had seized from Hungarian Jews, rewards for his bureaucratic and logistics triumphs, including a luxurious residence on Apostol Street, the former villa of Lipót Aschner, general director of the Egyesült Izzó electric bulb factory, one of the largest industrial firms in Hungary. Aschner had been sent to the Mauthausen concentration camp. Eichmann was said to have a riding horse at his disposal, and a special *Schwimmwagen* amphibious vehicle in which he was chauffeured over hills and through streams in the countryside outside Budapest. As Brand discovered, Eichmann also had luxurious private offices in the Little Majestic Hotel in the Buda hills.

Brand knew why he was there. For weeks, even before the Germans invaded Hungary on March 19, Brand's organization, the Vaada, had been secretly negotiating with the Gestapo and agents of the Abwehr, a counterintelligence agency established when Germany was forbidden to have offensive intelligence capabilities under the Versailles treaty. The agents sometimes mentioned Eichmann as the head of Department 4B of the Security Police, or passed on decisions that were attributed to Eichmann. For those who had tried to understand the complexities and nuances of the vast enterprise of deporting the Jews of Europe to camps in Poland and Silesia, the name evoked awe.

But standing only a few feet away, Brand was struck by the unremarkable ordinariness of Eichmann's appearance. He was not grossly fat like the Abwehr agents who overindulged on rich Hungarian pastries. He did not wear gaudy custom uniforms and jeweled decorations or surround himself with fine art and expensive *objets* like the infamous Hermann Goering. Eichmann had a small face, thin lips, and a sharp nose. He moved and spoke quickly, with a trace of awkwardness in his manners, as if he were uncomfortable with the meeting. He seemed humorless.

"I expect you know who I am," Eichmann said. "I was in charge of the actions in Germany, Poland, and Czechoslovakia. Now it is Hungary's turn. I have got you here so that we can talk business. I have already investigated you and your people of the Joint and the Jewish Agency. And I have verified your authority to make a deal."

Eichmann's words came out in clipped sentences punctuated by unexpected pauses, like staccato bursts from a machine gun. He spoke a horrible mixture of Berlin and Austrian accents, and even Brand, whose own German was not polished, noticed that Eichmann used a few words incorrectly. A tall, smartly dressed civilian stood behind Eichmann. A woman stenographer stood behind Joel Brand, writing down Eichmann's words. Brand was unable to sneak in a word, and nothing could have prepared him for what Eichmann would say next.

"Now then," Eichmann continued. "I am prepared to sell you one million Jews. Not the whole lot—you wouldn't be able to raise enough money for that. But you could manage a million. Blood for money, money for blood.

"You can take them from any country you like, wherever you can find them. From Hungary, Poland, the eastern provinces, from Terezin, from Oswiecim—wherever you will. Whom do you want to save? Men who can produce children? Women who can bear them? Old people? Children? Sit down and tell me."[26]

Brand did not sit down. The number Eichmann named—one million—was greater than the entire Jewish population of Hungary. The Hungarian Jews had enjoyed a privileged position since the beginning of the war, almost untouched by the restrictions, ghettoizations, and deportations that had marked German administration of the rest of occupied Europe. They had attributed their good fortune to the uniqueness of Hungarian Jewry, but that had all changed a month before when the Germans arrived in force. Hungary was now the largest intact Jewish population in Europe. Eichmann shockingly was bargaining for their freedom and their lives.

Eichmann didn't mention what he wanted in return, but there would surely be a price. Brand knew the demands would be enormous. In earlier negotiations, lower-level Gestapo agents had asked for $2 million to permit the emigration of a small number of Jews. That was already more than Vaada could hope to raise, especially with Gestapo agents on the streets of Budapest. Eichmann would certainly demand more than $2 million. Only the American Jews and the international organizations, or the governments of Britain and the United States, could conceivably provide the enormous sums Eichmann would demand. And so far there had been almost no help from the American Jews, the international agencies, or the western Allies. There had been some hand-wringing—messages with sympathetic words and a few stirring speeches from officials—but almost no money and no promises of rescue or aid for the Jews of Europe. Brand knew real help from the West might not come until British and American forces landed in Europe, the long-awaited second front. Then, there would be open communications channels to the West, the possibility of launching effective appeals and receiving direct aid from the American Jews and the international organizations. And the Allied forces would be in a position to intervene directly, to destroy the camps and rescue the Jews. But that would take time. Before he said a word, Brand knew his first priority was to bargain for time.

"Colonel," he said. "You are putting me in a most difficult position.

You are asking me to decide who shall survive and who shall be murdered. I cannot agree to do that. I do not want a single one of my people to lose his life."

Eichmann answered with a smile, as though Brand's words had been a compliment.

"I am a German idealist," Eichmann said. "I regard you as an idealistic Jew. Today I am able to sit at a table with you and discuss business. Tomorrow, maybe, I shall have to talk in a different tone."[27]

Eichmann didn't name a price. They would meet again, he said. Then they would talk about the specifics of the barter for one million Jewish lives. He told Joel Brand he was interested not in money but in goods. He liked one phrase enough to repeat it. *"Blut gegen wäre,"* he said. Blood for goods.

Brand was confused by Eichmann's phrase. He assumed they would want cash, Swiss francs or American dollars, but Eichmann said that money comes second. Only after Eichmann repeated the ominous phrase did Brand ask what goods Eichmann had in mind.

"Go to your international authorities," Eichmann said. "They will know. For example—trucks. I could imagine one truck for a hundred Jews, but that is only a suggested figure. Where will you go?"

Brand hesitated to answer. The only places where he could contact relief organizations or try to contact the Allies would be neutral Switzerland or Istanbul. From Switzerland he would be able to telephone London. But Istanbul was the forward base of the Jewish Agency, which had been supplying the modest funds they had smuggled into concentration camps and ghettos. He had contacts with the Jewish Agency representatives. And Istanbul was closer to Palestine.

"I need to think," Brand said.

"Yes," Eichmann answered. "Think it over."[28] Eichmann asked Brand if he had any family.

A wife and two children, Brand said.

"They will stay here," said Eichmann.

# 2

## When the Germans Came

*The German fears the defenseless, the weak and the sick. . . . That which drives the German to cruelty, to deeds most coldly, methodically and scientifically cruel, is fear. Fear of the oppressed, the defenseless, the weak, the sick; fear of women and of children, fear of the Jews.*

—Curzio Malaparte[1]

*What has been done in Germany, Austria, Czechoslovakia and Poland in years has been done in Hungary in a few weeks' time—it all came about very quickly, all the laws and oppressions against the Jews came in Hungary in a very short time.*

—Joel Brand[2]

The first yellow Stars of David appeared on the streets of Budapest on April 5, 1944, three weeks before Joel Brand's meeting with Eichmann. The crudely made stars had been hastily sewn on outer clothing the night before as Jews tried to comply with a newly issued order from the German occupiers. The Jewish community leaders had tried to negotiate the regulation, with one Jewish leader objecting that the stars would encourage the riffraff to attack and mock Jews on the streets, but a message arrived from Adolf Eichmann that he would absolutely not tolerate "the harming of Jews for wearing the Yellow Star, and that if any incident of this nature occurred it should be reported to him and he would deal with the attackers."[3] The Gestapo allowed a few exceptions to the regulation—Jews married to Christians, war veterans, and a few Jews who were favored for one reason or another—but outside those exceptions the Jews of Hungary were suddenly branded with a public marker, putting a dramatic end to the long hope and pretense that they would be treated differently from the rest of the Jews of occupied Europe. A few Budapest clothing shops quickly adapted to the new business of producing and attaching the stars, but for the majority of the Jews of Hungary the regulation was an unwelcome shock. When those who were familiar with the sequence of events in other occupied areas pointed out that the yellow stars had generally been the prologue to wholesale deportations, their suggestion of broadcasts to warn Jews not to wear the distinctive markings were hastily rejected.

For four years Hungary had been lucky. While much of central and eastern Europe had suffered wartime occupation, shortages, rationing, strict limits on travel, suppression of news and contacts abroad, and a long list of forbidden activities—a plunge into an abysmal and terrifying grayness that mirrored the color of the omnipresent SS uniforms— in Budapest the cafés and nightclubs had stayed open. In the evenings, lights twinkled along the shores and on the bridges over the Danube, and well-dressed people paraded on the Corso, strolling past the glorious parliament building. "We have everything one could want in the way of a parliament building," the saying went, "except a parliament." The country was ruled by Admiral Miklós Horthy, the former commander in chief of the Austro-Hungarian navy, who had arrived on horseback to seize power from the Béla Kun–led Communist republic that had taken power after the First World War. Horthy called himself the regent and took up residence in the Royal Palace. The humorists, and Budapest was full of humorists even in the spring of 1944, made much of the fact that Horthy was a regent of a country that had no monarchy and an admiral in a country that had no coastline or seaport, but the Horthy regime looked and acted like a proper authoritarian state, with an expansive and much-feared gendarmerie, secret police, and intelligence agents.

The victors of the First World War had redrawn the borders in the Balkans, turning former conquerors into the newly conquered, and leaving relations between Hungary and her neighbors a tangled catalog of bitter resentments. The despised 1920 Trianon Treaty forced Greater Hungary to surrender huge swaths of land and its only seaports and coastline to Yugoslavia, Czechoslovakia, Poland, Italy, and Romania. Hitler, well aware of Hungary's revanchist aspirations, courted Horthy on chamois hunts in Austria and stag hunts in Prussia, and after the fall of France in 1940, made a calculated play by forcing Romania to surrender the northern half of Transylvania back to Hungary. There was a price. "If you want to join in the meal," German foreign minister Joachim von Ribbentrop told Horthy, "you must help with the cooking." Three months later, long enough to allow both Germany and Hungary to deny rumors of a tit-for-tat, Hungary endorsed the Rome-Berlin-Tokyo pact, effectively becoming an ally of Germany. Horthy's interpretation that the pact did not oblige Hungary to join Germany's war, but only to render assistance if one of the parties was attacked, was initially popular.[4] There were some who resented seeing German officers strolling the streets of Budapest with pretty Hungarian girls on their arms, but the Germans were welcome customers at the luxury shops and restaurants, and Hungarian factories thrived on German orders of war matériel.

Even with German agents conspicuous in the cafés and nightclubs, most Hungarians trusted Hungarian exceptionalism to preserve their independence. Hungary was different, and Hungarians were proud of the differences. Their language was not related to any other European language, except for a few tenuous ties to Finnish or Turkish that only the linguistics professors discerned. Hungarian political and social development, the unique role of the nobility in Hungarian society, their history as part of the two-headed Austro-Hungarian Empire, even their ancient origins as a people and a nation had been different. And through the first years of the expansion of Nazi Germany, Hungary remained an exception. While much of Europe fell under direct or indirect German rule—annexed to the German Reich, like Austria, the Sudetenland, Memel, and Slovenia; declared protectorates like Bohemia, Moravia, and the General Gouvernement of Poland; or occupied by the German army, like much of France, the Netherlands, Belgium, and Denmark—Hungary remained independent. Hungary under Horthy's regency was not subjected to puppet governments or Nazi overseers. Officially, Hungary was an independent ally of Hitler's Germany. Many Hungarians thought Horthy had gotten the best of the Germans.

It was in the spring of 1941, when German forces used Hungary as a staging point for the invasion of Yugoslavia and Greece, that Hungarians learned the limits of their independence. Prime Minister Pál Teleki, who had signed a nonaggression pact with the Yugoslavian government, wrote to Horthy, "We have become faithless—out of cowardice . . . we have thrown away the nation's honor," and committed suicide.[5] A production of Beethoven's politically charged opera *Fidelio* was canceled at the Budapest opera house. The rest of the Hungarians consoled themselves with the Hungarian acquisition of three chunks of Yugoslavian territory (Bácska, Baranya, Prekmurje). By June, the betrayal of Yugoslavia seemed little more than a digression, as the German forces regrouped for Operation Barbarossa, the invasion of the Soviet Union. This time Hungarian army units were part of the assault force, and Hungary was rewarded for their contribution to the initial victories with Kamenets-Podolski, a strip of land wrenched from the Ukraine. The eastern campaign also consumed uniforms, equipment, arms, and ammunition in unprecedented quantities, some of it produced in Hungarian factories. If many Hungarians resented the loss of lives and independence on the eastern front, those who profited from the war remained sanguine if not enthusiastic about the alliance. As long as the war news reported German victories, they were content.

A few Hungarian officers and some of the right-wing parties sided closely with the Germans, especially after the Anschluss in 1938 created a common border between Germany and Hungary and facilitated German support of fascist movements in Hungary. But even Hungarian fascism was different. Ferenc Szálasi, the founder of the fascist Arrow Cross party, was a follower of a Magyarized Turianism, a nineteenth-century pseudoscience that claimed the Bible was written in a proto-Magyar language; that Turkic Hungarian tribes were the original biblical Semites, which made Jesus a Hungarian; and hence that European civilization was a gift of Hungary. Szálasi, his party, and their bizarre ideology had been marginalized between the wars, until he took advantage of German protection to revive his racist rants about the Jews and his advocacy of a Greater Hungary that would annex all of the lands lost after the First World War. In March 1943, the Hungarian general Ferenc Feketehalmy-Czeydner and his fellow officers were about to be put on trial by the relatively liberal Hungarian prime minister, Miklós Kállay, for the massacre of about six thousand Serbs and four thousand Jews at Novi Sad, when the Hungarian officers fled to Germany. Hungary sought their extradition, but Hitler granted them political asylum, telling Foreign Minister Ribbentrop to inform Admiral Horthy personally that "everyone in Europe should know that a person accused of persecuting Jews who would flee to Germany would be granted asylum. Anybody who fights against the Jewish pest in Europe, stands on our side."[6]

By late 1943, even wartime censorship and the strenuous German efforts to propagandize their own versions of war news with relentless newsreel scenes of victorious submarines heading into port and marching troops photographed from low angles with wide-angle lenses in the style of Leni Riefenstahl were not enough to hide the truth from those who read between the lines of the newspapers, listened for what the broadcasts did not say, and watched for what the newsreels did not show. The tides of war had shifted. American and British troops had driven the Germans from North Africa, Sicily, and the southern Italian peninsula. Mussolini had fallen, and German units had to rush to the Italian front to stop the Allied advances. At Stalingrad, the Soviet armies stopped the German advance and destroyed an entire German army. After the great tank battle at Kursk, the Soviet forces began to seem invincible, their advance toward the west inexorable. By early 1944, Soviet forces reached the Carpathian Mountains, close to the border of Hungary, where they were regrouping and poised for a massive attack across the plains of Poland and on a broad front toward Romania and Bulgaria. In the West, it was no secret that Britain, the United States, and their allies were preparing an invasion of France. Exactly where or when no one knew, but the café pundits talked of a landing force assembled in the east of

England, row upon row of tanks and trucks marshaled to attack the Pas de Calais, the shortest crossing to France. The same rumors said that the American general, George Patton, the victor in North Africa and Sicily and the one Allied general the Germans feared, would be in command of the invasion force. By the spring of 1944, anyone with a map and pushpins could begin to question the wisdom of Hungary's continued alliance with Germany.

Admiral Horthy, who had his own map and pushpins, quietly sent feelers toward the West. In the fall of 1943 he dispatched an official of the foreign ministry to Istanbul, a hotbed of diplomatic contacts and intrigues in neutral Turkey, to initiate secret talks with the British. In February 1944, he sent four scholar-emissaries to Istanbul, including the Nobel Prize winner Albert Szent-Györgyi and the legal scholar Ferenc Váli, with the secret message that the Hungarian military and government not only would not fight the British and Americans, but would join them against the Germans as soon as they approached Hungarian soil. The British were understandably hesitant to engage the Hungarian envoys in serious discussions. A Special Operations Executive agent (the SOE was established by Churchill in 1940 "to set Europe ablaze") named Basil Davison wrote Ferenc Váli that Hungary "can't behave like Germany's closest ally for three years . . . and expect to be treated any different from the way we are going to treat Germany."[7]

Horthy had been cautious with his peace feelers, but Hitler's intelligence services had long ears, and reports that Hungary was seeking a separate peace were enough to ignite Hitler's paranoia about betrayal by his supposed allies. In February 1944 Horthy wrote Hitler to demand the return of nine Hungarian divisions from the Eastern Front to defend the Carpathian border.[8] The Soviet advance was a genuine threat for the Hungarians, but Hitler saw the withdrawal of troops from the German battle order as yet another sign of treason, and in mid-March 1944 he summoned Admiral Horthy and General Szombathy, the commander in chief of the Hungarian army, for talks at Schloss Klessheim, the Führer's winter retreat at Salzburg. Hitler and Horthy met there alone, and Horthy, speaking German without a translator, tried to charm the Führer, dismissing the reports of Hungarian professors contacting the Allies in a neutral country as "malicious gossip," proclaiming Hungary Germany's oldest and most faithful ally, and assenting to the delivery of a few hundred thousand Jewish workers from Hungary to Germany. Hitler wasn't satisfied. He harangued Horthy on Hungarian perfidy and betrayal and demanded stringent measures against the Jews in Hungary.

That evening, while Horthy made preparations to board his special train to return to Budapest, air-raid sirens went off and a cloud of smoke appeared over the castle. Hitler announced that an Allied bombing raid had disrupted rail and phone service and sent a message to Budapest saying that the return of Horthy and General Szombathy was delayed. Only later would Horthy learn that the impressive smoke screen had been provided by the security detail at the castle. That night, a Saturday, while Horthy and General Szombathy were hostages at Klessheim, Hitler launched Operation Margarethe. Six German divisions entered Hungary on troop trains, ostensibly headed for the Eastern Front. The trains stopped in Hungarian stations, where the fully armed troops alighted and took up positions. Five other German divisions crossed the border from Austria. The Hungarian army was concentrated in defensive positions in the south and southeast; without orders from Admiral Horthy or General Szombathy, the Hungarian troops refused to fight back against the invading Germans. In a matter of hours German troops seized control of the major cities, highways, railroads, and communications. By Sunday morning the sky over government ministries in Budapest was gray with smoke from the fires burning incriminating papers.

At Klessheim, Horthy was presented with a joint communiqué announcing that the entry of German troops into Hungary had been arranged by mutual consent. "You may well have added," said the admiral, "that I begged Hitler to have Hungary occupied by Slovak and Romanian troops, which is another of the threats he [Hitler] made!" Ribbentrop, the German foreign minister, told Horthy that he would be allowed to return to Hungary on his special train as regent, but that a German plenipotentiary would be in charge of Hungarian affairs, and that Horthy had to agree to supply one hundred thousand Jewish workers for labor in the Todt Organization, a military engineering group in Albert Speer's armaments ministry; if he refused, he would return to Hungary as a prisoner. The admiral opted for his special train, and was accompanied on his journey by Ernst Kaltenbrunner, the head of the German security service, and Edmund Veesenmayer, the new German plenipotentiary for Hungary. When Horthy arrived in Budapest, German sentries were posted outside the palace.[9]

Over eight hundred thousand Jews lived in Hungary. With the exception of a mishandled 1941 deportation of foreign-born Jews to Kamenets-Podolski in newly acquired East Galicia, they had been relatively untouched by the war. Even while systematic deportations to camps in Poland and Silesia were instituted in Germany, Austria, Poland, the Netherlands, Belgium, Italy, France, Greece, Slovakia, and other occupied areas, the Hungarian Jews had not worn yellow stars, were not confined in ghettos, and did not have their personal property and residences expropriated. There was no need or demand for anything like the Transfer Agreement of 1933, which allowed some German Jews to emigrate in return for cash payments to the Nazis. The Hungarians had introduced their own anti-Semitic measures between the wars, beginning with a 1920 *numerus clausus* that restricted the number of Jews allowed in each profession to the Jewish percentage of the general population. The Jews of Budapest reacted to the measure with demonstrative gestures of loyalty to the state and were rewarded with a quiet disregard of the restriction; in 1939, more than half the members of the Hungarian bar were still Jewish. But by 1938, as Hungarian fascist groups demanded measures against the Jews in imitation of Germany, Admiral Horthy's government tried to steal their fire by reimposing the *numerus clausus* "for the sake of social and economic balance." This time the restrictions were enforced, limiting Jews to no more than 20 percent of those practicing white-collar professions of journalism, law, medicine, engineering, and acting and forcing many Jews out of their professions.[10] Other restrictions and special taxes were applied to Jewish businesses. In 1942 Hungary passed a law annulling all loans taken out by the government from Jews during World War I: the resultant savings were crucial to financing World War II in Hungary. A year later special legislation stripped Jews from the army officer corps and decreed that Jews would no longer serve in regular army units, but only in auxiliary labor corps. These anti-Semitic measures were humiliating, especially to Jewish veterans who had fought for the Austro-Hungarian Empire in World War I and proudly wore their medals on patriotic holidays. The conscripted labor service was under brutal conditions: wags called the labor brigades "thirty-kilogram people"[11] because the survivors came home gaunt, weak, and hungry. But Jewish Hungarians could still point out that they were not subject to the more extreme measures that had been imposed in German-occupied Europe. As late as 1943, on the evenings of the holiday services for Rosh Hashanah and Yom Kippur, white-gloved policemen still directed traffic and maintained order outside the main synagogue on Dohány Street in Budapest.

Despite the German efforts at censorship, Jewish labor battalions in the Hungarian armed forces on the Eastern Front witnessed the murders of Ukrainian and Russian Jews by German SS units. Jewish refugees fleeing the deportation policies in Poland and Slovakia brought stories of the roundups into ghettos and the cattle car deportations that carried hundreds of thousands of Jews to camps in Poland and Silesia. In the rural provinces of Transylvania and Subcarpathian Russia, poor and preponderantly Orthodox Jewish communities in shtetls and small towns were sometimes isolated from headlines and had little contact with visitors or refugees from abroad. But in the cities, especially in Budapest, news and rumors of what was happening in the rest of Europe was readily bantered about in the cafés. Eager listeners could weave fragments of information from rumors, visitors, and occasional uncensored news reports into the horrifying story of restrictions, humiliations, expropriations, ghettoization, and deportations, as Jews in much of western and central Europe were systemically stripped of their rights and quarantined from European society. German was widely understood in Budapest, and the café mavens who pieced together the rumors knew about the hateful signs in German shop windows denying service to Jews or urging them to leave the country, the horrifying *Kristallnacht* with its cascades of broken shop windows and desecrated synagogues, the humiliating requirement that Jewish men take the middle name Israel and Jewish women the middle name Sarah, and the highway signs on dangerous German Alpine passes exempting Jews from the speed limits in the undisguised expectation that they would kill themselves. In Budapest, the appalling reports were sometimes filtered through the Hungarian café tradition of holding distasteful news at arm's length with humor and sarcasm. For some Jews in Hungary, that distancing reinforced their sense of their own uniqueness and their conviction that they would be spared the horrors of the Nazi policies that had been applied to Jews elsewhere. Hungary, they assured themselves, had always been different.

The Hungarian Jews had their own myths. As they sometimes described the social and ethnic geography of Europe, other states had German Jews, Polish Jews, Russian Jews, Dutch Jews—separate populations that could be targeted by the Nazis because they identified themselves as Jews first, as part of a tribe or ethnic group, a separate nation within their state. But in Hungary, especially in the cities, the Jews proudly thought of themselves not as Hungarian *Jews*, but as *Hungarians* who happened to be Jewish. They spoke not the Yiddish of the Jews of Poland and Romania, but Magyar, a language named after the predominant ethnic group, and they identified with the history, culture, society, literature, and humor of Hungary. Some Jews claimed that their families had arrived in Hungary with the Romans, long before the Magyars. They told themselves and tried to assure their Christian countrymen that they were not part of some ancient tribe or nation, but Hungarians of the Jewish faith, as Hungarian as their Roman Catholic, Lutheran, or Calvinist fellow citizens. And the Magyars welcomed them because nationality in the Austro-Hungarian Empire and in the Hungarian state was determined linguistically, so the ranks of Magyar-speaking Jews strengthened the Magyars against the claims of the Croatians, Slovenians, Slovaks, Ruthenians, and other linguistic minorities. Jews in Hungary filled traditional economic roles in trades, industry, commerce, banking, and crafts—a burgeoning middle class for the Magyar nobility— but some Jews in Hungary were also farmers, landowners, and industrial moguls. A few wealthy Jews aped the styles of the Hungarian nobility, buying rural estates, taking up fencing, riding, and hunting, even dressing in the tall boots and feathered hats of the country gentry. But after 1890, as a depression in agricultural prices led to financial ruin for many of the nobles, Magyar nationalism turned increasingly anti-urban, anti–free trade, and conservative. Austrian and German anti-Semitism found new targets in Hungary, especially after a bizarre blood-libel trial in Tisza-Eszlár in 1883.

Jews had long been active in Hungarian politics, including some who held seats in the parliament. Béla Kun, the leader of the failed 1919 Communist revolution, was a lapsed Jew, as were thirty-two of his forty-five commissars, and even after the fall of the Communist regime, many Jews remained active in the Socialist and Communist parties. Those Jews who had ventured into politics and political parties saw themselves as loyal Hungarians, sometimes through rose-tinted glasses that blurred the open vilification and revilement of Béla Kun and his supporters, the White Terror instigated by Horthy's troops after they ousted the Communist government, and the occasional outbreaks of open anti-Semitism.

There were observant Orthodox Jews in the provincial towns, including Hasidic Jews with their rebbes, and there was a substantial Orthodox community in Budapest, but there was also a large Neologue movement in the cities, with values and practices close to Reform Judaism in the United States, and with members indifferent or opposed to visible Jewish symbols like a yarmulke. Many Jewish Hungarians observed Jewish rites, if at all, only at funerals, weddings, and on the most important of Jewish holidays. Whether observant or vigorously nonobservant, Hungarian Jews remained fierce in their devotion to Hungary, its language, and its culture, convincing themselves that even German occupation would not mean what it had meant elsewhere in central Europe. By early 1944, with the Germans seemingly in retreat everywhere, Hungarian Jews were inclined to assume the war was all but over, and that they had escaped the worst. Whatever they expected, the Jews of Hungary soon discovered that the Nazis did not read the battlefront news as they did and did not make the fine distinctions the Hungarian Jews had long assumed.

On the morning of the German invasion, March 19, 1944, the Neologue congregations of Budapest were holding their annual meeting under the leadership of Samuel (Samu) Stern, when German SS captains Hermann Krumey and Dieter Wisliceny appeared at 12 Sip Street, the headquarters of the Jewish community. Following the procedures first set out by Reinhard Heydrich, then chief of the Nazi Security Police, for the occupation of Poland in September 1939, the SS captains ordered Stern to form a Central Jewish Committee. Heydrich, in his infamous *Schnellbrief*, called the establishment of Councils of Jewish Elders an essential step toward what the Nazis privately described as "the ultimate goal."[12] Stern accepted the leadership of the new Nazi-ordered committee and summoned leaders of different factions to a meeting. Philip von Freudiger, the president of a large Orthodox congregation on Dob Street, and leaders of the other congregations showed up at the hastily summoned meeting and were seated facing three German officers in uniform, a female stenographer, and a soldier pointing a machine gun at the Jewish leaders. Two German officers, Krumey and Captain Otto Hunsche from the Office of Jewish Resettlement, began the meeting by announcing: "From now on all the affairs of the Jews of Hungary are under the jurisdiction of the *Sondereinsatzkommando* of the SS." Krumey, a short, thick man, blond and blue-eyed with an improbable button nose, announced: "We are here. There will be severe security degrees leveled against Jewish properties, Jewish freedom. Jews will wear yellow badges. But if you cooperate . . . the bad things will not happen."[13] Cooperation meant that the sixty Jewish leaders present would agree to maintain order and would deliver, in twenty-four hours, a complete list of every Jewish institution in Budapest and the names of the leaders.

When they were dismissed, the Jewish leaders and rabbis hurried back to their congregations to assure the anxious members that as long as order was maintained and certain restrictions were observed, nothing would happen to the Jews of Budapest. They later sent out messages to their congregants urging calm, and reminding their fellow Jews that they were not only people of the book, but also of the law, and that the Jews "must abide by all, even the most severe, measures without any deliberation and pondering."[14]

As a reward for their cooperation, the members of the Central Jewish Committee were granted 250 immunity certificates exempting them from many of the special restrictions imposed on the Jewish community, including the wearing of yellow stars. The one reminder of their real status was that they were required to report every two weeks to the Gestapo headquarters at the Astoria Hotel to get their exemptions renewed in a humiliating procedure. There were immediate criticisms of Samu Stern for cooperating with the Nazis and accepting his onerous position at the head of the Jewish Committee. Stern was admired as a successful businessman and a leader of the assimilationist Neologue community, and he had strong Jewish roots, but he was a man more comfortable in the Budapest of Franz Josef than with the sudden changes and demands of the Nazis. "A prisoner at the mercy of his jailer is not in a position to object to the cell into which he is thrown . . . ," he said in response to the criticism. "It is not good for the flock to change an experienced shepherd for an inexperienced one who just happened to be accepted in the midst of tempest."[15]

Britain and the United States had some forewarning of the German invasion of Hungary from agents inside Hungary, but from their perspective it was a squabble within the Axis. The only plans they had for action within Hungary was a mission that would parachute native Hungarian speakers into Yugoslavia, close to the Hungarian border, with a mission of reaching downed Allied pilots in Hungary. The only qualified volunteers were young Zionists in Palestine who had made *aliya* from Hungary, and the parachutists understood that once their primary mission was accomplished they could gather useful intelligence or work with the local resistance units and provide moral support to the Jews. The American OSS lent support to the parachute missions, and had earlier parachuted spies into Hungary to gather military intelligence,[16] but they left the drops of Zionist parachutists to British intelligence.

The missions were daring and bold, but hampered by poor intelligence and timing. Of the thirty-three Jewish agents parachuted into occupied Europe, seven died in landing accidents or were murdered shortly after they landed. Many of the others were dropped in the wrong place or arrived after the local Jewish population had already been relocated to a detention camp or deported. Three of the parachutists were on missions to Hungary: twenty-six-year-old Emil Nussbacher (his Hungarian name was Yoel Palgi), nineteen-year-old Peretz (Ferenc) Goldstein, and Hannah Senesh, a twenty-three-year-old native of Budapest who had volunteered for the mission in the hope of seeing her mother, who still lived in Budapest. They parachuted into Croatia in mid-March 1944 on two separate flights, met up with local partisans, and were told that there was no possibility of crossing the border into Hungary because well-equipped German units had taken over the borders. A few days later they learned that Hungary had been invaded by Germany. "We knew only too well what that meant for the last great Jewish community in Hungary," wrote Nussbacher.[17] The eager young Zionists, determined to do something for the Jews of Hungary, were stuck in Yugoslavia.

Adolf Eichmann celebrated his thirty-eighth birthday the day the German army occupied Hungary. The next day he arrived in Budapest and set up a temporary office in the Astoria Hotel. He would soon be followed by the staff of his Special Intervention Unit Hungary (*Sondereinsatzkommando Ungarn*). Even before their arrival, Hitler and other senior Nazi officials were closely following events in Hungary.

By noon on the first day of the German occupation, SS Reichsführer Heinrich Himmler was asking for detailed reports, including updates on the number of Jews taken into custody. Initially, there were no large-scale roundups of Jews, but Himmler was so insistent that SS *Standartenführer* Dr. Hans-Ulrich Geschke, the commander of the Gestapo in Hungary, wrote down the names of lawyers and doctors with "Jewish-sounding" names from the Budapest phone book and proudly informed Berlin that two thousand leading members of the Hungarian Jewish community had been taken into custody.[18]

By the end of March, 3,441 detainees were being held. Guests and tenants were expelled from the villas and hotels in Swabenberg to make room for Nazi security offices in a bucolic, private, and secure setting. Geschke moved the Gestapo offices into the commodious Majestic Hotel. Eichmann and his group took the Little Majestic Hotel across the road. With offices and bureaucratic apparatus in place, the security agents switched from their uniforms to plainclothes, ransacked the offices of leftist political parties and trade unions, banned 126 newspapers, and began the systematic arrests of British, American, and French pilots who had been shot down, Hungarian civil servants, ordinary citizens who had belonged to any of the leftist parties, journalists, scientists, and scholars who were considered potential opponents of the Nazis. By mid-April, 6,461 detainees were in custody or had been sent to Vienna for what the Gestapo called "protective custody." Effective the morning of the invasion, Jews were forbidden to withdraw more than 1,000 pengős (approximately $280) from their bank or postal savings accounts, and Jewish safe-deposit boxes were sealed.[19] On March 27, 1944, an initial set of formal anti-Jewish restrictions was imposed: a ban on Jewish ownership or use of telephones, followed days later by regulations forbidding Jews from employing other Jews, practicing law, or working in the media or theater, and requiring Jews to declare all motor vehicles, which would later be seized. By April 16, Jews were required to declare all of their property and any transfers to non-Jews made after March 22 were declared invalid. Through the month of April Jews lined up at postal savings banks to turn in their savings, jewelry, gold, and valuables, which were placed into special envelopes, with the contents noted on receipts that were signed and stamped before copies were handed to the Jews. It was a perfect illusion of security for their life savings.

Nazi officials had long talked about the wealth of some of the Hungarian Jews. The day after the invasion of Hungary, the Wehrmacht leadership met at the garrison town of Jüterbog, south of Berlin, to sign a treaty of friendship with the Hungarian military. Over the objections of some of the German financial officials, it was agreed that the cost of the German occupation of Hungary would be recuperated by selling off Jewish financial assets. On April 26, all Jewish assets and securities were to be surrendered to the Hungarian National Bank. The Hungarians also agreed that any Jew leaving Hungary would forfeit all assets to the Hungarian state. A month later, the German Economics Ministry concluded that Jewish assets accounted for at least one third of the total wealth of Hungary, and "we can assume that we will have numerous opportunities to liquidate Jewish wealth."[20]

Kurt Becher, the chief of the economic department of the SS, was sent to Hungary in March 1944, supposedly to buy twenty thousand horses for the German army. Youthful, tall, and well dressed, Becher had been a grain salesman before he joined the SS cavalry. He brought his own horse when he signed up, was thought to be an aristocrat and experienced with horses, and soon became an expert at procuring horses for the SS, before graduating to more important duties as an expert at expropriating the property of Jews. In Budapest he promptly initiated negotiations with Frederic Chorin, managing director of the enormous Manfred-Weiss Works on Csepel Island in the Danube, one of the largest steel complexes in central Europe.[21] The Manfred-Weiss industries were owned by the interrelated Weiss, Chorin, Kornfeld, and Mauthner families, all assimilated or converted Jews. Chorin—who was born a Jew but was later baptized as a Christian was also Baron Manfred-Weiss's son-in-law—held high positions in Hungarian banking circles, was Admiral Horthy's favorite bridge partner, and owned an enviable country house and a spectacular villa on Andrássy Avenue in Budapest that some thought the finest private house in Hungary. The Nazis found him hiding in a monastery, and after he was put into what they told him was "honorary protective custody," he was threatened, interrogated, and humiliated until he agreed to give up his factories and properties in return for being allowed to escape with thirty-six members of his extended family by car to Vienna and then on a special flight to Portugal. Becher took over the magnificent Chorin House on Andrássy Avenue as his private residence in Budapest. Foreign Minister Ribbentrop and the Führer took a personal interest in the Manfred-Weiss expropriation.[22]

Becher was only one of many Nazi bureaucrats who found ways to expropriate city houses, country villas, art, jewelry, and other wealth in transactions that promised special freedoms to the owners and their families. Samu Stern received requests for women's lingerie, eau de cologne, typewriters, and an original Watteau painting. A music-loving transport expert in Eichmann's command asked for a piano and was offered eight pianos. "I do not desire to open a piano shop," he said. "I merely want to play the piano."[23] Budapest had a reputation as a city of Jews and a city where one could live well. The new German occupiers were determined to share in that booty.

At nine o'clock on the morning of March 19, the day of the German invasion, Joel Brand was in his bath when Josef Winniger and two other Abwehr agents he knew from the cafés and nightclubs burst in and took him to the offices of the Danube Steamship Company, a front that served as the Abwehr office in Budapest. There the mysterious Dr. Schmidt explained that they would hold Brand in "protective custody" because the Gestapo and the Wehrmacht would know his address. After three days in custody, Brand was released. He paid $8,000 in cash and a gold cigarette case to Winniger to hide out in an apartment Winniger had rented for one of his dancer friends from a Budapest club called Arizona.[24] The bribe was not Brand's own money, but from funds Vaada had collected for rescue efforts. The detention was a good introduction to the overlapping and conflicting bureaucracies and authorities in the Nazi empire. After the days in custody, Brand feared that his relationships with the Abwehr counterespionage agents would not protect him from the Gestapo.

Brand did not like Schmidt. Ten days before the invasion, he had lunch with Winniger and Schmidt at an elegant restaurant, the Lukács-Bad, where Schmidt warned Brand that the Germans would soon invade Hungary and asked Brand to give him details of his activities with the Abwehr agents, including the occasional smuggling of funds from Istanbul into Hungary and on to concentration camps in Poland, and the aid provided to Jewish refugees fleeing Poland and Slovakia for Hungary. Brand, who thought Schmidt an "unpleasant, sadistic, sexual, disgusting character," assumed Schmidt was collecting "a good testimonial for himself" in case the Allies won the war.[25]

After that forewarning of the German invasion, Brand's wife Hansi and his children had gone into hiding in Andreas Biss's apartment at 15 Semsey Andor Street, in a gentile neighborhood southeast of the Városligct Park. Biss was a cousin of Joel Brand by marriage, a wealthy manufacturer who had been raised as a Protestant by his *Volksdeutsch* (Transylvanian German) stepmother. Although born of Jewish parents, he had German identity papers. He was no great friend of Brand, but he identified with the Jews after the Germans invaded Hungary, and his apartment, which served as the office of his pottery and faience stove business, was large enough to accommodate meetings and other clandestine activities. With beds for more than a dozen, a radio, and a telephone, it was quickly set up as a temporary office for Vaada. Those who stayed there called it the "bunker."[26] Hansi Brand and the Brand children moved in, along with Rezső Kasztner, a lawyer from Cluj, and Otto Komoly, a construction engineer who was raised in a Zionist home and had been active in the negotiations with Abwehr officials and rescue efforts to assist Jews fleeing Poland and Slovakia. Hansi Brand, who had already proved herself a good manager in the knitwear business, took over the paperwork and organizational work for Vaada. From the safe house he shared with the dancer, Brand maintained contact with his colleagues at the house on Semsey Andor Street so they could plan the next stage of their rescue efforts. Overnight, the German occupation had turned the Jewish rescue problem on its head. Instead of finding funds and counterfeit papers to bring a trickle of refugees from Poland, Slovakia, and other German-occupied areas to Hungary, Vaada now needed to protect the Hungarian Jews. The only contacts they had were Brand's Abwehr connections.

Brand quickly learned that with the arrival of the Wehrmacht troops and the Nazi bureaucrats, Abwehr agents like Dr. Schmidt and Winniger were no longer senior intelligence officials in Hungary. Franz von Papen, the German ambassador to Turkey, a former ambassador to Austria, and the former chancellor who had been instrumental in Hitler's rise to power, had been privately scheming with the chief of military intelligence in Turkey to bring the Abwehr operation in Turkey under his control.[27] Foreign Minister Ribbentrop and Heinrich Himmler also resented the prestige and fame of Admiral Canaris, who had been a hero of the submarine service in World War I before he became the head of the Abwehr. They feared competition from Canaris's independent organization and used their access to Hitler to campaign against the Abwehr. When a former Rhodes Scholar, anti-Hitler Catholic, and Abwehr spy named Vermehren defected in London in early 1944, an enraged Hitler fired Admiral Canaris and abolished the Abwehr, leaving the entire espionage responsibility to SS Reichsführer Himmler's Nazi-loyal Sicherheitsdienst (Security Service) and the Gestapo. Hitler's new orders left the former Abwehr agents in Budapest powerless. Realizing that the most they could hope for was bribes from Brand and his colleagues to put them in touch with Gestapo officials, the Abwehr agents began revealing information about the Nazi plans for Hungary in the hope that their revelations might make them indispensable to any future negotiations between the Vaada and the Nazis.

Brand and his Vaada colleagues were not surprised by what they heard. They had followed the German pattern in Slovakia, Poland, and the Ukraine through their rescue efforts, and had not subscribed to the hopeful vision that Hungary would somehow be exempted from the policies that had been applied elsewhere. As Zionists they had also long believed there was no future for the Jews in Europe. If many Jews in Hungary tried to remain hopeful, Vaada was openly cynical, recognizing that to the Nazis they were only Jews; that Béla Kun and his commissars and Jewish members of the Hungarian Socialist and Communist parties were to the Nazis leaders of the Judeo-Bolshevik conspiracy, the enemy against which Germany was waging its war; that Jewish writers, artists, and scientists who proudly proclaimed their loyalty to Hungary were to the Nazis promulgators of decadent Jewish culture; and that the distinguished Jewish Hungarian merchants, bankers, and factory owners, with their villas on Andrássy Avenue and proud patronage of charities and the arts in Budapest, were admired by the Nazis only as targets for expropriation. The Vaada members had seen and heard enough elsewhere to realize that the arrival of the Nazi bureaucracy signaled the beginning of a plan to eliminate the Jews from Hungary. Overnight, what had once been an interesting rescue mission for Jews fleeing to Hungary had become a desperate race to save as many Jews in Hungary as possible before the Nazis instituted their draconian measures. If they did not, the Jews of Hungary—the last relatively intact population of Jews in Europe—would face the same fate as the Jews of every other area occupied by the Nazis.

On April 5, the day the first yellow stars appeared on the streets of Budapest, Joel Brand had his first meeting with the new Nazi officials. Brand had given Josef Winniger and Dr. Schmidt a bribe of $20,000 plus $1,000 for each of their colleagues to arrange a meeting with SS *Hauptsturmführer* Dieter Wisliceny.

Wisliceny had been in charge of the ghettoization and deportation of the Jews in Greece and Slovakia in 1942. In Slovakia the distinguished rabbi Michael Dov-Ber Weissmandel and a bold woman named Gizi Fleischmann had organized the Bratislava Working Group to try to save the Jews. Their feelers to outside organizations like the American Joint Distribution Committee and the International Red Cross were focused on what Weissmandel called the Europa Plan, by which the Nazis would spare the Jews of Europe in return for payments in cash. Rabbi Weissmandel had written to Philip von Freudiger in Budapest for financial help and advice after Wisliceny had demanded $2 million to delay and ultimately end the deportation of Jews. When Gizi Fleischmann sought clarifications from the Nazis, she learned that the Jews of Germany and Poland would be excluded from the proposed plan and that the Nazis' demands for payments had escalated to $3 million, far more that the Slovakian Jewish Committee could raise without help from abroad. Bratislava was close enough to Hungary that couriers could bring reports to Budapest daily. Brand and his colleagues had followed the negotiations and knew what to expect when Wisliceny was assigned to Budapest after the German invasion.

At their meeting on April 5, Brand and his colleague Rezső Kasztner met the German officials at an elegantly appointed apartment overlooking Szent István Park in Budapest. SS *Hauptsturmführer* Erich Klausnitzer, who hosted the meeting as a representative of the Gestapo, had requisitioned the apartment. Josef Winniger and Dr. Schmidt were there, but it was Wisliceny who did the negotiating.

Dieter Wisliceny—his nickname was Wili—was enormously fat, and his carefully tailored uniforms with their vast expanse of gray accentuated his bulk until he seemed to fill a room. He did not cultivate the harsh, forbidding mien of some of the German officers, and his square, unthreatening face and gentle manner could seem reassuring and friendly, especially when he would go out of his way to tell the Jews with whom he negotiated that he cared about their interests and concerns, and that he personally did not subscribe to the more extreme measures that had been imposed or threatened. Privately he collected what he called "bonbons" from Jews—family jewels, strings of pearls, gold watches, and cash. If he was pleased he would remark that "the bonbons were good."[28]

Too fat to sit in any of the chairs in the elegantly furnished apartment, Wisliceny strutted around the room, addressing Brand and Kasztner in a series of mini-lectures in pseudoscientific language, as if what he was talking about was not human lives, but a social-engineering problem. The German objective, he said, was not to ghettoize or deport the Hungarian Jews, only to eradicate Jewish influence at all levels of Hungarian society. There would be no wholesale killing of the Jews: there had been a change of policy higher up and the Jews would be used for manpower. There would also be no wholesale concentration in ghettos or camps, although Jews living in small villages and townships would have to be transferred to larger towns, which might necessitate some confinements. Deportations, he said, depended solely on the Hungarians, and while the Germans had no plans for killing the Jews in Hungary, the SS would not be detailed as a protective guard for the Jews. He added ominously that "when you do some planing, shavings are bound to fly." Finally, he said that the Germans were very much interested in emigration of the Jews—not a select few, who would presumably be the wealthy Jews and the leaders of the Hungarian Jewish community—but a mass exodus of Jews from Hungary, sufficient to eradicate the Jewish culture of Hungary.

Brand and Kasztner were ready with a proposal of their own. They wanted no extermination of the Hungarian Jews (their delicate euphemism was *Erhaltung der Substanz*, preservation of those existing); no deportations of Jews from Hungary; no setting up of ghettos or concentration camps; and permission for Hungarian Jews to emigrate to Palestine. In exchange for those guarantees, they offered $2 million, which they knew was the sum Wisliceny had asked from the Slovakian Jewish leaders in 1942. They told Wisliceny that because of their limited resources and the financial restrictions on the Jews in Hungary, the best they could do was to pay the sum in ten monthly payments of $200,000 each.

Wisliceny said that the "paltry" offer of $2 million "could not be considered since there was no comparison of the numbers involved," that in Slovakia there had been only 10,000 Jews, while Hungary had 1.2 million Jews. (Both of Wisliceny's numbers were exaggerations: there were around 60,000 Jews in Slovakia before the Germans began their deportations, and the total Jewish population of Hungary was closer to 850,000.) Wili did allow that he would accept an initial payment of $200,000 from Brand and Kasztner as a fee for his "pains" in presenting the proposal to higher authorities and as demonstration of their "good faith and financial solvency."[29]

Brand and Kasztner responded with a revised proposal for the emigration of 150,000 Hungarian Jews to Palestine, a figure they arrived at because they had heard there were a total of thirty thousand permits available under the British restrictions that limited Jewish immigration to Palestine. Rezső Kasztner argued that each permit was valid for a family of five.[30] Their new proposal, like the first offer, was a bluff: Jewish immigration to Palestine was strictly limited to very small numbers by the British White Paper of 1939, and neither the Jewish Agency nor the British had given the slightest indication that they would allow the available Palestine immigration permits to be used by Hungarian Jews. Kasztner either was dissembling or did not realize that each immigration permit to Palestine was not for a family, but for an individual. Kasztner and Brand made the offer because they needed a concrete proposal to take a measure of Wisliceny. And at all odds, they needed to keep the negotiations going.

Wisliceny, still pacing, said that their request was impossible, that the grand mufti of Jerusalem, Haj Muhammad Amin al-Husseini, was in Berlin, was in agreement with the Nazis on Jewish policy, had helped recruit Bosnian Muslims to serve in the SS, and had made an agreement with the Nazis regarding Palestine; hence any mass exodus of Jews to Palestine from Europe was out of the question. Instead, he said, Brand and Kasztner and their colleagues should pursue emigration for the Hungarian Jews to North or South America, Australia, or North Africa. He all but admitted that the reference to the grand mufti was a red herring when he slyly added that "of course, if they subsequently went from North Africa to Palestine, then it was no longer any concern of his." Kasztner and Brand agreed to meet with him again a few days later.

At their second meeting, Brand and Kasztner, aware that the long negotiations in Slovakia had ultimately gone nowhere and ended up with the deportation of the Slovakian Jews, said that to raise the enormous sums the Germans were demanding Vaada would need to be able to present some evidence of concrete results. Kasztner said that a ship in the Romanian Black Sea port of Constanţa was preparing to leave for Turkey, and that if the Germans would grant seven hundred emigration certificates to Hungarian Jews for travel on that ship, all at once, it would be sufficient evidence of good faith to help Vaada raise the balance of the funds they had offered.

Wisliceny asked for a list of names of those to go on the ship, and in another strutting lecture declared that the Germans were ready to let out 750 Jews. But, he said, he could not direct the Hungarian authorities to let Jews go to Palestine, or anywhere else. As he put it, he could not "sell Hungarian Jews directly from Hungary." The Jews would have to first be brought on a Danube steamer to German-occupied territory, Vienna or Slovakia. Only after they became "German merchandise" could they travel back down the Danube to Constanţa and board the ship for Turkey and points beyond. Kasztner and Brand were appalled by Wisliceny's ominous and casual use of terms like "sell Hungarian Jews" and "German merchandise."[31]

When they asked for details of the proposed transaction, Wili said that the Jews on the list would have to be concentrated in a camp in Budapest while transportation details were arranged. To Brand, it sounded like a ghetto, exactly what they hoped to avoid for the Hungarian Jews. However friendly Wili's square face, smile, and manner, his words matched his reputation: the fat man in the enormous SS uniform was a formidable negotiating opponent.

Brand also knew payments to Wisliceny would be only the first step. Vaada would have to find a country willing to accept the Jews, at a time when no country anywhere in the world was willing to issue visas to Jewish refugees. They would have to arrange transport and documents—not forging a few papers in an attic or basement workshop or concealing an individual in the trunk of a private car, but for unprecedented numbers. They would have to support the emigrants before and during their long journeys. And they would surely have to pay more bribes. Once the process started, and Jews were in the limbo of emigration, the whole operation was susceptible to further extortionate demands from Nazi and Hungarian officials at every step. Even this tentative proposal from Wili was a daunting challenge, dwarfing their years of efforts to save a few individuals from Poland and Slovakia.

Brand also realized they would have to sup often with the devil: the first meetings with Wili would be followed by many more. In Slovakia Wisliceny had negotiated, or at least pretended to negotiate, for months. And if that was a precedent, the possibility of reaching an agreement, of coming up with the funds he would demand, and of making the complex transactions work, was remote. Wili could fill a room and lecture them with great authority, but every delay in the negotiations was a potential excuse for someone higher up than *Hauptsturmführer* Dieter Wisliceny to throw aside his negotiations and suddenly impose the extreme measures of ghettoization and deportation that had prevailed in Poland, Slovakia, and elsewhere.

What kept Brand and his Vaada colleagues talking was the hope that dragging out the negotiations with more meetings would at least delay the imposition of harsh measures against the Jews of Hungary. Solid war news was hard to come by in Hungary, but stories about the staggering

German defeats at Stalingrad and Kursk were intertwined with rumors of Allied war plans on the Eastern, Italian, and Western fronts. If they could delay any German measures against the Hungarian Jews until the western Allies landed in France and renewed their attacks in Italy, and the Soviets renewed their inexorable advance from the east, crushing the Germans in a gigantic three-jawed vise, there was a chance of saving the Hungarian Jews from the fate of the Jews of Poland and the rest of occupied Europe. Brand and his colleagues had to balance that hope against the possibility that the negotiations might suddenly collapse, or that a higher-up in the Nazi hierarchy, even Himmler or Hitler, might reach the end of their patience and suddenly order a massive roundup and deportation of the Hungarian Jews, or that the Soviets would overrun Hungary before the western Allies arrived.

After a few meetings, Brand discovered that Wisliceny and his colleagues seemed as eager for more meetings and talk as he was. When Brand wondered why out loud, Wisliceny told him, "Your news service is quicker than ours."[32]

That remark suggested another danger for Brand and his colleagues in Vaada: the more they met with Nazi officials, the more likely their efforts would be discovered and misunderstood or that they could be accused of collaboration.

The $2 million that Wili had already refused was so far beyond the fundraising capabilities of Vaada that Brand's first step was to see if other Jewish organizations would cooperate in making an appeal to the Jewish community in Budapest and to Jews and relief organizations abroad. When he went to the Central Jewish Committee, Brand discovered that he wasn't the only one who had tried to deal with the Nazis. Philip von Freudiger, one of the co-chairmen of the Jewish Council and a leader of Vaad Hatzala, a rescue committee formed by the Orthodox Jews in Budapest, had already met with Wisliceny at the Majestic Hotel in the Swabenberg hills. Wisliceny had shown Freudiger a letter from the famed Rabbi Weissmandel in Slovakia lamenting that it was the turn of Hungarian Jewry to suffer the bitter fate of the rest of the Jews in

German-dominated Europe. "May the Almighty have mercy on us all," Rabbi Weissmandel had written, urging the Jewish leaders to continue negotiations on the stillborn Europa Plan.

Wisliceny held the letter out. "Have you read it?" he asked Freudiger. Wisliceny then defiantly tore the letter up and tossed the pieces into a burning stove. "Till then—the money coming—we need it," he said.

"We or I?" Freudiger asked. He had little experience with the Nazis, but knew about their extortionate demands and Wisliceny's reputation.

"That is no affair of yours," Wisliceny answered. He dismissed Freudiger in a huff, presumably as a man who didn't know how or was not willing to play their game.[33]

Brand and Freudiger were on opposite poles of Hungarian Jewry. Freudiger was a baron, a successful businessman, and a devout man, a leader of the Orthodox congregation on Dob Street. His noble name earned him respect in a city that worshipped nobility. He was scrupulously formal, always dressed in a suit and tie, his head covered with a hat or a yarmulke. He proudly refused to request an exemption from the rule requiring Jews to wear the yellow star on the grounds that it would be unfair to the thousands who came to the synagogue on Dob Street wearing yellow stars on their clothing.

Brand lived in a working-class neighborhood, had no formal education, no association with any synagogue; he had a prison term on his résumé, had dabbled with the Communists, and was affiliated with the Zionist labor movement. Freudiger and the Orthodox were not entirely opposed to Zionism, but they had little patience for what they saw as radical Zionism with its socialist experiments of kibbutzim. Brand almost made a point of never being in a synagogue, and he was more often to be found in a café than in a business office. To the more "respectable" Jews of Dob Street Brand seemed shady-looking. One colleague of Freudiger said of Brand, "even his eyes are not straight."[34] Brand also had no qualms about accepting special privileges. He, Kasztner, and Hansi Brand got themselves special immunity cards signed by Krumey, one of the Nazi officials.

Freudiger saw Brand as an opportunist, a Zionist freethinker who had abandoned the laws and faith of Judaism for dreams of a secular state in Palestine. The mistrust was mutual. To Brand, Freudiger represented the closeted, self-interested, cliquish Orthodox, as buttoned up as Freudiger's waistcoats, determined to keep their old ways, seeking either to move their lives intact to another country like the United States or to stubbornly remain in a doomed Europe.

When Brand asked Freudiger how much the Orthodox would contribute toward the $200,000 down payment they needed to keep negotiations with Wisliceny alive, Freudiger pointedly asked about the funds Vaada was rumored to be receiving, through contacts in Istanbul, from Mapai, the Zionist labor party in Palestine. Brand countered by asking about the sums Freudiger and the Orthodox organizations had been getting from American Jews and Orthodox institutions. In the end they put their posturing aside. Freudiger realized that however despicable Brand might be in the eyes of the Dob Street Orthodox, his negotiations with the Nazis might be the only hope for the Jews of Hungary. He agreed to help and quickly raised $80,000 from wealthy Jews in Budapest.

Brand and Kasztner also raised funds, although as longtime Zionists their connections among the wealthier Jews of Budapest were not as solid as Freudiger's. By April 12 they were still 500,000 pengős (around $14,300) short of the $200,000 initial payment they had promised in the first negotiations. April 14 and 15 were the last days of Passover, important religious holidays to the Orthodox Jews, so on the eve of the holidays Freudiger committed 100,000 pengős from the Orthodox treasury and loaned a further 400,000 pengős from his own factory, which was exempt from the monetary restrictions on Jews because it was producing war matériel. Brand came to Freudiger's office with suitcases to fetch the money.

The Nazi power structure was built of overlapping and sometimes conflicting spheres of authority, a deliberate structure of bureaucratic tension that kept officials on their toes and dependent on the decisions of higher-ups. The scheme owed much to Friedrich the Great, who had pioneered the techniques of bureaucratic competition to centralize his own power. The result was that different agencies in the Nazi bureaucracy sometimes converged on the same targets. In Budapest, Gestapo agents and Abwehr counterintelligence agents plied the same cafés, seeking the same individuals, asking the same questions, and negotiating the privileges or information they would offer for the right bribe. It was not unusual that while one agency, or even one individual in an agency, was negotiating emigration schemes with Jewish representatives, another agency or individual might be implementing procedures for expropriation, ghettoization, or deportation.

While Joel Brand and Rezső Kasztner were meeting with Wisliceny, in the Hungarian provinces, reaching to the borders of Romania, the Ukraine, Slovakia, and Austria, SS units were already implementing the ghettoization routines that had been tried and perfected in Poland and other areas. Jews from shtetls were swiftly moved into selected towns. In the larger towns and provincial cities, Jews were confined in demarcated neighborhoods or at large, open facilities like brickyards. Learning from previous experience in Germany, Austria, Poland, and the Netherlands, Eichmann met with two Hungarian officials, László Baky and László Endre, and through them secured the cooperation of the Hungarian gendarmerie. Eichmann knew the capabilities of the available forces and bureaucratic agencies, and made a deliberate decision to start with the outlying areas and leave Budapest for later. They agreed to divide Hungary into six discrete zones for the operation, to cut off all communications between the zones, and to begin their operations in Zone I (Carpathian Ruthenia) and Zone II (North Transylvania), where as many as 290,000 Jews were confined to ghettos. Always a stickler for proper paperwork, Eichmann insisted that a member of the Hungarian government submit a formal request for the evacuation of the Jews. The procedures in the northeast and east were followed later in Zone III (northwest Hungary and the area north of Budapest), Zone IV (southern Hungary east of the Danube), and finally in Zone V (Transdanubia and the outskirts of Budapest). Budapest would wait.

As the Jews in the provinces were confined to ghettos, experienced Nazi bureaucrats began the process of systematically stripping them of their possessions: jewelry, money, furniture, clothing, tools, musical instruments, art, residences, business property—anything that would be of value to the Reich or to enterprising individual officers in the various German programs and agencies involved in the occupation. From prior experience, every step was covered with legalistic paperwork, specifying regulations about the property of minors and reimbursements for the cost of the expropriations.[35] The transfer of property from Jews to non-Jews was called *aryanization.* An observer recorded a dialogue between a young lady and an older woman on a streetcar:

> Have you taken it away from the Jew, my dear?
> Yes, we have, Aunt Magda.
> Did you ask for it, or did they give it?
> We asked for it and they gave it.[36]

News of the Nazi roundups in the provinces was no secret in Budapest: Jews in Budapest had relatives and business acquaintances in provincial cities or the countryside. The Zionists of Vaada were not surprised by the reports. They knew from their negotiations that the Germans were greedy, that expropriation of money, property, and goods from the Jews was at least one motivation for the entire program of ghettoization and deportation. Every step on the path was another opportunity to expropriate more goods and funds from the Jews. Higher-ups in the Nazi bureaucracy would use the threat of each stage as another opportunity to negotiate bribes. Joel Brand and his colleagues also knew that if they were to have any chance of saving those Jews, their negotiations had to move beyond the dilatory talks with the fat man. With that on his mind, Brand was ready when the shiny Mercedes showed up at the Opera Café and took him to Adolf Eichmann's headquarters at the Little Majestic Hotel in the Swabenberg hills.

# 3

## Negotiations

*I know from years of work that everyone of them can be bought. I know this from years of work—I am not saying that I have bought Eichmann or Wisliceny. In my work very many of them have been bought and I do believe that criminals of such low sort as these men are always receptive to offers of money. It is natural that people who do such terrible things will not have clean hands where money is concerned either.*

—Joel Brand[1]

*Eichmann's cleverest trick in these difficult negotiations was to see to it that he and his men acted as though they were corrupt.*

—Hannah Arendt[2]

B rand was given no ride back from his meeting. He walked down from Swabenberg and took a streetcar over the Danube to Sip Street, the heart of Jewish Budapest. The long trip was a good opportunity to think about Eichmann and his shocking proposal.

Joel Brand knew little about Eichmann. The officials he knew—Abwehr agents and SS officers like Dieter Wisliceny and Hermann Krumey—talked about the aloof Eichmann with a sense of awe. Wisliceny, who liked to distance himself from the harsher measures that had been administered to the Jews, often hinted that Eichmann was the heavy who initiated orders for ghettoization and deportation of the Jews, or at least efficiently carried out orders from above, meaning Berlin. But if he didn't know Eichmann, Brand felt he knew the Germans. After years of furtive negotiations in cafés and parked cars, he knew they were greedy.

He had heard Oskar Schindler's descriptions of what bribes and induce-ments could buy from the Germans, and had heard Dieter Wisliceny's lecture on what he would need to be paid for his "pains." The greed was not confined to the low-level Abwehr stringers. The ranking SS officers might be more formal and correct in their negotiations, but however lofty their rank, language, and proposals, the Nazi officials seemed always to include a fee for themselves. In the end they all seemed to want money, fine houses, good brandy, and pretty girls.

Was it also true of Eichmann? Dr. Schmidt and the Abwehr offices were in a warehouse space, masquerading as a Danube steamship com-pany. Many of the counterespionage agents used the same makeshift office Brand had long used—the Budapest cafés. As an *Obersturmbann-führer*, the SS equivalent of a lieutenant colonel, Eichmann enjoyed an entirely different level of luxury—an office suite upstairs in a luxurious villa, surrounded by trees, and nestled in the cool foothills of Buda. He had a beautiful expropriated house, a special car and driver, assistants at his beck and call, a riding horse kept ready for his whims. What could a bribe provide him that he did not already have? He was potentially a candidate for promotion to *Standartenführer*, or colonel—a huge leap in prestige, authority, and prerogatives, far more than the English equiva-lent of the rank suggests.[3] In the SS ranks a *Standartenführer* was almost a general officer. They were like gods. They did not need bribe money for brandy or pretty girls.

The Abwehr agents and Wisliceny had all talked money on the first meeting, as if there were price lists for whatever they offered. The only thing Eichmann said he wanted in exchange for one million Jews was goods—in his ominous phrase, blood for goods. Was the proposal sin-cere? Would he make a deal with the Jews and pass up the opportunity to show his efficiency and perhaps earn a promotion to *Standartenführer* by dealing with the Jews of Hungary, the only large and still intact popula-tion of Jews left in Europe, as he had dealt with the Jews of Poland? For Joel Brand, who had long prided himself in sizing up men in café meet-ings and anticipating where the negotiations would go, the assessment of this man was suddenly the most important decision he would ever make.

Before Brand's meeting with Eichmann, Brand and Vaada had been content to operate alone, using their relative secrecy to good advantage. The German invasion, and Eichmann's shocking proposal, had changed the stakes dramatically. The Vaada members concluded that the proposal was too important not to be shared with the Central Jewish Committee in Budapest and its two leaders, Philip von Freudiger from the Orthodox, and Samu Stern from the Neologues. Samu Stern was a *Hofrat*, an honorary Austro-Hungarian title that entitled him to be addressed as "Excellency," and Freudiger was the wealthy owner of textile factories. As the official representatives of Hungarian Jewry, accustomed to dealing with the government, they and the committee had not been surprised to find themselves the first organization the invading Nazis contacted. But they found themselves overwhelmed by the suddenness and gravity of the Nazi invasion. Even as they learned about the anti-Jewish measures under way in the provinces, their lack of preparation or plans to deal with the Nazis, and a sense of resignation that followed the collapse of their long faith that Hungary would somehow not fall victim to the measures introduced elsewhere, left them paralyzed in inaction, repeating the same calming words to their congregations and making no efforts to warn provincial Jewish leaders of the measures the Nazis were taking. Yet Freudiger and Stern were ultimately realists, and to Brand's surprise, when they were told about the meeting with Eichmann, they immediately recognized the gravity and import of the proposal that had been made to Brand and promised their full support.

Brand's acquaintances among the Abwehr agents were not as enthusiastic. Josef Winniger, who had been Brand's primary contact with the world outside his safe house, told Brand that Dr. Schmidt would definitely oppose Brand going abroad alone to negotiate this or any other proposal, since he might give away important military information. Brand laughed, pointing out that he knew no military information, and that even if he had known military secrets, a companion would hardly make a difference. Surely it would be impossible to watch him every minute he was in Istanbul.[4] Winniger's caution was a bluff, since with the Abwehr officially abolished he, Schmidt, and the other agents were themselves no longer privy to important military or policy information, and they had no official responsibility to preserve German military security. Like so many of their interactions with Brand and his colleagues, their moves seem to have been motivated primarily by worries that they would not get a share of the bribes that might be part of any arrangement with Eichmann.

Brand was outgoing and well traveled. He spoke serviceable German and some English and was experienced at dealing with the German agents in Hungary. But a meeting abroad would mean travel to Switzerland, or more likely Istanbul, and he had never been in Istanbul. He told Josef Winniger that he would welcome traveling with a companion who knew the city and the Turkish bureaucracy.

If Joel Brand had few doubts about his abilities, others would question his qualifications to negotiate for the lives of the Hungarian Jews. To some, he wasn't even Hungarian. He was born in 1906 in Mukachevo in northern Transylvania, a region of forest and mountains where the borders of Hungary, Ukraine, Slovakia, and Romania converge at the edge of the Hungarian steppe.[5] Russian, Ukrainian, Slovakian, and Hungarian were all spoken in the area, and Gypsies, Romanians, and members of ancient Slavic tribes like the Rusins sometimes appeared in the markets. Towns like Mukachevo were far from the urbane culture of Budapest.

Joel was four years old when the family moved to Erfurt, in the German state of Thuringia, where his father established a company called Priteg (an abbreviation of *Privattelefongesellschaft*) that sold and installed telephones. Joel attended a private primary school and a technical high school, but he was restless as a student, and after passing his *Abitur* in 1923, he left the Polytechnic Academy, worked for three months as a technician and salesman in his father's firm, then sailed for the United States, where he lived with a well-to-do uncle on Spruce Street in New York and worked at a German firm making leather hats before setting off to work in Philadelphia, at an architectural firm in Atlanta, in auto factories in Detroit, and bouncing between hard labor and unemployment in San Francisco. He was in the United States long enough to notice the prominence of Jews like Schiff, Morgenthau, Strauss, Lehman and Loeb in investment banking; Ochs and Sulzberger at the head of the *New York Times*; and the East European Jews who owned and controlled the motion picture industry in California. The years in the United States were also an introduction to the vagaries of an unbridled capitalist society. When he returned to Erfurt in 1927, his father was dead and his brother-in-law was managing Priteg.

Germany is a land of credentials: every position has its necessary lock-step qualifications; even factory workers carry their lunches in what look like briefcases. Brand had no higher education and no experience in an apprenticeship, a necessary stage for advancement as a skilled worker, but he had spent time around the Priteg workshops, knew the work, and was adept enough at dealing with authorities to talk his way into a certificate of apprenticeship. Despite his lack of training in engineering, he talked his way into the title of Engineer by Diploma; by 1930 he had become codirector of Priteg with the responsibility of traveling to branches in major German cities like Leipzig, Stuttgart, Jena, Breslau, Weimar, Brunswick, and Frankfurt am Main to sell telephone systems.

Joel was already interested in politics, perhaps in rebellion against a father who had been intently focused on the Priteg business and disengaged from politics, Jewish observance, and community activities. In 1919, when he was fifteen years old, too young to be a full member, Joel had joined Poale Zion, the Zionist workers party, which represented the secular and socialist wing of Zionism that attracted those who opposed both Jewish orthodoxy and capitalism. When the party split into socialist and communist factions in 1923, he joined the communist youth movement and remained a member until Hitler became chancellor. A few days after Hitler came to power in March 1933, Brand was arrested as a leftist, accused of complicity in the Reichstag fire, sentenced to prison, and incarcerated according to the changing whims of the German justice system in Erfurt, Fulda, Frankfurt am Main, and Kassel.

He was released from prison in late summer 1934 and left for Cluj (Klausenburg in German) in Transylvania, a former Hungarian province that had been awarded to Romania by the Trianon Treaty. He prolonged his stay there by bribing the immigration officials each time a deportation order arrived, until he tired of paying the bribes and moved to Budapest for a job as a workman in the Budapest Priteg, a branch operation his father had sold. In Budapest he rejoined the Zionists and enrolled at a *hachsharah*, a training farm where young people learned agricultural skills and agronomy in preparation for work on a kibbutz or moshav in Palestine. It was there that he met Hansi Hartmann. As committed Zionists Joel and Hansi weren't overly concerned about the formalities of marriage ceremonies or even the conventions of romance. They agreed to marry in the hope of getting permits to emigrate to Palestine, where they hoped to found a telephone company similar to Priteg.[6]

The permits never came through, and as the Nazis put pressure on the Jews in Erfurt and all but expropriated the family's remaining interest in Priteg, Joel's mother and three sisters fled to Budapest. With a large family to support, Joel and Hansi put their dream of making *aliya* to Palestine on hold and started the knitwear business. Hansi had learned to make fashionable leather and wool gloves from an aunt, and Hansi's parents provided the money to start the business. Under her management the business prospered, expanding from a single machine to the workshop on Rozsa Street. While Hansi ran the business, Joel assumed leadership positions in the Poale Zion party, the Zionist Land Organization, and the Zionist Building Fund—organizations that disseminated information about Zionism, ran training programs to prepare Jewish youth for agriculture and industry instead of the "black-coated professions," and looked for chinks in the restrictive British immigration policies so they could send Jews to Palestine. Joel Brand was one of as many as eighty people working actively in Zionist programs in Budapest.

In 1938, when Hungary resolved to retake Transylvania from Romania, Joel was drafted as an officer cadet in the Hungarian military, only to be expelled from the officer corps under the new regulations that assigned Jewish soldiers to labor brigades. As the Hungarians continued to ramp up their army, he dodged more draft notices as long as he could, and finally got himself admitted to a hospital, where he persuaded a friendly physician to declare that he suffered from diabetes and could not serve. With the war approaching he had no time for labor brigades. He was already at work aiding victims of the Nazis.

After Germany and Russia invaded Poland in September 1939, he and his Zionist comrades began smuggling cigarettes and food to internment camps in isolated rural villages in Poland. The camps were built without fences, relying on remoteness and guards to keep the prisoners in, which made it relatively easy for Brand's Vaada rescue group to smuggle in contraband and aid escapes. They also sent money into the newly established ghettos in Poland, and tried to aid Polish Jews living underground in Vienna by bribing the driver of a *Völkischer Beobachter* delivery truck to smuggle food along with the copies of the Nazi party daily.

After Hungary received new territory as a reward for their participation in the attack against the Soviet Union in 1941, the chief of Hungarian police, Lieutenant Colonel Ferenczy, ordered fifty thousand foreign-born Jews in Hungary—mainly Poles—into temporary camps, announcing that they would be "resettled" in the newly acquired territory of Kamenets-Podolski in East Galicia, a Siberia to most Hungarians. The actual roundup was bungled—the Hungarian bureaucracy had picked up habits of Austrian *Schlamperei* in the long years of the dual Austro-Hungarian Empire—and many native-born Hungarian Jews who did not meet the criteria for deportation, including Hansi Brand's sister Lenke Stern and her brother-in-law Lajos, found themselves included on the lists and held in detention, without resources or recourse, awaiting transport to the remote area of the Ukraine. When Hansi went to see her sister and brother-in-law, they were being held in a police cell, a "cage," as Brand described it. Travelers to the Hungarian provinces had come back to the Budapest cafés with stories about the deportations on cattle trains and the appalling conditions in Kamenets-Podolski. Hansi begged Joel to do something to get her sister and brother-in-law back.

Brand did what he usually did with a problem: "I must confess that I am very fond of visiting coffeehouses. When I am worried, I like to sit at a table and think things over. I nearly always get an idea, or else I meet someone who can help me. And so it happened on this occasion. I had hardly sat down when a man came in whom I knew slightly. But I immediately said to myself, 'There's your man.'"[7]

The man Brand spotted was a Hungarian intelligence agent named Josef Krem. Brand agreed to pay him 10,000 pengős (approximately $2,800) to get Hansi's relatives released and brought back to Hungary. A week later Krem showed up with four Jews hidden in the trunk of his car. They were not Hansi Brand's relatives. After more under-cover café meetings and negotiations Krem brought back Hansi's sister and brother-in-law on the fourth try. Krem and Brand began working together, locating other deportees who could be rescued and arranging under-the-table bribes to bring them into Hungary. Through Krem, Brand met German counterintelligence agents working in Hungary who were also willing to make arrangements.[8]

As Jewish refugees from Austria, Slovakia, and Germany fled across the borders into Hungary, Brand would meet newly arriving refugees, provide them meals, and hide them while they waited for forged Christian birth certificates and military service records. He and Hansi bought a small printing press to forge false documents, and they and their Vaada colleagues learned techniques like using egg whites to erase stamps and signatures on documents, which could then be overprinted with new names and information. He and Hansi eventually spent so much of their time on rescue operations and negotiating with the German counterintelligence agents that they handed control of the knitwear business over to one of the weavers, Kovesdi Pálné, who looked plump and provincial enough to not attract police attention and was willing to hide guns and refugees in the workshop. Their cook, Rozsi Varsoni, also joined the effort.[9]

While many Jews of Hungary were content to trust Admiral Horthy and Hungarian exceptionalism to protect them from the Nazis, by October 1943 Brand was urging his Vaada colleagues to prepare for armed resistance in case the Germans invaded Hungary. They called this part of their work *Hagana*, "the defense" in Hebrew. Hagana was also the name of the Jewish self-defense forces in Mandate Palestine. Refugees from

Poland had smuggled a few weapons into Hungary, and Brand and his colleagues in the Hagana group planned to steal additional weapons that soldiers left unguarded in restaurants and barbershops. They were further inspired in January 1944 when Heike Klinger, who had been active in the Berlin underground, lectured about her experiences and the valiant stand of the Jewish fighters in Warsaw.[10] At a retreat near Lake Balaton the Hagana group met for lessons in martial arts and Morse code, and to plan for armed resistance. Their plan was that when they had sufficient members and arms they would attack small police stations and military outposts to "liberate" the weapons there. By the time of the German invasion they had succeeded in collecting 150 pistols of mixed ages and origins, 40 hand grenades, 3 small Hungarian carbines, 2 machine guns only one of which was serviceable, and very little ammunition. If they were going to successfully resist the Germans, it would not be with arms.

While the self-defense effort remained a pipe dream, Vaada did succeed in establishing reliable courier services for information and funds to Bratislava and Istanbul, and sent occasional couriers to Bucharest, Switzerland, and Austria. Sam Springmann, a diminutive diamond dealer and watchmaker who sold fancy brooches to the wealthy of Budapest, had used his jewelry business as a cover for trips to Istanbul. In 1941 he opened contact with the Jewish Agency office there, which provided communication to Palestine and modest funds for relief and rescue operations. Other couriers for Vaada were businessmen with excuses for travel like rug merchants, journalists sympathetic to their efforts, and German counterespionage agents eager for a percentage of the funds Brand and his colleagues brought from the Jewish Agency. Brand trusted the Abwehr agents because those assigned to Hungary were Austrians who reportedly resented the German Nazis, and because the couriers were so eager for bribes and the 10 percent commissions they received from the funds they transported that Brand was sure they would do anything possible to avoid killing the goose that laid those golden eggs.

In addition to the German copies of the Auschwitz Protocols that were smuggled out of Slovakia, copies were hidden behind a picture of the Virgin Mary in an apartment that had been rented temporarily for Vrba and Wetzler, and one copy had been translated into Hungarian for delivery to the rescue groups in Budapest. The German occupation of Hungary sharply curtailed the courier traffic between Bratislava and Budapest, but not long after Joel Brand's first meeting with Eichmann, Rezső Kasztner received the Hungarian copy of the Auschwitz Protocols. Philip von Freudiger in Budapest also got portions of a copy of the Protocols.[11]

The Nazis had done a good job of compartmentalizing Europe, restricting news so that the population of one occupied area heard little about what had happened elsewhere. But the members of Vaada had stayed in regular contact with Gizi Fleischmann and Rabbi Weissmandel in Slovakia, and probably heard from them about the preparations at Auschwitz for the mass murders of Hungarians.[12] They were also in contact with relief organizations and exiles in Switzerland and Jewish Agency officials in Istanbul. For the Vaada leaders, the Auschwitz Protocols were a confirmation of what they had long feared and suspected, proof that the rumors of annihilation of the Jews were true.

As early as May 1944, Kasztner and his Vaada colleagues made a quiet but fateful decision that they would not disseminate details or even the general contents of the Auschwitz Protocols revelations in Hungary. Their reasons—which they never explained in letters or memoirs— have long been debated. They may have been so confident of their plan to negotiate with the Nazis that they were afraid that a panicked reaction to the report from Auschwitz would complicate their negotiations. They may have intended to use their detailed knowledge of Auschwitz as a bargaining card or feared that revelation of their knowledge of the ultimate fate of the Hungarian Jews would accelerate the German plans for deportations. They may have concluded that revealing the horrifying details about Auschwitz would turn the masses of Hungarian Jewry against them as bearers of ill tidings. Or they may have regarded the secret knowledge of what was happening at Auschwitz as a token of their power and authority within the complex political and social structure of Hungarian Jewry and feared that disseminating it would dilute or destroy their authority. Whatever the actual balance among their possibly complex motives, a leading historian of the period has called their refusal or unwillingness to disseminate the shocking contents of the Auschwitz Protocols to the Jews of Hungary "a conspiracy of silence."[13] It was an accusation that would later come to haunt them.

But even as they refused to disseminate the revelations, they could not ignore at least one detail in the Protocols. The report included specifics of recent construction at the Auschwitz-Birkenau camp, particularly the new unloading ramp that had been built to facilitate the processing of arriving trains of Jews and the new crematoria that had been added to the facility, which would raise the capability of Auschwitz-Birkenau to "process" twelve thousand individuals per day. The timetable for the new construction had the additions completed in early 1944, on the eve of the invasion and occupation of Hungary. Only one explanation of that timetable made sense: the increased capacity of the camp was to enable the swift annihilation of the 850,000 Hungarian Jews. They knew that the ghettoization of the Jews in the Hungarian provinces was already almost complete. It remained only to load them onto trains of cattle cars for the short journey from Hungary across Slovakia to southern Poland. With the expanded capacity at Auschwitz-Birkenau, it would take the Nazis only a few months to murder the entire Jewish population of Hungary. Wisliceny had said that the goal of the Nazis was to destroy Jewish culture in Hungary. The Auschwitz Protocols confirmed that the Germans were prepared to achieve that goal in the gas chambers at Auschwitz-Birkenau.

In early May, Brand and his Vaada colleagues also learned that the Hungarian government was taking no action to stop the German-directed ghettoization of Jews in the provinces. At a meeting on May 13, the foreign minister read into the record a letter from Angelo Rotta, the papal nuncio, urging that the government distinguish between Jews who had become practicing Christians and those who had not, and not force the former into ghettos.[14] His request was acknowledged, but the government gave no assurances about the rest of the Jews of Hungary.

Following the practiced procedures Reinhard Heydrich had laid out in his 1939 *Schnellbrief*, a skeleton crew of German experts had supervised the roundup of the Jews in the provinces into temporary ghettos. The holding camps were dire: cattle markets, tile factories, and brickyards, devoid of sanitary facilities, with thousands of men, women, and children, including the aged and the ill, forced to live in the open in conditions of extreme crowding. The roundup of the Jews relied less on German efficiency than on the whimsy of rural Hungarian gendarmes who had long resented the relative wealth of local Jewish families. An observer wrote that it was "tragically obvious that a great many will die of exposure, disease and slow starvations even before they are jammed 80 to 100 to a wagon into cattle cars for deportation."[15]

Incredulity made many of the Jews of provincial Hungary easy victims. Veterans of World War I responded to the ghettoization orders wearing their medals and carrying briefcases full of their diplomas and birth certificates, assuming that their contributions to the Hungarian state would be recognized and rewarded. A disabled and much-decorated officer from Cluj reported that when he tried to warn local Jews of the Nazi roundup and urged them to try to escape to Romania or go underground with false papers, his warnings were dismissed as *bobemayses*—old wives' tales. In one town the chairman of a Jewish burial society assembled his fellows and told them: "Don't listen to him. The president of our devout community is a blasphemer. He says that God will allow it to come to pass that our very devout community, which has done so much good and has helped so many of the poor, will be exterminated. Do not listen to him and his schemes. May the will of the Almighty be done. Pray to God, for He alone is our protection."[16] Gentile neighbors averted their eyes as the Jews were taken away to the temporary camps; many then swept in to confiscate the long-coveted property of the Jews.

Railway officials talked about the transport of three hundred thousand individuals to Košice, Slovakia and from there to Poland. "Both the public as well as many authorities are being told that the plan is to employ the Jews as a fresh source of labor," wrote Jean de Bavier, the Budapest representative of the International Red Cross. "However, the deportees include both old people and children, which indicates that the real purpose is something very different. I was actually told, and not even by Jews but by high-ranking government officials, that the final destination of the trains is Poland, where there are up-to-date installations for the gassing of people."[17] When rumors about deportations of the Jews spread, the gendarmes unleashed an orgy of looting. They knew that once the Jews left Hungarian soil, anything they had managed to conceal would become the property of the Germans.

A week after his first meeting with Eichmann, Brand was summoned back to the Little Majestic Hotel.[18] This time Eichmann was joined by his senior assistant Hermann Krumey, Friedrich Laufer from the economics department of the Gestapo, and Edmund Veesenmayer, Hitler's plenipotentiary in Hungary. The gray SS uniforms and high-ranking insignia gave an imprimatur of gravity to the meeting. When Brand arrived, Jewish forced laborers were working in the woodsheds behind Eichmann's villa.

Eichmann expressed surprise that Brand was still in Budapest and not already on a journey to negotiate Eichmann's proposal. Brand explained that Dr. Schmidt would not let him leave Hungary without Winniger or another of Schmidt's men as a companion, lest he reveal military secrets. In what Brand thought a "cautious and diplomatic voice," Eichmann told Brand to ask Schmidt to let him travel even without one of Schmidt's men. Brand was astonished that a "senior German official should ask a Jew to convey such a message to another high-placed German official." Eichmann's condescending sarcasm was an admission that Schmidt and the other Abwehr agents were on the outs with the Nazi higher-ups, but it was also another example of the controlled Eichmann Brand had glimpsed at the first meeting.

Again, Eichmann proved mercurial, switching from the calm voice to brusque ultimatums. When Brand said that the proposal for a trade was so vague, with such imprecise hints of what Eichmann expected in return for the lives of one million Jews, that it would be difficult to negotiate with the Allies or the relief agencies, Eichmann curtly said that Brand would have concrete proposals before he left Hungary. Even with a specific proposal, Brand said, he was not sure he could persuade "his people" to send goods, because they might not have confidence in the German promises. Eichmann again answered without hesitation. If Brand delivered or tele-graphed an acceptance of the proposal by the Allies, Eichmann would release the first group of Jews over the frontier, as many as one hundred thousand, even before any goods were delivered. He added a detail: the Jews would be released to neutral Spain. It would be the responsibility of the Allies or the Jewish organizations to take them from there. Previous refugees from Hungary had not utilized the route to Spain, and no one had even begun to consider where the huge numbers of emigrants Eich-mann had proposed could ultimately be sent, but the detailed specifica-tion added to the shock of Eichmann's proposal.

Brand asked about the forced gathering of Jews in the Carpathian provinces, protesting that the roundups, in caravans of horse- and oxen-drawn wagons or on foot escorted by gendarmes with bayonets had been done with utmost cruelty. The Jews had not been allowed to take anything with them, had been subjected to humiliating and unhygienic body exams, sometimes with gendarmes watching, and were confined in conditions that guaranteed that they would suffer and perhaps die from hunger and disease.[19] Eichmann snapped back that he had personally ordered the concentration of 310,000 Jews in the Hungarian provinces as a necessary part of his timetable. The conditions there, he said, were not his responsibility and strictly the fault of the Hungarian gendarmerie. He added that one of his men had just returned from the Carpathians and reported that he had seen no trace of these rumored cruelties, only truckloads of bread and foodstuffs being taken to the Jews. Before Brand could respond, Eichmann abruptly dismissed the issue, saying that if an answer to his proposal was not received in time, the confined Jews, along with their countrymen in other provinces and Budapest, would all be shipped off to Auschwitz.

Coming after what Brand and his colleagues had just read about the preparations at Auschwitz, Eichmann's unhesitating answer was a per-fect stick to his earlier carrot. As if to emphasize the point, Eichmann told Brand that he was going to Berlin, implying that his proposal and threats were serious enough to warrant discussion at the highest levels of Nazi policy.

Eichmann's assistant Krumey spoke up to clarify that there were definite conditions on the proposal Eichmann had offered. The Germans would under no circumstances allow mass emigration to Palestine, only to Africa west of Tunisia, South America, North America, and Australia. Brand knew from the earlier negotiations with Wisliceny that the Germans had promised to control Jewish emigration to Palestine in return for the grand mufti's promises of Arab support. Brand also knew, through Vaada's Jewish Agency contacts in Istanbul, that Turkey, although officially neutral, had put pressure on the Germans to not allow Jews to transit Turkish territory, and that even if the Germans permitted Jewish emigration to Palestine, the British White Paper policy severely restricted the immigration permits available to Jews. Krumey and Eichmann's repeated emphasis that Jewish emigration would only be allowed to Africa, the Americas, and Australia had more behind it than diplomacy or expediency. Brand had spent enough time with Nazi agents to realize that they believed their own propaganda: they actually *believed* that the Jews were a dangerous spiritual disease, a threat to European civilization and *Kultur*. Carried to its logical end, that ideology meant that any concentration of Jews in Europe or in Palestine could become a center from which the threatening Jewish "spiritual disease" could be exported. Hence the Nazi goal was to see the Jews widely dispersed, especially in Africa, the Americas, and anywhere the Allies had colonial and homeland interests, so the Jews "would do great harm to the Allies."[20]

As the discussion went on, Eichmann and Krumey listed problems Brand might encounter on his journey to negotiate with the Allies, and then turned to the goods they expected in return for allowing Jews to emigrate. They mentioned many items—trucks, machines of all types along with spare parts, raw materials, leather, and hides. Veesenmayer added coffee, chocolate, tea, and soap to the list.[21] Brand was struck by the casualness of the requests, as if they were somehow of little importance. Or perhaps they anticipated that the Allies would somehow know exactly what they wanted in return for saving Jewish lives. The meeting that began with Eichmann pretending surprise that Brand hadn't yet left on his journey ended with the announcement that there would be more meetings before Brand departed.

News of the second meeting spread quickly among the Jewish organizations in Budapest, and Brand found himself again a center of attention, not just from his Vaada colleagues and Jewish community leaders eager to hear a progress report but from men he barely knew, hangers-on who had hovered between the underworld and café society, finding profitable niches in the crevasses between the Jews and the Germans. A few weeks before he had been hiding in a safe house with the dancer friend of an Abwehr agent. Now he was a minor celebrity, with an identity card signed by Krumey and the Hungarian authorities that allowed him to walk freely on the streets, travel on a tram, or ride in a taxi. "It enabled me to get around," he later testified.[22]

It was after the second meeting that Brand learned that a man named Bandi Grosz was looking for him. Brand knew Grosz well enough to dislike him intensely. Grosz's real name was András György. He was also called Andor Gross. Short and ugly, with red hair and protruding teeth, Grosz called himself a carpet merchant, although he had no shop and few customers. His putative business was a cover for a life on the run as a smuggler and illegal courier. He was Jewish, but had little contact with the Jewish organizations in Budapest. He was known to work with the Hungarian police, including the feared secret police, and took frequent trips to neutral Turkey, ostensibly to buy and sell carpets, but actually to smuggle papers, cash, and gold. Some of his smuggling was black market speculation, but he had also carried papers and information to Istanbul for Vaada, including funds from the Jewish Agency, and had traveled to Istanbul for the Abwehr agents.[23] It didn't bother Brand that Grosz dealt with the Hungarian police and the German agents; after all Brand had dealt with the same men himself. He didn't like the ugly red-haired man because no one could say for sure which side Bandi Grosz was on.

By May 1944 Grosz was dropping names like Krumey, Wisliceny, and Eichmann in a way that indicated or pretended a familiarity that went beyond bribes for smuggling. A few days after Brand's second meeting with Eichmann, Grosz arranged to pick up Brand in his car and take him to what Grosz called an important meeting. They drove to a village twenty kilometers outside Budapest, where, in a comfortable villa, Brand was introduced to Rudolf Laufer. On the way Grosz told Brand that he had once had issues with Laufer, who "had wanted to put a rope around his neck," but that they were now good friends. Brand did not know what to make of the comment.

When he had stood behind Eichmann in the Little Majestic Hotel office, Laufer had worn a gray SS uniform. That and the luxurious villa he had appropriated certified him as a senior official, but at the villa Laufer wore civilian clothes and never mentioned his rank. He told Brand that he was in the security service, but was actually an economist. He was gentlemanly, even courtly, in his manner, although like so many of the German officers he lectured rather than conversed, explaining that the Germans, including Himmler, were sincerely "interested in a solution to the Jewish problem," but only in a "decent" way; that most of what Brand might have heard about the SS were "fairy stories"; and that if the SS men were occasionally severe or cruel, they always kept their word and could be trusted. He was openly apologetic about the language and manners his colleagues had used, and repeatedly came back to the term "goods for blood," apologizing that the concept had been brought up so crudely. He said he knew that Schmidt, Winniger, and the other Abwehr agents had swindled Brand, and wanted to hear all the details about their dealings with Brand. When Brand answered that those private transactions did not concern Laufer, Laufer recounted crude stories about the "sexual appetites" of the Abwehr agents, and said he knew about the large sums of money they had slipped into their pockets from what they claimed were official dealings. Laufer, who was rumored to have Jewish ancestors, had a reputation for bragging about getting Aryan documents for himself and his family through Gestapo friends, and anti-Nazi Hungarians warned new arrivals to Budapest that Laufer was dangerous.[24] Brand understood that Laufer was distancing himself from the Abwehr agents, as if to say, "I am someone you can trust."

Laufer also asked Brand about his negotiations with Hermann Krumey. Krumey had picked up the discussions that had started with Wisliceny about the ship in Constanţa waiting to take Jews to Palestine via Turkey. When Brand reported that Krumey had demanded 10 million pengős (approximately $2.8 million) to allow 750 Jews to emigrate on the ship, Laufer told him that it was "far too much," and that they "could not do business on such a basis." Only days before Brand had been shocked when Eichmann had given him an apparent order to pass on to Dr. Schmidt. He was fascinated by Laufer's apparent candor about other Nazi officials and the backbiting and gossip that seemed to go on behind the public façade of uniformly gray uniforms and stern expressions.

Our discussions are only beginning, Laufer told Brand. He said they had much to talk about before Brand left on his journey, and that they would see one another again soon. Then he cautioned Brand never to use his name, not to anyone. He was only to be referred to as Herr Schroeder. The mysterious pseudonym, and the scheming and apparent conspiracies between and among the Nazis in Budapest, added to the exciting aura around the Eichmann proposal.

By the first week of May, Brand found himself meeting almost daily with Nazi officials or with Grosz, who frequently claimed to have messages from one or another of the officials. The exception was Schmidt, Winniger, and their Abwehr colleagues. Café gossip about them seemed to echo the comments Laufer and Eichmann had made, including stories about their avarice and sexual peccadilloes. While the gossip continued, the Abwehr agents disappeared from Budapest. Rumors circulated that they had been executed.[25]

Eichmann asked for another meeting on May 10. This time Krumey and *Hauptsturmführer* Gerhard Clages, Himmler's intelligence agent in Budapest, joined them. Clages, slim and well dressed, was the archetypical special agent—close-shaven "like an actor" and full of "wit, intelligence, and sly humor."[26]

"I've sent for you because I want to give you something," Eichmann said to Brand.

He then threw two large envelopes on the table. The outsides of the envelopes were marked with the names of some of Brand's colleagues. The envelopes were from Switzerland, had been opened, and the contents spilled out on the desk—letters in French with false nationality documents from San Salvador for Budapest Jews. Brand recognized the documents: some carried photographs he had sent to Switzerland. There were letters in Hebrew and German on Zionist business, including one that mentioned in a roundabout way that the package was being brought to Hungary by the Swedish military attaché. There were also private letters addressed to Jews in Budapest. None were addressed to Brand, and none of the private letters had been opened. Eichmann pointed them out and declared that he and his colleagues would not open private mail, but that they knew what Brand was doing. And since he was not "politically naïve," they could trust him, but that if he was to deal with them he had to promise to report anything political in his correspondence. If they found out that he was meddling in politics, Eichmann threatened, "They would take the ground away from all his work."

Eichmann then threw a smaller envelope from his pocket onto the desk. "Look at this," he said.

Inside was $32,750 in U.S. currency. Eichmann explained that it had had been brought by Grosz, and that the Germans had to pay his commission as a courier, implying that it was secret funds that were being imported by Brand's organization. Eichmann pushed the money across to Brand—indicating that it was for Brand's expenses—and said that he hoped Brand would be ready to leave in a few days, and return with "plenty of goods," after which there would be "great emigrations, not to Palestine, but through Spain." He added that he had gotten confirmation from Berlin that the goods, by which he meant the heavy-duty all-weather trucks he had mentioned in an earlier meeting, would be used only on the Eastern Front, and not against the Allies in the West. Eichmann casually mentioned the exchange rate: one truck for every one hundred Jews. The price for one million Jews was ten thousand heavy-duty all-weather trucks. Eichmann explained that he needed new transport for his own work— Brand knew the "work" was transporting Jews to death camps—and that he had hoped to get trucks from the SS, but the Waffen SS units on the Eastern Front needed new all-weather trucks to prepare for the expected Soviet spring offensive. When Brand got new trucks for them from the Allies, Eichmann said, the Waffen SS would give their wornout trucks to Eichmann for his own transport needs.

Between his meetings with Eichmann, Brand had gotten a secret telegram from Jewish Agency officials in Istanbul suggesting that it might be possible to find railroad undercarriages that could be traded to the Nazis. Brand suggested substituting railway undercarriages for the heavy-duty trucks. Eichmann dismissed the offer, saying they already had as much rolling stock as they needed. Brand then said that he was not sure he could get trucks and the other goods Eichmann had asked for, that while he might be able to guarantee payments of money, it wasn't clear that the Allies would trade potential war matériel like heavy trucks, even if they were only used on the Eastern Front.

"The International Jews control the world," Eichmann answered. "They control every British and American official, so they could lay their hands on anything they want."

Agitated, Eichmann stalked up and down the office. "Now I feel absolutely sure of myself," he said. "I know you Jews would like to kill me, but now that I am so important for you and do business with you, you will not touch me. But even if the worst comes to the worst, you will never get me, because I will first shoot my wife and child and then myself."

When Eichmann finished his histrionics, Brand was told to produce two photographs, and that Krumey would go to Vienna to arrange a passport and a plane to Istanbul. Eichmann asked Brand how long he expected to remain abroad. Brand said that he thought the mission would take him two or three weeks. Eichmann said he would lay down no definite time limit, but that "the quicker the negotiations were concluded the better it would be for the Jews."[27]

Brand and his colleagues agreed. They learned that on May 15 and 16 trains of cattle cars left the Hungarian provinces for Auschwitz, each packed with seventy-five or more Jews, with the doors padlocked and the windows barred. A witness described "the ruthless demeanor of the Hungarian gendarmes . . . as bloodthirsty as the Gestapo of Germany," as they herded the Jews into the cars "with rifle butts and a whip was even used by one gendarme." As many as forty-five cars—3,375 individuals— made up a train. It would take four trains each day to achieve Eichmann's target of deporting twelve thousand Jews daily.

There were already rumors about the trains. One said that Jewish girls on the trains were sent to Germany and forced to wear armbands inscribed *Kriegshure* (war harlot). The official explanation for the deportations was that Germany needed labor to build fighters, especially the new jet fighters that were supposed to turn around the air war against the Allies. In his moments of optimism, the Führer had boundless faith in his new superweapons, the V-1 and V-2 rockets that were supposed to bring Britain to its knees and the new jet aircraft that were supposed to restore air supremacy to the Luftwaffe. German factories requested one hundred thousand Hungarian Jews for war production. The youngest and strongest of those who were sent to the slave labor factories might survive a few months before they were too sick to work effectively. Then, with a virtually infinite supply of new labor available from the deportations, they too could be sent to one of the death camps. A few trainloads of potential slave laborers left from Hungary for factories in Germany, but most of trains ran from Csap (then on the Ukraine border, now part of Ukraine) through Košice, Presov, Orlow, and Motins to Auschwitz-Birkenau.

For Eichmann, the deportations were routine and hardly worth mention. His message confirming the deportations was written in the usual bureaucratic obfuscation: "The consignment intended for special handling is proceeding along its designated route."[28]

But for Vaada, the beginning of deportations marked a desperate shift in German policy in Hungary. They responded by sending a message to their contacts in Istanbul, Venia Pomerany and Menachem Bader, representatives of the kibbutz movement in Palestine who worked closely with the Jewish Agency mission. The message announced that Joel Brand would be coming to Istanbul as an emissary to make contact and negotiate with the Allies.

Sending a *shaliach,* or emissary, abroad for special missions is a long-standing tradition in Judaism. It may have begun with Eliezer, who was sent by Abraham to find a wife for his son Isaac.[29] *Shaliach* is used not only to describe emissaries of communities and organizations, but also to refer to an intermediary between man and God (the *hazzan,* or cantor, in a Jewish service is the *shaliach tzibur,* emissary of the congregation), and even to the messenger of the Messiah.

Joel Brand also started thinking about his own role. He had come a long way from the Budapest cafés. He was now being asked to be the savior of the Hungarian Jews. He began calling himself the Emissary of the Doomed.

# 4

## Dissembling

*Brand's mission is not the brainstorm of a minor Gestapo leader in Budapest.*

—Leslie Squires, American vice-consul, Istanbul[1]

*My men had as one of their basic orders that all unnecessary harshness was to be avoided. This fundamental principle was also accepted by the Hungarian officials. In practice they may not have adhered to it 100%. But that did not and could not interest me, because it was not my responsibility.*

—Adolf Eichmann[2]

I n early December 1943, President Franklin Roosevelt quietly named General Dwight Eisenhower commander of Operation Overlord, the code name for the Allied invasion of Europe.[3] Ike was not chosen for his battlefield prowess: he had seen no frontline experience in the war and very little before. For much of his career he had been an aide to the flamboyant and notoriously difficult General Douglas MacArthur. But as a member of the war planning staff in Washington, Eisenhower had demonstrated talents for diplomacy, leadership, and organization, precisely the skills he would need to deal with the complexities of an invasion and difficult allies and field commanders like Winston Churchill, Field Marshal Bernard Montgomery, General Charles de Gaulle, and General George Patton.

Eisenhower attended West Point in the early years of the twentieth century, not long after Admiral Alfred Mahan at the Naval War College had made geopolitics and global thinking a strategic focus for the U.S. Navy. West Point did not articulate a comparable world strategy for the

U.S. Army, but the academy developed its own strategic axioms. Cadet Eisenhower graduated in the middle of his class, but he learned the tenets of the academy well, especially the credo that the most important, indeed the *only* object of war was to engage and defeat the enemy. The corollary of that axiom became an inviolable tenet of American military strategic thinking: any distraction from this singular and focused mission was to be avoided at all cost.

With that principle in mind, Eisenhower, as the Supreme Commander of the Allied Expeditionary Force (SCAEF), gathered a staff in England to plan Operation Overlord. Napoleon had planned an amphibious invasion of England, and Hitler had planned Operation Sea Lion with the same goal. But nothing compared with the assault Eisenhower was planning. He would bring together the largest amphibious force ever assembled, more than 7,000 ships manned by over 195,000 naval personnel from eight countries. An initial landing of 133,000 British, Canadian, and American troops would be followed in short order by the construction of temporary ports and the transport of 850,000 men, 148,000 vehicles, and 500,000 tons of supplies. The scale of the plans was staggering. So many convoys of ships sailed to England with arms, artillery, uniforms, landing craft, tanks, jeeps, trucks, tents, ammunition, and rations that wags said the UK would sink from the sheer weight of stockpiled American war matériel. The same British wags rued that there were only three things wrong with the Yanks arriving daily in the packed transports: they were overfed, oversexed, and over *here*.

By May 1944, planning for the invasion reached fever pitch. From his headquarters in London and later his command trailer in Portsmouth, Eisenhower directed a vast team: oceanographers to map the tides, meteorologists to predict the weather for the invasion, Coast Guardsmen who would pilot the landing craft, airborne troops who would secure bridgeheads and road junctions in advance of the amphibious landing, naval and air cover for the assault forces, engineers to build artificial ports on the French coast. A new computer at Bletchley Park, the Colossus Mark II, would come on line on June 1 to gather and process information for the invasion. The south of England ran out of berthing facilities, airfields, and temporary billets for the gathering force. And while supplies, ships, landing craft, aircraft, and troops were secretly marshaling in the southern ports and airfields, an enormous task force of inflatable dummy tanks and trucks, made in an American factory, was arrayed in the east of England, deliberately visible from the air or by spies. The location of the decoy force pointed to the shortest crossing to France, directly across to the Pas de Calais—the reciprocal of the route Hitler had chosen for his aborted plan to invade England. Rumors were floated that George Patton would command that invasion force, in the hope that German spies in the pubs would pick them up. Eisenhower was aware from the North African and Sicilian campaigns that the Germans feared Patton. The preparations for the dummy invasion were meant to be noticed.

The real invasion plans were kept secret. And in January 1944, the Allies had made another fateful decision that was also meant to be secret. The significant paragraph of Eisenhower's orders from the Combined Chiefs of Staff read: "You will enter the continent of Europe, and in conjunction with the other Allied Nations, undertake operations aimed at the heart of Germany and the destruction of her Armed Forces."[4] Accompanying orders stressed that the Allies would focus their war aims on engaging and defeating the Germans; they would not use military means for rescue or aid missions. It was an internally self-contradictory policy: the Allies were fighting to liberate the civilian populations of Europe, and rescue plans that did not impede the overall effort on the battlefields—like negotiations to slow down the pace of deportations and death camp operations; promising neutral nations on the borders of occupied Europe that refugees reaching their borders would not be a burden on local economies; dropping leaflets declaring that bombing was a retaliation for the Nazi murder of Jews and other citizens; exerting pressure on the Red Cross to intervene on behalf of those held in concentration camps; and providing food, clothing, and medicines for internees in the camps—could only advance the goal of liberation. Even more direct measures, like aiding Jewish resistance efforts, bombing the railroads leading to extermination camps, or bombing the gas chambers and crematoria at the death camps, would not have materially hindered the overall military effort or prolonged the war effort.[5] But the strategy agreed on in January, known as the Victory First policy, became the guiding principle and mantra of political and military strategy for the war, especially as the Allies approached the all-important moment when they would land troops on French soil to open the Western Front against Germany.

Eisenhower, a skillful politician and a meticulous man, was determined to execute that policy and profoundly reluctant to allow any diversion—not the egos of politicians and generals or the demands and pleas of special interests—to detract from the success of the sacred mission that had been entrusted to him.

While Eisenhower planned in London and Portsmouth, in Berlin and Berchtesgaden Hitler raged at his generals for their failure to carry out his wide-ranging orders. He cursed his allies, especially Finland, Italy, and Hungary, for their perfidy and weakness. And, as always, he excoriated the Jews for their diabolical plans and what he claimed was their behind-the-scenes control of the Allied war effort against Germany. The relentless bombing campaign against German military targets and cities, British Lancasters at night and Americans B-17s and B-24s by day, had begun to take a toll: 30,000 to 40,000 civilians were killed in the firestorm after the bombing of Hamburg alone. German forces had been forced to yield ground along the entire length of the Eastern Front, and only troops rushed from the already short-manned defenses against the Soviets had been able to halt the Allied advance up the Italian peninsula. But Hitler was far from considering the war lost. Whenever one of his generals pointed to the superior manpower, supplies, and armaments that the Soviets and the western Allies could bring to the war effort, Hitler talked about new designs for jet planes that would put an end to the Anglo-American bombing campaign, the long-range V-1 and V-2 rockets that would destroy London and wreak havoc on any Allied plans to invade Fortress Europe, and newly formed Waffen-SS divisions that would renew the attacks on the Soviets with Panther and Tiger tanks, the heaviest tanks in the war. He ignored reports that the V-1 and V-2 rockets actually did minimal damage, and the caution of the famed aviator and glider pilot Hanna Reitsch, who said of the jet planes: "Mein Führer, you are speaking of the grandchild of an embryo."[6] Determined to fight on all fronts, Hitler was unshakeable in his conviction that the coalition against him was so unstable that a few months of stalemate on the battlefields would see the alliance of the western Allies and the Soviets torn apart by internal political and military tensions.

When public opinion in Germany became sensitive to the reversals on the Eastern, North African, and Italian fronts, Hitler answered the doubts with a new campaign to whip up an anti-Jewish frenzy. Josef Goebbels delivered a "total war" speech before a huge, carefully selected audience in the *Sportspalast*, justifying the German war effort as a response to Jewish villainy: "Behind the onrushing Soviet divisions we can see the Jewish liquidation squads—behind which loom terror, the specter of mass starvation and unbridled anarchy in Europe. Here once more international Jewry has been the diabolical ferment of decomposition, cynically gratified at the idea of throwing the world into the deepest disorder and thus engineering the ruin of cultures thousands of years old. . . . We have unmasked Jewry's rapid and infamous maneuvers to deceive the world. . . . The aim of Bolshevism is the world revolution of the Jews."

The radio broadcast of the speech to Germany and the world ended in wild applause and orchestrated shouts of "Out with the Jews!" But even Goebbels admitted the show was a fraud. "What an hour of idiocy!" he said to his entourage after the speech. "If I had told these people to jump from the fourth floor of the Columbus House they would have done it."[7] Through 1943 and into 1944, on patriotic holidays like the Memorial Day for Fallen Soldiers, at the funerals of high Nazis, and in radio broadcasts timed to reach massive audiences inside and outside Germany, Hitler and Goebbels ratcheted up their anti-Jewish rhetoric. The Jews as inciters of terror attacks became a leitmotiv. In early 1944, Hitler complained to the Hungarian prime minister: "We did not yet hear that in Hungary there had been complaints against the Jews who were responsible for the mass murder of women and children in the Anglo-American bombings. It should be clear to everybody that only the Jews could be the agitators behind these horrifying terror-attacks."[8] The Allied bombing raids in Budapest focused on industrial areas, where few Jews lived. Rumors floated, or were instigated in Hungary, that the Allies were sparing the Jews as coconspirators in the war against the Axis. Trusting their own propaganda, the Germans believed the Allies would spare Budapest from the bombing, making the city a self-enforced ghetto.

There was method behind Hitler's anti-Semitic madness. The Jews had been central to his thinking from the beginning of his spectacular rise to power. On January 30, 1933, he prophesied to the Reichstag that a second world war would bring about "the annihilation of the Jewish race in Europe." He convinced himself that his crusade against the Jews was a just cause and a motivation for the German people, and believed that by endlessly repeating that the war was a *Jewish* war, launched only for the sake of *Jewish* interests, and that he had exposed the *Jews* as the hidden link between capitalism and Bolshevism, he could influence foreign opinion and reawaken a buried antagonism between the West and the Soviet Union. Through 1940 and 1941, his diplomatic bluffs, strategic daring, and lightning strikes had shown up the caution of his generals and demonstrated a ruthlessness and audacity that his enemies feared to the point of near-collapse. But in the face of the cascade of reverses after 1942 in Africa, in Italy, and on the Eastern Front, Hitler became reckless. Fantasies of victory supplanted his strategic intuitions of the early war. He fervently believed in the infallibility of his own strategies, discounting the analyses of the generals, convinced that their estimates of the growing differences of manpower, logistics, supplies, and production in favor of the Allies could be overcome by secret new weapons, the superiority of the German fighting man over those of other nations, and by the irresistible force of his own will. He had convinced himself that if only the western Allies understood that the Jews had started and controlled the war, that the Judeo-Bolshevik powers threatened not just Germany but the entire world, then surely, in a matter of months, Britain and the United States would recognize and join his crusade against the Jews and Bolsheviks.

On occasion Hitler addressed his officers collectively, hectoring them on their duty to National Socialism or lecturing them on the ideological basis of the war. "If Providence should actually deny us victory in this battle of life and death," he told hundreds of generals and admirals at Rastenburg on January 26, 1944, "and if it is the will of the Almighty that this should end in catastrophe for the German people, then you, my generals and admirals, must gather around me with upraised swords to fight to the last drop of blood for the honor of Germany—I saw, gentlemen, that is the way it actually *must* be!"[9] But collective histrionics were an exception. More frequently, especially with his close advisers and staff, Hitler used Friedrich the Great's managerial technique of dealing with his underlings individually and privately, playing them against one another. He feared conspiracies, and knew that when he dealt one-on-one the sheer power of his convictions and rage could erase dissent. The technique enabled him to manage difficult men like Heinrich Himmler, the Reichsführer, commander in chief of the SS and the German security services, and, after Hitler, Goering, and perhaps Martin Bormann, the most powerful man in Germany.

Himmler was a gifted administrator, pedagogue, and organizer. He followed Hitler's orders with sycophantic enthusiasm and unrestrained brutality and never wavered in his belief that the Jews were the cause of the war, that Allied bombing was the work of the Jews, that the removal of the Jews was crucial for the future of Germany, and that the policies to implement that removal were legal.[10] In a speech to a secret meeting of SS officers in Poznan, Poland, in October 1943, he spoke frankly about the ongoing extermination of the Jews, claiming that although the Jews were being killed, their property would not be taken for personal gain, so the SS would retain the decency that was the root of their strength. The extermination of the Jews had to be kept secret, he said, because in a future world without Jews people would not understand the fierce measures that were necessary to rid the world of Jews.[11]

Beneath the bravado, Himmler was insecure about his middle-class origins, shopkeeper appearance, and omnipresent eyeglasses, especially around the aristocratic Wehrmacht officers, and he could be superstitious and indecisive, ordering sudden policy about-faces that left his staff and the chain of command below him befuddled. Few were aware that

Himmler's bouts of tergiversation were associated with incapacitating attacks of stomach cramps. No medications or treatment would help with the excruciating pains until March 1939, when Himmler met a Baltic German masseur named Felix Kersten, who had a Finnish passport and a magic touch on the massage table.[12] A few hours with Kersten would work wonders on the incapacitating cramps, much like the effect of Rasputin on the young tsarevitch. Himmler and Kersten spent many hours together, and the usually reticent Himmler confided in his masseur.

According to Kersten, in 1942, even before the surrender of German armies at Stalingrad, Himmler confidentially said that the German losses of troops, matériel, and territory on the Eastern Front were far more significant than Hitler was admitting publicly; by late 1943, Himmler privately said the war was heading toward at best a stalemate; and by the summer of 1944, he was willing to discuss the "eventuality of a German defeat."[13] Himmler was staunchly loyal to the Führer, but in his private confidences to Kersten his strident repetitions of the party line were intermixed with qualms and reservations. In November 1941 he said: "The Jews cause the rottenness on which they thrive. They dominate the entire world through the centers of news, the press, the cinema, art and practically everything else. The damage which the Jews have been doing for centuries—and the future would only be worse—is of a kind so comprehensive that it can only be met by eliminating them entirely." Five days later he opposed the idea of a Final Solution: "You're right, the extermination of peoples is un-Germanic. You can demand everything from me, even pity, but you cannot demand protection for organized nihilism. That would be suicide." A year after that he was adamant that "the Jews had to leave Germany," and on the same day explained why he would not use neutral channels to seek "an honorable understanding with England and America . . . it would shake the prestige of the National Socialist Party and the Führer would prefer anything to that."[14] Kersten noticed that whenever Himmler had to talk to the Führer, the stomach cramps would act up and the Reichsführer seemed terribly afraid, as if he were torn between loyalty to the Führer and his own doubts about the future of the war and of Germany.

As his doubts mounted, Himmler quietly collected information that could be useful to him later. In December 1942, he wrote himself a note: "I have asked the Führer with regard to letting Jews go in return for ransom. He gave me full powers to approve cases like that, if they actually bring in foreign currency in appreciable quantities from abroad."[15] The note could have been justification for a special policy for dealing with wealthy Jews, as Nazi representatives like Becher would later do in Budapest, but it was also a cover if Himmler had motives for direct negotiations with the Jews.

As head of the security apparatus, with eyes and ears in every sector of military and civilian society, Himmler was aware that others also had qualms about the Führer's total war policy. He followed developments in Turkey, where Franz von Papen, who had been chancellor of Germany and had made decisive moves that ultimately brought Hitler to power, was the German ambassador, an important position because Turkish chromium reserves were needed to produce high-grade steel for weapons. Papen had wide contacts in Turkey—his wife watered the plants at the office of the Vatican nuncio, Angelo Roncalli, the future Pope John XXIII—and he followed politics in the United States, predicting a Republican victory in 1944: "with a Republican Congress and perhaps a Republican President Germany can come to terms for a compromise peace." Through the chief of military intelligence in Turkey, Papen arranged a conversation with Himmler in August or September 1943. American intelligence got wind of the meeting and pondered the possibility that Himmler and Papen so distrusted each other that each man thought he was using the other as "an instrument" for independent peace negotiations with the West.[16]

Felix Kersten, with his connections in neutral Sweden, persuaded Himmler to send Walter Schellenberg, head of the espionage agency of the SS, to Sweden in October 1943 to meet a representative of the American OSS named Abram Stevens Hewitt. Their discussions of peace prospects went nowhere, but it was a start. With Himmler's knowledge, Schellenberg later explored other contacts, some through the Abwehr, including attempts at negotiations in Switzerland and Istanbul. Whenever these contacts or others were exposed, Himmler would distance himself by acting with fierce determination to arrest the alleged conspirators, including well-known figures like Hans von Dohnányi; his brother-in-law the Protestant pastor Dietrich Bonhoeffer; Admiral Canaris of the Abwehr; Graf Helmut von Moltke, scion of a family that had produced two chiefs of staff of the German army; and a lawyer named Carl Langbehn, a personal friend of Himmler, who met in Switzerland with Allen Dulles of the OSS. The cautious policy kept Himmler fully informed of negotiations without breaching his long-nurtured reputation for absolute loyalty.

Himmler also tracked Wisliceny's negotiations with the Jewish leadership in Slovakia, carefully keeping his distance and retaining the option of repudiating his subordinate if the Führer or other, more orthodox Nazis objected. When an attaché with the Swiss legation in Berlin named Anton Feldscher passed along a British proposal in 1943 for an exchange of interned Germans in return for Jewish children in the General Government of Poland and Soviet territories being allowed to emigrate to Palestine, Himmler gave permission for Eichmann's involvement, and either Eichmann or Himmler specified an exchange ratio of four Jewish children for every German (or pro-Nazi non-German) internee released, with the proviso that the Jewish children would not be allowed to go to Palestine: "The Reich government cannot lend its hand to the ousting of such a noble and valiant people as the Arabs from their Palestine homeland by the Jews."[17] The British objected to the exchange ratio and finally rejected the deal when it was clear that they would have to accept the Jewish children in Britain. But Himmler had gone far enough along to acknowledge to his staff, including Eichmann, that the Jews could be traded instead of killed. The negotiations with the British over *Judenkinder* did not end until March 1944, on the eve of the invasion of Hungary.

Himmler did not waver in his belief that Bolshevism (or as he would have described it, "Judeo-Bolshevism") was the principal threat to Germany, and he recognized that the survival of the nation depended on the Wehrmacht and the Waffen-SS defending Germany from the Soviet armies regrouping on the plains of eastern Europe. The Wehrmacht was officially exempt from investigation by the Gestapo, but Himmler was aware that some conservative and aristocratic elements in the German army did not subscribe to the political and ideological agenda of National Socialism and that a core of Wehrmacht officers, many with roots in Prussia, were so convinced that Hitler's war policies and leadership were a disastrous course for Germany that by the spring of 1944 they were talking privately about the possibility of assassinating the Führer. Himmler seems not to have known the details of their plans and did not share their belief that their planned act was a gesture of loyalty to a Germany that predated and would long survive Hitler, but he knew frontline Wehrmacht commanders had warned that Germany did not have the resources and manpower to fight on two fronts, and he agreed that defending Germany from the threat of the Soviet hordes might require a separate peace with the western Allies.

But how would separate peace negotiations begin? Himmler was not a man to venture a gesture as dramatic and quixotic as Deputy Führer Rudolf Hess's 1941 flight to Scotland. Hess, then the third most powerful man in Germany, was trying to reach the Duke of Hamilton, whom he had met briefly at the 1936 Olympics in Berlin, with a proposal that would have divided the world between Britain and Germany. Himmler's hopes were only slightly more modest. Despite the failed secret efforts to negotiate with the Allies, including the prolonged negotiations over the *Judenkinder,* he believed that the one issue that would draw the attention and interest of Britain and the United States was the fate of the Jews. To Hitler and Himmler it seemed obvious that the American and British governments were beholden to the Jews, and that Churchill and Roosevelt would bend their policies to Jewish interests. The Führer and Goebbels would rattle off the names of Jewish financiers like Morgenthau and Schiff who controlled Wall Street. The *New York Times* was owned and run by a Jew. So were the Hollywood studios that poured out propaganda films. The way to approach the western Allies, Himmler concluded, was to incorporate a rescue of Jews in the approach. The Führer had already approved ransom schemes involving the Jews if they were done for a proper purpose. What purpose was higher than the future and sanctity of the Fatherland? And even if the negotiations failed to lead to a separate peace with the West, the approach was good insurance. If the war was lost, Himmler and the other Nazi leaders could argue that they had made efforts to save the Jews, only to have their proposal rejected by the Allies. Carried to its logical end, that reasoning made the Allies as complicit in the destruction of the Jews as the Nazis.

Himmler wasn't alone in worrying about the future of Germany. On April 3, 1944, days before the yellow stars were introduced in Budapest, German plenipotentiary Edmund Veesenmayer cabled Berlin that renewed Allied bombings of Budapest had exacerbated anti-Jewish feelings. He raised the possibility of executing one hundred Jews for each Hungarian killed in the bombings, but wanted to know whether alternate plans were still being considered: "In reference to the suggestions made by Herr Reichsaussenminister [Foreign Minister Ribbentrop] to the Führer about offering the Jews [of Hungary] as a gift to Roosevelt and Churchill, I would like to be informed whether this idea is still being pursued."[18]

Veesenmayer gave the credit to Ribbentrop, but it was Himmler's plan he was writing about.

When it suited his purposes, *Obersturmbannführer* Adolf Eichmann could affect a tone and demeanor of fairness, honesty, and openness. He could look Joel Brand straight in the eye and say that all he wished was "to play fair with the Jews." He did exactly that when he made his proposal to Joel Brand, but he was dissembling. The proposal Eichmann made to Joel Brand was not his idea. He had other plans for the Hungarian Jews.

Eichmann had made the Jews his career. As a young SS-*Obersturmbannführer* (first lieutenant), shortly after the German Anschluss with Austria in 1938, he had been given the responsibility of establishing a Central Office for Jewish Emigration in response to a Jewish initiative to facilitate emigration by allowing property from the wealthy to pay for exit permits granted to poorer Jews. He later claimed he had visited Palestine for research,[19] and that after reading Herzl's *The Jewish State* he had concluded that Zionism "fell in with our desire for a political solution: the Zionists wanted a territory where the Jewish people could finally settle in peace. And that was pretty much what the National Socialists wanted."[20] The Nazi higher-ups rejected his early schemes to deport the Jews of Europe to Palestine or Madagascar, and when the infamous Wannsee Conference in 1942 decided on a Final Solution for the Jews of Europe, Eichmann was appointed head of a new bureau for Jewish Affairs and Evacuation within the Reich Central Security Office, and assigned the responsibility for assembling and transporting the Jews of Europe to camps.

With its Jewish population of over 850,000 virtually intact, Hungary was the final challenge for Eichmann's practiced specialty. He and his staff had moved to Budapest immediately after the invasion to prepare for the deportation of the Jews of Hungary, and even while he was meeting with Joel Brand, Eichmann's staff was using the procedures he had refined in Poland and the Netherlands, and the ready forces of the Hungarian gendarmerie and police to gather the Jews of the Hungarian provinces into temporary ghettos. The roundups were completed in record time, using fewer resources than any previous ghettoization. Eichmann prided himself in his efficiency. And he stood to gain promotions and recognition by completing the destruction of the Hungarian Jews.

His behavior during the negotiations with Joel Brand was strikingly uncharacteristic. Because his specialty was subject to misunderstanding and negative propaganda, Eichmann usually operated without interference from outside, and without other high-ranking SS officers present. Gerhard Clages from Himmler's intelligence staff, Kurt Becher from the economic office, plenipotentiary Edmund Veesenmayer, and Friedrich Laufer, another Gestapo official who did not report to Eichmann, were present in his office at various points during the meetings with Brand, presumably to make certain that the negotiations did not get off the track that would lead to Himmler's goal of initiating talks with the western Allies.

Although he had little difficulty lying when it suited his purposes,[21] Eichmann was also not a man to give vague replies. He was accustomed to being unchallenged, and his responses to questions were usually precise and definitive. But when first asked by Brand what he expected from the Allies, his only answer was that "they will know what we want." His later laundry list of materials read like an outsider's speculation of what *might* be demanded. It was only when Friedrich Laufer and later Kurt Becher entered the negotiations, along with Himmler's personal representative Clages, that Eichmann finally narrowed the request to heavy-duty military trucks, one truck for every one hundred Jews. Eichmann's explanation that the trucks were for the Waffen-SS, who would then turn their old trucks over to him, seems far-fetched. The roundup of provincial Hungarian Jews was almost finished and had proceeded efficiently without additional trucks. The further transport of the Jews from Hungary to camps in Poland or Silesia would be by rail. Eichmann did not need trucks.

When Brand said that heavy trucks were war matériel, which the Allies were no more likely to supply to the Germans than tanks or fighter planes, Eichmann had a ready answer, so ready it seemed prepared: "I can give your Allies a definite assurance, on my word of honor, that these trucks will never be used in the West. They are required exclusively for the Eastern Front."[22]

It made sense. Heavy-duty, all-weather trucks were crucial in the infamous spring mud of eastern Europe, where the Soviet forces were poised. The Germans had learned in three years of fighting against the Soviet Union that there was never enough transport. But Eichmann's assurance that the trucks would only be used on the Eastern Front, said in front of Himmler's agent Clages and other senior officials, had another purpose. Brand could be depended upon to pass that assurance along to the western Allies: it was as close as the Nazi diplomatic initiative could come to an open invitation to Britain and the United States to consider a separate peace with Germany. "Offering the Jews [of Hungary] as a gift to Roosevelt and Churchill" was the bait to establish contacts, the opening agenda for talks.

The proposal remained known to only a small group, and was vague enough for Himmler, Eichmann, and the other SS officers involved to have left almost no documentation of their moves. But by mid-May 1944 it had taken on some urgency. The pace of meetings was stepped up, and at his third meeting with Brand, on May 14, Eichmann said: "I've been traveling around the entire country and have seen only wagons loaded with bread for delivery to your Jews"[23]—a message meant to answer Brand's objections about the treatment of the Hungarian Jews, but more accurately a statement of how many Jews were already confined in ghettos, and hence a threat of what awaited the rest of the Jews of Hungary. The temporary ghettos were a perfect situation for Eichmann's expertise with the carrot and the stick. "Twelve thousand Jews will be transported daily," he told Brand, "But I am prepared to send them to Austria and not to Auschwitz. I will keep part of them in Slovakia. The transports will wait there until you come back, and they can then easily be rerouted to the Spanish frontier. If you don't return or if you aren't back in good time, these people will go to Auschwitz."

Brand registered surprise and dismay, and asked for a demonstration of good faith. Eichmann was ready.

"If you come back in a week's time," Eichmann said, "or shall we say at the latest in two weeks' time, and bring me a definite decision, then I'll blow up Auschwitz and the people I am deporting today will be sent to the Spanish frontier as the first consignment of those I have promised you." This was the relief Vaada and every rescue group had dreamed of. Then came the stick. "I can't just put your Jews on ice," Eichmann said. "Those who are able to work can, it is true, be given some casual labor, but the women and children and the old people must be got rid of. . . ."[24]

Joel Brand was also dissembling. He and his colleagues knew that Eichmann's threats were not bluffs. Although they had not publicized the information, they had seen the smuggled Auschwitz Protocols, which confirmed the construction of new crematoria and a second unloading ramp at Auschwitz, raising the capacity of the camp to enable the extermination of twelve thousand Jews per day—exactly the number Eichmann threatened to deport. Private reports to Vaada told of horrifying conditions in the new temporary ghettos in the Hungarian provinces. Independent reports from Slovakia described the readiness of the rail lines that led from Hungary across Slovakia to Auschwitz, and the availability of cattle cars in sufficient numbers to meet the efficient schedule Eichmann had threatened.

Brand had spent enough time with Abwehr agents to distrust the Germans. He would bargain and negotiate, and even lose at poker when he had to, but he had learned not to believe what they said. Although Eichmann was many levels above Joel Brand's former café contacts, from Eichmann's references to Berlin Brand had a strong sense that Eichmann's entire proposal was a propaganda stunt, scripted so the Germans would later be able to say that they had tried to get the Jews out of the country and had sent someone to arrange a reasonable deal, but nothing came of their offer and they were *forced* to kill the Jews. Eichmann and his SS colleagues knew that Joel Brand had no special access to Britain and the United States, the only powers who could possibly supply the trucks that Eichmann was demanding. Even if Brand could reach the Allies, the possibility that he could negotiate an exchange of frontline war matériel for Jewish lives was close to zero. It was possible that the Allies, along with relief organizations and wealthy American and British Jews, would pay cash or gold to ransom Jewish lives, but Eichmann had never asked for cash. And even if he had agreed to accept cash, Brand had no contacts with access to the enormous sums needed to ransom a million lives. The only people Brand knew in Istanbul were minor officials affiliated with the kibbutz movement, who used neutral Istanbul as a base to recruit refugees arriving from Europe. Even if he could somehow find his way to qualified Allied officials who had access to ransom funds, his experience negotiating Jewish rescues had been with German counterintelligence agents and Hungarian secret police in Budapest cafés. The cafés were no background for negotiating with ambassadors and foreign ministers.

Brand went along with the extended discussions and preparations for his journey to Istanbul because it was exciting, and because he knew that the alternative was deportation and annihilation of the Hungarian Jews. He and his colleagues had heard of Eichmann's efficiency. Every day that the deportations were postponed meant twelve thousand Jewish lives not snuffed out in the gas chambers of Auschwitz. Every day that Brand and his colleagues could stall Eichmann was another day that might bring the Allied invasion of western Europe, British and American forces who would be eager to relieve the situation in Hungary and rescue the Jews. Brand and his colleagues knew about the wealthy and powerful American Jews. They were confident that those influential Jews already had a voice in American policy, enough to make certain that an invasion of Europe and the opening of a Western Front against the Nazis would bring immediate pressure on the Germans to end the deportations and murder of Jews. They were confident that rescue of the Jews was an Allied priority.

"Eichmann put a million human beings on my back," Brand wrote.[25] If traveling to Istanbul to talk to the Jewish Agency officials there could buy time, it was a worthy mission. Even if he only managed to delay the deportations by two or three weeks, it was something. Every death postponed was maybe lives saved. Soon the Allies would come. The nightmare would end.

It was around the time of Joel Brand's third meeting with Eichmann that Vaada got a telegram from their contacts in Istanbul. The cables to and from Istanbul were terse. The Zionists had no access to secure telegraph facilities and often wrote in crude code, substituting transliterated Hebrew words in their mostly German messages—*Ashkenaz* for German, *kessef* for gold, *sechora* for goods, *Erez* or *Eretz* for Palestine, *shaliach* for emissary, *Sochnuth* for the Jewish Agency, *Kusta* or *Kuschta* for Istanbul or Constantinople. Sometimes they used coded words, like *Stefan* for the United States, *Brodeczky* for England, *Rasha* (Hebrew for "damned") for Himmler, or *Moledet* (Hebrew for "homeland") as an alternate term for Israel. The codes were nothing that would fool a trained agent or cryptographer, but perhaps enough to keep messages away from the attention of bribed telegraph operators. But this message was not coded; it was clear and unambiguous. "Let Joel come," the telegram read. "Chaim is waiting for him."[26]

Brand and his colleagues were overjoyed. Brand was sure the Chaim of the telegram could only be one man: Chaim Weizmann, the president of the World Zionist Organization. Weizmann had negotiated with presidents and prime ministers. He had persuaded the British to issue the Balfour Declaration promising a Jewish homeland in Palestine. He had signed agreements with emirs. He had stood up for Zionism at the Paris Peace Conference and stood up against the British over issues affecting Mandate Palestine. Eichmann had said, "The Jews control the whole world." If the occupied states of Europe had governments in exile and kings in waiting, Chaim Weizmann was the president in waiting of a future Jewish state. That he had taken a personal interest in the negotiations, and was willing to meet Brand in Istanbul, suddenly elevated the proposal and Brand's role to the world stage.

Brand told Eichmann he was ready to leave: "The president of our organization is awaiting me in Constantinople."[27]

# 5

## Bandi

*The situation in Hungary . . . does not at the present time constitute an acute problematic situation. On the contrary, as you are undoubtedly informed, the Hungarian Government has recently been relatively humane in its attitude towards the minorities in offering them means of entry into Hungary from the German-occupied countries and permitting the organization or methods for their safety and safe exit to other countries.*

—Ira Hirschmann[1]

*Pronto question Georgy and Brandt concerning "Brandt Plan."*

—William Donovan, Director, OSS[2]

No one trusted Bandi Grosz. He was agile and inventive, never at a loss to explain away the inconsistencies in his stories, able to invent clever if unconvincing reasons for his actions, and unfailingly sincere. An interrogator who questioned him for a full week declared that there was no point cross-examining Grosz, even when his statements contradicted reliable information, because of Grosz's "inability to tell the truth," and that he was "much too glib and too eloquent to be taken seriously." The interrogator summed up Grosz's testimony with one word: "smoke."[3]

After years of calling himself a rug importer or a gold merchant, covers that fooled no one, by 1944 Grosz openly gave his profession as smuggler. He had tried business as a younger man, bought a café that went bankrupt, and later founded a transport firm that had to close when he could not pay the fines after customs officials caught him with smuggled goods. He went into exile in Algiers to avoid imprisonment and, when he returned to Hungary in 1931, started black market smuggling. After the Anschluss in 1938, he switched to smuggling gold and founded a "firm" that would provide Hungarian passports and visas to Jews escaping Austria. His growing reputation as the Smuggler King in Budapest attracted the attention of both the police and the Abwehr counterespionage agents.

The Smuggler King soon found himself showing Germans "the alcoholic sights of the Hungarian capital" and catering to their interests in women and money. To anyone who questioned his loyalties or called him a procurer he announced that he was not involved in espionage but only "assist[ed] the German war effort in the fields of commerce." He gained enough of a reputation in Switzerland and Istanbul from his smuggling trips that he was sought out by the Hungarian counterespionage service, by various sections of the Abwehr, by the British and the Americans, and finally by the Zionists in Budapest. In Istanbul, Teddy Kollek, who would later become mayor of Jerusalem and was then a resident agent for the Jewish Agency, recruited Grosz to smuggle funds and documents to Jewish refugees in Europe and promised to introduce Grosz to British agents in return. Grosz claimed that he had carried messages in lead medicine tubes and a special lead pencil with radio codes, and admitted delivering payments to lady friends and "a certain priest," as well as to the refugee camps. When he was caught at a border with suspicious materials, he bribed the customs agents with carpets. He turned down no one: he was an equal-opportunity smuggler with no qualms about who employed him or who received smuggled funds. Some funds went to the girlfriends of Abwehr agents, some to officials as bribes, some to Jewish relief groups for delivery to labor and concentration camps. Sometimes Grosz wasn't sure whom the funds were for. No matter. Whoever used his services, he was a stickler for his commissions: 10 percent of the sum he smuggled. If he used a courier to move cash or gold, he got a precisely agreed cut. He alternated between passports in the names André György, Andreas Grainer, and András Grosz. Those who knew him called him Bandi and checked their pockets after they spent any time with him.

Bandi was always open for an opportunity. When he heard about Joel Brand's negotiations with Eichmann, he met Clages at the Café

Negrescu in Budapest to ask about Brand's arrangement with Eich-mann. Laufer later joined them, and the three of them went to the rakish Arizona cabaret for dinner. Bandi spent enough time with the Germans to pick up the jargon and banter they used privately among themselves, like calling the Reichsführer "*der Mann mit den Augengläsern*,"[4] a nick-name SS officers used behind his back because of Himmler's omnipres-ent wire-rimmed eyeglasses. Bandi privately called Laufer "the fat man." Clages and Laufer explained that the Germans had picked Brand for the negotiations because Brand's Zionists essentially agreed with the Ger-mans that the Jews had no future in Europe.

Grosz didn't care about politics. And he was sure the Allies would not give ten thousand trucks to the Germans. But they might offer dol-lars or Swiss francs, and if they did, someone would have to smuggle the money into German-occupied Europe. A 10 percent commission on the cash equivalent of ten thousand heavy-duty trucks was too inviting to resist. Grosz pointed out that he knew Istanbul and had been there many times, while Brand had never been there. Grosz didn't mention that he had already rented an apartment in Istanbul and had his wife living there, safe from the hands of the Germans. They talked and drank until four in the morning. Grosz asked if he could go along on Brand's mis-sion, but even after Clages said he would like to spend the evening with a "beautiful, plump girl about 30," and Grosz agreed to fulfill his request, the two Security Police men said no.[5]

A few days later Grosz went to lunch at Laufer's country house. Laufer explained that the whole Brand mission was a sop to the German Foreign Office and the German ambassador to Turkey, Papen, who was fiercely jealous of the expanding power of the Security Police. The real objective of the negotiations, Laufer said, came from "Heinrich with the eyeglasses." Laufer asked Grosz whether he thought he could make con-tact with high British or American officers who would be willing to meet with two or three Security Police officers to discuss a separate peace, then wondered out loud whether the negotiations should be with England alone, the United States alone, or with both. Laufer answered his own question. Negotiating with only the Americans would not work because the Americans would not act without the British. Negotiating only with the British would not work because of the strength of Zionism in America and because "the Americans, not the British, would rule the European roost after the war."[6] Hence they would need to set up negotiations with both. In the car on the way back to Budapest, Bandi and Laufer talked about a money equivalent to the trucks. If the Germans wanted $2,000 for every Jew leaving Europe—a number that had been bantered around—the sum for one million Jews came out $2 billion. Grosz and Laufer agreed that the sum was ridiculous.

Perhaps because he had been so visible as the Smuggler King and seemed to have access to the British and the Americans as well as the Zionists, Laufer and his colleagues apparently decided that Grosz could find and meet with responsible representatives of the western Allies. Bandi had talked big, and the Germans were listening.

The preparations for Joel Brand's departure went quickly. Most of the arrangements were made with Lieutenant Colonel Krumey from Eichmann's staff. In a final meeting, Eichmann laid his revolver in its holster on the table as if for emphasis, and told Brand that if he had to, he should go to London or New York. "But first send me a cable and I will put the brakes on."[7]

It is impossible to sort out the conflicting accounts of how Grosz ended up on the mission. Grosz claimed that both Brand and the Jewish Committee demanded that he accompany Brand because of his knowledge of Istanbul, and that he had been in on discussions of the Jewish Committee in Budapest. Brand claimed that Grosz repeatedly insisted that he be taken along, and that after Grosz met with Laufer and Clages, Grosz was forced upon Brand as a traveling companion. Brand later thought he should have resisted Grosz's company. He claimed that he knew nothing about Grosz's discussions with Laufer or his separate "mission," which was almost certainly true.

Rezső Kasztner argued privately that he should take Brand's place, that his own education as a lawyer, experience as a leader of Zionist training camps in Transylvania, his flawless German, and his previous communications with Chaim Weizmann made him the most qualified to deal with the Allies. Hansi Brand, who was unhappy in her marriage to Joel Brand and had begun spending more time with Kasztner than their joint work for Vaada required, argued that there would never be another chance, and that Kasztner was the man to go on the all-important mission.[8] Joel Brand answered that it was he who had been summoned to Eichmann's office, and he who was recognized by the Germans and by the Central Committee of Hungarian Jews as the official *shaliach*. The argument persisted until Samu Stern and Philip von Freudiger, as joint leaders of the Jewish community, prepared a letter of introduction for Brand, naming him as the representative of "the whole of Hungarian Jewry," and requesting that "all qualified Jewish people and institutions accord him the full support in their power." On May 17, 1944, Brand was told to meet Bandi Grosz at the Café Opera the next morning, and to bring photographs of himself. That evening they held a family gathering in anticipation of their departure. Joel Brand and Bandi Grosz talked as if "they were gods who would save the Hungarian Jews."[9] The title of *shaliach* and the stately letter of introduction had gone to Brand's head.

In the morning Hansi drove him to the café. It was probably a difficult good-bye: he already knew Hansi was spending time with Kasztner. The ongoing negotiations with Eichmann made it temporarily possible for Kasztner and Hansi to travel openly in Budapest, and Hansi Brand was told to see Eichmann in his office that day. Eichmann was friendly, even charming, and tried "to create an atmosphere as if it was purely a business deal, a straightforward transaction, and that we were business partners."[10] But Hansi Brand had been in business long enough to see through charm. She realized that Eichmann was reminding her that she and her children were hostages. They did not have to be held in custody: there was no escape from the Gestapo in occupied Hungary.

Krumey picked up Brand and Grosz at five that afternoon and drove them to Vienna. On the drive Grosz pulled a typed letter from his pocket and said he had to learn it by heart. Brand, absorbed in his own mission, did not ask questions but noticed that for the whole drive Grosz was studying his instructions.

They arrived in Vienna in the dark and were driven directly to a hotel reserved for German officers and the SS. Grosz had a Hungarian service pass that he had used on his smuggling runs, but Brand had no passport, so Krumey took Brand's photographs to get an official passport made. Brand and Grosz were not locked in their room, or even in the hotel for the evening, and were free to explore and eat in a restaurant. In the morning Krumey brought back a new German passport for Brand, identifying him as an engineer from Erfurt named Eugen Band. Krumey explained that the Security Police had issued permits for Brand and Grosz to leave, and that he had reserved two seats on the weekly German courier flight to Istanbul, but the courier planes were run by the Foreign Office, and they might not be able to fly or might fly only as far as Sofia and need to take a train from there. It wasn't until they got to the airfield early on Friday morning, May 19, that Krumey came back from the plane and confirmed that they would be allowed to board. At the airfield Grosz gave the instructions he had been studying to Krumey, and Krumey gave him an empty briefcase in return. Brand, no doubt jealous of the espionage symbols, tapped his chest pocket. "My secret instructions," he said. "I have to learn them by heart and then destroy them."[11]

The Junkers-52 was an ungainly three-engine transport, designed when Germany was forbidden an air force. The corrugated metal skin resonated with the loud BMW radial engines, and the spartan interior, engineered so the plane could be converted to a bomber, was noisy. The top speed was only 170 miles per hour, so with a landing in Sofia, where Grosz deplaned and chatted with local officials he seemed to know, the 850-mile flight took most of a day. During the flight Brand reread his instructions and finally ostentatiously tore the sheets into tiny pieces. He and Grosz were already competing.

They landed in Istanbul in late afternoon. Brand, anticipating a welcoming delegation, including Chaim Weizmann, let everyone else deplane before he stepped onto the tarmac, only to discover that no one was waiting for them except Grosz's wife, a low-level representative of the Hungarian consulate, and Turkish officials, who pointed out that neither Brand nor Grosz had a Turkish visa, and hence they would not be admitted to Turkey, would not be allowed to leave the airport, and would have to return on the plane in the morning. It was not the greeting Brand expected.

They stood on the tarmac, pleading with the Turkish officials, until a car showed up with someone from the Jewish Agency who breathlessly announced that he had been running around all day trying to get papers for the two envoys, and had finally gotten a letter from the British authorities requesting that Joel Brand be temporarily admitted to Turkey. The Turkish officials compared the letter with the name on the passport Brand was carrying, Eugen Band, and denied the British request. The Jewish Agency official then introduced himself. He was the head of the Istanbul office, and his name was Chaim Barlas. Brand had not imagined that the Chaim who would be waiting for him in Istanbul would be anyone but the famous Chaim Weizmann, the head of the World Zionist Organization.

The stalemate with the Turkish officials did not end until Grosz's wife dashed into the city and returned with a representative of the Antalya Transport Company, which had long been a cover for some of Grosz's smuggling. Against the personal guarantee of Mehmet Bey, the head of the Antalya company, Brand and Grosz were given temporary entry visas and *permis de séjour*. No one said so afterward, but they probably also paid bribes to the officials. They left together in a car and drove through Sultanahmet and across the Golden Horn to the Pera Palas Hotel.

Two days before Brand and Grosz left Budapest for Vienna and Istanbul, Dr. Imre Reiner, head of the Judicial Department of the Jewish Committee, heard from his parents in Nyíregyháza, in northeast Hungary, that the Jews there were notified during the night that they were to leave in a few hours. They were allowed only one suitcase each and had to leave everything else in their homes. By morning many were rounded up in brick factories and similar open but fenced areas. Some were interned in a camp at Kistarcsa, where an official reported sarcastically: "The Whole Nice Gang Is Together."[12] Reiner went with Philip von Freudiger to see Krumey at the Majestic Hotel to protest the mistreatment of the provincial Jews. While Reiner and Freudiger were waiting in an ante-room, Eichmann passed by and asked, "What are the handsome ones doing here?" Told they were waiting for Krumey, Eichmann invited the agitated Reiner and Freudiger into his office. A large map of Hungary was on one wall.

"This is border territory," Eichmann said, pointing at northeast Hungary on the map. "Over these mountains are Russians, and unreliable elements cannot be allowed to move about freely, that is clear. It concerns 310,000 Jews."

"Nyíregyháza is border country?" Freudiger asked. "It is three hundred kilometers from the border."

"You should ask your Hungarians why it nevertheless belongs to the border corps," Eichmann said. "It is up to you to guard against epidemics. The rest will be all right."

Reiner asked how it was possible to ensure hygiene when each person was allocated one square meter of space.

Eichmann shouted: "Shut up with this atrocity propaganda! Where do you get this from?"

Reiner answered calmly that he knew about the conditions because his ninety-year-old parents had been included in the roundup in Nyíregyháza.

When Krumey showed up, Eichmann ordered him to "have the first-degree relatives of Council members brought to Budapest."[13] It was a typical Eichmann gesture: he did not enjoy unpleasant meetings.

But of course he would not extend the special privileges accorded to a few to the rest of Hungarian Jewry. "I knew Eichmann's mind," Wisliceny would later recall. "His idea was to carry on the deportations in such a manner that the negotiations ordered by Himmler would in any case be frustrated by an accomplished fact." Eichmann admitted as much: "Such an idea about the ten thousand trucks would never even have crossed my mind. I would not even have thought of it. . . . I always preferred to see the enemy dead than alive. But when I got Himmler's order to equip two SS divisions with ten thousand trucks, then let a million Jews go to hell. . . . In the last resort I would have promised them even two million, because I would have squeezed out everything possible from the bargain."[14]

Eichmann was determined to deal with the Hungarian Jews his way. The day Brand and Grosz traveled from Budapest to Vienna and on to Istanbul, Eichmann went to Auschwitz-Birkenau. There he met with the former commandant of the camp, Rudolf Höss, who had been replaced as commandant in December 1943, then had been recalled on May 8, 1944, to supervise *Aktion Höss*, the liquidation of Hungarian Jewry. When Eichmann asked if the camp was ready for transports from Hungary, Höss equivocated, telling Eichmann that despite the newly built additional ramp and crematoria, he was not sure they could process the large numbers Eichmann demanded all at once. The selection procedure at the arrival ramp, where the camp adjutant and medical officers like Josef Mengele would choose which new arrivals were to be sent to labor and which were to be sent directly to the gas chambers, was so time-consuming that some of the transports might have to be shunted to sidings and guarded, sometimes for days, before the deportees could be unloaded. Eichmann was not pleased by Höss's answer. He ordered that to speed up the process there should be no selection procedure: *all* of the new arrivals from Hungary should immediately be sent to the gas chambers.[15]

The Pera Palas, the unofficial terminus of the *Orient Express,* was in the Europeanized Taksim neighborhood of Istanbul, a quick ride up from the shore of the Golden Horn on the cog railcar in the *Tunel.* Generations of European travelers arriving at Surkeci Station on the *Orient Express* had crossed over to Taksim on the pontoon bridge to stay at the Pera Palas, marveling at the ornate brass-trimmed elevator in the center of the hotel, the gracious formal dining room, and the familiar sounds of German, French, and English in the lobby and café. Across the street from the Pera Palas stood the large, neoclassical building that everyone still called the American embassy, even though it was now only a legation, with the real embassy hundreds of kilometers away in Ankara. Until 1941, when a bomb concealed in a suitcase turned the first floor into a shambles, killing six people and injuring twenty-five, the Pera Palas had been considered luxurious and secure. Even after the bombing, it was a convenient place to meet emissaries, agents of rescue groups, smugglers, and spies. The Jewish Agency rented a suite in the hotel as their Istanbul office. Other Jewish organizations in Istanbul divided their offices between the Pera Palas and the Continental Hotel, close to the British legation. Both were comfortably far from the German legation and the Nazi agents at the Park Hotel.

For Joel Brand, the Pera Palas would have seemed comfortably European. The ornate portico of wrought iron and glass echoed the familiar art nouveau shapes of Budapest. Coffee and tea were served in cups with saucers like any European café, not in the tiny glasses of the souks, and the trays of pastries on the marble counters and tables of the café were reminders of the familiar haunts where Brand had negotiated in Budapest. The exaggerated courtly rituals of the Sublime Porte had disappeared with the last sultan, but in Taksim many Europeans still called the city Constantinople, not quite acknowledging the new Turkish Republic, with its capital in Ankara and its insistence on Istanbul. By the 1940s, so many Jews lived in the area around the Pera Palas that they had outgrown their tiny synagogues and used the reception area of the Jewish primary school for holiday services.

Brand checked into the hotel alone, a far cry from the reception he had anticipated for his mission. Two local representatives of Jewish organizations showed up while he and Grosz were still in the lobby: Venia Pomerany, the kibbutz movement official they had originally cabled from Budapest,[16] and Benjamin Griffel, a representative of Agudas Israel, the Orthodox political party. The officials said little until Grosz and his wife left for their private apartment. Then Brand handed them the letter of introduction he had been given by Freudiger and Samu Stern in Budapest, and offered them cakes that Hansi had made. "I never eat with a stranger," Griffel said, "for I am afraid the food might not be strictly kosher. But from your hands I would accept anything, for they are holy hands."[17] Finally, Brand was being received as a *shaliach*.

The two men took Brand down the hall to the office of Chaim Barlas, where a group of close to a dozen Jewish officials had gathered. Brand was not a public speaker—cafés were his venue—but with the representatives of Jewish organizations as his audience he described the miseries and terror of Jewish life under German occupation, the details of his negotiations with the Nazis, and the incredible stakes of his mission. He ended up speaking for hours. The group was stirred. Some of the men wept openly. Others, shocked by what they heard, shouted: "All lies! A deceptive, villainous proposal!"[18]

Brand spoke about his disappointment in not finding Chaim Weizmann waiting at the airport. What issue could be more important to the Jewish Agency? he asked. "Is one single member of the executive here today? With whom am I expected to deal? Have you the authority to make decisions in this matter, decisions on which the fate of millions of people will depend? How are we to proceed? It is a question of days, of hours. Eichmann will not wait. Every day twelve thousand people are being driven into cattle cars. . . . Are you prepared to accept the responsibility for the slaughter of even a thousand more Jews, just because no one with the authority of the Executive has turned up at the right time in Constantinople?"[19]

The group began to argue. Each man had an opinion, and their gesticulations added to the chaos. To Brand it was cacophony. Some tried to be optimistic, while others cried in despair at how little they could do. Ludwig Kastner, an Orthodox representative from Slovakia, suggested that they could telegraph Budapest that negotiations were in progress pending the arrival of an authoritative representative from Palestine. Someone answered that they should not "throw down the gauntlet." Others put the blame on the Americans and British for their inaction. "When we win this war, and perhaps those who committed the crimes are called to the prisoner's dock," said Benjamin Griffel, "the Americans and the English will also belong in the prisoner's dock." He explained that it wasn't just the Americans they had encountered in Istanbul that he was talking about, but "those in America know enough from our reports exactly what is happening, yet none of them come forward to help, the feeling of Jewishness and sense of solidarity of the Jews does not exist [there]."[20]

Brand interrupted, explaining that he did not understand Hebrew well enough to follow the conversation, that they would have to speak German or English, that it was imperative that he understand every word, and that he would not be content with a majority decision from the group. He had expected to meet with Chaim Weizmann, someone empowered to respond to his proposal. Instead, he was faced with a cacophony of opinions that except for the languages probably sounded like a committee of representatives of Jewish organizations in Budapest.

He said that a cable had to be sent to bring someone from the executive of the Jewish Agency, someone who had the authority to make a "serious counterproposal" to Eichmann. Brand acknowledged that the British could never be persuaded to transfer army trucks to the Germans in the middle of the war. But the details of the goods didn't matter. What mattered was for him to be able to cable Eichmann that the proposal had been accepted in principle. He told the Jewish representatives that he knew that "the man with the eyeglasses" was behind the whole proposal.[21] It was proof that the Germans were desperate, he said. They knew that a catastrophe loomed. If a transfer of trucks was impossible, the Nazis could be bribed with food, even with money. All it would take was a cable, a simple agreement in principle, and Eichmann would blow up the gas chambers at Auschwitz and release one hundred thousand Jews. And once Eichmann made that first step, the killing would end. "Can you believe," he asked, "that once Eichmann has blown up the gas chambers of Oswiecim, has started official negotiations with the Jewish Agency and has sent one hundred thousand Jews abroad who will inform the world about what has happened in Poland, can you then believe that after half a year he will once more start gassing our people, just because we cannot give him a thousand trucks?"

Even if everything miscarried, even if they could not deliver on any of their promises, he told them, at least they would have saved one hundred thousand lives. "Is that nothing? Furthermore, we will be able to carry on our normal work. We can incite the people; we can build strongholds. Many will join the partisans. We will be giving them precious time, comrades. Every hour means five hundred saved from death. . . . I am absolutely convinced that this offer of the Germans is a serious one. If we accept it, or if we pretend to accept it, then our people will live. It may be that I shall have to bluff these Germans, but I cannot bluff if I don't see someone here who has real authority. The Germans will know if anyone has been here who has real authority to make a deal."[22]

Menachem Bader, the other representative of the kibbutz movement, pointed out that they couldn't just cable Jerusalem for someone to come to Istanbul. Telegraph communications were insecure. They had no way to know whether their cables arrived, were intercepted, or were garbled in transmission. He could have added that they also had no way to know whether a cable might be misunderstood, that Joel Brand might not be the only one to confuse a reference to Chaim Barlas, their local station chief in Istanbul, with Chaim Weizmann in London.

Brand buried his head in his hands. Even in occupied Hungary, he said, his little group was able to establish communications with enemy countries. Was it really possible that from neutral Turkey they could not send a telegram to Jerusalem, in Mandate Palestine under British control?

He made two requests of the group, first that they not let the British know the details of the German offer, because if the British were to refuse outright Brand would no longer be able "to play Eichmann along." His second request was that they put him in touch with Laurence Steinhardt, the American ambassador to Turkey. Brand and the Vaada in Budapest had heard that Steinhardt, a German Jew from New York, a lawyer and a New Deal Democrat, was "a good Jew, and above all a fine man." Steinhardt had a reputation for brash self-confidence and for tweaking the staid British diplomats. He was reported to have told the British guests at one dinner party: "We won the last war for you by throwing our money and our soldiers into the struggle. We are going to win this war for you but with a difference." The war would end with the United States and USSR the world's principal powers, and the Europeans would have to face up to how important a part the United States was going to play in their lives. More important than his baiting of the British, Steinhardt occasionally opened the code room of the American embassy in Ankara for the use of the JDC and other relief agencies, and seemed sympathetic to the Zionist cause.[23]

Chaim Barlas had a good relationship with Steinhardt, and promised to telephone and ask for an appointment. He also agreed to cable Jerusalem and ask that Moshe Shertok, the head of the political department of the Jewish Agency—the equivalent of a foreign minister for the Jewish state in waiting—come to Istanbul to discuss the proposal. Someone suggested that a cable wasn't enough; Venia Pomerany should take a train to Jerusalem to brief Shertok in person and bring him back to Istanbul.[24]

That would take a week, Brand said. "Why doesn't Venia take a plane, if possible, tonight?"

Told that it was not that easy to arrange air travel, Brand said that he had gotten the Germans to provide him with a courier plane to Istanbul. He did not let on, or perhaps conveniently forgot, that his transport was arranged by the Germans on their schedule and on their plane. "It was apparent," he later wrote, "that we in Budapest had greatly overestimated the influence of our Constantinople delegates."[25]

For the twenty-four hours until Venia Pomerany could leave for Jerusalem by train, Brand was caught up in individual discussions with the Jewish representatives in Istanbul, each obsessed with his own priorities. Chaim Barlas talked about the pressures from different groups, like the Agudas Israel representatives who wanted immigration permits to Israel assigned only to Orthodox rabbis and the heads of Orthodox communities. Others in the group talked about *aliya bet*, the code name for illegal immigration to Palestine—a challenge to both the Germans, who would not allow Jewish emigration from occupied Europe, and to the British authorities, who strictly limited Jewish immigration to Palestine. The operation had been organized by young Palestinian Jews called "the boys," men of twenty to thirty-five, bold and unafraid, who communicated in Hebrew codes, running what they called the *tiul* ("walk") from Poland through Slovakia, Hungary, and Romania to the Black Sea, hoping to prove to the Allies that Jews could be evacuated from Europe and ultimately to persuade the Allies to put pressure on the Turks to treat the Jewish refugees as stateless persons and not as potential enemy citizens. How many ships could be illegally chartered from Constanța to Haifa? they asked Brand, who pointed out that at best they might get one hundred refugees per month onto ships. What was that compared to the deportations from the Hungarian provinces that were sending five hundred Jews per *hour* to Auschwitz?[26]

Menachem Bader asked about the Hagana and the preparations for military resistance against the Germans. Another representative talked about forming a new Jewish Legion, an armed uniformed Jewish unit to fight against the Germans. Brand did not even try to explain the impossibility of armed resistance to the Germans, realizing that no one who hadn't lived under German occupation could understand the totality of the experience and the futility of schemes of armed resistance. Instead, he sketched out the ground plan of the Auschwitz camp, showing the layout of the new ramp and crematoria that he had learned about from the Auschwitz Protocols. He asked if the Zionists could contact the Allies to ask that they bomb the gas chambers and crematoria, and the railway junctions on the lines leading from Hungary to Auschwitz. The targets were compact, and it would take only a few bombs to wreak tremendous damage. Even if the Nazis tried to repair the damage, every hour spent repairing the railway tracks, gas chambers, or crematoria, he reminded the Zionists, meant five hundred Jews who were spared.

Brand was filled with ideas and a sense of urgency. The Zionists, in the relative isolation of Istanbul and Jerusalem, had been so cut off from the battlefronts, and from the immediacy of the deportations and death camps, that they lost themselves in incessant talk of politics. Even the next day, when they all accompanied Venia Pomerany to Haydarpasa Station on the Asian side of the Bosporus where he would board the weekly *Taurus Express* from Istanbul to Aleppo and Damascus, the group argued politics. The ferry across the Bosporus landed directly at the immense neoclassical station, built on eleven hundred wooden pilings, a pre–World War I gift to the sultan and people of Istanbul from Kaiser Wilhelm, and yet another reminder of the complex politics and loyalties in Turkey that Joel Brand had not anticipated.

Brand had not been prepared for Istanbul. It had been so easy to fly there on a German courier plane from Vienna, yet from supposedly neutral Turkey it was impossible to get a British plane to Palestine. He knew that the Zionists in Turkey had campaigned to bring Jewish refugees from Europe, via Turkey, to Palestine. From an apartment in the Beyoğlu neighborhood they sent postcards to Zionist groups all over Europe with the message: "Please let me know how you are. *Eretz* is longing for you."[27] Yet for years it had been virtually impossible to persuade the Turks to allow ships with refugees through the strategic Bosporus and Dardanelles, the only route from Romania, the Ukraine, and Bulgaria and the most direct route from much of central Europe.

On December 16, 1941, the *Struma*, a tramp steamer chartered in Constanţa, Romania, limped into Istanbul. The ship was rated for one hundred passengers, underpowered, leaky, and in terrible condition. A Jewish representative in Istanbul said of the ships available for charter by the Jewish organizations: "the word ship has the same relationship to these transport vessels as a tortoise to a lion."[28] The only transport the desperate refugees could find, the *Struma* carried 769 Jewish refugees bound for Palestine, a journey across the notoriously rough Black Sea, through the Bosporus and Dardanelles, and across the eastern Mediterranean. The passengers had paid exorbitant sums for passage under the impression that they would be allowed to land without visas. The ship barely made it to Istanbul before the engine failed. They asked permission to tie up at a wharf while they effected repairs to the engine, and seven passengers with Turkish visas were allowed off, but the Turkish authorities refused permission for the others to land. Representatives of the passengers begged the British authorities to issue them immigration permits for Palestine, which would have been sufficient documentation for the Turkish authorities to permit them ashore as transients, but the British refused. The British high commissioner in Palestine wrote to London that the ship should not be allowed to proceed to Palestine because there might be enemy agents among the passengers and that the passengers were mostly professionals, at a time when Palestine was short of provisions, suffering a locust plague, and could not absorb more "unproductive" immigrants. With no other option, the ship waited in Istanbul, short of food and sanitary facilities, while representatives of foreign agencies and rescue organizations argued that refusing to allow the passengers to land would mean certain drowning or recapture by the Nazis. By Christmas, the temperature was below freezing and it was snowing. The passengers had no fuel, food, heat, or sanitary facilities aboard the ship. They pleaded on humanitarian grounds, but the British and Turkish authorities steadfastly refused to let them off the ship or allow supplies on. After two months of waiting in those abominable conditions, on February 24, 1942, with crowds of curious Turks watching from the shores, a Turkish tug, the *Alemdar*, towed the crippled *Struma* through the Bosporus and up into the Black Sea, cutting it adrift three miles from shore. A few minutes after the towline was cut, a terrible explosion rocked the *Struma*.[29] Of 762 passengers, all but five drowned as the helpless ship listed and sank. Two survivors died the next day, two more a few days later. Only one man, David Soliar, survived the sinking.[30]

The American ambassador's reaction to the *Struma* sinking was to suggest that the Turkish authorities require that any vessel used in the evacuation of refugees receive prior clearance from the American or British naval authorities.[31]

In defiance of Brand's request, the day after Venia Pomerany left for Palestine, an intelligence agent from the Jewish Agency secretly approached Harold Gibson, the head of British intelligence in Istanbul, to feel out his reaction to the Eichmann proposal. Gibson's reaction was "cold as ice." He was not willing to recommend to his superiors in London that they allow the emissaries in Istanbul to negotiate with the Germans, or even pretend they were negotiating. He wasn't candid with the Jewish Agency officials—although they pretended to be allies, the British and the Agency had very different agendas—and did not admit his fear that the Soviets would find out and suspect the West of negotiating not to save lives but to pursue a separate peace. "We became entangled in a network of international intrigue and high diplomacy," Ehud Avriel wrote, "and from then on the British followed our every step."[32]

American ambassador Laurence Steinhardt heard about the arrival of Brand and Grosz and the rough terms of the Eichmann proposal before Chaim Barlas phoned him. He was willing to clear his calendar to see Barlas and Brand, though not to come to Istanbul. He had a member of his staff draw up a memo about Brand, which reported that Brand's traveling companion Grosz was regarded by American and British intelligence as a Gestapo agent and "completely unreliable"; that Brand's own bona fides, including his letter of introduction from Stern and Freudiger, might be a Gestapo trick; and that the motives for the proposed negotiations were probably mitigation of German reputations if the war were lost, a German effort to relieve themselves of the burden of the Jews, or a need for Allied sympathy because a putsch was in the works.[33]

Brand, knowing that any contact with the British would have to take place through the Jewish Agency and that the British would resist any immigration of Jews to Palestine, looked forward to direct talks with the American ambassador. There were no seats available on flights to Ankara, so Barlas and Brand arranged to take the train from Haydarpasa Station, the terminal where they had seen Venia Pomerany off to Jerusalem days before. They purchased their tickets and were waiting for the train when a group of excited Zionists showed up, pulled Brand aside, and told him that he did not have permission to leave Istanbul, he would not be allowed to take the train, and the police had a warrant for his arrest on the grounds that he had entered Turkey illegally.[34] There was no point arguing, they explained. He had to return to the Pera Palas. Chaim Barlas agreed to go on to Ankara alone to meet with the American ambassador.

Brand's confidence in his mission plummeted. "If you can't arrange a traveling permit to Ankara for two people," he told the Zionist delegates, "from where will you draw the strength to lift the heavy burden the offer involves?" He tried to suppress his nervousness and to give an impression of calm confidence, but Eichmann had given him two weeks. Four days were gone, and so far he had gotten nowhere. The Jews were still being rounded up in the Hungarian provinces. Hansi and the children were hostages in Budapest. If he went back empty-handed his own life would be worth nothing. When he got back to the Pera Palas Hotel he dictated a will to Menachem Bader.[35]

He and Bader were in Brand's room when the porter called to say that that two detectives from the foreign department of the Turkish police wanted to see Brand in the lobby. Brand asked one of the Zionists, Akiba Levinsky, to sneak him out of the hotel. "If I am arrested all is lost," Brand said. "The Germans will hear of it through their agents at once, and that will mean the end of our pretense of power. They will realize how small our influence is in this country."[36]

Levinsky started calling Zionist delegates to explain the situation. People were willing to call friends and arrange bribes, but it would take time. Levinsky was on the phone when the two Turkish detectives barged into the room and took Brand into custody, escorting him to the special police station that handled matters relating to foreigners. He was not locked up, but was allowed to wait in a large office that was open to the public. A policeman accompanied him to the washroom. It was a strange custody: police and members of the public with questions or business for the police came and went through the office. Finally a senior Turkish official arrived. "They're going to send you off to Svilengrad today," he told Brand, referring to the border station on the rail line through Bulgaria to Budapest. "Have you got all your luggage with you?"

Brand protested that it was all a misunderstanding, that they couldn't seriously mean to expel him. He demanded that they telephone the Palestine office and ask about him.

"We already know all about you," the officer said. "The expulsion order is irrevocable and there is no appeal against it."[37]

On May 27 three agents of the Hungarian secret police raided the covert Vaada offices on Semsey Andor Street in Budapest. They confiscated currency from Switzerland and Istanbul, but did not find the hidden suitcase where Vaada kept blank baptismal certificates and fake military ID cards for their mobile forgery workshop. The police arrested Kasztner, Hansi Brand, Sándor Offenbach, and Kasztner and Offenbach's wives; at another location, Menachem Klein, a leader of the Zionist youth organization, was found with forged travel documents and arrested.

The Hungarian police, suspicious of German negotiations with the Jews, of which they had been told nothing, had decided to conduct their own investigation. The prisoners were taken to an office where Peter Hain, the head of the Hungarian secret police, had them interrogated for five days. Guards beat them when their answers were deemed inadequate. Hansi confessed that she had been responsible for arranging forged documents, but said that she had no idea why her husband had been sent to Istanbul. The others also denied knowledge of Brand's journey or of negotiations with the Germans. On the sixth day, as the Hungarians were beginning their interrogation of Rezső Kasztner, the phone rang, an SS officer appeared, and the Vaada members were all released. Hansi had been beaten so severely that she was unable to stand on her feet and for a long time afterward had difficulty walking.[38]

The next day, Hansi and her colleagues learned that despite Eichmann's assurances that there would be no deportations to Auschwitz, the trains of Jews loaded into cattle cars at the provincial stations were being routed not to Austria and Germany for slave labor, but toward Slovakia and the rail line to Auschwitz. Hansi determined to pursue the issue, but realized "that it was not for a woman to bear such responsibility." She decided she would bring Rezső Kasztner with her when she went to see Eichmann.[39]

On that same day, in Istanbul, Joel Brand had been brought to the police station. Bandi Grosz was also arrested by the Turkish police and brought to the same office at the special branch for foreigners. Grosz, who assumed that he was safe once he reached Turkey, was furious, and blamed the Zionists for the trouble they were in. "If we're sent to Germany," he said. "We shall be shot like dogs as soon as we cross the frontier."[40]

Brand had also been thinking about their fate. If they were deported in the direction of Bulgaria and Hungary, he said, they could jump off the train before they crossed the border and could travel underground. Then once they reached Budapest he would tell Eichmann that the Zionist delegation had accepted his offer completely, but that in order to get temporary residence permits, they would have had to tell the Turks the purpose of their mission, and to avoid disclosing anything to the Turks, they were waiting to hear from Jerusalem before proceeding.

Grosz dismissed Brand's scheme as a pipe dream. "Joel," he said, "you're blind as a bat, and you simply do not understand what is going on behind the scenes. Do you really believe that Eichmann wants to free a million Jews in order to get dollars or trucks?" He then told Brand about his own mission, explaining that the Germans knew that the war was lost, and that Himmler wanted to make use of whatever contacts he could establish to start conversations with the Allies. "The whole of your Jewish business was just a side issue. We might have saved the Jews, but that would have been only an incidental result of my own mission. . . . "[41]

They argued. Brand refused to believe Grosz's explanation, which made his own mission and the possibility of saving Jewish lives so peripheral. Grosz, blaming the incompetence of Brand's Zionist friends for getting them arrested, was adamant that he would not allow himself to be put back across the border.

In the evening, the police office was closed to public traffic. The detective on duty told Brand and Grosz that they would not be locked up, but would have to spend the night there. Grosz protested: Where were they supposed to sleep? On the floor? When the Turkish detective suggested that they push a couple of tables together to make a bed, Grosz hysterically waved his arms, shouting in a mixture of Turkish, French, and German that the situation was intolerable, that he must be allowed to speak to his wife. Confronted with an apparent madman, the Turkish detective gave in and let Grosz use the phone. Half an hour later Grosz's wife arrived with blankets and bedclothes. When the detective left, locking the door behind him, Grosz used the office phone to call everyone he knew in Istanbul and urged Brand to call Menachem Bader of the Zionist group.

Bader was astonished and cautious. "What's happened," he asked. "Have you been released? . . . Have you escaped then, Joel? This isn't

Budapest. You'll get us all into trouble if you do things like that. The Turks might deport the whole delegation."

Brand calmed him down and explained that he and Bandi Grosz were being held in an office, and that Grosz had already had visitors. "It is vital that someone should visit me," Brand said. "But not one person has come. I just cannot understand your behavior."

Bader answered with vague assurances. The only plan he and his colleagues could come up with was a scheme to lock up Brand's passport so he could not be deported.[42]

After calling everyone he knew in Istanbul, Bandi Grosz changed tone and asked the detective guarding them personal questions, learning that he was a poor man with a large family. Grosz boldly suggested that the three of them take a room at the Pera Palas for the night, where they could have a good supper and sleep in real beds; the detective could lock the door and in the morning bring them back to the police station before anyone else arrived. To Brand's astonishment, the detective appreciated the logic of Grosz's suggestion. They cemented their friendship on the taxi ride to the hotel, where they ate and drank well. Under Bandi Grosz's ministrations the detective was soon oblivious, letting Brand and Grosz move freely around the hotel. Brand called his Zionist colleagues, and despite their qualms that illegal behavior could put the Zionist mission in Istanbul in peril, he got them to come to the hotel around midnight. Bader explained that the order for Brand's expulsion came from the highest levels and could not be canceled.

"In that case," Brand said, "we shall leave the hotel tonight and you can hide me somewhere."

It is not that easy, Bader said. Turkey was a police state.

"Budapest is under the control of the German Gestapo," Brand answered. "But when we have to, we can hide a thousand people there. You say you can't conceal me, illegally, for just one week?"

No one answered. Brand said that if he could leave Turkey freely on the German courier plane all would not be lost. He could bluff Eichmann and say that the local Zionist delegates in Istanbul, representing the Jewish Agency, had in principle accepted the Eichmann proposal. The delegates were intrigued with the idea. For hours, while the Turkish detective slept, they drafted a tentative document, promising that authorized delegates of the Jewish Agency were on their way to Istanbul (and if necessary to another country to be mutually agreed upon with the Germans) to discuss implementation of the Eichmann proposal. In the interim they proposed a temporary agreement: the Germans would agree to stop deportations in return for payments of 1 million Swiss francs ($250,000) per month; allow emigration to Palestine in return for payments of $400,000 for every thousand Jews; allow emigration through neutral countries such as Spain at a cost of $1 million for every ten thousand persons; and allow food, clothes, shoes, and medical supplies into ghettos and concentration camps in return for payment equal to 50 percent of the value of the goods sent. The arguments and drafting took most of the night and the agreement, "drawn up in a very complicated manner," was soon covered with Hebrew comments.[43] The proposed ransoms in American dollars and Swiss francs were generous, but there was no mention of heavy-duty all-weather trucks or the other goods that Eichmann had demanded.

Bandi Grosz left the hotel to be with his wife at their apartment. In the morning the detective took them back to the police station, where a Turkish official announced that the authorities had obtained transit visas for Brand and Grosz to take a train through Bulgaria, Yugoslavia, and Hungary. Both knew that a journey back to German-occupied Europe would probably mean death. It was noon when Menachem Bader arrived at the police station with the news that the expulsion order had been temporarily postponed as long as Brand reported to the police each day.

For days, nothing happened. Brand cabled to Budapest that they had reached a provisional agreement and that special delegates were on their way to Istanbul from Jerusalem to commence serious negotiation of the Eichmann proposal. Brand had established a code with his Vaada colleagues before he left: any message signed with a surname as well as a first name meant the opposite of what was written. He knew the temporary agreement he had drafted with the Zionist representatives would not satisfy Eichmann. Whatever his ultimate motives, Eichmann wanted to deal with Allied authorities, not a group of lower officials faking an interim agreement. In a coded reply to Brand's cable, Hansi reported that the Germans had not made any improvement in the Jewish situation in Hungary, which, if anything, was worse.[44] Each day Brand renewed his temporary *permis de séjour* at the police station. Mostly he ticked off the days Eichmann had given him, and waited for the expected results of Venia's mission to Jerusalem, the arrival of Moshe Shertok to begin serious negotiations of the proposal as the official representative of the Jewish Agency.

Chaim Barlas returned from Ankara and reported that the American ambassador had listened keenly to his presentation of the proposal, promised to send a report to Washington, appointed an assistant to follow the situation closely, and asked to be kept informed. It wasn't the reaction Brand had hoped for. Barlas also reported that Ira Hirschmann, a vice president at Bloomingdale's department store in New York on temporary assignment with the War Refugee Board, would soon visit Turkey and would be interested in the proposal. Hirschmann had met with some of the Zionists in Istanbul during his first visit to Turkey in February; he was Jewish, nonjudgmental, and a good listener. "Turkey is the observation tower into the Balkans," he said. "It's a window. What we tried to do was to make a door of it."[45] The Zionists had liked him and found him sympathetic, but he had explained that the War Refugee Board had no funds to aid in the emigration of Jewish refugees. Steinhardt's and Hirschmann's tentative support were not much of a foundation for serious negotiation of Eichmann's proposal by the Americans. There was nothing to do but wait.

While Joel Brand waited, Bandi Grosz was a bundle of activity, constantly meeting with people, always in great secrecy. After days of nervous waiting, Grosz proposed that Joel join him in traveling to Aleppo in British-occupied Syria, the entry point for British Mandate Palestine. They could get papers for the journey from the British, and from Aleppo they could arrange travel to Jerusalem. "There's no point in talking with these local Jewish Agency delegates," Grosz said. "I have good relations with the Allies, Joel. And the British and American attachés have definitely advised me to go to Syria. If there is anywhere that the fate of our mission will be decided, that is the place."[46]

Brand was wary. From the little he had seen—a lack of regular and reliable communications or transport and a cautious relationship to the British—it wasn't clear that productive negotiations would take place in British-controlled Mandate Palestine. And traveling from neutral Turkey to British-occupied Syria or Palestine meant crossing the enemy lines, tantamount in the eyes of the Germans to going over to the other side. The Zionist delegates, aware that Brand's days in Turkey were numbered, had discussed the possibility of getting permission from the Turks and the British for him to travel to Jerusalem, where at least he would be safe from the Germans. But it wasn't clear that the British would allow anyone who went to Palestine back out. The issue had also come up in Chaim Barlas's meeting with Steinhardt in Ankara. Barlas reported that the American ambassador had strongly recommended that Brand *not* travel to Jerusalem unless he first received assurance from the British that he would be allowed to return.

For Grosz, whose wife was already safe in neutral Turkey, it was an easy decision. If Brand crossed into Palestine he might never see Hansi and his children again. With good reason—he had heard Eichmann's threats and seen his temper—Brand feared what the Germans would do if or when they learned that their emissaries had defected to the British side of the battle lines. Despite Brand's reluctance, the Zionists tried to keep the possibility open, presenting British and Jewish Agency documents to the Turkish police, proofs that Brand would be allowed to travel to Palestine, urging that the alternative to deportation back to Budapest or Germany be explored. The police and the Turkish governmental offices did not reply to his appeals: the Turkish bureaucracy had inherited the Ottoman method of avoiding the unpleasantness of saying no to a petitioner. On May 28 the Turkish police announced that the deportation order was final. That evening Brand's and Grosz's belongings were sent to Surkeci Station, the terminal for trains through Bulgaria to Hungary and Germany.

With the days Eichmann had allowed him quickly running out, and deportation from Turkey looming, Brand seemed to find an inner calm. He stopped haranguing the Zionists about the importance of his mission and their lack of an appropriate response, and instead focused on details: financial arrangements for the few Jewish refugees who could escape to Palestine and future budgets for Jewish Agency support of the activities of the Vaada inside Hungary. He quietly asked Menachem Bader to get him a cyanide capsule, so he would not reveal secrets if the Germans tortured him. "Not just for us does a bullet wait in Svilangrad," Brand said. "This will be the death of the last hope of those who sent us." Bader got the cyanide, but decided not to give the capsule to Brand.[47]

While Brand contemplated a heroic stand, Bandi Grosz hid in the Polish embassy and made plans to leave for Palestine with support from the British ambassador in Ankara. Brand and some of the Zionist delegates begged Bandi Grosz not to leave, at least not until June 1, when Moshe Shertok was supposed to arrive from Jerusalem to begin serious talks about the Eichmann proposals. If their mission showed fragmentation and dissension, it would weaken their negotiating position. Getting the cooperation of the British, the Americans, or the Jewish Agency depended at the very least on showing a united front.

Grosz answered that he had his orders and could as easily carry out his own mission from Palestine as from Turkey. It wasn't true—he had been sent to talk to British and American military representatives, who were more likely found in Istanbul than in Palestine—but Grosz was eager to save himself and his wife. And Palestine looked safe. On the night of June 1, thirteen days after they arrived in Turkey, and one day before Eichmann's two-week deadline expired, Grosz boarded the *Taurus Express* to Aleppo. The British were waiting for him at the Syrian border, but not with the reception he anticipated. British intelligence had learned that Grosz had been arrested by the German security service in Hungary before he left for Istanbul, and that he had penetrated Allied intelligence services in Turkey. He would have a lot of questions to answer in Aleppo.[48]

Joel Brand got even worse news. The day Bandi Grosz left Istanbul, a cable arrived from Jerusalem with the news that Moshe Shertok, the foreign minister of the Jewish Agency, the one official who seemed to have the authority to act on Brand's proposal from Eichmann, was unable to obtain a visa to enter Turkey.[49] Joel Brand's mission was nowhere.

# 6

## Playing for Time

*It is not contemplated that units of the armed forces will be employed for the purpose of rescuing victims of enemy oppression unless such rescues are the direct result of military operations conducted with the objective of defeating the armed forces of the enemy.*

—U.S. War Department, January 1944[1]

*It was as if [we] were convened to watch the performance of death.*

—Isaac Gruenbaum[2]

On June 2, 1944, General Dwight Eisenhower, Supreme Commander of the Allied Expeditionary Force, moved from his London headquarters at Bushey Park to Portsmouth, close to the ports where the invasion forces were marshaling. Characteristically, Ike passed up the luxurious Southwick House that had been assigned as his temporary headquarters to live and work in a cramped and spartan trailer, decorated only with photos of his son John and his wife Mamie. He ate little and slept less, smoked four packs of cigarettes a day, and drank one cup of coffee after another. His personal secretary, Kay Summersby, wrote in her diary that her boss was "very depressed." Ike had a thousand worries. England was sinking under the weight of American troops and equipment. The logistics experts had run out of storage and bivouac space. The strategic planners in Washington and London were concerned about the speed of the Russian advance across Europe, the vulnerability of the Allied forces in Italy, and the possibility that German defense measures in France would outstrip the invasion plans. Most of all, Eisenhower worried about the weather.

He received daily weather briefings from RAF Group Captain Stagg, a dour and canny Scot who served as his chief meteorologist, heading a staff of British weather experts and brash Americans like Irwin Krick, a young Caltech meteorologist who based long-range forecasts on an innovative and controversial theory that weather systems formed not on the surface but higher in the atmosphere. Krick's private forecasting company in California had catered to the movie studios and other high-profile clients. To the British meteorologists Krick's talk of the upper atmosphere and mathematical modeling sounded like astrology, but he had been spot on with his forecasts for the amphibious invasions of North Africa and Sicily.

The invasion plans depended on a moonlit night for the parachute and glider units that would land on the eve of the invasion to secure critical bridgeheads, a low tide on the Normandy coast in the hours after first light so demolition units could clear the obstacles the Germans had placed on the beaches to block landing craft, and a window of fair weather long enough to establish and reinforce a beachhead. Statisticians studying tide charts, climate records, and weather reports from aircraft flying over Newfoundland picked June 5 as the ideal date for the invasion. The early summer date was also politically advantageous, potentially forestalling a German summer offensive that could force the fighting to a place and time of the Germans' own choosing.

After an unsettled May, with freakish hot spells that left everyone edgy, at the beginning of June the skies over Britain and the Channel cleared and temperatures moderated. Then on June 3 Stagg reported that the meteorologists predicted the arrival of a cold front that would produce heavy cloud cover, winds of force 5 and greater, and heavy seas—impossible conditions for an invasion plan that depended on overwhelming air superiority, a risky night parachute drop and glider landing, and calm seas for the landing craft with their low freeboard. Eisenhower knew that postponing the invasion would have serious political and military consequences. The earliest it could be rescheduled was two weeks

later, which would give the Germans time to prepare defenses or a coun-
terattack. American, British, and Canadian field and naval commanders
had been training their forces for months, aimed toward a peak of readiness for the amphibious assault. The intricate plans for transporting men
and material from temporary bivouacs and depots to the southern ports
were precise and lock-stepped. The transport trucks and trains had to
go into motion days before the fleets of ships, aircraft, and gliders were
launched across the Channel. Details of the planned invasion had been
kept secret, but rumors and barracks gossip had energized the troops, and
deliberately leaked false information had been dribbled out to waylay the
Germans. A postponement would blow the cover of General Patton and
his phony army in East Anglia, jeopardize the preparedness of the actual
invasion forces, further tax the stretched logistics, and require retraining,
redeploying, and re-energizing hundreds of thousands of men.

But the meteorologists, who rarely agreed on anything, were unanimous
about the approaching front. Eisenhower ordered a twenty-four-hour
postponement. Soldiers, sailors, and airmen stood down in place as the
great armada treaded water. June 4 dawned bright, clear, and almost
windless. Later that day naval forces that had been mobilized early
reported rough seas, and when the weather system finally hit England,
troops already loaded onto landing craft were virtual prisoners as ram-
pant seasickness multiplied the discomfort of the crowded conditions
and prebattle anxiety. Between visits from an argumentative General
de Gaulle, Eisenhower polled Stagg and his meteorologists: How long
would the cold front stay in position? When would the clouds break, the
wind drop, and the seas calm? Finally, the deputy supreme commander,
Sir Arthur Tedder, asked Stagg point-blank: "What will the weather be
on D-day in the Channel and over the French coast?"

Stagg pondered in silence for a full two minutes before he said: "To
answer that question would make me a guesser, not a meteorologist."

The German forces in France also watched the weather. Their forecast
for June 6 concluded: "Invasion possible, but not probable." Field Marshal
Rommel, who had been given command of the defenses of France, used
the bad weather as an excuse to depart for his home near Ulm early on

June 4. He planned to celebrate his wife Lucie's birthday on June 6, and also hoped to see Hitler to make a personal appeal for greater priority for his army group in France. The weather forecast convinced Rommel that nothing untoward would occur in his absence.

The final go, no-go decision was Eisenhower's. On the evening of June 4 he polled his staff officers, then let them leave the room. Reports from Italy suggested that the Allies were close to victory in the battle for Rome, but the fighting there was still critical and no additional units could be brought from Italy to supplement the invasion force. It was 9:45 PM when Eisenhower made his decision and told his commanders. He seemed remarkably calm, but Kay Summersby heard him mutter, "I hope to God I know what I'm doing." When he was alone again, Ike handwrote an "in case of failure" message, explaining that his "decision to attack at this time and place was based upon the best information available" and that "if any blame or fault attaches to the attempt it is mine alone."[3]

In Istanbul, Chaim Barlas, as head of the local Jewish Agency executive, was determined to keep the Eichmann proposal secret, lest an early exposure put the negotiations at risk. Barlas ran a tight ship, with the insistence on security and secrecy the Zionists called Hagana discipline. When Joe Levy, a reporter for the *New York Times*, showed up in Istanbul and began asking questions about the Zionists and what the *Times* called the "refugee question," Barlas forbade Brand to speak to him. Calling himself a disciplined Zionist, Brand did not violate his orders.[4] At the same time, Barlas had been in Istanbul long enough to have friendships among the many emissaries and agents posted there. One friend was Angelo Roncalli, then the apostolic delegate to Greece and Turkey. Ira Hirschmann, the special American envoy to Turkey, had visited Roncalli at his palace on the island of Principio in the Sea of Marmara, where Trotsky had been in exile before his move to Mexico, and found the palace a "gem." Roncalli reminded Hirschmann of Fiorello La Guardia, with his "charm and humor and cleverness . . . his little eyes sparkled and rolled; his stomach protruded, his body swayed."[5] The Vatican was officially neutral in the war, and the friendly Roncalli could be diffident in his politics. He had coordinated the support of some Catholic priests for Jewish refugees and occasionally let Barlas and Menachem Bader use papal couriers to send funds and messages to Hungary. When Cardinal Spellman visited in 1943 and asked about a bust of Mussolini in Roncalli's office, Roncalli said, "What we think in our heart and say with our mouth are not necessarily the same thing." But the wife of German ambassador von Papen still arranged flowers and sometimes swept the floors in Roncalli's chapel.[6]

Before Joel Brand arrived in Istanbul, Barlas had asked Roncalli to relay three requests to the Vatican: Would the pope ask neutral states to grant temporary asylum to Jews who managed to escape occupied Europe if American relief organizations paid for the relief? Would the Vatican inform Berlin that if Germany would free some Jews, the British had fifty thousand immigration certificates to Palestine? And would Vatican Radio declare unambiguously that "rendering help to persecuted Jews is considered by the Church to be a good deed"? The Vatican secretary of state, Cardinal Maglione, answered on behalf of the pope a resounding no to all three requests. His explanation was that the Vatican would not assist the Jews because a Jewish presence in Palestine might interfere with the holy places. It wasn't a promising precedent for Roncalli or the pope to help with Joel Brand's mission.

Once Joel Brand was put under arrest and forced to spend his days in the waiting room at the police station, he could do nothing during the day. But after five o'clock each evening he was escorted back to the Pera Palas Hotel, where he and the detective guarding him would spend the night. There, Brand was free to meet with the Jewish Agency representatives and other Zionist officials. They talked over the Eichmann proposal for hours. Brand bragged about his adherence to Zionist discipline. Despite the looming American legation offices across the street from the Pera Palas, his only official contact with the Americans was with Vice Consul Leslie Squires, who interviewed Brand and reported to Ambassador Steinhardt in Ankara that Brand "had little hope of actually getting many Jews out of Europe" and was "playing for time."[7] Aside from the Zionist agents, Brand's only other official meetings were with a Polish official he met in Chaim Barlas's office—they spoke only about affairs in Poland—and a violinist named Lili who lived in Bandi Grosz's Istanbul flat. Lili was from Budapest and asked about her family. Brand knew her mother had been deported from Hungary, but could tell her nothing.[8]

Brand and the other Zionists had no way of knowing that the British and Americans were already sharing documents on the Brand mission, that the British high commissioner in Jerusalem had dismissed Brand's faith in the possibility of prolonging the negotiations or substituting cash payments for useful war matériel as naïve, that the British embassy in Washington had ridiculed the proposal as "a sheer case of blackmail or political warfare . . . equivalent to asking the Allies to suspend essential military operations," that the British were claiming that even Chaim Weizmann agreed Eichmann's proposal "looked like one more German attempt to embarrass the United States and United Kingdom governments," or that Churchill had already instructed Anthony Eden, "On no account have the slightest negotiations, direct or indirect, with the Huns."[9] The Zionist efforts had been single-mindedly focused on getting a full hearing from Moshe Shertok, whose position in the Jewish Agency and close connections with the British made him the linchpin of the hoped-for negotiations. Brand was stunned when he heard that Shertok was not coming to Istanbul because he could not get a visa. "I found this quite incredible," Brand remembered, "for even then I regarded Moshe Shertok as the foreign minister of the Zionist movement, and of the nascent Jewish state. The Jews were the truest allies of the Western powers and Turkey was England's friend. Why then was the representative of the Jewish Executive now refused a visa to a country he had already visited frequently during the war?"[10]

Barlas and his colleagues were slightly more familiar with the policy backgrounds of the Jewish Agency and the British Foreign Office, but they could not answer Brand's question. When Shertok's telegram arrived, Barlas, Ehud Avriel, and Brand decided that with Grosz already gone, and no prospect of beginning serious negotiations with the Jewish Agency or the Allies in Istanbul, Brand too had no option but to go to

Aleppo, in British-occupied Syria, the closest point where he would be able to meet with Moshe Shertok. Eichmann's deadline had expired. The Turkish authorities were impatient for him to leave Turkey, and made it clear that they were not particular which exit he took—whether through Bulgaria and back to Budapest or Germany, or the long train ride across Anatolia to Aleppo—as long as he left Turkish soil. Others outside the close Jewish Agency executive in Istanbul were not sanguine about the idea of Aleppo. Kastner, the Orthodox representative from Slovakia, begged Brand not to leave neutral Turkey, saying the Germans would not let him back, and that it was naïve to assume that he could actually travel to Palestine.[11] For months he and his colleagues had struggled for each immigration permit to Palestine from the British. Why did Brand think they would make an exception? Some of the Jewish Agency offi-cials thought the British were planning to trap Brand, but made no move to stop him from traveling to Syria "out of awe and respect for the Emis-sary of the Doomed."[12]

Brand knew that the Orthodox competed with the Zionists for funds, exit permits, and Allied attention, which could in part explain Ludwig Kastner's opposition to his going on to Aleppo. But he also had his own qualms. The American ambassador had warned that the British might not allow him to leave Syria or Palestine once he entered, and no one on the German side had ever mentioned Palestine as an appropriate venue for the negotiations. From the inability of the Jewish Agency executive even to communicate reliably between Jerusalem and neutral Istan-bul, it seemed unlikely that he would be able to get or send messages to Budapest from British-controlled Aleppo or Jerusalem. He might never see Hansi or his children again. And for what? So far no one from the United States, Britain, or the Jewish Agency had heard him out about the proposal, let alone seriously negotiated or offered a counterproposal.

Barlas and Avriel assured Brand that he *was* being taken seriously, that they had cleared the entire matter with the British and the Ameri-cans, that he would be able to travel freely from Aleppo, including air passage back to German-occupied Europe, and that Aleppo was as far as Shertok could travel without a visa. Brand continued to raise objections and reservations, right up to the day scheduled for his departure, June 4. Barlas finally said that the Jewish Agency had made a decision, and that as a good Zionist soldier Brand had to abide. Ehud Avriel, who had handled much of the liaison with the British for the Jewish Agency executive in Istanbul, agreed to accompany Brand on the train. In preparation for their departure, Brand signed blank telegram sheets that could be used to communicate with Budapest in his name, and gave Barlas the codes he had used for messages to and from Eichmann. Finally, he sent a cable to Eichmann saying that he had to go farther afield to pursue negotiations "at the highest level," and that the text of an interim agreement should reach Budapest in a few days.

On the morning of June 5, 1944, the seventeenth day after his arrival in Istanbul, Brand and Avriel took the ferry from Katiköy, at the mouth of the Golden Horn, across the Bosporus to the great Haydarpasa Station. He had made that journey before to see Venia Pomerany and later Barlas off. It was different to be traveling himself. The ferry took him to a new continent. If Taksim and the Pera Palas had seemed familiarly European, Haydarpasa and the Asian side of Istanbul were a strange, unfamiliar world. Atatürk had abolished the fez, but men on the Asian side still wore baggy black pants, the crotch reaching down to their knees, with colorful brocaded jackets and vests. Women covered their hair, and sometimes their faces, dressing in abayas or robes over pants, a pastiche of styles and colors that were strange and different.

The *Taurus Express* was one of only two international trains out of Turkey (the other was the train from the European side of Istanbul through Svilangrad in Bulgaria to Budapest and Vienna, the old route of the *Orient Express*). The weekly departures of the *Taurus Express* from Haydarpasa Station drew crowds eager to say good-bye to those leaving neutral Turkey for a war zone. The entire Zionist delegation came to see Brand and Ehud Avriel off. There was an air of solemnity as they said their good-byes.

The two men shared a sleeper compartment. The train hugged the coast of the Sea of Marmara, where ships of all sizes and shapes anchored in schools along the shore, waiting for free wharves to load and unload their cargoes. When the Princes Islands faded from view the train route led past Hereke with its famous carpet weavers and Iznik where the glorious Ottoman tiles had been made, before turning back from the shore into a countryside of apple and pear orchards, fragrant with June blossoms. Apiaries dotted the fields. The apple and pear honey would be a specialty in the markets. The rural houses were built of wood in the Ottoman style. The orchards gradually gave way to wheat fields punctuated with occasional patches of grapevines or melons and upliftings of schist spotted with pines and weatherworn limestone. Rows of poplars grew as windbreaks between the fields. Only the occasional sight of shepherds and farmers in their traditional attire, with their flocks of fat-tailed, black karakul sheep, and a few heads of cattle relieved the bleakness of the plain and the loneliness of the journey. Brand and Avriel talked most of the way, with the intimacy that a cramped sleeper car promotes. Avriel was an ardent Zionist, working for the agency in Istanbul under the cover of being a journalist. If the journey across Turkey was familiar to him, it was not to Brand.

After eight hours the train stopped in Ankara.[13] A delegation was waiting at the station, Joseph Klarmann and Eli Jabotinsky (the son of Ze'ev Jabotinsky) of the Revisionist Zionist Party and Benjamin Griffel of the Orthodox Agudas Israel Party. Griffel had eaten cakes Brand brought to Istanbul, saying, "Your hands are holy." The men pulled Brand and Avriel aside and earnestly and emphatically said: "We have information that Joel Brand is being lured into a trap. Shertok was not granted a visa because the British want to entice Brand onto British-controlled territory and then arrest him. . . . In this matter the British are not our friends, and they do not want Brand's mission to succeed."[14]

After weeks of hoping and waiting for a meeting with Shertok, the warning was a shock to Brand. He knew that the Orthodox and the Revisionists had long been rivals of the Jewish Agency and were jealous of the inroads the Zionists had made in many countries; accusations had long flown back and forth between the groups as each accused the other of political maneuvering, or even collaboration with enemies of the

Jews. And while the Zionists were perhaps the most controversial in their aggressive recruiting of immigrants for Palestine and their dealings with Britain as the Mandate power in Palestine, Brand had assumed from the outset that the maneuvering of the Zionist executive in Istanbul and Jerusalem was all directed toward the goal of bringing the British into negotiations. He had harbored doubts about the possibility that the British would supply trucks to the Germans, but at the very least he assumed that the British would respect him as an emissary, an "officer bearing a flag of truce" and "the duly appointed representative of the Jewish underground movement in Europe." Avriel, who had been in Istanbul with the Jewish Agency long enough to know the ropes, and had served as the official liaison to the British there, seemed even more distressed by the warning than Brand.

The OSS—the Office of Strategic Services, the predecessor to the CIA—maintained an office in Istanbul on a tiny street near the exquisite Rustem Pasha mosque, a Salim masterpiece close to the spice market. The cluster of agents in the office worked hard and long enough in June 1944 that the lights and fans in the office were blowing fuses and burning up the wiring. The head of the OSS mission in Turkey was Lanning MacFarland, a Chicago banker and friend of William ("Wild Bill") Donovan, the director of the OSS. MacFarland made up for his lack of intelligence experience by wearing a slouch hat and trench coat. In secret communications from Washington, his code name was Abdul.[15]

MacFarland's chief source was an informer code-named Dogwood, a Czech Jew whose real name, Alfred ("Freddy") Schwarz, was not revealed until after the war. Schwarz was educated in Prague. In 1928 he came to Istanbul, where he built a business as an importer of agricultural and transport machinery. Schwarz learned Turkish, claimed to have been in contact with Kemal Pasha (Atatürk) and to have been involved in the adoption of Latin script for the Turkish language. Like many of his claims, those could not be confirmed.

When Hitler came to power in Germany, Schwarz assembled a secret circle of anti-Nazi intellectuals who were in Turkey as professors, lecturers, and teachers. He was recruited by both the Czech and the British intelligence agencies. He did not ask to be paid, and when the OSS set up their Istanbul office in July 1943, the Americans took him on and dubbed him Dogwood. His contacts also received the names of flowers—Verbena, Trillium, Camellia, Canna, Sage, Jacaranda, Iris, Crocus, and Azalea, among others.[16] Someone in the OSS had access to a good florist's guide. Dogwood claimed to have connections with dissident elements in the Abwehr and to know prominent anti-Nazis, including Helmut von Moltke. By the end of 1943, he was calling himself a representative of influential German anti-Nazi staff officers and officials who "in order to save Germany from complete annihilation are determined to work together, and collaborate with the Allies, for the defeat and destruction of the Nazi regime."[17]

Dogwood's organization used the Western Electric Company as a cover, which let him establish offices with a manager and a secretary, code-named Lily. For the newly established OSS, Dogwood initially seemed a gold mine of information, but before long the Americans discovered that much of the information he supplied them could not be confirmed. One of Dogwood's flowers, Pink, provided eight reports about Hungary that found their way to the OSS; none of the reports survived local checking.[18] The information on Hungary from some of Dogwood's other flowers, including those he had recruited from his Abwehr contacts, was equally suspect, especially the reports provided by Trillium and Iris. Trillium, who had made eight trips to Istanbul from Budapest in 1943, was Bandi Grosz. Iris, in real life, or as close as he got to real life, was Frederick Laufer, aka Director Schroeder. As Trillium, Grosz purported to report on negotiations or potential negotiations between the Germans and the Allies, the same expertise that had drawn him to the attention of the Germans in Budapest. He once met in an Istanbul apartment with Allied officials, bet them that the Americans would be in Budapest by December 1943, and, when the officials accepted the bet, passed that along to the OSS as a report. He was the classic double agent, often smuggling documents, money, or goods for the Germans on the same missions on which he was supposedly bringing information to

Dogwood for the OSS. Laufer, who had spied for the Czechs early in the war, remade himself as a Nazi, squelching the rumors that he was Jewish, and managed to hover in the middle ground between the German Security Police, whose uniform he occasionally wore, and a role as an independent economist and businessman. At one point, as Iris, he suggested through Dogwood that there was a possibility of "using a Jewish Refugee deal, in which refugees in Central Europe would be exchanged for either material or money."[19] But that leak, which was no doubt deliberate, was one more item amid the flood of misinformation and irrelevant reports that Dogwood passed on to the OSS. With so many proposals buzzing back and forth among the flowers like pollinating bees, the OSS routinely disregarded most of the information they received from Dogwood.

Dogwood's goal was to facilitate negotiations between anti-Nazi Germans and the Americans, exactly what Bandi Grosz, as Trillium, proposed in Istanbul in late May 1944. His proposal ran smack against the increasing doubts of the OSS about the reliability of the Dogwood flowers and the agreements FDR and Churchill made with Stalin at their February 1943 Casablanca meeting. Stalin's insistence on an unconditional surrender categorically precluded a separate peace between the western Allies and Germany. Like most of the intelligence agencies, the OSS was willing to probe beyond the limits of national policy, but proposals like the one Grosz made were screened with skepticism: "Nazis now expected to make preposterous claim to the effect that bargain concluded and Berlin to receive American trucks and other war material in exchange for refugees. Believe this devilish scheme aimed to destroy allied harmony, embarrass USA especially Roosevelt. Nazis expected to say Roosevelt prefers rescuing Israelites to winning of war." They also considered some of the agents serious risks: "whole Dogwood chain including Dogwood is dangerous . . . a general concerted effort to penetrate is being made against which we have warned all areas."[20]

There was another reason for the OSS diffidence to what they heard about the Jews of Hungary, and all of occupied Europe. The OSS engaged Charles Irving Dwork, a recent University of Southern California PhD who had studied under the Hollywood rabbi Edgar Magnin, to create a Jewish desk,[21] but the Jewish refugee problem, as it would be called in the OSS and in official American policy, was not a priority for the OSS, or for the Departments of State, War, or Navy. The reasons for this unstated but widely observed policy were a combination of a conviction that the real and weighty issues were the war itself and planning for the peace to follow, an inescapable if well-mannered disdain for Jewish issues among the Ivy League and military academy graduates who held prominent positions of power in the departments, a trace of anti-Semitism in the reaction to lobbying efforts by Jewish organizations and individuals, and a legitimate fear that appearing to favor one minority or one group of refugees could generate serious domestic and international issues if the favoritism were protested by other groups. The Roosevelt administration was eager to avoid an entanglement in the refugee issue, and while the United States had sent a representative to the 1938 international conference on refugees at Évian-les-Bains on Lake Geneva, neither that nor the Bermuda conference in April 1943 addressed the problem with substantive solutions. Until the establishment of the War Refugee Board in January 1944, there was no American agency or department to handle the refugee issues. The creation of the underfunded and understaffed WRB then became a license for other departments and agencies to ignore refugee issues because the jurisdiction belonged elsewhere. That cavalier disregard for the Jewish refugees, a quasi-official attitude among the OSS officers and agents, may explain why the copy of the Auschwitz Protocols that reached OSS offices in Switzerland early in the summer of 1944 did not find its way to Washington until the end of the summer. In the view of the OSS, it was not their problem.

Despite the presence of Laurence Steinhardt, an experienced diplomat, as the U.S. ambassador in Turkey and the visits of Ira Hirschmann as an official envoy of the War Refugee Board, studied indifference to the Jewish refugees and standoffishness toward the Zionists was also the policy in the Istanbul office of the OSS. The OSS agents established a caïque navy in Turkey for spying missions but refused to use the small boats for the rescue of Jews who had escaped Europe on boats from Black Sea or

Mediterranean ports. Instead, they collected newspaper reports on the "scandal" of Steinhardt allegedly "continually" trying to bring Jews to Istanbul to organize the office with "an exclusively Jewish staff."[22] The agents in Istanbul do not seem to have realized that their chief informant, Dogwood, also maintained close contacts with the Zionist representatives in Istanbul, especially Teddy Kollek, who was living in Istanbul with the cover of being a hazelnut merchant. Dogwood also had contacts with Ehud Avriel, one of Barlas's assistants in the Jewish Agency office in Istanbul and Joel Brand's traveling companion on the *Taurus Express* to Aleppo.

At the moment when Brand and Avriel reboarded the *Taurus Express* in Ankara for the long journey across the plains of Anatolia to Aleppo, an armada of nearly 7,000 ships, manned by 195,000 naval personnel, and carrying 133,000 Allied troops and masses of military hardware, embarked across the still cloudy and roiled English Channel toward the beaches of Normandy. In his stirring Order of the Day to the "Soldiers, Sailors and Airmen of the Allied Expeditionary Force!" Eisenhower called their mission "the Great Crusade."[23] The Germans, trusting Hitler's insistent prediction that an invasion would come to the Pas de Calais, the route Hitler had chosen for his own plans to invade Britain, were totally surprised by the massive amphibious assault, and with Rommel celebrating his wife's birthday in Ulm, the German defenses in France were scattered, unprepared, and slow to rally. The landings on three of the beaches, Juno and Gold by the Canadians and British, and Utah beach by the Americans, went well. On the fourth beach, Omaha, the Americans battled equipment failures and a desperate German defense until Omar Bradley, the American commander, came close to giving up the effort. But by the morning of June 7, after fierce fighting, heavy casualties, stunted progress through the dense Normandy hedgerows, and difficulties in linking the amphibious assault force up with the airborne troops who had landed on the night of June 5, the Americans succeeded in establishing a beachhead. For General Eisenhower, his commanders, the vast forces under his command, and for General Marshall, President

Roosevelt, and the State and War departments in Washington, the doctrine they had learned at West Point—the need to engage and destroy the enemy without distractions from the central mission—now had a fulcrum. Before the first day was over on the beaches of Normandy, the plans were under way to establish temporary docks and move men and matériel to France, entire armies, shipload after shipload of equipment, enough aircraft to block out the sun. They had one mission: the destruction of the German army. Nothing would be allowed to distract them from the Great Crusade.

General Eisenhower broadcast an announcement of the invasion over the Allied propaganda transmitters. Despite German efforts to block and counter the broadcasts, news of the Allied invasion quickly reached much of occupied Europe, including Hungary. The first reports were electrifying café fodder. The news of the invasion was spotty enough that anyone could read his or her own message into the reports. Some thought the war would be over in weeks. Others thought the beachhead would not hold, that Rommel would gather forces and drive the Allies back into the sea. For those desperate for good news, like the Jews of Hungary, the Allied landings meant a sudden hope for liberation. The Soviet troops were closer, almost at the borders of Hungary, but from long experience the Hungarians did not trust the Soviets. It was to the West that they turned for relief, and the successful Allied beachhead in Normandy, followed by the expected flood of troops, material, and equipment, meant the end of the war, liberation from the German occupation, and the end of the ghettos and the deportations to Auschwitz.

Aboard the *Taurus Express,* Brand and Avriel heard nothing of the invasion. From Ankara the train rode over the vast Anatolian plain, past fields of wheat and maize, where limestone outcroppings and weathered hills rose up from the plains, and flocks of sheep and black goats grazed under the watchful eyes of shepherds and trained dogs. If Brand did not hear wolves howling at night, he surely could have imagined them from the size and ferocity of the Akbash and Kangal guard dogs that had been bred for centuries to protect the flocks. The land was arid but fertile, green from the spring rains. Occasionally they came across stuccoed timber or stone houses with sagging tile roofs, alone or clustered around a tiny, rude mosque. As the train turned south toward Adana, the land-scape gradually became more Mediterranean, with shimmering olive and palm trees taking the place of oaks and pines. At Adana, where the train stopped for water, they could see black basalt citadels that crusaders and Armenians had once contested on the distant hilltops.

Brand and Avriel were asleep in their couchettes when the train approached the Syrian border. French officials demanded their papers, and were almost apoplectic at the sight of Brand's German passport, turning the passport over repeatedly and talking among themselves with great animation. When Brand pointed out the British visa for travel in Syria that he had gotten in Istanbul, the officials relented and stamped his passport. They didn't check his or Avriel's luggage.

Half an hour later the train stopped at another checkpoint, this one manned by British officials who waved Brand and Avriel through without looking at their passes. When they were clear of the officials, Avriel said, "If we should unexpectedly be parted, you must follow these instructions implicitly." He told Brand not to allow himself to be ques-tioned except in the presence of a Jewish Agency representative. "You must request that Moshe Shertok be informed, and you must answer no questions whatsoever before his arrival."

The train approached Aleppo through stony fields and quarries. With no guards on the grade crossings, the train whistle wailed almost con-tinuously until it pulled up at the station, a sheltered platform that led out to the two tracks. The station building was small, and city streets came right up to the tracks on either side of the platform. Brand and Avriel expected to see someone waiting for them at the station, but they recognized no one on the platform. While Brand gathered their luggage, Avriel got off the train to fetch a porter. Brand watched him run down the platform, and a while later a porter appeared for the luggage. Brand handed the luggage to the porter and was about to follow him across the platform when an Englishman wearing civilian clothes entered the sleeper compartment and said, "Mr. Brand?"

"Oh, yes," he answered.

"This way, please."

Brand wanted to follow the porter, but the Englishman barred the way and pointed in the opposite direction. More men arrived and forced Brand to go in the direction the Englishman had indicated. It all happened quickly, and before Brand could collect his wits, he was escorted into a waiting jeep with its engine running. He tried to resist, and shouted for Avriel, but his companion was nowhere to be seen. Once Brand was in his seat, the jeep drove off fast toward the outskirts of Aleppo.[24]

# 7

# Aleppo

*When we will have won this war, and perhaps those who committed the crimes are called to justice, the Americans and British will also belong in the prisoner's dock. Ultimately, the Jews of America will also be answerable for their leading role.*

—Benjamin Griffel, May 26, 1944[1]

*In the matter of Joel we acted correctly from an international-political point of view, in accordance with the interest of the Hungarian Jews and the interests of world Jewry.*

—Eliezer Kaplan, Jewish Agency[2]

Moshe Shertok looked like a diplomat. Tall and slender, and generally dressed in a suit and tie rather than the ideologically correct Zionist uniform of an open-necked, short-sleeved shirt, he had served as an interpreter with the German army in Palestine during World War I, later studied economics in England, and was fluent in German, English, Arabic, and Turkish, as well as the Hebrew of his education in the Ukraine and Palestine. As political secretary of the Jewish Agency, responsible for dealing with the British mandatory authorities and for relations with other nations, Shertok had the frenetic agenda and wartime diplomatic challenges of a foreign minister—all he was missing was a country. The Jewish Agency carried on detailed diplomatic negotiations with the Allies. and coordinated underground programs to bring funds into war zones and bring refugees out and to Palestine, their actions limited at every step by the British. In his effort to broker with the Allies, and especially the British Mandate, Shertok flew between Jerusalem and London so often that he was accustomed to the roundabout route across North Africa and the multiple refueling stops needed to avoid overflying occupied Europe. Each circuitous flight was a reminder of how much of Europe was under Nazi occupation, how much of the Jewish population of the world was subject to ghettoization and deportations to the labor and death camps, and how little the Jewish Agency could do about the situation.

The Jewish Agency walked a narrow line in 1944. When it was established in 1933, it was supposed to have a significant non-Zionist representation to voice the views of groups and organizations that were committed to the idea of Palestine as a refuge for Jews who had nowhere else to go, but who were reluctant or unwilling to support the Zionist aim of establishing an independent Jewish state or commonwealth in Palestine. Some Jews and organizations on both ends of the spectrum, from ardent assimilationists to ultra-Orthodox Jews, were opposed to the Zionist aims and campaigned hard and effectively against the Zionists, both in Palestine and abroad. With the rise of the Nazis and the emigration crisis that followed in the 1930s and especially in the war years, the Jewish Agency faced the dilemma of pursuing its own Zionist agenda and advocacy as a state in waiting, while at the same time negotiating with and appealing for funds to groups and organizations opposed to its Zionist goals. It also had to deal with the widespread myth, subscribed to by some in both Axis and Allied governments, that the Jews of the world were organized in a vast, semisecret, and infinitely powerful network. The origins of the myth are obscure, but it was fed by literary examples, not only in openly anti-Semitic tracts like the infamous Protocols of the Elders of Zion, but in popular novels like Sir Walter Scott's *Ivanhoe*, with its hints of worldwide Jewish financial connections, and by tales that grew up around Jewish interventions in events like the Damascus Affair of 1840 and the Dreyfus Affair. Men like Slovakian rabbi Michael Dov-Ber Weissmandel, who wrote letters on stationery from Swiss hotels authorizing himself to negotiate with the Nazis in the name of "representatives of the rabbis of the world," fed the myth and faced the Jewish Agency with claims that they were a spearhead for an all-powerful, organized world Jewry, with political leaders like Winston Churchill and Franklin Roosevelt in their pockets. And because the need for Jewish immigration to Palestine trumped many other Zionist concerns, the official Zionist agencies sometimes found themselves with strange bedfellows. In the early 1930s, they had been so eager to maintain good relations in Europe that when President Hindenburg died, the Zionist Organization sent a cable of condolence to Hitler. They could also never escape the irony that their goal—getting the Jews out of Europe—paralleled the primary goal of the Nazis.

Shertok was in Tel Aviv in late May 1944 when he learned that an urgent telegram had arrived in his Jerusalem office reporting that someone was flying from Istanbul to meet him in connection with the Hungarian situation. Shertok had followed reports about the Nazi occupation of Hungary and was eager for more news, but he was too busy to get to the airport at Lydda, and the man he sent in his place returned alone, reporting that no one showed up on the only flight from Istanbul. Later that night Shertok heard that the messenger from Istanbul was Venia Pomerany from the Jewish Agency executive there, that he had missed the plane and was traveling by train and bus. Pomerany arrived in Jerusalem close to midnight, carrying a summary of the Eichmann proposal concealed in a tube of shaving cream. He promptly met with Shertok to report on the Vaada negotiations with the Germans, Eichmann's proposal, and the missions of Joel Brand and Bandi Grosz.[3]

Shertok was sufficiently impressed by what Pomerany reported to summon a special meeting of the Jewish Agency executive the next morning. He knew the agency representatives in Istanbul had previous experience with Grosz, who had occasionally carried funds destined for concentration camp inmates back to Hungary, and once had come to the Jewish Agency in Istanbul claiming that he had been commissioned by "a very important Hungarian group to arrange for them to meet British and Americans—primarily Americans—with whom certain members of the Hungarian General Staff were alleged to wish to make arrangements with the Allies for 'resistance' and anti-Nazi activities in Hungary." The Jewish Agency officials had taken that story with a large grain of salt, concluding that it was nothing more than a Nazi intrigue. They saw nothing different in Bandi Grosz's alleged new mission of setting up a meeting with Allied officials.

The Jewish Agency executives knew less about Joel Brand—Venia Pomerany was their only source, and he had spent only one day with Brand before leaving for Jerusalem—and they had not yet talked to other Jewish Agency representatives in Istanbul. The proposal Brand brought from Eichmann wasn't the first they had seen for ransoming Jewish lives from the Nazis, but there had never been an offer on anything approaching this scale before, and with the fortunes on the battlefronts turning against the Nazis, it seemed at least possible that the Nazis would seriously negotiate. At the same time, the Jewish Agency had few resources to offer. Their own financial resources were limited, and many of the agencies and groups with funds, like the JDC and other international relief organizations, were not interested in Zionist proposals to bring refugees to Palestine. Even if the Jewish Agency had access to funds or goods to ransom refugees, the British had repeatedly and adamantly made it clear that they would not allow increased Jewish immigration to Palestine. The British had occasionally issued eloquent responses to pleas on behalf of refugees—they too had to face the public relations issue of appearing uncaring—but in the end they would not allow any substantial increase of the Jewish population of Palestine lest they offend the Arab population. Appeals of this policy from abroad and from the Jewish community in Palestine did not change the official British position. Nor did the open alliance between Hitler and the grand mufti of Jerusalem, who claimed to be the spiritual if not the political leader of the Palestinian Arabs, change the adamant British resistance to more Jewish immigration to Palestine. The British did not seem to be aware that the Germans had plans for a continuation of the Holocaust in Palestine.[4]

Although the possibility of getting any of the Hungarian Jews out of Europe and to Palestine seemed nil, the numbers in the proposal Brand brought made it impossible to ignore. Reports from Hungary and Slovakia confirmed some of what Brand reported, including his references to the wholesale annihilation going on at Auschwitz. If even a tiny fraction of the one million refugees in Eichmann's proposal could be ransomed, it would be a spectacular rescue, tens or hundreds of thousands of European Jews saved from the death camps or the slow death of labor camps and the ghettos. The odds of actually negotiating a trade of goods for lives were minuscule, but *something* might come of the negotiations, if only a delay in the deportations. And to not negotiate would be criminal. The Jewish Agency was also acutely aware of its image and reputation, and of the potential reaction of the British and Americans. When the executive met to talk about the proposal, Eliahu Dobkin, director of the immigration department, and Isaac Gruenbaum, head of the rescue committee, wanted to conceal the Brand proposal from the British; Gruenbaum also wanted to conceal it from the Americans, for fear the Allies would somehow sabotage the proposal. David Ben-Gurion argued that without the Allies "we may not be able to move."[5]

Ultimately, the Jewish Agency could not risk being blamed for callously ignoring a proposal to save Jewish lives. In some quarters the Zionists had been criticized repeatedly for seeming to care more about the Zionist enterprise of building a Jewish state than about the fate of the Jews in Europe under the Nazis. In an instinctive response to those criticisms, the hastily called meeting of the executive, presided over by Ben-Gurion, decided to follow up on the Brand proposal by asking the British high commissioner for "facilities for the thorough exploration of the whole business," which translated to getting permission and transport for Moshe Shertok, their most senior foreign policy person, to go to Istanbul to investigate the offer.

Early the next day, May 26, Shertok presented the matter to the British high commissioner in Palestine, Sir Harold MacMichael, assuring him that Shertok would promptly report whatever he found in Istanbul to the British embassy in Ankara. The high commissioner regarded the matter seriously but skeptically, asking whether the purpose of the Jewish rescue mission was to undermine Allied unity. As far as he was concerned, he told Shertok, the Eichmann proposal was one more Nazi intrigue, and Joel Brand and Bandi Grosz were Nazi agents. At the same time he agreed that nothing should be left undone to explore the proposal, lest there later be accusations that someone had missed the chance of saving people. He agreed to report the matter to London and wire the embassy in Ankara to inquire about a Turkish visa for Shertok.

Days went by and no visa came. Once before, when an important matter arose, the British had allowed Shertok to fly to Turkey without a visa. They wired their embassy in Ankara, and a consular official was sent to Adana, in the south of Turkey, to meet Shertok's BOAC flight and arrange the necessary papers. When Shertok pressed for the same consideration on the Brand matter, MacMichael said the British government was willing to use a similar procedure to get him to Istanbul to meet Brand, then suddenly at the end of May announced that he had been told by the British embassy in Ankara that on "no account" should Shertok attempt to travel to Turkey without a visa. He did not say who had made the decision or why.

By then, the Turkish officials in Istanbul were insisting that Brand's welcome in Turkey was exhausted and that he either return to Hungary and Germany or travel onward to Palestine. A British intelligence official in Palestine suggested that while the British could not guarantee that Brand would be able to return to Hungary from Palestine, Shertok could meet with him in Aleppo, in British-occupied Syria. Aleppo was close to the Turkish border, and there would be no objection to his returning to Hungary from Syria. The Jewish Agency officials in Istanbul agreed, and with the approval of the chief secretary and the chief of military intelligence in Palestine, Shertok left by train from Haifa, coordinating his departure so he would arrive in Aleppo at the same time as Brand's train from Istanbul.

For hundreds of years, trains of as many as a thousand camels each brought goods—gold, frankincense, myrrh, hand-woven carpets, spices, fine wool, silk—from Persia and the East to Aleppo, the commercial center of Syria. When railroads replaced the camel trains, Aleppo remained the great souk where goods from the East met those from Turkey and Europe. Aleppo textiles, and the centrality of the city for trade with the

East, faded by the 1940s, but the city and northwest Syria remained strategically important because of their connection to Turkey and the Caucasus. After France fell to the Nazis, British and Commonwealth troops invaded Syria in 1941 to prevent Vichy or the Germans using Syria as a base to attack Palestine and Egypt. Moshe Dayan, a native-born Jewish Palestinian, fought with the British forces and lost an eye in the action. Later, when pressures were mounting to take Jewish refugees into Palestine, the Colonial Office suggested the possibility of Syria as a refuge for Jews.[6] The idea was never followed up.

By 1944, British-occupied Aleppo had become the point of entry to Palestine and the Middle East for war refugees fleeing Europe via Turkey. The British determination to limit Jewish immigration to Palestine turned the city into a restrictive gateway: Many of the arriving refugees, fresh from enforced ghettos, labor camps, or concentration camps, exhausted from the long and harrowing overland journeys and perilous voyages on marginal steamers in the rough waters of the Black Sea and the Mediterranean, and terrified of the Turkish bureaucracy that had harassed them or thwarted their travel, found themselves detained in British camps outside the city for as long as a fortnight while their immigration status was reviewed. Many found the British interrogation procedures terrifying, especially when their passports or other travel documents were seized and the interrogators put marks next to their names on an interview sheet, a secret judgment that might not be revealed for days or weeks while they waited in a desert limbo.[7]

Joel Brand was spared the temporary refugee camps, and taken instead to a nearly empty dormitory on a military base outside Aleppo. It wasn't the diplomatic reception he expected, but despite his kidnapping at the Aleppo station and the drive to a secret location, he wasn't made to feel like a prisoner. When he arrived at the military base, the British sergeants sitting around a table reading newspapers ignored him. He was given his choice of cots, his luggage was delivered, and in the morning he was invited to join the noncommissioned officers for an excellent breakfast. It wasn't until after breakfast that an officer asked his name.

"I am not permitted to answer any questions," Brand said defiantly. "I am a Jewish emissary, and I am not allowed to make any statement except in the presence of a representative of the Jewish Agency." Long accustomed to the give and take of café negotiations, and proud of his ability to deal with authorities, he was willing to flaunt Zionist discipline when it served his purpose.

The British officer was nonplussed. He asked if Brand had any information for the British authorities, left for a while, then came back to report that on the morrow Brand would be able to see "Mr. Shertok, and speak to him in our presence." The news reassured Brand. If his treatment by British intelligence and security agents had been closer to a kidnapping than to the diplomatic reception appropriate for an emissary on a life-or-death mission, at least, after weeks of waiting, he would finally have his chance to hammer out a counterproposal for Eichmann.

The next morning he was driven by jeep to a villa, again somewhere on the outskirts of Aleppo. The interior of the villa was lushly furnished in the Arab style, with a tile floor, fine carpets, and low divans. British officers and civilians were seated around inlaid tables. A tall, middle-aged man with a thin moustache rose and greeted Brand, introducing himself as Moshe Shertok. He had arrived in time to meet Brand's train, but had to wait four days in a hotel in Aleppo while British security held Brand in isolation.[8] The Englishmen in the room said nothing, but seemed to pay close attention to what Brand and Shertok said.

Shertok offered Brand a drink. "Our English friends here are most interested in your report," Shertok said, "and we have nothing to hide from them." When Brand said that he could understand English but hadn't spoken it for many years, Shertok told him to speak German so the nuances of his report could be precisely conveyed. A stenographer was ready to take notes of the conversation.

Before he began, Brand asked Shertok: "Am I going back?"

Shertok said that it seemed doubtful that Brand would go back to Hungary.

"I *must* go back," Brand said. He became agitated, shouting that it was inconceivable that he not be allowed back, that if he did not return the situation would be worse than ever. No one in Hungary would believe that he had not been given permission to travel back.[9]

Shertok assured him that everything possible would be done. He begged Brand, in the interest of his mission, to collect himself and give a calm and dispassionate report.

Brand then spoke for ten hours.[10]

He began by describing the misery and hopelessness that had overtaken the Jews of Poland, Slovakia, and then Hungary; the history of Vaada and their rescue efforts; the long record of negotiations with the Germans, in Bratislava and then in Budapest. His report went slowly because Shertok periodically had him pause while he translated for the English officers and the stenographer. Even with the frequent interruptions, the small audience of English officers and civilians seemed moved by what Brand said. The only sound when he paused was the scratching of the stenographer's pencil.

Shertok asked Brand whether the Germans were "really so stupid as to think that the Allies would give them trucks, which were war equipment?" Brand answered that Shertok's question betrayed a lack of understanding of Nazi psychology, that the Germans honestly believed that the Jews were all-powerful in the Allied world, that they appointed and dismissed American senators, and that Churchill and Roosevelt were, so to speak, in their pockets. "It would therefore be a mere trifle for the Jews to get the Allies to send 10,000 trucks."[11] Brand added that Eichmann and his confederates hoped to enter into the "good books" of the Allies, and anticipated that their offer would ensure sanctuary for themselves and possibly better treatment for Germany as a whole.

"You must always remember," Brand said, "that we are dealing with thieves and murderers. Supposing you catch a thief red-handed, stealing £100. He will say: 'Here are £20 for you—and keep quiet about the £80.' Similarly, the Nazis believed that by offering to release the remaining two million Jews, they might get away with the killing of six million."

Shertok looked incredulous at Brand's numbers, which were far beyond the count anyone had given for the Jews sent to Nazi death camps. "Please believe me," Brand claims he said. "They have killed six million Jews; there are only two million left alive. They come now to the world and say: Take this remaining two million. It is a way of exonerating themselves."[12]

Brand also explained why the Nazis would allow refugees to depart via Spain or Portugal, but not to Palestine—because they were aware that the Turks could not or would not cope with transports of the needed number, even in transit. Also the Jewish refugees were primarily Hungarian and Romanian, and the Germans, as sticklers for quasi-legal procedures, would need to transport them to Reich territory before they could be deported. The Germans did not want to antagonize the Arabs, and they also did not want a strong Jewish Palestine which, if Germany were to rise from the postwar ashes, would confront them. They regarded the Jews as a disease and wanted to infect their enemies, particularly the United States and England, which would not happen if the Jews were concentrated in Palestine.[13]

Brand returned again and again to the demand that he be allowed to go back to Hungary. Even if the situation had changed in Hungary and he risked being shot on his return, he insisted that he could not abandon his wife, children, and friends. He contrasted himself with Bandi Grosz, who after discovering he could not get in touch with the people he was supposed to meet in Istanbul had quickly decided not to return to Hungary. Grosz, the comparison suggested, had no interest except saving his wife and his own skin. Brand insisted that he not only had a duty to his wife, children, and family, but, as the Emissary of the Doomed, to the hundreds of thousands of Hungarian Jews whose lives were in the balance while Eichmann awaited a response to his proposal.

Shertok asked Brand three questions: What would be the result if he were to return to Budapest with an affirmative reply? A negative reply? Or if he did not return at all?

Brand thought for a long time before answering. Too long, he concluded later.[14] "A week ago," he said, "I would have answered the first question firmly and my answer would have been this: If we accept Eichmann's offer, he will destroy the gas chambers in the extermination camps, stop the deportations, and send one hundred thousand Jews across the Spanish frontier. Now, however, Bandi Grosz has made me feel somewhat less certain. It may be that the Germans have intertwined our journey with other plans of theirs. It may be that the establishment of contact with the Allies is more important to them than are these negotiations of ours."

For the second option, Brand was more emphatic. "The second possibility does not exist for me. If I return to Budapest, I will never admit that my mission has failed and that you have refused Eichmann's offer without making some counterproposal. For that would be both murder and suicide. It would mean a terrible catastrophe for the remaining Jews in central Europe."

He was equally firm on the third option. "In the case that I don't return to Budapest, Eichmann would at once arrest my wife, my relatives, and all the leaders of the Vaada. Every day twelve thousand people would be deported to Auschwitz, and in two months the survivors would number no more than the few persons who escaped from the Warsaw ghetto."

When Brand finished, it was already late afternoon. Shertok and the English officers withdrew to a corner of the room, where they spoke softly but expressively. Then Shertok came back and put a hand on Brand's shoulder.

"Dear Joel," he said. "I have something very bitter to tell you. You must now go on farther south. The British insist on it. I have done all I can to make them alter their decision, but it is an order from the highest authority and I cannot change it."

For a moment Brand was uncomprehending, unable to grasp the meaning of what Shertok was saying. South of Syria could only mean British-controlled Palestine or Egypt. Then he realized that he was about to be arrested.

"Don't you understand what you're doing?" he shouted. "This is plain murder! Mass murder! If I don't go back, our best people will be slaughtered! My wife! My mother! My children! They will be the first to go. You've got to let me return."

He shouted that he had come under a flag of truce, that he was on a special mission, that he was not an emissary from the enemy, that the

Germans were as much his enemy as they were enemies of the Allies, that he was the delegate of one million people condemned to death. "Who gives you the right to lay hands on me? What have I done to England? So far as has been within our power, we have helped the Allies." He begged, he threatened, he wept. "What do you want from me? What do you want from me?"

Shertok assured Brand that he was personally sympathetic, and that as soon as he could he would fly to London to appeal the decision: "But now, at this moment, we are powerless and must do what we are told, you as much as I."

The other Englishmen said nothing.[15]

Hannah Senesh, the only woman among the trained Palestinian parachutists who had been sent to Hungary to find downed Allied airmen and aid the Jews of Hungary, had spent almost three months living with partisans in Yugoslavia, waiting for her opportunity to enter Hungary. On June 9, 1944, she finally got permission to cross the border. She was eager to pursue the mission for which she had trained and prepared, and knowing what possibly awaited her, asked a colleague for a cyanide capsule before she went across. He refused to give her one. She gave him a four-line poem she had written while waiting with the Yugoslavian partisans.

*Blessed is the match consumed in kindling flame.*
*Blessed is the flame that burns in the secret fastness of the heart.*
*Blessed is the heart with strength to stop its beating for honor's sake.*
*Blessed is the match consumed in kindling flame.*

Hannah Senesh was captured within hours of crossing the border and taken to a Budapest jail. Her comrades Nussbacher and Goldstein crossed the border on June 13, and made it to Budapest a week later, planning to meet up with Hannah Senesh at the Great Synagogue. But Hungarian police and German agents were already tailing them and caught them when they retraced their steps to retrieve a radio transmitter they had hidden. They managed to escape from the Germans, and with their fake Swedish and real British passports, they found their way to the Vaada office. They had heard of Rezső Kasztner as a leader of the Zionist movement in Budapest and asked him to help them find British and American pilots who had bailed out of their planes. Their primary mission, along with contacting and providing relief to the Jews in Hungary, was to meet up with the Allied pilots to gather information and provide escape information and funds.

Hansi Brand was at the office with Kasztner. "And how do you imagine we do that?" she said to the two young Palestinians. "We put an ad in the paper and suggest they contact us? We put our address in the advertisement? In June 1944, in Budapest!"

Nussbaacher pulled a sock out of his pocket with fifty gold Napoleon coins inside. Hansi laughed at the idea that the intrepid parachutists thought they would save Hungary's remaining Jews with fifty Napoleons.[16]

Kasztner was equally unsympathetic. He had discussed the parachutists with Eichmann, who said the matter was not within his competence.[17] Hansi and Kasztner assumed the Germans had tailed the Palestinians to the Vaada office and hence had put the Vaada operation in peril. It was one thing to negotiate with the Nazis, including Eichmann, for Jewish lives, but another matter altogether to be caught with agents who had been parachuted in by the British. Kasztner told the two young men that he was in no position to hide them or facilitate their escape, that there was no hope of armed resistance by the Jews, and nothing they could do for the Jews of Budapest. He gave them two options: they could try to hide from the Gestapo and police, and possibly imperil the Jewish community of Budapest and the Vaada organization. Or they could turn themselves in to the Germans. The two young men hesitated: they were native Hungarians, fluent in Hungarian, had prepared for their mission for months, and had waited for long months in Yugoslavia before crossing the border. Nothing in their training had prepared them for this impossible choice poised by a Jewish leader. Kasztner would later claim that "out of awe

and respect to the emissary of Jewish Palestine," he did not allow Nussbacher to hand himself over to the Nazis.[18]

Shertok returned to Jerusalem on June 13 and met with the Jewish
Agency executive the next day. He had been impressed by Brand, finding him "a very solid type: squarely built, broad-nosed, peasant-like; a
bit slow and heavy, but with a very clear head and a firm grasp of facts.
He breathes honesty." He admired Brand's courage—"Every minute of the day in Budapest he was risking his life in conspiring against
the Germans"—and reported that the British officers who met Brand
in Aleppo seemed to share his opinion of the man.[19] Bandi Grosz, he
assumed, was totally irresponsible, that he "would sell his own mother
for money." But the way Grosz had been tagged onto Joel Brand's mission suggested that the Germans were desperate and serious. Shertok was
cautious in his report, using double negatives to couch his recommendations: "it did not follow that by skillful handling, further negotiations
might not save . . . if not tens of thousands, at least thousands, of Jewish
lives," as he argued that if the Germans thought they might get something from the negotiations, they might let some Jews go, and as long as
they believed important negotiations were impending, they might temporarily halt the deportations. The goal, Shertok thought, was to gain
time, not by doing nothing but by taking action.

On June 15 Shertok and David Ben-Gurion met again with the high
commissioner for Palestine. Shertok reported on his meeting with Brand,
and they jointly recommended that Brand be allowed to go back to Hungary, that Shertok go to London, and that a meeting be set up between
the Germans and suitable Allied representatives. Although Shertok
wanted nothing to do with Grosz, the latter was essentially what Grosz
had been sent to arrange. Shertok suggested the American War Refugee
Board, the British Inter-Governmental Committee, or the International
Red Cross as the appropriate group to meet with the Germans, on the
grounds that any of the three organizations was sufficiently imposing
and official to impress the Germans with the seriousness of the Allies

and that all three groups were sufficiently divorced from official policy that their negotiations would not be misinterpreted or misrepresented as a peace feeler, which would raise havoc with the Russian allies and, if discovered, with the popular press. Shertok and Ben-Gurion urged that even though the commodities side of Eichmann's proposed agreement sounded ridiculous, it might be an opening gambit, and that whatever the details, the negotiations should be pursued, without, of course, "jeopardizing the higher interests of the war." In a diplomatic deference—the Jewish Agency was only a tolerated organization in Mandate Palestine— they allowed that "of course" the Foreign Office was "more competent than we" to decide the proper agency for a meeting and even whether a meeting should take place.

The high commissioner was inured to the supplicating language in Shertok's report: he had heard the same regularly from both the Arabs and the Zionists in Palestine. He acknowledged that in London Chaim Weizmann had met with Foreign Secretary Anthony Eden to discuss the proposal, and that the latter had agreed "to avoid anything that might look like slamming the door." With regard to Shertok's specific suggestions, the high commissioner was less encouraging. He saw absolutely no possibility that Brand would be allowed to go back to Hungary. As far as the British were concerned he was potentially a German agent, and they would no more let him return to German-occupied Hungary than the Germans were likely to allow a British agent who had penetrated into the Reich to return to Britain.

Shertok answered that if they were truly to avoid slamming the door on the German proposal, Brand should be allowed to go back. Indeed, he said, "Brand would not have left Turkey for Syria were it not for. . . ."

"I know what you're going to say," the high commissioner interrupted. "You are going to argue that there has been a breach of faith. Don't go on. The answer is very simple: This is war!"[20]

The most the high commissioner would agree to was to transmit Shertok and Ben-Gurion's requests to London, including Shertok's request for air priority. With no other option, Shertok and the Jewish Agency waited. Cables came from Istanbul asking when Brand would return.

Assuming that any answer would be passed along to Budapest, Shertok wired back that Brand had been delayed, but that he was flying to London. It was a lie, of course, but wartime diplomacy depended on lies.

Joel Brand knew nothing of the negotiations on his behalf. He only knew that from an emissary with a life-or-death proposal on behalf of Hungarian Jewry, he had become a prisoner, held against his will and not allowed to return to Hungary. Instead of the serious negotiation he had anticipated, a back-and-forth of offer and counteroffer that would at least buy time for the Jews of Hungary, he had been dealt with as if he were a witness, or even the accused, in a trial. From Aleppo, he was taken by rail south, through Beirut and Haifa and onward to Cairo. He was escorted on the train, as he had been since arriving in Aleppo, but he was given a sleeper compartment and treated with courtesy. When the train stopped at Beirut and Haifa, he was allowed to go to the buffets, and when the train crossed into Palestine in the early morning he was allowed to stand on the platform of the railcar to gaze out into the distance and breathe the air of Zion. He had been a Zionist since he was a teenager, dreaming of living on this land that he was seeing for the first time. He thought of escaping from the train. He was a Jew, he could speak a little Hebrew and some Yiddish. He might find sympathetic people who would help him return to occupied Hungary. He was a good negotiator; it was the one skill he could contribute to Vaada and to the resistance against the German extermination of Jews. At least in Hungary he could arrange meetings in the cafés with Nazi officials. Maybe he could negotiate bribes and save a few Jewish lives.

He decided not to try to escape, telling himself he had made the decision because he was under Zionist discipline, but also wondering about his own capabilities. "Perhaps that [escaping] is what I really should have done," he wrote. "But I felt so small, so insignificant—a man thrown by chance into the boiling caldron of history—that I did not dare take on my own shoulders the responsibility for the fate of a hundred thousand people. I lacked the courage to defy discipline, and therein lay my true guilt."[21]

When the train arrived in Cairo, Brand and his British escort took a cab from the station to a small, private house. The escort left Brand waiting in the cab while he went inside for an hour. When he came out, he gave directions to the driver, but said nothing to Brand and avoided his gaze while they drove out of town to a fortresslike building. There were no guards outside, but as they drove up, an iron door swung open to a courtyard where a dozen Abyssinian soldiers stood with bayonets fixed. Inside, a British noncom challenged Brand's passport and his explanation that it was a false passport, that he was not German, and that his name was not Eugen Band. After some argument, they agreed that Brand could sign his real name to the false information from his German passport.

A corporal then led Brand to a large and well-furnished room, leaving the door open. An Arab waiter served him excellent food, offered him a choice of wines, and replenished a bowl of fresh fruit. Brand's suitcase was delivered undisturbed. Twice a day an Arab servant washed the floor to keep the room cool. Brand was allowed books. No one bothered him, but he was still a prisoner. A corporal took up a post outside the door. Whenever anyone passed by in the corridor, the corporal locked Brand's door. Enjoying the luxury but fuming at his incarceration and the refusal of the British and the Jewish Agency to take his mission seriously, Brand protested that they had no right to hold him prisoner.

The corporal was prepared for the question. "How can you say you're a prisoner, sir? A prison doesn't look like this. You have only been brought here for a few days in your own interest." Everything will be explained in time, he assured Brand. "There's a war on."

Ira Hirschmann was happy as a vice president at Bloomingdale's department store in New York, and well liked in the position. He was forty-three, had a good family life, and was active in the classical-music world of Manhattan. But as the war waged into 1944, Hirschmann felt removed from the great effort. He had been concerned about the refugee situation in Europe, and when the War Refugee Board was established as a late and minimal response to the demand for American action on the refugee question, Hirschmann volunteered. Through connections in Washington and New York, he was assigned to work on the refugee situation in Turkey. Bloomingdale's agreed to pay him $1,000 per month for six months while he worked for the WRB. Before he went abroad, Hirschmann wrote Isador Lubin, FDR's economic adviser, to ask for a letter of introduction from the president.[22] When they later met in the West Wing of the White House, Lubin warned Hirschmann that the British "run things in the Middle East and hold the keys to the success or failure of your work."

As a member of various Jewish organizations Hirschmann had followed the sporadic news about refugees fleeing occupied Europe through the back door of the Black Seas ports, especially Constanţa in Romania, and had read about the challenges the refugees faced on the perilous route through the Black Sea and the Bosporus, and the humiliating and sometimes impossible restrictions the Turkish authorities imposed on arriving refugees, or more often, their refusal to give a definite reply to requests for transit visas for refugees. He had also followed with horror the story of the *Struma* and had read the comments by politicians afterward, including D. L. Lipson, who had said in Parliament, "If the *Struma* had been an enemy ship, German, Italian, or Japanese passengers would have been interned," and Lord Cranborne, who dismissed complaints about the *Struma* and other denials of aid to refugees curtly: "Under the present, unhappy situation in the world it is to a certain extent inevitable that we should be hardened to these horrors." Hirschmann appreciated the irony that the same week that the British refusal to admit the refugees to Palestine had precipitated the *Struma* tragedy, Anthony Eden, the British foreign minister, announced that half the Arab followers of the former grand mufti had been readmitted to Palestine.[23]

Hirschmann learned about the young Palestinians, called "the boys," who had organized the secret *tiul* ("walk") to bring Jewish refugees to the Black Sea ports. The U.S. intelligence services placed great value on information they got from the young Palestinians. On his first visit to Turkey Hirschmann met secretly with Jewish officials and told them, "As a Government official I cannot approve of your illegal work, but go ahead, by all means." He regularly saw Joe Levy, the *New York Times* reporter in Istanbul, and met Cyrus Sulzberger when he visited Istanbul, although the scenes they witnessed and the matters they discussed seem to have had no impact on the *Times* policy of relegating news of the impact of the war on the Jews to small articles buried on back pages.[24] With Judas Magnes, the president of the Hebrew University, Joseph Schwartz of the JDC, and Joe Levy, Hirschmann watched as 758 Jewish refugees were loaded onto a special train to take them from their ship to Haydarpasa Station, where they could board the train for Aleppo, a direct transit the Turks had arranged to effectively quarantine the refugees.[25]

The British were not enthusiastic about Hirschmann. "Mr. Hirschmann is a go-getter," the British ambassador in Ankara cabled, "somewhat tenacious of his own ideas, and impatient of official methods. He is looking at the whole Jewish refugee question mainly from the point of view of the coming Presidential election in the United States and is I think inclined to resent the fact that it is not being dealt with by the United States alone as a purely American concern."[26]

After his first mission in February, Hirschmann had been in Cincinnati visiting family when he got an emergency message about two Hungarians, "both Nazi agents"—Brand and Grosz—who had been flown to Istanbul by Himmler's assistants to make a proposal to the Allies. As he rushed back to Washington on a train, Hirschmann worried about the problem that was about to be thrust into his lap: "It suddenly occurred to me that there might be something flimsy or without substance to the entire proposal and that when I get there I may have to send a reply that would be very disappointing . . . there is that possibility."[27] In Washington he was shown an *aide mémoire* from Lord Halifax to Secretary of State Hull taking strong exception to any participation in this "psychological warfare," and was told the dangers of this newest Nazi initiative were so great that the British would have nothing to do with it. He also saw Hull's reply explaining the American position that "every effort should be made to convince the Germans that this Government is sufficiently concerned with the problem that it is willing to consider genuine proposals for the rescue and relief of the Jews and other victims . . . the sole purpose of conveying this fact to Brand is to let it be known that this Government has not closed the door." Hirschmann's own instructions were to "Keep talking. Keep the negotiations going. While you are talking, the Jews will be alive. And you are bound to pick up some information. Keep cabling back everything you have."[28] Before his departure, Hirschmann had a brief private meeting with FDR, who also urged him to keep talking and gave him a personal letter saying his mission has "our Government's full support and hearty wishes for success."[29]

From Washington Hirschmann was flown on C-54s (the military equivalent of the Douglas DC-4) as far as Adana, Turkey, then on to Ankara in a British Dakota (the C-47, a military DC-3), a journey considerably easier and speedier than the route most of the OSS agents had to take, from New York by ship via the Chesapeake, Key West, and Panama, down the coast of South America, across to Cape Horn and Durban, up the east coast of Africa to Aden, via the Suez Canal to Port Said, from there by train to Beirut and across to Aleppo, and finally via the *Taurus Express* to Ankara or Istanbul.[30] When Hirschmann reached Ankara, he went immediately to the embassy to see Ambassador Steinhardt.

Steinhardt had not met with Brand or Grosz, but he had discussed the situation with Chaim Barlas. He had also gotten a lengthy analysis of the Brand proposal from Leslie Squires, the American vice consul in Istanbul, who had concluded that Grosz, "already known as a double agent," had sold out to the Gestapo of his own choice or under pressure; that Brand's "illegal pro-Jewish activities" linked him to the Gestapo; that it wasn't possible to determine whether Brand's mission represented "German manipulation or Jewish desire"; that the orders for the mission could not have been so widespread and sure unless they came from a relatively high source; that the proposals were almost certainly not from Hungarians or Germans through the Hungarians, but "directly from the Germans"; and that the Germans knew the plan would fail and that it was all "part of an elaborate propaganda campaign, primarily to split the Allies from the Russians."[31]

Hirschmann asked the whereabouts of the two Hungarians.

"The British have captured them and spirited them over the border into Syria," Steinhardt said. "They are out of my jurisdiction."

"Where in Syria?" Hirschmann asked.

"Nobody seems to know."[32]

It took Hirschmann an hour with the British minister in Istanbul to learn that British intelligence was holding Brand and Grosz in Cairo, and that the entire matter had been placed under the authority of Lord Moyne, cabinet member, resident minister of state in Cairo, and Churchill's confidant. It took Hirschmann two days to get to Cairo on BOAC. He arrived in the midst of a sandstorm. The sticky, superheated air of the city was cloudy with insects.

Walter Edward Guinness, 1st Baron Moyne, was never known for the moderation of his views. His great-great-grandfather, Arthur Guinness, had established the Guinness brewing firm, and Lord Moyne grew up in a life of privilege and connections. He served with distinction in the Boer War and in Egypt, and later at Gallipoli and Paschendale in World War I, was elected to the House of Commons as a Conservative, and took a harshly conservative line on issues from the Marconi scandals to President Wilson's peace proposals, of which he said: "Since the days of Mahomet, no prophet has been listened to with more superstitious respect."[33] He and Winston Churchill became friends at the Other Club, an informal dining club for politicians which had a rule calling for members to freely express their opinions. Churchill freely vented his spleen on the British politicians in the 1930s, and Lord Moyne shared his opinions. In 1934, Moyne took a voyage from Marseilles to Greece and Beirut on a seven-hundred-ton ferry he had converted to yacht service, with the Churchills as his guests. He later cruised the Pacific with Clementine Churchill as a guest.

With the outbreak of World War II, Moyne used his office and influence to pursue the internment of Diana Mosley, who had divorced Moyne's son to marry the British Fascist leader Sir Oswald Mosley in Berlin, with Hitler and Goebbels witnesses at the wedding. A detention order for Diana Mosley was signed when Churchill became prime minister in May 1940. A year later Churchill appointed Moyne colonial secretary. Moyne spoke out frequently against the Zionists, supporting the Arab position that the Jews were foreign in both culture and blood, and urging that they be forced to settle in Lebanon, Syria, and Transjordan instead of Palestine. Despite protests from scholars and representatives of the Jewish community, in 1942 Lord Moyne was appointed deputy resident minister in Cairo, and in January 1944 he was promoted to resident minister, which gave him responsibility for Persia, the Middle East, and Africa.

Hirschmann, despite his credentials from the War Refugee Board and from FDR, got no response to his requests for a meeting with Lord Moyne. Instead, he was told that Foreign Secretary Eden would arrange a special flight for him to London to discuss the matter at the highest level there; hence there was no reason for him to meet with Lord Moyne. Hirschmann finally told Minister Tuck at the American legation in Cairo that he had had enough flying for a while, that it was his mission to see the two men from Hungary, and that he demanded a meeting with Lord Moyne.

The insistence worked, and Hirschmann went from the unguarded American legation to the heavily barricaded British embassy in Cairo, with its sentries, checkpoints, and prickly protocol. He was ushered into a room, and promptly at noon a tall, thin, angular man of sixty-five or seventy appeared. To Hirschmann, "the entire atmosphere surrounding him seemed gray. His eyes were cold and unemotional." Hirschmann made a gesture to shake hands, only to watch Lord Moyne look away and refuse the overture. Instead of the usual embassy meeting around a circular table, which minimized rankings, Moyne insisted on sitting on one side of a desk, with Hirschmann and various uniformed secretaries and assistants lined up on the other side.

With the reserve and haughtiness of a British peer, Moyne outlined the attitude of the British Empire, that it would not be put in a position of accepting bribes or being caught by psychological tricks, that these so-called emissaries could be one more Nazi trick, that the whole idea of exchanging money or matériel in the midst of war was "revolting," and that "of course" the British would not participate in such a scheme "as it was contrary to principle."

Hirschmann was not surprised by what Moyne said, although he was surprised that Moyne said so much. He answered that his government was also unwilling to bribe Nazis or be caught in any nets, but that they felt a broad responsibility to talk to anyone who had a plan to save human lives, and that by talking to the men from Hungary they were bound to discover information that might be useful.

Lord Moyne answered that the British had been talking to the two men for eight days of interrogation, and that one had already revealed that he was a double agent, selling information to both sides indiscriminately. Hirschmann knew Moyne was talking about Grosz. The reports he had gotten on Grosz indicated that the man was unreliable, and he told Moyne that as far as he was concerned they could keep Grosz in prison; he had no desire to see or talk to the man. But at the same time he insisted on seeing Joel Brand. Moyne countered by repeating Anthony Eden's invitation that Hirschmann go to London. Moshe Shertok, he said, had accepted the same invitation.

Hirschmann and Moyne sparred for an hour and a half. Hirschmann allowed that he would like to go to London some day and meet Anthony Eden, but that he took his instructions from Washington, not from London. Finally Hirschmann got up as if to leave. "Mr. Minister," he said. "I come from a sporting people. So do you. I will agree to take my instructions from Mr. Eden if you will agree to take yours from Mr. Hull. I will go to London if you will go to Washington." He showed Moyne the letter from President Roosevelt and asked Moyne to cooperate in settling the matter on the spot, where the two of them, as envoys with authority, could do so without delay.

Moyne turned to an aide, Brigadier Mark Maunsell, and said, "Arrange for Mr. Hirschmann to meet Joel Brand this afternoon at 3:00 PM."[34]

The brigadier suggested that before meeting Brand, Hirschmann be briefed on the organization of the German Gestapo so that he would at least recognize the names of the individuals Brand might refer to. He led Hirschmann through a labyrinth of British intelligence offices to an air-conditioned room, where a green shade was raised to reveal an organizational chart of the Gestapo on a blackboard. Looking at the secret chart, Hirschmann reflected that his temporary assignment had taken him far beyond any frontier he might have imagined when he took a leave from Bloomingdale's.

# 8

## Brand's Last Stand

*Mr. Shertok, of the Jewish Agency, has just arrived in London, bringing a firsthand account of his talks with Brand, the Hungarian Zionist who recently arrived in Turkey, accompanied by a German secret service agent, with proposals from the Gestapo . . . to release 1,000,000 Jews in return for certain concessions. Mr. Shertok's talks in London with the Foreign Office and the Jewish Agency will bring to a head the question of what further is to be done over this fantastic affair.*

—Lord Halifax, June 1944[1]

*The British are lazy realists who get away with murder.*

—Ira Hirschmann[2]

The Auschwitz Protocols, the secret report on Auschwitz that Walter Rosenberg and Fred Wetzler dictated in the Slovakian village of Zilina at the end of April 1944, traced torturous and furtive journeys from Slovakia, emerging from underground into the light slowly and unpredictably.

A German copy of the report had been sent by courier to Geneva for the attention of Nathan Schwalb, the head of the Hechalutz office of the World Zionist Organization. Hechalutz had been founded to train young people in Europe and later in the United States for agricultural work in Palestine. Schwalb was bright and enthusiastic, had an energetic staff, enjoyed a reputation for honesty and effectiveness, and mostly kept himself outside the competition for credit, influence, and attention that put some of the relief organizations at loggerheads with one another.

He had also been in Geneva long enough to have a wealth of contacts there.

Geneva was a hornet's nest of diplomats. From elegant lakeside embassies, chargés d'affaires sent announcements and invitations on behalf of governments and nations that had effectively disappeared under German or Soviet occupation. Swiss neutrality, the charms of the city, and the attractive location had also long attracted the headquarters of organizations like the defunct League of Nations, the International Red Cross, and smaller private or semiprivate organizations that would later be known as NGOs. Some organizations, like the Red Cross, were officially neutral; others, like the American Joint Distribution Committee, had strong sympathies on one side or the other of the war. For all of them, the neutral air of Switzerland was the closest they could get to refugees and to those incarcerated in Nazi labor and concentration camps in German-occupied Europe.

The clusters of diplomats and relief agencies indirectly supported a third and perhaps even larger constituency of spies. Most were diplomats and agency staff members leading double lives as espionage agents. Everywhere and anytime in Geneva—in hotel lobbies, restaurants, bars, on park benches, in parked cars, in supposed courtesy calls, at diplomatic receptions, on hired boats, in quiet walks on the lakeside paths—there were secret meetings, well-dressed individuals talking quietly and discreetly, exchanging, selling, and freely passing information and misinformation. So many rumors and alleged revelations were whispered and passed about that picking out the truth was like searching for a diamond in a souk filled with fakes. A shocking new document like the Auschwitz Protocols might readily be passed from hand to hand, but it ran the risk of being lost in the surfeit of information or dismissed as horror propaganda created by a belligerent against a mortal enemy. Schwalb's copy of the Protocols found its way around the relief agencies that followed the fate of the Jews, but without corroborating evidence from one of the neutral powers—Sweden, Switzerland, or the Vatican—it was hard to present the revelations of the conditions and operations inside Auschwitz-Birkenau as fact. Many dismissed the report as propaganda.

From Budapest, Moshe Krausz, the secretary of the Palestine Office there, who had been in close contact with the Swiss consul, sent another copy of the Protocols to Switzerland, adding a report that 435,000 Hungarian Jews had been deported between May 15 and June 19, and that another 350,000 were assembled in and near Budapest, awaiting deportation.³ Still another copy was brought to Berne by a courier of the Czechoslovakian underground movement on June 18, and delivered to Dr. Jaromir Kopecky, the Czechoslovakian minister, who sent it to the World Jewish Congress in Geneva and to the Swiss press. In the next few days articles about the document appeared in Swiss newspapers, although they were censored everywhere in occupied Europe. Copies of the Protocols eventually found their way to Saly Mayer, the dour, stiff Swiss who ran the office of the JDC in Switzerland; the Agadut office that represented the interests of Orthodox Jews; the British Foreign Office; and the Jewish Agency, which sent it to Palestine, where it was promptly translated into Hebrew.

While copies of the Protocols quietly circulated, two other internees, Czeslaw Mordowicz and Arnost Rosin, escaped from Auschwitz on May 27, 1944. They tried to go east to Krakow and Warsaw, but discovered that able-bodied men were being conscripted for forced-labor brigades to build tank defenses, so they turned south, reached the Slovak border on June 6, and made contact with the Slovak Jewish leaders. Their report emphasized that the preparations Rosenberg and Wetzler had described a month earlier had been put to use on the arriving trains of Hungarian Jews. "Wetzler and I saw the preparation for the slaughter," Rudolf Vrba later wrote. "Mordowicz and Rosin saw the slaughter itself."⁴

A copy of the Protocols reached Roswell McClelland, the head of the Geneva office of the War Refugee Board. The word "refugee" in the title of the agency was in some sense a euphemism, as the jurisdiction of the War Refugee Board covered the millions of Jews and other internees who were held in concentration camps in Germany or the occupied countries, or had been deported to what the Germans claimed were labor camps in Poland and Silesia. McClelland was sincerely committed to the agenda of his new agency, but the budget of the War Refugee Board did not match the breadth of its charter. Basic staff salaries were paid from discretionary presidential funds, and staff were allowed access to secure communications through the local U.S. legations and occasionally through OSS offices, but the only funds they could deploy for actual relief work were from private organizations. And after so many years of American inaction on refugees and especially the situation of the Jews in Europe, the staff the WRB recruited were inexperienced, novices tossed into the hotbed of rumors, misinformation, propaganda, and occasional real information. They had little experience separating the kernels of important intelligence from the bushels of chaff, and little clout in Washington to do anything about what they perceived as important information.

In Bratislava, a German copy of the Auschwitz Protocols had been passed to Monsignor Giuseppe Burzio, the Vatican's apostolic delegate in Slovakia.[5] As far back as 1942, Burzio had indicated his sympathy for the situation of the Jews in Slovakia. When the deportations of Jews began he sent a telegram to the Vatican with an ominous last sentence: "The deportation of 80,000 people to Poland, at the mercy of the Germans, is equivalent to the condemnation of a majority to a certain death."[6] The Vatican did not react to his warning, but Burzio had reason to hope that direct testimony of witnesses to what was happening at Auschwitz might change minds in the Vatican. As a papal chargé d'affaires, Burzio was able to send telegrams to the Vatican in cipher, but the Protocols was too long to encode, so he resorted to the papal courier service which transported the equivalent of diplomatic pouches. By May 1944, with Allied and German forces engaged in a fierce renewed battle for Rome, the courier service was using a roundabout route to reach the Vatican. Burzio's copy of the Protocols, with his covering letter, went first to Berne, whence it was forwarded to Madrid, and then by diplomatic pouch to the Vatican.[7] Given the sanctity of the diplomatic pouches, and the protection provided to the pope by both the Italian government and the German forces, Burzio had every reason to assume that the report, with its sensational news about the camp at Auschwitz-Birkenau, would quickly find its way to the appropriate office and ultimately to the Holy Father himself. Like many in the church hierarchy, Monsignor Burzio believed that the pope was compassionate and concerned about the victims of the war and would immediately address the issue.

On June 23, 1944, while Joel Brand was in Cairo, Chaim Barlas in Istanbul got a German copy of the Protocols. The next day he brought it to his close, trusted friend, Angelo Roncalli, the apostolic delegate for Greece and Turkey. Roncalli did not read German, so Barlas sight-translated passages of the report into French for him. "With tears," he recalled, Roncalli "read the documents I asked him to transfer to his Patron in Rome." Roncalli immediately sent the document on to the Vatican, and it arrived there late on June 24. Although Roncalli urged immediate attention to the revelations of the document, the Vatican conducted its own diplomacy, for its own ends, and was obsessed with the precariousness of its position between the Allies and the Axis. Before and during the war, the pope and his officials had carefully balanced what they perceived as the advantages of their relations with Germany against information like reports from Roncalli in Istanbul or the eyewitness testimony in the Auschwitz Protocols. Their papal delegates enjoyed diplomatic immunity and the security of diplomatic pouches, and sent steady streams of information about the situation of the Jews to Rome, but the Vatican played its policy cards close to the chest and was fiercely secretive about how much the pope knew. It has maintained that secrecy to this day[8] and consistently defended the pope's inaction. Alienating Germany would have risked its last shred of authority over one of the largest Catholic populations in Europe and whatever leverage the papacy maintained over the Nazis, and any direct intervention would have worsened the situation by prompting a retaliation from Hitler. The Vatican, like the British and the Americans, made no public statement about the shocking information in the Auschwitz Protocols.

The British prison in Cairo was comfortable, but it was still confinement and hard on a gregarious man who loved the cafés of Budapest. Brand had set off on his mission to negotiate. He did not do well in solitary confinement.

On his first day as a prisoner Brand was alone in his room when he heard Hungarian songs and a familiar whistled tune from the court-yard below. He rushed to the window and saw Sam Springmann, the former member of the Vaada group in Budapest who had established their courier network. Brand hadn't seen Springmann for six months. Springmann's nerves could not tolerate the German occupation, and he had left Budapest on a legal emigration visa to become the Vaada representative in Istanbul. Despite the efforts of the Jewish Agency officials there, the Turks ordered Springmann deported, his appeals were denied, and after a sarcastic "Thank you very much, comrades, for all your help" to the group in Istanbul, he was taken to Aleppo and from there to Cairo, arriving six weeks before Joel Brand.[9] At the prison Springmann and Brand arranged a system of whistles and songs to communicate, allowing Brand to enjoy both the sense of company and the feeling that there was at least someone who would listen to his story.

His joy was short-lived. After three days of confinement, an official took Brand's suitcase from his room. The next day Brand was taken to a room where an interrogator, speaking from a raised platform as if it were a criminal proceeding, addressed Brand as "Doctor"—perhaps a stereotype of a Budapest Jew for the military interrogator—and told him that he was not imprisoned, had not been charged with any offense, but was being held in his own interest for "reasons prescribed by military necessity." When Brand questioned this, he was told that he would soon return to Hungary where the Germans would almost certainly use extraordinary means to get him to report what he had seen in the British war theater, and that it was therefore in his interest to be able to avoid torture by claiming that he had been imprisoned and had seen nothing. The interrogator also said that he was being questioned because Moshe Shertok was en route to London, and that Brand's answers would provide information for those London discussions. Brand, who still thought of England as "the home of freedom" and an ally, wanted to believe what he heard. It was better than the haunting thought that his mission, and the peril his wife and children faced after he left Budapest, was to no end.

The next day, June 16, British lieutenant N. Savigny began an exacting interrogation.[10] Brand was uncooperative. He had already told Moshe

Shertok what he considered the important information about his mission and the Eichmann proposal, and while that meeting hadn't been satisfactory, Shertok was at least a high official of the Jewish Agency with access to British foreign secretary Anthony Eden and other influential Allied representatives. He wondered what purpose was served by talking to this inquisitive lieutenant who asked about every person Brand had ever met. Brand would mention a name, and the lieutenant would follow up with questions about how Brand had met that person, the life story of the person, names of others known to that person, and exactly when and where Brand had seen him or her. The lieutenant wanted every detail of Brand's travels, his youthful adventures in the United States and with the Communists in Germany, and the earliest days of the Vaada rescue operations. How would any of that help the Jews of Hungary?

The questioning went on eight hours a day, day after day. Brand was by nature garrulous, but he resented the relentless and repetitive questioning and was exasperated that this seemed to be the only British interest in his mission. With his firm sense of himself as an official emissary, he could not grasp that British intelligence was trying to uncover contradictions in his story, that they had reason to suspect he might be a German agent, or at least to try to discredit him. Assuming that he and the British had the same interests, he could not understand why they put him in the position of the accused facing a prosecutor,[11] and why Lieutenant Savigny seemed scarcely interested in the possibility of a rescue or ransom of the Hungarian Jews who were condemned to death in the Nazi extermination camps.

It wasn't until the fourth full day of interrogation that the lieutenant finally asked: "Do you believe that the Germans intended this offer to be taken seriously?"

"Completely seriously," Brand said. He explained that he was convinced that Eichmann, Wisliceny, and Krumey were acting with the authority of Himmler; that the entire German security services in Budapest, Vienna, and Bratislava were involved; and that at every step in the negotiations with Eichmann "they were in continuous touch with Himmler in Berlin."

"So you are convinced, Mr. Brand," Savigny asked, "that the Germans will give the remaining Jews their freedom, if their offer is accepted? . . . And all for ten thousand army trucks?"

"For less," Brand said. "For a few million dollars. I am absolutely convinced of that."

The lieutenant was openly skeptical. Why would the Germans, who had provoked the hostility of the entire world by their insane project of exterminating the Jews, let the rest of the Jews go free for a few million dollars? The sum was trifling. Compared to the daily war expenses of the Germans, even $100 million was nothing. "What possible sense is there in such a policy?" he asked.

Brand answered angrily that he had not come to theorize about the Germans, and that he was absolutely certain that their offer should be accepted, or that at the very least he should be allowed to continue to negotiate with the Germans. "What does England stand to lose by this?" he asked. "Maybe in the end the Nazis will kill me, and in that case instead of five million Jews destroyed there will be just one victim more." [12]

As he had said to Moshe Shertok and the Jewish Agency officials in Istanbul, Brand once again explained that the German power apparatus was not a monolithic block, that there were groups and cliques competing with one another, and that the advance of the Allies and setback of the Germans had exacerbated the internecine squabbles. The SS officers in particular, he told the lieutenant, were sensitive to the impending catastrophe for Germany and desperate to fabricate covers and excuses for their past acts. They continued to believe that the Jews possessed immense power to influence governments, still believed in the fairy tales of the Protocols of the Elders of Zion and a secret global Jewish ruling class, and were convinced that they would establish contact with the western Allies before the onslaught of the Soviet juggernaut destroyed Germany. Himmler in particular, Brand explained, was trying to conclude a secret peace with the Allies, maybe even by sacrificing Hitler, in the hope that an arrangement with the western powers against Russia would somehow obtain a pardon for himself, his people, and maybe even the German nation. He and the SS officials realized that they would lose the occupied lands of Europe and at best be left with the German homeland, and that they would not succeed in killing all the Jews. But they even made that part of their strategy. Brand explained that Eichmann had always been in favor of mass emigration of the Jews: he believed that by infecting the Allied countries with what the Nazis thought of as the "Jewish plague" they would weaken Germany's enemies. And if the Allies refused to accept the Jews, then the Germans could claim in the all-important court of world opinion that they tried to expel the Jews, and that it was only because the Allies would not accept them that they had to be exterminated.

Brand described the strange Nazi ideology calmly. He had lived in occupied Europe and dealt with the Nazi officials long enough that the twisted logic was no longer surprising.

"But," Brand said, weary of the explanations and interrogations. "That is high-level politics and no concern of mine. I have a definite mission to fulfill. I am here to ransom a million Jews."

When the lieutenant suggested that Brand seemed almost to agree with the bizarre ideas of the Nazis, Brand answered: "For me a murderer is a murderer. But an onlooker who does not intervene when murder is being committed must also bear his share of the guilt."[13] The victory the Allies anticipated might come too late, he said. Unless they released him from prison and sent him back to Budapest with authority to negotiate with the Nazis, thousands, maybe millions, of lives would be lost.

"You are not in prison, Mr. Brand," the lieutenant repeated.

"That is a quibble. I am not allowed to return to the one place where I can do something."

"Do you really imagine that we would deliver ten thousand trucks to the Germans in the middle of the war?"

"I have already said a dozen times that we don't want any of your trucks. Give us a promise that you will never have to carry out, and on the strength of that alone I can save a hundred thousand lives."

He explained once again that Eichmann's offer stipulated the immediate release of one hundred thousand Jews as soon as Brand confirmed that the negotiations were serious. Later, he explained, the Jewish Agency and the Allies could dishonor the agreement and deliver nothing to the Germans. "There is no need to keep one's word with murderers."

The lieutenant answered that the Allies would have to take those hundred thousand people to some neutral frontier and then put them on ships. "Have you any idea what such an operation would entail in time of war, or how much shipping space would be required for such a mass transportation?"

"The Germans are poorer than you," Brand answered. "But they managed to collect sufficient railroad cars to take millions of people to the gas chambers in eastern Poland. They moved them clear across Germany, and in the middle of a war, when their railway system was already overstrained by the requirements of their Eastern Front. Yet you say that now, with the enemy beaten to his knees, you are unable to find enough ships to move a hundred thousand people who have narrowly escaped from hell."

Lieutenant Savigny was telling the truth when he told Joel Brand that Eichmann's proposal was under consideration in London and Washington. On May 26, 1944, a week after Brand and Bandi Grosz flew from Vienna to Istanbul, Sir Harold MacMichael cabled the secretary of state for colonies in London to report that Moshe Shertok and David Ben-Gurion had visited him and told him about Brand and Grosz, their journey to Istanbul, and the proposal Brand had brought with him.[14] The cable was considered sensitive enough to be classified SECRET. MacMichael summarized Eichmann's offer, Brand's report that three hundred thousand Hungarian Jews were already in concentration camps in Poland and twelve thousand were being deported every day, and Brand's opinion that the negotiations could be prolonged and modified from the demands for war matériel to cash payments. He added that Brand's reports of deportations from Hungary had been corroborated by eyewitness reports,[15] and that the Jewish Agency was maintaining secrecy on the proposal but wanted the details communicated through official channels to Washington and to Zionist leaders Chaim Weizmann in England and Dr. Nahum Goldman in the United States. Copies of MacMichael's cable were also sent to the British ambassador in Ankara and Lord Moyne in Cairo, the former because Brand and Grosz were then in Istanbul and the latter because the Foreign Office and the prime minister routinely consulted Lord Moyne as the senior resident official in the Middle East.

Except for the terms of Eichmann's proposal, nothing in MacMichael's cable was shocking to either the British or the Americans. By May 1944 they had received reports of Nazi atrocities against the Jews from their own intelligence services, diplomatic listening posts, and relief and rescue organizations. The reports came in the midst of a flood of information and misinformation from groups promoting other agendas, which until the Auschwitz Protocols with their firsthand account arrived, could be and were dismissed as hearsay, unreliable, or propaganda.

The Jews were not popular in either Britain or the United States in 1944. Instances of open anti-Semitism could be heard in pubs and bars, and even in polite society there was widespread resentment and disdain for "those people," especially toward the lobbying and propaganda efforts of Jewish organizations and individuals and the influence of Jews in Hollywood, the media, and the intelligentsia. By 1944, Britain saw an uptick of anti-Semitism because the Jews were perceived as having avoided playing their full role in the war effort; they were accused of being responsible for the black market, and of always being the first to evacuate London.[16] Despite Allied awareness that the Germans had an organized program to persecute the Jews, American and British experts and the popular press failed, or refused, to understand the uniqueness of Nazi attitudes toward the Jews, and did not acknowledge the differences in scale and degree between the Nazi persecution of the Jews and the persecution of other minorities, such as the Jehovah's Witnesses, Gypsies, and homosexuals. The one distinction the British would make was that the Jews, under the guidance of the Zionist movement, were pressuring to go to Palestine. Even before the war, the British recognized that the Zionists and the Nazis shared an interest in getting the Jews out of Europe, and that their mutual interest could be construed as a challenge to British war aims and Palestine policy.[17] The threat that Nazi policy might promote increased immigration of Jews into Palestine—which the Foreign and Colonial offices had determined was against British interests in maintaining good relations with the Arab populations of the Middle East—was as decisive in molding British policy as the information they received about the Nazi ghettoizations, deportations, and annihilation programs.

In Britain, resistance to special efforts on behalf of the Jews became an unspoken agreement among civilian politicians, the general public, and the military. Even as evidence emerged that the numbers and proportion of Jews dwarfed all other persecuted groups among the victims of the Nazis, British politicians cited a sense of fairness in defense of their conviction that appearing to favor any persecuted minority would generate harsh criticism in the press and among other minority groups. The general public, with no love lost for the Jews and no sense yet of the extent of the German measures against the Jews in occupied Europe, quietly supported the government policy of treating the Jews as one more minority. That attitude accorded well with the military conviction in both London and Washington that the answer to *all* grievances against the Nazis was a total Allied victory, as soon as possible, and that incremental or special relief measures would only detract from the war effort and possibly delay that victory.

Public and military attitudes toward the Jews in the United States were close to those in Britain. FDR had Jewish friends, Jews in his cabinet, on the Supreme Court, and as advisers, and he occasionally spoke eloquently on the fate of refugees in occupied Europe. But he also tolerated Ambassador Joseph Kennedy's friendliness with the Nazis for too long and consistently supported Assistant Secretary of State Breckinridge Long, who was using every bureaucratic trick to prevent Jews from entering the United States under the existing quotas. The reality was that for Roosevelt other priorities took precedence over the plight of the Jews in Europe. His war policies balanced political necessities at home with long-term geopolitical interests. The fate of the Jews did not matter enough to influence his policies or to override the American military doctrine that the central war effort could not be distracted by auxiliary concerns.

FDR's unstated positions were echoed and supported in the American press. Even by 1944, the daily press continued to ignore news of the implementation of the Final Solution and downplayed the need for relief efforts. The *New York Times* would devote a lengthy page-one story to gangster Louis Lepke's efforts to get a stay of execution at Sing Sing, but relegate a story on the pitiful budget of the Intergovernmental Committee on Refugees to sixteen lines on page four. On May 18, 1944, after the deportations from Hungary had begun, page one reported that the New York Republican Committee had chosen to honor its new leader by making "Yankee Dewey Dandy" its theme song; *Times* correspondent Joseph Levy's report that as many as one million Hungarian Jews were doomed was consigned to a few lines on page five.[18] The few voices campaigning vocally for action on behalf of the refugees were individual cries in a wilderness of public apathy. In 1943 Kurt Weill showed Ben Hecht a clipping from a Swiss newspaper reporting that the Romanian government would allow seventy thousand Transdniestrian Jews to leave Romania if someone would pay the cost of $50 each for transport to the border. Hecht took out full-page advertisements in the New York papers:[19]

FOR SALE

70,000 JEWS

AT

$50 APIECE

GUARANTEED HUMAN BEINGS

Initially, the only governmental organization dealing with the refugees was the Intergovernmental Committee for Refugees, which one diplomat called "nothing more than a decorous façade concealing the inactivity of the thirty-two governments which had set it up."[20] But through 1943, a group of young, non-Jewish Treasury officials obtained proofs of the State

Department's deliberate avoidance of the refugee problem and compiled a "Report to the Secretary on the Acquiescence of This Government in the Murder of the Jews" for Treasury Secretary Henry Morgenthau, the highest-placed Jew in the American government. Morgenthau had the report toned down and submitted it to FDR early in 1944 as a "Personal Report to the President." The tone was still sharp enough to threaten to expose FDR's nonaction policy toward the Jews. "You can't hold it," Morgenthau's report warned. "It is going to pop, and you have either got to move very fast, or the Congress of the United States will do it for you."[21] In response, FDR created the War Refugee Board by executive order in January 1944, charging it with "all measures within its power to rescue victims of enemy oppression who are in imminent danger of death and otherwise to afford such victims all possible relief and assistance consistent with the successful prosecution of the war," and directing all departments to cooperate with the new WRB. John Pehle, who had drafted the original report to Morgenthau and helped tone down the version submitted to FDR, thus demonstrating both conviction and political astuteness, was named the head of the WRB. FDR promised administrative funds for the new agency from discretionary accounts he controlled, but the funds he provided were only enough for salaries and expenses, and would not cover relief or rescue operations. The War Refugee Board also had no counterpart in Britain, so while its requests for cooperation from the British were answered with assurances of support and sympathy, there was little possibility of concerted concrete efforts on refugee issues. The qualifying clause in the WRB charter—"consistent with the successful prosecution of the war"—gave the War and Navy departments and the OSS an effective veto over proposed rescue or relief operations and meant the War Refugee Board had no authority to act on matters of intelligence or substantive proposals like the one from Eichmann that Joel Brand had brought on his mission.

The official British response to High Commissioner MacMichael's cable came from the British War Cabinet Committee on the Reception and Accommodation of Refugees, answering that in its considered opinion the entire proposal from Brand had been put forward by the Gestapo as blackmail or political warfare.[22] The committee saw nefarious German scheming in every element of Eichmann's proposal: ten thousand heavy all-weather trucks would be of significant military assistance to the Germans and hence could not possibly be offered as a ransom; the designation of Portugal and Spain as the sole exodus for refugees would "embarrass" Allied military operations in Europe; and any agreement to the blackmail of the proposal would be "inseparably connected" to the raising of the Allied blockade of German-occupied Europe and hence would inevitably lead to further blackmail. The committee memo, which purported to speak for both the British and the Americans, was careful to urge that all parties understand that the U.S. and British governments "are engaged in schemes designed on a practical basis to rescue Jews from death by means which would not have the effect of interference with the vital needs of the war effort," that large numbers of Allies are held by the Germans "in terrible conditions," and that "exchange of German prisoners for persons to be selected by Hitler, leaving Allied internees and prisoners in German hands, would lay Governments open to very serious criticism." A copy of the reply to MacMichael was sent to the British embassy in Washington for transmittal to the U.S. government, asking that the United States concur with the British opinion and cautiously urging that the scheme not be mentioned to Chaim Weizmann or Dr. Nahum Goldman.

Both the State Department and the WRB had reservations about the British response. They recognized that Shertok wanted a further carrot to the Germans in the shape of agreement by the United Kingdom and United States to discuss the question of Jewish rescue. Shertok had urged that "we should decide what *quid pro quo* could be offered to the Germans" in advance. The Americans were not ready to articulate an offer, but they wanted a forum "which would not (repeat not) involve any direct negotiations with the Germans, but would leave the door open for subsequent offers."[23] Hence, the State Department urged, any serious suggestion by the Germans to release Jews or other persecuted minorities should not be rejected without "full consideration" as long as the proposal was "not inconsistent with the successful prosecution of the war," since from the available information it was not possible to judge the real nature of the Eichmann proposal, and in any case the proposal should be kept under discussion as long as possible in the hope of saving lives, at least during the period of discussions. To that end, Ira Hirschmann of the War Refugee Board, although not authorized to enter into any "understanding with the Germans," was to explore the matter, "thereby indicating to the Germans that [the] matter is still open." The Americans also urged that it be made clear to the Germans "by actions as well as words" that the British and U.S. governments would find temporary asylum for all Jewish and similar persons in imminent danger of death whom the Germans are willing to release, and that the British ambassador in Ankara be instructed to take steps similar to those being taken by the American ambassador, "in order to keep negotiations open, without in any way committing either Government to an understanding with the Germans."[24]

The differences between the American and British positions might have led to serious discussions of the proposal between the Allies, but with all information about Brand and the proposal arriving in Washington second-, third-, or even fourth-hand, and the invasion in Normandy taking priority over every other strategic and tactical decision, the differences between the Foreign Office and the State Department remained mostly unspoken. For the sake of internal peace the two allies had agreed to disagree. Washington awaited Hirschmann's report, and London awaited both Shertok's report and the recommendations of Lord Moyne and other British advisers. While they waited, there was no response to Eichmann's offer.

In the weeks while they waited, according to a report German plenipotentiary Edmund Veesenmayer assembled from Eichmann's data, 147 trains of cattle cars left Hungary, carrying 437,402 Jews to Auschwitz.

Brand's first relief from the frustrating interrogations came on June 21, when he was told that an emissary from the United States was coming to see him. After weeks of pointless interrogation and the broken promise of a return to Hungary, Brand had lost the last shreds of his faith in the

Britain he had once thought of as the land of freedom. Perhaps something would come of Moshe Shertok's mission to London; otherwise Britain seemed determined to ignore or derail him. But he still hoped the United States could be a very different story. He had been there as a young man, had traveled to both coasts, held jobs in many cities, worked alongside ordinary people. He was familiar with the expansiveness of American visions and opportunities, the deep reserves of industrial might, funds, and goodwill that the Americans could muster in support of a war or a cause. Vaada had been in touch with American organizations like the JDC, and he knew that some American Jewish organizations and individuals had contributed generously to Zionist causes and to relief efforts in Europe.

He did not know how much American policy on what the statesmen still called "the refugee problem" was determined by military considerations or the staunch American military doctrine that no distractions should be allowed from the primary military mission of meeting and engaging the enemy. And from his confinement in Cairo, where he was allowed no newspapers or radio, he knew little about the progress of the Allied landing in Normandy. The extent of the unanticipated American and British struggle in the hedgerows of Normandy, where the invading troops were bogged down and scarcely able to advance, was not broadcast widely. Brand, like many did in occupied Europe, assumed that with American troops now on the European mainland, and with the famed Atlantic bridge of ship convoys bringing seemingly limitless reserves of supplies, equipment, and manpower from North America, it was only a matter of time before the Americans would sweep to the rescue of the Jews of Europe, roaring across the plains of Europe in their tanks like the cavalry in the western movies from Hollywood that Hungarians had long delighted in watching. That a senior American official had found him in Cairo seemed a harbinger of that scenario. It was exactly the news Joel Brand needed after the many frustrating weeks in Istanbul, Aleppo, and Cairo. "My affairs would soon be in order," he thought.

The next day, June 22, he was taken to a private house on the banks of the Nile, the borrowed residence of a British officer. A dozen people were waiting for him, including British officers and stenographers. Through the windows behind the seated men he could see views of the yellow-green river. Brand was introduced to a slim man of medium height in his early thirties. "I am Ira Hirschmann," the man said. "President Roosevelt has sent me here to talk to you, Mr. Brand."

Hirschmann wore a business suit and tie and had a reserved and businesslike manner. Brand thought he seemed conceited and pompous.[25]

"Why did you leave [Hungary]?" Hirschmann asked.

"Because I had been sent to come and try to make . . ."

"Who sent you?" Hirschmann interrupted. He quickly moved the discussion to the specifics of Eichmann's offer. "Did you have confidence in his [Eichmann's] word?" he asked Brand.

"I did not have the right to question my own conscience," Brand told him. "There is no other way besides legal means in which we can help. We cannot wait for that invasion of Budapest."

"Then it was a matter of conscience with you, not a matter of confidence—is that correct?" Hirschmann asked.

"No—" Brand told him, "there is only one chance, perhaps it is no good, but there is no other chance." He explained: "They need things. Besides, I know from years of work that every one of them can be bought. Many of them have been."

Hirschmann asked about Bandi Grosz: "Who was he working for, really?"

Brand grinned at the question. "I do not understand you," he said. "He was working for money."[26] It was an answer that anyone who had dealt with Grosz would understand.

The interview went on for two hours. As Joel Brand was escorted away, Hirschmann said: "I beg you to believe me, Mr. Brand, when I say that my government entirely disapproves of the way in which the English are handling this matter. I shall fly to London and shall there, and also in Washington, demand your immediate release. You will be given the opportunity of continuing your mission."[27]

It was exactly the response Brand had been hoping to hear. But after the interview, Hirschmann dictated his report on the meeting with

Brand piecemeal under the pressure of time and a midsummer temperature of 118 degrees in Cairo. Perhaps forgetting the difficulties Moyne
had presented earlier, Hirschmann shared the transcript of the interview with Lord Moyne and claimed that the British resident minister
"was (along with me) genuinely enthusiastic regarding possibilities which
might develop provided that this matter was handled with care and skill."
Hirschmann was eager to have his interview accepted "as the basic and
accepted report on the Brand case" and cited Moyne as evidence that he
had gathered new information, which had "heretofore been unknown to
British intelligence." The State Department—their minds already made
up—paid little attention to Hirschmann's report, except to send him a
stinging telegram urging him not to talk about "broader matters connected with [his] conversations with the enemy."[28]

After the interview Brand was taken back to the British prison, where
Lieutenant Savigny resumed his interrogation, asking more detailed
questions about Brand's acquaintances, travels, and obscure couriers
who had occasionally carried documents or money into or out of Hungary. Brand heard no more from or about Ira Hirschmann, and from
the British there wasn't even the pretense of an interest in the Eichmann
proposal or the fate of the Hungarian Jews. Despite Ira Hirschmann's
parting promise, and the many promises of the British, Joel Brand was
still a prisoner, treated as if he had been accused of some crime. After a
few more days of the interrogation routine he revolted, telling the British officers that they had no right to keep him; that their actions were
contrary to international law, to their own interests, and to the interests
of the Jews of Europe; and that if he was not released in three days he
would go on a hunger strike.

The guards and officers tried to placate him, but Brand was adamant. On the fourth morning, he refused to eat his breakfast. The
guards responded by bringing him especially appetizing dishes, which
he refused. For three days of hunger strike it took all his strength to keep
from nibbling the food. Then he found that it was suddenly easier. He
had ceased to feel hungry.

One month after the exchange of cables between the Foreign Office and the high commissioner in Palestine, Moshe Shertok arrived in London to report on his own meeting with Brand. He had already sent repeated cables to London urging that Brand be released and sent back to Budapest: "According text telegram from friends in Budapest transmitted by Istanbul unless Brand and other person who accompanied him to Istanbul return to Hungary immediately everything will be lost. . . . Brand came as emissary remnant European Jewry who in interests its rescue accepted mission from enemies on clear understanding that he return with reply." There was no reply to his pleas.

In London, Shertok argued to the Foreign Office: (1) that Brand should be sent back to Hungary at once, if possible with Grosz, and with a message that the offer was under consideration, lest an impatient Gestapo murder Brand's family and other Jews; (2) that he was convinced of the bona fides of Brand and that the proposals really did come from high and responsible German circles; and (3) that however fantastic and unacceptable the proposal from Eichmann seemed, the British and American governments should examine it carefully and make a counterproposal urging that the Jews be released by the German authorities.[29] Shertok made his recommendations knowing full well that they were unlikely to be accepted by the British. He and the Jewish Agency also knew that the proposal and any subsequent negotiations were unlikely to result in more Jewish refugees coming to Palestine.

Accompanied by Chaim Weizmann, Shertok met with Under Secretary Hall at the Foreign Office to clarify the views of the Jewish Agency. Ben-Gurion had already sent messages about the readiness of the Nazis to release one million Hungarian Jews. Fully aware of the necessity for buzzwords and conciliatory language in an appeal, Ben-Gurion had urged that the Allies "not allow this unique and possibly last chance of saving the remains of European Jewry to be lost although it is fully realized that the exigencies of war are primary consideration." Along with his other arguments, Shertok suggested that in addition to initiating immediate negotiations with the other side, perhaps through the WRB in Istanbul, and allowing Brand's return to Hungary, the Allies could put pressure on the Hungarians by issuing a warning that railway men in Hungary could be prosecuted as war criminals for their participation in the deportations.[30]

Others also appealed to the Foreign Office. Nahum Goldman met with the British ambassador in Washington, urging him to consider that Eichmann's offer was not a psychological warfare ploy based on the certainty of the British refusing, but an effort by the Gestapo leaders ("certainly Eichmann and possibly Himmler") to obtain foreign exchange for their own use when they would have to flee a defeated and occupied Germany, and that the discussion be kept open on the prospect of saving "at least some Jews' lives." He and the distinguished and respected American rabbi Stephen Wise were strongly opposed to any publicity about the proposal on the ground that it might jeopardize the possibility of saving lives.[31]

Anthony Eden paid little attention to Shertok's arguments and any other arguments urging a response. He noted: (1) that Brand should be held at least until Shertok completed his talks. (It isn't clear what would have constituted Shertok finishing his talks, since the only place he could safely travel was to London. Noting that the "disposal of the German agent [Grosz] has been left to the British intelligence authorities" seemed his way of suggesting the appropriate "disposal" of Brand); (2) that there was independent evidence that Grosz was of dubious reputation and "Brand no more than a terrorized instrument of the Gestapo," and that the plan really was put forward "with the knowledge of very high German authorities," which in his view only strengthened the estimation that the proposal had been put forth solely for blackmail and propaganda; and (3) that the vagueness of the German references to a quid pro quo might in fact conceal a demand for chromium or some other war essential, and the request that Jews be allowed to emigrate via Spain and Portugal was clearly designed to embarrass the allies. On the basis of those arguments, Eden urged that Brand not be sent back to Hungary, and that the only reason the entire proposal should not be perfunctorily rejected was that the Jewish Agency in Britain, the Jewish leaders in the United

States, and "the highest circles of the United States Government . . . will be—understandably enough—filled with emotional anxiety and we should not precipitate the further horrors threatened by the Gestapo, or leave ourselves open to the charge of neglect of any means within our power, in existing circumstances, of saving a substantial number of Jews from certain death."

Eden wanted Shertok informed that the plan Brand brought "arrived in circumstances so suspect, and was worded in such a mixture of terrorist threats and blackmail," that the British and American governments would surely be justified in rejecting it forthwith, but "with our well-known solicitude for the Jews and for all who are suffering under the German terror, we have, however, carefully considered what, arising out of this affair, can be done by both Governments." Congratulating himself and His Majesty's Government for adhering to its own restrictive quotas for immigration to Palestine, he urged that the German government be called upon to "show its good faith" by agreeing to allow the International Red Cross to visit the principal internment camps for Jews and report on the conditions there; suggested that the UK and the United States would intervene with the Spanish and Portuguese governments to urge hospitality, to be paid for by the Germans, "to a stated number of Jews and others not included in earlier proposals"; and that pending the "practical working-out of all these suggestions," the German government was to undertake "no more extreme measures against the Jews." With his empty offers and intentionally embarrassing demands on the Germans, Eden was doing exactly what he accused the Germans of doing: drafting a proposal based solely on its value as propaganda.[32]

Anticipating Shertok's reaction, that he would claim that the Foreign Office counterproposal provided no material inducement to the Germans and that ignoring the German proposal would lead to dire consequences, Eden preemptively argued that the Germans "will be relieved of the burden of Jews in substantial numbers; that should be sufficient inducement" and that in any case it would be impossible for the UK and the United States to have anything to do with the Gestapo or the German government on the basis proposed by Brand, "above all in face of the firm refusal of the Soviet Government, whose military interest, as being nearest to Hungary where most of the remaining compact Jewish communities are planned, is most important."

Nothing in Eden's memo is as revealing as this last line. He mentions the alliance with the Soviet Union almost in passing, but it was a dominating concern for the British and the Americans. Stalin and the Red Army had been in a death struggle with Germany for three years. The Soviet armies had absorbed the brunt of the fighting against the Nazis and had seen vast areas of their homeland invaded, occupied, and laid waste; they finally held the upper hand, with their forces advancing toward Germany and along the broad front from the Baltic to the Black Sea and the Balkans. Though British and American relations with Stalin and officials in the Soviet hierarchy had never been warm, and fear of Soviet intentions consumed a disproportionate share of energy and time at Whitehall and Foggy Bottom, the long negotiations leading up to the Casablanca Conference had established unconditional surrender as the only acceptable outcome of the war. To Stalin, unconditional surrender was not open to interpretation and precluded *any* dealings with the Germans. The British embassy in Moscow had already warned that the Soviet Government "does not consider it permissible or expedient to carry on any conversations whatsoever with the German Government" on the question of any bargaining for Jewish lives.[33] No matter how the Eichmann proposal or a reply was couched, Stalin would see a betrayal in any negotiation with Himmler. He did not have to articulate what he could do in response. When British and American troops finally landed on the European continent, opening up the long-awaited Western Front, Stalin could simply order his troops to stand down in place, which would have allowed the Germans to move the bulk of their armies to the west and repel the invaders back into the Channel. It was a risk neither Britain nor the United States was willing to consider.

The Allies were eager to point out that they had addressed the issue. Within three days of the German occupation of Hungary, in March 1944, Franklin Roosevelt had issued a warning that those who took part in the annihilation of European Jewry would not "go unpunished." Describing the "wholesale systematic murder of the Jews" as one of the "blackest crimes of all history," he promised that "all who knowingly take part in the deportation of Jews to their death . . . are equally guilty with the executioner." His strong and eloquent comments were reported on the front pages of the *Los Angeles Times*, the *Christian Science Monitor*, the *New York Times*, and the *New York Herald Tribune*.[34] But like most wartime news, the speech and the issue had come and gone in the United States. Attention was now on the Allied landings and the promise that it was the beginning of the end of the war.

A few in Britain, like the archbishop of Canterbury and some of the trade union leaders, also spoke out in favor of rescue and relief efforts directed toward the Jewish refugees. In a note to the BBC the archbishop confirmed that he had proof that twelve thousand Jews per day were being sent to Auschwitz; he may have seen or heard rumors about the Auschwitz Protocols. He wrote to the prime minister: "I am sure the only Christian attitude in the face of this horror is to say, we will do what we can, however trifling. If the result were the saving of one Jew, it would be worth it."[35] His and other delegations to the Foreign Office and the prime minister were received politely with the explanation that His Majesty's Government was doing all it could under the circumstances, that there remained a grave danger in any negotiation with the enemy, and that it was imperative that no one lose sight of the ultimate war goals. The delegates were so thrilled to be received by Anthony Eden or in some cases the prime minister himself that they would leave with fawning thanks for the audience, either not realizing or not concerning themselves that they received no promises of action on the refugee issue. As pressure mounted, and stories about the Auschwitz Protocols began to circulate in Britain in July 1944, Churchill responded to the issue in confidential memos and personal replies to appeals: "I fear we are the witnesses of one of the greatest and most horrible crimes ever committed in the whole history of the world. And this was done with the aid of scientific devices and by a so-called civilized people. It is clear beyond a doubt that everybody involved in this crime who may fall into our hands, including those who only obeyed orders in committing these butcheries, must be killed."[36] He would later use the same language in a dramatic public speech.

But even as Churchill was trying out his eloquent comments about "the most horrible crimes ever committed in the whole history of the world," British policy remained adamant. The agendas prepared for the meetings with church leaders and other appeals were unyielding: "It has been decided that there should be no negotiations with any enemy government and that no emissary should be sent to Budapest." And the British were prepared to stand firm even if the Americans—whom they assumed would be influenced by their own large Jewish population—took a less rigid position. As early as March 1944, Anthony Eden reported "serious differences of opinion between HMG and the United States Government over details of refugee policy."[37] If D-day, the joint Western Front, and the focus on bringing the war to a speedy end brought the Allies closer on many issues—a notion Eisenhower might have disputed after some of his testier meetings with Field Marshal Montgomery—the Brand mission and proposal aggravated and accentuated fundamental differences between the United States and Britain on rescue policy. By July, when Anthony Eden was warning of the danger of sending Brand back to Hungary because the scheme was a cover for peace talk feelers, he worried in confidential memos that Treasury Secretary Morgenthau, the highest-ranking Jew in the American government, would "play" with any scheme that could be viewed as an effort at rescuing Jews.[38]

Anthony Eden had his qualms about Morgenthau and the influence of the Jews on American policy, but in reality there were few protests in the United States to the existing policy of inaction. Peter Bergson's Committee for a Jewish Army of Stateless and Palestinian Jews aggressively picketed, paraded, and raised funds, calling for "an all-out campaign to save European Jewry," including the establishment of camps in Palestine to house those who escaped Europe.[39] But when Bergson organized a visit of five hundred rabbis to Washington in October 1943, FDR quietly rearranged his schedule to leave the city early enough to miss the rabbis. The press either ignored the event or reported inaccurately that the rabbis were there to support emigration to Palestine.[40] Bergson encountered enough entrenched anti-Semitism to point out in his speeches that "Justice Frankfurter is not a Hebrew. He is an American of Hebrew descent, practicing the Jewish religion, exactly as Justice Murphy is an American of Irish descent, practicing the Catholic religion."[41]

Bergson and his group hoped to also inspire a propaganda effort across the Atlantic, but the British Foreign Office dismissed his committee as "a racket thought up by Bergson and other terrorist elements . . . who had previously been ejected from official Zionist circles." On the recommendation of the Foreign Office, Churchill refused to acknowledge communications from Bergson's organization.[42] The American State Department reciprocated in kind, blaming mass demonstrations in support of Jewish refugees on "England, where certain emotionalists and impractical dreamers adopted it and shipped it on to Rabbi Wise and Goldman in New York."[43]

It wasn't just radical action that the British government resisted. Lord Moyne and other senior advisers urged that the potential dangers and military and political burdens of an effort on behalf of the Jews of Hungary or elsewhere in occupied Europe outweighed any public relations benefits to Britain or to the war effort. Lord Moyne would later deny it, but it was widely reported that after hearing about the Eichmann proposal and the perilous situation of the Hungarian Jews, Moyne said: "What am I going to do with a million Jewish refugees loose in Europe? It will completely disrupt our war logistics."[44]

# 9

# The Lull

*If there is no place for us on this planet, then there is no alternative to the*
*gas chambers for our people.*

—Joel Brand[1]

*Brand is convinced that the lives of one hundred thousand Jews absolutely*
*depend on the success of his mission, convinced that even in the most desper-*
*ate period the Germans can organize the emigration . . .*

—Ludwig Kastner[2]

E ven before Joel Brand left Budapest for Istanbul, his colleague on
Vaada, Rezső Kasztner, moved into the leadership of the organization. He also moved into Hansi Brand's bed.

Hansi later claimed she had never been in love with Joel, that she
appreciated him as a loving father to the children and admired his skills
as a salesman and his adeptness with the café meetings that had once
been so important to their knitwear business and the early days of the
Vaada rescue committee, but that she had doubts about his adequacy for
the task of negotiating for the lives of the Jews of Hungary.

Joel Brand was a *schlub*, his red hair unkempt, his suits rumpled, his
German colorful but never elegant, his posture and manner the louche
slouch of the cafés. Awed by the powerful and famous, he compensated
for his lack of formal education with bravado and patter and was besot-
ted with naïve idealism, an exalted sense of his mission, and the firm
belief that he was a *shaliach*, a Jewish emissary, following an age-old tradition and representing the doomed Jews of Hungary. Hansi and Rezső

Kasztner thought Joel too naïvely unaware of the twentieth-century web of deceits, self-interests, and power diplomacy to be capable of serious negotiations with those who would decide the destiny of the Jews. They criticized him for taking on more than he could handle, for failing to complete his negotiations, and for not returning with a counterproposal, contrasting what they saw as his bumbling with Kasztner's own adeptness.

By contrast, Rezső Kasztner was sophisticated and self-confident, always well groomed, a polished lawyer with little faith in those he dealt with and few doubts about his own capabilities. He seemed to relish the role of power broker, and was convinced he understood the Nazis. "There was an exemplary collaboration between the various SS organs," as he saw it. "The *Judenkommando* [Jewish unit] murdered, the economic staff cashed in."[3] If Joel Brand had been awkward around Eichmann or Laufer, Kasztner was comfortable with Eichmann, Krumey, Clages, Laufer, and Becher. And he took advantage of his relationships with them. While the Jews of Budapest huddled in crowded apartment blocks under harsh restrictions, Kasztner was allowed to live in an unmarked house, was exempted from wearing a yellow Star of David, and enjoyed the use of a telephone, a car, a passport, and a ready supply of cigarettes—all thanks to the Nazis. Dressed in his tailored suits, he drove from meeting to meeting, utilizing the ready access to the phones that were allowed to him by special permission. At dinners with Becher and Becher's mistress at the luxurious Chorin House on Andrássy Avenue, and late at night at the casino with other senior Nazis, Rezső Kasztner was spared the solitude, terror, and frustrations of Joel Brand's lonely mission to Istanbul, Aleppo, and Cairo. If others criticized the relative luxury of Kasztner's privileged life while so many were crowded, cold, starving, and terrified, he never mentioned it in his memoir. He would probably have dismissed the criticism by pointing out that his relationships with the powerful and well placed required that he look and act the part.

After Joel left Budapest, Kasztner and Hansi protested the deportations from the Hungarian provinces. Kasztner complained to SS Captain Hunsche that hundreds of Jews were confined and transported in deplorable conditions, with no food, water, or sanitary facilities. The captain angrily answered that he had heard enough of the Jewish "atrocity tales," that he had followed up on the facts himself, and that not more than fifty to sixty people on each shipment died in transit. Later, in Eichmann's office in Swabenberg, Kasztner and Hansi protested that they had gotten reports that in Carpathian Ruthenia as many as ninety individuals were packed into each cattle car. "The Jews in that area have many children, and children don't need much space," Eichmann sneered. When they urged Eichmann to stop the deportations altogether, he answered that if he stopped, the Zionists would have no reason to negotiate with him.[4]

They met often enough with Eichmann for Hansi Brand to become accustomed to Eichmann's heavy smoking and drinking—"you could smell the brandy from way off"—and the chatty moods that would follow his cruel comments as he would switch to a calm voice and make efforts to show that "he understood the Jewish business very well." Eichmann stressed that what a German officer promises he will always honor, protested that Vaada was too slow in fulfilling its part of the agreements, and argued that since Vaada had nothing to show, no agreement or counterproposal sent back by Joel Brand, he could postpone the releases of Jews he had promised. He enjoyed taunting them. "If I don't get a positive reply from Istanbul in three days," he said once, "I will let the mill in Auschwitz go to work." At another meeting he asked, "What is up with our emissary? Why hasn't Brand come home from Istanbul? Make sure the Jews and Allies understand something, that the German Reich will not let you lead it around by the nose."[5]

Hansi and Kasztner were remarkably outspoken, even as Eichmann toyed with them. When Hansi Brand pleaded for Eichmann to spare children from the deportations and he refused, she said, "You probably do not have any children, and that is why you have no pity on them." She must have impressed Eichmann or touched a nerve: few ever risked defying him so boldly. He answered her without his usual rage: "You are taking a great liberty, Mrs. Brand; if you speak to me like that I advise you to stop coming to see me."

Once, Kasztner pressed Eichmann to bring Jews with Palestine certificates to a safe haven in Budapest. When Eichmann refused—"Once I've said no, it's no!"—Kasztner got up from his chair as if to leave the room, a taboo in protocol before German officials until you were formally dismissed. "Kasztner!" Eichmann said, "Your nerves are shot. I'll send you to Theresienstadt to recover. Or would you prefer Auschwitz? Get me straight, I've got to clear the Jewish shit out of the provinces."[6]

If Hansi seemed to understand Eichmann's limits, Kasztner seemed to enjoy Eichmann's threats: being the recipient established his bona fides as the leader of the rescue efforts. Eichmann remembered that when they were together Kasztner smoked cigarettes "as though he were in a coffeehouse," taking one aromatic cigarette after another from a silver case and lighting them with a silver lighter. He described Kasztner as

> an ice-cold lawyer and a fanatical Zionist. . . . With his great polish and reserve he would have made an ideal Gestapo officer himself. . . . As a matter of fact, there was a very strong similarity between our attitudes in the S.S. and the viewpoint of these immensely idealistic Zionist leaders. . . . I believe that Kasztner would have sacrificed a thousand or a hundred thousand of his blood to achieve his political goal. . . . "You can have the others," he would say, "but let me have this group here." And because Kasztner rendered us a great service by helping keep the deportation camps peaceful, I would let his groups escape. After all, I was not concerned with small groups of a thousand or so Jews. . . . That was the "gentleman's agreement" I had with Kasztner.[7]

Before long, Kasztner was contrasting what he hoped to achieve in his own plans with the long weeks during which Brand seemed to have accomplished nothing. He had effectively taken over the leadership of the negotiations in Budapest, and he and Hansi Brand had become inseparable. When Kasztner sent messages to Istanbul, Hansi would sometimes add a postscript, asking the recipient to give her regards to Joel. Eichmann may have tolerated Kasztner's efforts because it took pressure off the Brand mission. Hansi recalled that Eichmann was relieved when Joel Brand's efforts seemed to come to naught. "I can say this quite confidently," she later testified. "That he was very pleased. He was very pleased that this transaction had not come off."[8]

In late May 1944, when Joel Brand was still in Istanbul, Kasztner reminded Eichmann that the Allies would want a sign of good faith before they trusted the Germans in negotiations, and that if the deportations continued at twelve thousand per day, the Germans would run out of Jews to trade. Eichmann told Kasztner that he would redirect thirty thousand Jews (excluding Jews who were "ethnically and biologically valuable elements") to Austria, where they would be "put on ice." Eichmann's price for this "gesture of goodwill" was SFr 5 million. What sounded like a gracious gesture was in fact only Eichmann's response to the mayor of Vienna, who had prevailed upon the German Security Police to supply him with additional slave labor for the arms factories. Kasztner collected $100 from each person selected for the new program, a bargain price to escape what many thought of as the death sentence that awaited Jews on the deportation trains. On Sip Street, where the Orthodox and Neologue communities had their offices, people fought for the privilege of being slave laborers, offering everything they had as bribes. Special trains then carried some eighteen thousand to twenty thousand Hungarian Jews toward Vienna, where they were incarcerated in the Strasshof concentration camp.[9] Kasztner gave the funds he collected to Wisliceny.

Reports of the Hungarian deportations reached the OSS and the State Department in the United States, and MI6 and the Foreign Office in Britain, but the details and even the terrible statistics drew little attention. The War Refugee Board had references to the Auschwitz Protocols in their files as early as May 22,[10] but they were precluded by their charter from involving themselves in intelligence activities and hence had little leverage in Washington. The semi-official position in government circles in both countries was that while atrocities were obviously being committed, there was no definitive proof of annihilations on the scale that lobbyists for the Jews and certain relief organizations claimed. Failing that proof, the military and civilian authorities argued, it was inappropriate and deleterious to detour from the strategy of total victory.

In Jerusalem, Istanbul, and Budapest, the rescue groups talked among themselves about the incredible horror they were witnessing. Anyone who had seen or heard the reports about the loading of the cattle cars could do the simple arithmetic. The café talk was that 450,000 Jews had already been deported from the Hungarian provinces, and that another 350,000 from Budapest and the surrounding areas would follow in weeks. More Jews had been murdered in Poland, but this time those who were willing to believe the reports were watching the annihilation in real time, not learning about it weeks or months later. In desperation, the Jewish Agency proposed dramatic rescue schemes, like awarding every Hungarian Jew Palestinian citizenship or getting the Allies to bomb the railroad tracks leading to Auschwitz. And even as they made these proposals to what they hoped were sympathetic audiences in Britain and the United States, they knew there was almost no possibility that anything would happen.[11] Apart from the Jewish rescue groups themselves, among the Jews outside Europe who managed to get word of what was going on, and the still nascent WRB, no one was listening.

The OSS, in charge of American intelligence, was obsessed with long-range planning for the end of the war, the need for Germany to remain the most powerful economic power in Europe, and for Austria to remain German; some of their agents floated wild ideas, like having the head of the agency, William Donovan, negotiate directly with the German ambassador to Turkey, Franz von Papen. With rescue efforts a low priority, they never forwarded the copy of the Auschwitz Protocols they had received, or even a summary, to the president. With no systematic collection or review of evidence of the extent of German atrocities against the Jews, requests for relief or rescue efforts fell on deaf ears in the White House, the Pentagon, and at Foggy Bottom.

On June 24, Roswell McClelland at the American legation in Berne sent a cable to Washington repeating a desperate request of Rabbi Weissmandel of Slovakia that the Allies bomb the railways leading from

Hungary, through Slovakia, to Auschwitz. It was not the first time this request had been made. On May 25, when Brand was en route to Istanbul, Isaac Sternbuch, a representative of the Union of Orthodox Rabbis in the United States, had written from Switzerland passing along requests from Slovakia for air raids over Košice, as a "transit place for military transports" and also the "junctions for deportations coming through Košice." The requests were precise, describing vulnerable bridges and pointing out that the stretch was "the single near route from Hungary to Poland . . . [and] that bombing should be repeated at short intervals to prevent rebuilding." More requests to the U.S. Army Air Corps and the British Air Ministry to bomb Auschwitz arrived through every channel the Jewish organizations could muster, including Shertok, Chaim Weizmann, and Nahum Goldman in the United States.[12] U.S. reconnaissance photos of the area taken on April 4, 1944, showed the large camp at Auschwitz. The photos and interpretation had been sent to both American and RAF intelligence for analysis, but none of the photo interpreters and analysts commented on the huts and other camp features or the vulnerable railroad line. On June 6, a report based on those reconnaissance photos, augmented by "information from available ground sources," was circulated to British and American air intelligence, but again the bombing planners were interested only in the industrial facilities near the camp. The photo analysts dismissed the rows of barracks at Auschwitz as typical of a labor camp and the smoke pouring from a crematorium chimney as typical of a "boiler plant for heating." On one desperate telegram from Rabbi Weissmandel, an American official scribbled: "The old 'Noteschrei' [distress cry] technique!"[13]

Although the political authorities remained cautious in their interest in the Auschwitz Protocols, Vrba's drawings of Auschwitz, included in the Protocols and showing the placement of the gas chambers and crematoria, were submitted to military authorities, who were urged to utilize their precision bombing capabilities to destroy those facilities and hence stop the murder of Jews at the camp. Churchill, a few weeks after D-day, read a short but detailed report about the deportations to Auschwitz with suggested responses, including bombing the tracks leading to Auschwitz,

The Opera Café on Andrássy Avenue, where Brand waited.

The Little Majestic Hotel, Eichmann's headquarters in the Buda hills.

Joel Brand (taken after the war).

Adolf Eichmann, in the uniform of
an SS Obersturmbannführer (major),
before he arrived in Budapest.

Walter Rosenberg (Rudolf Vrba),
taken before the war.

Dieter Wislicenzy.

Kurt Becher, the Nazi expert in expropriation, taken after the war.

The Chorin mansion on Andrássy Avenue, thought by many to be the finest house in Budapest, expropriated by Becher as his personal residence.

Hansi Brand, taken after the war.

Resző Kasztner, passport photo.

Members of Vaada, the rescue committee. *From left to right:* Otto Komoly, Hansi Brand, Resző Kasztner, Zvi Goldfarb, and Peretz Reves.

Heinrich Himmler, *mit dem Augengläsern*, in the uniform of an SS Obergruppenführer before he was named Reichsführer.

German passport photos of Bandi Grosz (András Győrgy) (*left*) and Joel Brand (*right*) for their journey to Istanbul.

Jewish youth in Transcarpathia with their newly issued yellow stars, awaiting confinement in a ghetto, 1944.

Hannah Senesh before her mission.

Emil Nussbacher (Joel Palgi), Hungarian-Palestinian parachutist who survived the war.

Peretz (Ferenc) Goldstein, Hungarian-Palestinian parachutist.

bombing Auschwitz, and bombing government buildings in Budapest. He scribbled on the report: "What can be done? What can be said?" Eden argued that doing anything, or making further warnings, would make the "anti-Jewish atrocities worse."[14] After taking due time to demonstrate that they had taken the requests seriously and done due diligence on the proposals, the British and American bombing authorities denied every request. The reasons they offered were that the Auschwitz facility was beyond the range of the available bombers, that the distance was too great for a night attack, that they lacked precise targeting information, that without escorts the missions would be too dangerous for the crews, that no aircraft were available for the proposed missions, that there were no aircraft capable of such precision bombing, that interrupting the railways "is out of our power," and that even if the rail lines and camp facilities were bombed they could quickly be rebuilt.[15]

The Allied failure to bomb Auschwitz and other death camps has been debated for over sixty years. The Americans and British repeatedly argued that Auschwitz was beyond the range of available bombers. Bombing from airbases in the UK would have required unescorted flights of two thousand miles over enemy-held territory, but airfields in Italy were available and closer, and on June 2, the Allies began Operation Frantic, which used a Soviet airbase at Poltava for turnaround and refueling on long-range bombing missions from Foggia, Italy. Oil refineries and factories within a few miles of Auschwitz were repeatedly bombed, and missions of even longer distance had been undertaken with B-24 heavy bombers, including raids on the Ploeşti oil fields in Romania flown from fields in Tunisia. Many of those missions could have easily reached Auschwitz, a vulnerable target that lacked the ground-based aircraft and dense arrays of antiaircraft guns protecting the Axis oil fields and the factory sites and railways in Germany that were the usual targets of American daylight and British night raids. And while the big B-24s, B-17s, and British Lancasters could not do the kind of precision bombing necessary to take out crematoria or gas chambers without risking collateral damage to the internees in the Birkenau camp, aircraft like the Mitchell B-25 or the British Mosquito light bombers had been designed and used for low-level precision bombing, and had been successfully used in missions like the raid on Amiens to free prisoners of war, where the targets were more precise and better protected than the Auschwitz gas chambers and crematoria. It took the Germans eight months to build the new gas chambers at Auschwitz. If they had been destroyed in a successful bombing run, they could not have been rebuilt in time to be utilized again.

Taking out the rail junctions in Slovakia and southern Poland, which would have stopped the rail traffic bringing deportees to Auschwitz, at least until the rail lines were repaired, could be done with high-altitude bombing from heavy bombers. Indeed, bombers from the Fifteenth Air Force flew missions along and across those same rail lines while attacking oil refineries in Silesia. Portions of the rail lines would have been relatively easy to repair, but stretches of the single line that led from Hungary to Auschwitz ran on steep slopes along rivers and would have required heavy equipment and time-consuming repairs. Every day that the lines could have been out of commission would have meant trains held up and twelve thousand Jewish refugees who would not reach the loading ramps at Auschwitz. The British bomber command authorities also declared that even if the missions were possible, there were no aircraft available. At the time this explanation was given to the various Jewish groups lobbying for bombing, one hundred heavy bombers were tied up to deliver containers of arms and supplies to scattered Polish units of little military value to the advancing Russian forces; the British had decided that the missions were necessary to keep "faith with its ally" and bolster relations with the Polish government in exile and with the Polish communities in the UK.[16]

On the ninth day of his hunger strike, the guards brought Joel Brand a letter from Ehud Avriel in Istanbul. Avriel, who had escorted Brand to Aleppo, reported that Hansi Brand and the children were alive and well in Budapest, and that Brand's colleague Rezső Kasztner had been able to make some progress negotiating with the Germans. The letter was mercifully short on details about Kasztner's relationship with Hansi; it also had no information about the negotiations with Shertok in London or the British and American refusal to bomb the railway junctions leading to Auschwitz and the gas chambers and crematoria. But the good news that Hansi and the children were still alive in Budapest and that some efforts were going ahead to save the Hungarian Jews was enough to persuade Joel Brand to stop his hunger strike.

He began accepting food, and the British officers and guards became increasingly friendly, joking with him, joining him for meals, inviting him to movies and parties, and nicknaming him "Hess number two." He felt like he was being paraded before senior British officials on their arrival in Cairo as though he were a trophy. He also saw their attention as a refined form of the earlier interrogation, a fishing expedition for intelligence that was unrelated to his mission. But after the weeks of isolation he relished the outings to clubs and cafés. Brand did not know that Shertok had reported to the Jewish Agency from London that every proposal for a meeting had been turned down, that no similar proposal involving Palestine would be considered, and had asked whether in the present circumstances Joel Brand's return would be "at all desirable."[17]

On June 14, 1944, Rezső Kasztner wrote from Budapest: "the provinces are already without Jews . . . In Budapest we wait in the next days, maybe already hours, the establishment of ghettos to which the majority of approximately a quarter million Jews will be confined."[18] His prediction was close.

On June 17, the Budapest City Council ordered all Jews in Budapest— close to the quarter of a million in Kasztner's letter—into 2,680 apartment buildings that were marked outside with large yellow six-pointed stars against a black background. A family of four was entitled to one room. With no room for their belongings, many hurried to sell what they owned before their property was seized by the government or by covetous gentile neighbors. The superintendent or another appointed chief of each building in the new ghetto had to keep a list in triplicate of the Jews who lived there, with copies submitted to the city authorities and posted at the entrance to the building.

A week later, on Sunday evening, June 25, posters went up in Budapest announcing that henceforth Jews were forbidden to leave their places of residence except between two and five in the afternoon, and then only for medical visits, purchases of food, and visits to the public baths. No occupants of "Jewish houses" were to receive visitors, and Jews were not allowed to visit any city park, travel in any but the last streetcar on a train, or use any public shelter unless a separate Jewish area had been marked off. The Gestapo began going from house to house, shooting Jews *"sur place"* in random executions.[19] Eichmann also ordered the construction of camps in Budapest for what he called "sample goods"—inside the Aréna synagogue, near the Városliget, the biggest Budapest park, and later at 46 Columbus Street in the fourteenth district, at the Israelite School for the Deaf, Dumb and Blind.

No longer allowed in the cafés, the Jews of Budapest debated privately about what the Germans would do next. As weeks went by and nothing happened, they began calling the tense, quiet days "The Lull." The Lull had come so suddenly that it seemed that the next round of deportations could happen just as suddenly, and also without warning. On the streets, people speculated that the Germans had already decided the order of deportations from Budapest, beginning with childless women and able-bodied girls, then able-bodied men, and finally children and all persons "unsuited for work." Dreadful as it sounded, it was a hopeful rumor, letting those in the ghettos believe that the first two categories would actually be sent to work in factories as slave labor, and that only the last category would be sent directly to Auschwitz.[20]

Horthy had become a puppet of the Nazis. He was allowed to retain the trappings of his office and insisted on formality, protocol, and regal gestures, including his public appearances on horseback or in horse-drawn carriages, but the pretense of Hungarian independence fooled no one. Horthy had no means to resist the orders from Berlin or from local German officials. He stayed in his palace with plenty of time to move pushpins on the maps and contemplate what the advancing Soviet armies on his eastern border and the advancing British-Canadian-American invasion force in France meant for the future of his regime. By late June 1944, representatives of the International Red Cross and heads of state in neutral Sweden and Switzerland sent pleas to Horthy to stop the deportations of Jews. Hungarian counterintelligence also saw Roswell McClelland's June 24 cable requesting bombing of the railways leading to Auschwitz, a hint that the Allied governments might join the neutral governments and relief agencies in campaigning on behalf of the Jews. On June 26, the day after the Vatican received Roncalli's report on the Auschwitz Protocols, Horthy received a papal appeal urging that he intervene in the deportations.

Horthy was no defender of the Jews. He did not share the values of the Nazis, but the admiral probably believed that *Ostjuden* were a different biological and ideological race and a potential threat to Christian Magyars.[21] He was also a cautious politician, and balanced his growing awareness that the Allies might consider him and his government war criminals against the pressure of the Germans and his concerns about domestic rivals for power. As the Allies closed in he was less afraid of the occupying Germans than of a right-wing coup by fascist and anti-Semitic Hungarian elements who had been empowered by the German occupation and were eager to settle long resentments toward the Jews of Hungary. His strongest instinct remained survival. The day he received the papal appeal, June 26, 1944, Admiral Horthy quietly requested that the Germans cease all deportations of Jews.

A week later, on July 2, an American daylight bombing raid targeted Budapest. The railway station was hit, but the largest concentration of bombs fell on factories in the outskirts of the city and did little damage, though enough for the cafés to soon be full of talk about the arrival of the Americans and the end of the war. Because the bombing spared the ghettos of the well-to-do Jews in the fifth (Leopold) district and the poorer Jewish neighborhoods of the sixth (Maria Theresa) and seventh (Elizabeth) districts, rumors circulated that Jewish agents on the ground had coordinated with the Allied bombers. Admiral Horthy assumed the Allied bombing was a Jewish-motivated act of revenge.

As his military situation deteriorated, Adolf Hitler became reclusive, rarely appearing in public or visiting Berlin. In the isolation of his headquarters at the Wolfschanze near Rastenburg in East Prussia, and occasionally at his Bavarian aerie at Berchtesgaden, he became increasingly paranoid and fiercely self-protective, surrounding himself with the web of Himmler's security apparatus, trusted guards, and stringent special security procedures as he micromanaged the smallest details of the German campaigns on multiple fronts, including the situation of the Jews in Hungary.[22] It wasn't only his putative allies like Admiral Horthy that Hitler distrusted. At his own headquarters at the Hotel Prinz Albrecht in Berlin, Himmler received a steady flow of reports about suspicious army officers on the German general staff. He and Hitler worried about the possibility of a plot against the Führer.

Their suspicions were well placed. To those on the German general staff who had long been contemptuous of Hitler's background and held doubts about his military strategies, the toll of the day-and-night bombing by the Americans and British, the steady advances of the Soviet forces on the Eastern Front, the success of the long-feared Allied invasion of France and the creation of a second front, and the revelation of the enormous advantages of manpower, equipment, and fuel supplies enjoyed by Germany's enemies signaled pending doom for Germany. The idle talk among a small group of officers months before became a full-blown conspiracy to assassinate the Führer and end what they saw as the suicidal course on which Hitler was leading Germany. They did not have a plan of how and where they would assassinate the increasingly reclusive and protected Führer, but the rest of their conspiracy began to fall into place.

In anticipation of a potential disaster, the German Reserve Army had developed a plan called Operation Valkyrie, to be used in the event that Allied bombing or a rising by the hundreds of thousands of slave laborers in German factories threatened a breakdown of law and order. Under the plan, General Friedrich Olbricht, head of the General Army Office headquarters at the Bendlerblock in central Berlin, controlled an independent system of communications to reserve units all over Germany.

When Olbricht and Colonel Henning von Tresckow, a nephew of Field Marshal Fedor von Bock and a member of his Army Group Center staff, joined the secret conspiracy against the Führer, they brought to the plot access to this communications system, with direct connections in the army staff, and the framework of a plan for the Reserve Army to take control of German cities, disarm the SS, and arrest the Nazi leadership. General Carl-Heinrich von Stülpnagel, the German military commander in France, secretly agreed to take control in Paris after Hitler was killed and to negotiate an immediate armistice with the Allied armies.

The conspirators did not know about Himmler's own secret scheme to open negotiations with the Allies through Grosz and Brand. Himmler had always been thorough in covering himself. As late as June 1944, he had insisted privately that he would not be pointed to "as one of the greatest murderers on record" because "he had done nothing wrong and only carried out Adolf Hitler's orders." He explained to his trusted masseur Felix Kersten that although he would let the Jews go abroad, it would be done only in absolute secrecy and without his name being used, because "firstly, extermination was a dirty business; and secondly it aroused a good deal of ill-will, as innocent people abroad were too stupid and too ignorant to realize the necessity for it."[23]

Indeed, news of the scale and hurried timetable of the mass annihilation of Hungarian Jews may have attracted additional senior German staff officers to the conspiracy against Hitler, less because they were sympathetic to the Jews than because they considered the efforts devoted to the mass-murder of the Jews a diversion from the essential military task of defending the Fatherland—a position ironically parallel to the American strategic axiom of eschewing any distraction from the main mission of engaging and defeating the enemy. Suggestions were floated that the Reichswehr conspirators make an arrangement with Himmler, perhaps through Himmler's lawyer friend Carl Langbehn,[24] but they never communicated directly with the Reichsführer. They also seem not to have realized that Himmler's spy network inside Germany kept him informed about their conspiracy.

Himmler took no action against the conspirators, probably because he did not realize the extent of their contempt for him and the rest of the

Nazi leadership. He probably assumed that if they succeeded in assassinating Hitler, the conspiracy could serve his own goals, and that as the Führer's designated successor, he would be in a position to negotiate a peace settlement before Germany was destroyed. He also no doubt realized how unlikely it was for an assassination plot to succeed, and was clever enough to leave no footprints that might later entangle him with the conspiracy. Even as he received regular reports about the conspirators, he carried on as if nothing were awry. In mid-July he met with Hitler to outline his proposed future course of action on the "Hungarian Jewish question" and recorded Hitler's approval with a check mark on his written agenda.[25]

Despite their broadening network of connections inside the army, the circle of conspirators was unable to get anyone within pistol or bomb range of the reclusive Führer. Then on July 1, 1944, one of the original conspirators, Claus von Stauffenberg, was appointed chief of staff to General Fromm at the Reserve Army headquarters in Berlin; this made him a member of the small group eligible to attend Hitler's military conferences at the Wolfschanze and in Berchtesgaden. Twice in the first weeks of July, Stauffenberg attended Hitler's conferences, carrying a bomb in his briefcase. Both attempts were called off because neither Goering nor Himmler were present at the conferences, and the conspirators had concluded that they would also have to be executed for the plot to have a chance of succeeding. On July 15 Stauffenberg again flew to a meeting in East Prussia. By then the requirement that Goering and Himmler be present had been dropped from the plans, but that attempt was also called off at the last minute, though not in time to halt a partial mobilization of Operation Valkyrie, which had to be canceled and concealed at the last minute. When Stauffenberg returned to Berlin, he heard rumors that the Gestapo was closing in on the conspiracy and that they would have to act at the next opportunity. Hitler had another conference called for the Wolfschanze on July 20, and Stauffenberg again flew to East Prussia. Despite Hitler's mania for security, the briefcases of the officers attending the meeting were not inspected, and the two-pound block of plastic explosive and pencil detonator in Stauffenberg's briefcase were not detected. This time the meeting was not in the underground *Füh-rerbunker* where most of Hitler's meetings were held, but in a wooden hut that served as an alternate command and briefing room. Stauffenberg activated the detonator before the meeting and, once inside the hut, placed his briefcase under the conference table. At twenty minutes after noon, ten minutes into the meeting, he made an excuse and left the room. The bomb went off at 12:40, demolishing the room.

German army officers in France and Berlin were poised to unleash Operation Valkyrie, seize power from the Nazi leadership, and begin immediate negotiations for peace with the allies. Because of the confusion in the aftermath of the explosion, including the time it took Stauffenberg to fly back to Berlin, it was four o'clock that afternoon when General Olbricht issued the orders to mobilize Operation Valkyrie. By then, news had leaked out that Hitler had survived the blast. Some attributed his survival to his fierce will to live or his self-proclaimed destiny as Führer; others noted that the briefcase had been leaning against the leg of the massive conference table or possibly had been moved to the opposite end of the table from the Führer, and that the relatively flimsy wooden hut did not effectively confine the blast, which had been designed for the enclosed underground bunker. When news of Hitler's survival reached Himmler, the Reichsführer issued orders countermanding the mobilization of Operation Valkyrie, and separate orders for a roundup of the conspirators. By early evening Hitler telephoned Josef Goebbels at the Propaganda Ministry and spoke to some of his commanders, confirming his survival to those who had received contradictory reports. At one o'clock the following morning, Hitler broadcast from Rastenberg. "My German comrades!" he began. "If I speak to you today, it is first in order that you should hear my voice and should know that I am unhurt and well, and, second, that you should know of a crime unparalleled in German history." His peroration ended four minutes later with a reference to the conspirators: "This time we shall settle accounts with them in the manner to which we National Socialists are accustomed." The executions began later that day. To persuade others of his own loyalty, Himmler ordered especially vicious deaths for the conspirators.

Though badly shaken up by the assassination attempt, Hitler did not forget his obsession with the Hungarian Jews. While the reprisal executions were going on, the Führer spoke with Hungarian Field Marshal Miklós, criticizing Horthy's intercession on behalf of the Jews and blaming the Jews as the force behind Allied bombing of Hamburg and other cities. If the Jews threatened to destroy Europe, he promised, they would find themselves destroyed first.[26]

# Revelation

*What they had done, by publicizing the matter, is the worst kind of bestiality, and it emerged from a calculation in which the blood of our brothers plays no part. It is an unheard-of provocation.*

—Isaac Gruenbaum[1]

*Immigration which is not entirely aimed—from beginning to end—at our wartime needs, is not beneficial.*

—David Ben-Gurion and Israel Galili[2]

Goebbels's propaganda machine officially suppressed foreign news reports of the attempt on Hitler's life for five days, and the embargo was effective. Kurt Becher, despite his high-level SS connections, did not hear about it for a full week, and the foreign press had to wait even longer. Hannah Senesh's mother, in prison in Budapest, did not hear for weeks.[3] But there was no lack of news in the West. On the day of the assassination attempt, newspapers and radio stations on both sides of the Atlantic had another sensational story. This one was leaked by the British Foreign Office, printed in the *New York Herald Tribune* on July 19, and picked up elsewhere, including by the London papers and BBC, on July 20.

## A MONSTROUS "OFFER"
—
## GERMAN BLACKMAIL
—
## BARTERING JEWS FOR MUNITIONS

The German authorities, the *Times* of London reported, "have reached a new level of fantasy and self-deception" in putting forth an offer "to exchange the remaining Hungarian Jews for munitions of war—which, they said, would not be used on the Western front."[4] The article repeated the language Anthony Eden had used to respond to Joel Brand's proposal: "The British Government know what value to set on any German or German-sponsored offer. They know there can be no security for the Jews or the other oppressed peoples of Europe until victory is won." The article also reported that the International Red Cross had announced that the Hungarian government had agreed to put a stop to the deportations and even allow some Jews to leave, and that in light of that announcement "the German 'offer' seems to be simply a fantastic attempt to sow suspicion among the allies." "Fantastic" seemed to be the key term of the Foreign Office leak: the concluding lines of the *Times* article assured readers that "Fantastic though it was, London made sure that Moscow and Washington were quickly in possession of all the facts."

The next day Wickham Steed broadcast a fuller version of the story on the BBC, concluding: "There is not the slightest possibility that the British and American governments will agree to enter into any negotiations of this sort, although they would like to help the Hungarian Jews."[5] The story was quickly picked up by newspapers as far away as Cairo and Jerusalem, and by German counterintelligence in Vienna. The Germans quickly answered with counterpropaganda; those who had never been informed of the ongoing negotiations, like Foreign Minister Ribbentrop, sent angry telegrams demanding explanations.[6]

As news of the broadcast and newspaper reports spread, those who had been working quietly to negotiate for lives were appalled. Even a vague revelation of the stillborn negotiations could embarrass the Germans and reassure the Soviets—no doubt the goals of the Foreign Office leak—and end any possibility of saving the remaining Jews in Hungary. "BBC's reference to 'creating a division among the Allies' may have some significance," wrote J. K. Harrison, the American ambassador in Switzerland. "It might just possibly refer to those in the U.S.A. who are working so unreasonably in this War Refugee affair—and to those in London who are trying to make the Trading with the Enemy laws stick."[7]

The public had mixed reactions. A Jewish office manufacturer in Shoreditch wrote to Anthony Eden that he trusted "the Allies will not accept this offer in any way whatsoever," but that it would be appropriate "to make a Public Statement to the effect that those 400,000 Jews (if they will be slaughtered by the German Methods) be classed as soldiers fighting in the front line helping the Allied War Effort."[8] The Jewish Agency equated the publicity about the proposal to a death sentence for the Hungarian Jews and called it a grave breach of confidence.

For the Vaada members still in Budapest, it was one more item in a relentless cascade of bad news. By July 1944, the Budapest public was speculating on Horthy's actions. Rumors floated that he had quietly agreed to use his efforts to stop the deportations, but there was no information about what would happen to those who had already been deported and were in the pipeline to the gas chambers and crematoria at Auschwitz, those still in transit in Slovakia and Poland, and those who had been deported to labor camps in Germany to work on desperate new weapons for the defense of the Reich—the V-1 and V-2 rockets and jet aircraft. For the members of Vaada, the rumors meant little. They had lived through months of German occupation. They had seen the efficiency of Eichmann's *Sonderkommando* units and how quickly they had been able to train and organize the Hungarian gendarmerie to carry out the work of deportation. They realized early in the occupation that resistance was futile. And when the first reports of Joel Brand's mission were not the enthusiastic reception by the Allies Brand had expected, but a wary and almost hostile standoff, their initial enthusiasm for the scheme had been tempered with resigned skepticism bordering on the pessimism they had all learned in the Budapest cafés. The wags had said early in the war that the first item on the long list of what the Nazis would declare *verboten* was optimism. By summer 1944, no one in Vaada thought Brand could still buy time by initiating negotiations with the Allies.

Quietly, Vaada launched new efforts to save Jewish lives. Because the success of Joel Brand's mission depended on his never wavering in his belief that his mission was the only hope for the Jews of Hungary, they told him little about their other negotiations. Knowing nothing about their alternate efforts made the newspaper and BBC revelations a death-blow for Joel Brand's own hopes.[9]

Despite their public outcry, the revelation of the aborted negotiations with Eichmann had little consequence for the Jewish Agency. They had always faced an impossible balancing act. Officially, the Jewish Agency was sup-posed to have significant non-Zionist representation, but the organization worked indefatigably for the long-term goal of a Jewish state in Pales-tine, the ancient Zionist dream that had been the object of Jewish prayers and longing for millennia and finally seemed possible after the collapse of the Ottoman Empire at the end of World War I. For more than two decades following the postwar peace conferences, the Zionists had made an uneasy arrangement with Britain, supporting the British Mandate in Palestine as a necessary compromise that would allow them the opportu-nity to recruit the necessary Jewish population, consolidate Jewish land and property holdings, and build the economy and institutions of a Jew-ish state. A Zionist bureaucracy shadowed the Mandate government and was at once more expansive, more experienced in Middle Eastern issues, and more determinedly dedicated than the British civil servants and mil-itary officers. The British had come to Palestine with attitudes bred in the administration of India, where a tiny coterie of British military and civil servants had governed a vast native population. The same concept failed disastrously in Palestine, where the British had to balance Jewish and Arab interests, compete with a zealous Zionist bureaucracy, and deal with often-violent expressions of Arab nationalism.

Until 1930, British policy toward the immigration of Jews into Pal-estine had been based on estimations of the Jewish economy and its ability to absorb a larger Jewish population. In October 1930, Colonial Secretary Passfield reinterpreted the Balfour Declaration as imposing an equal obligation to both the Jews and the Arabs of Palestine. He proposed a White Paper that would not allow any Jewish immigration that would put Arabs out of jobs, promise millions of pounds of investments to improve the Arab economy of Palestine, and allow the immigra tion of a few tens of thousands of individuals, most of them Arabs, thus guaranteeing that for the long term the Jews of Palestine would remain a minority with at best a measure of cultural autonomy. The Zionists promptly attacked the policy, labeling Passfield the worst enemy of the Jewish people since Haman in the book of Esther. After much lobbying Chaim Weizmann succeeded in getting a new interpretation of the pro- posed policy from the prime minister that effectively canceled the Pass- field White Paper. Weizmann's victory depended on his persuading the British that the fifteen million Jews in the world could be organized as an effective enemy of British policy. The British, and others, including the Germans, believed Weizmann. For those who believed the Protocols of the Elders of Zion, the episode was another proof that the Jews of the world were united in a sophisticated, highly organized political force able to dictate to prime ministers and presidents.

After the withdrawal of Passfield's proposal, and with the rise of the Nazis and the introduction of harsh anti-Semitic measures in many Euro- pean states, Jewish immigration to Palestine grew dramatically, rising to forty thousand to sixty thousand per year in 1933–1935 as the Zionists provided refuge for early victims of Nazi restrictions and those who saw the writing on the wall in Germany. "We want Hitler to be destroyed," Ben-Gurion said, "but as long as he exists, we are interested in exploit- ing that for the good of Palestine." In the lead-up to the beginning of the war, Ben-Gurion assumed correctly that the British would allow the Jews of Palestine to serve in the British military, providing military expe- rience that the Zionists could later put to use in the Hagana and Palmach self-defense forces that would someday become the nucleus of the Israeli army. A few fervent Zionists put the same military training and experi- ence to work in the Irgun, which would later directly and more violently challenge the British Mandate. The growth of those self-defense forces, and the cycle of violent incidents between Arabs and Jews in Palestine, especially in 1929, 1933, and the orchestrated violence of 1936–1939 that

Arabs called the Great Arab Revolt, convinced the British that fighting between Arabs and Jews in Palestine was inevitable, and that increased Jewish immigration would only fuel the smoldering resentment that led to outbreaks of violence. The official British answer to the tensions and threats in Palestine was the White Paper of May 17, 1939, a statement of pro-Arab, anti-Zionist regulations that strictly limited the number of Jews allowed to settle in Palestine for five years and required Arab agreement for Jewish immigration after that interval. The policy admitted no exceptions, even in extreme situations.

The British participated in selected relief efforts directed at the Jews, like the *Kindertransport* of Jewish children from Germany, Austria, and occupied Europe to the UK, and a tentative but never serious plan to settle Jewish refugees in British Guiana. But as long as the White Paper governed immigration to Palestine, the Colonial and Foreign offices would not consider increased Jewish immigration to Palestine and viewed issues everywhere in the light of the impact on that Palestine policy. Churchill opposed the White Paper, which went against both his own policy as colonial minister and private assurances he had given Chaim Weizmann, but he had not been willing to resign over the policy. He later told the War Cabinet: "Our chief aim at the present time should be to keep the situation as quiet as possible and to avoid bringing the Jewish-Arab problem into undue prominence." When the U.S. election loomed in 1944, secret British internal memos worried that both American parties had adopted "pro-Zionist positions," which was of particular concern because "Arab unity discussions may shortly be taking place."[10]

This aggressively anti-Zionist British policy was not what the Zionists had anticipated as the next stage of the evolution that began with the Balfour Declaration. David Ben-Gurion's policy of *havlagah* (moderation) in Palestine had survived the frequent Arab rioting and effectively negotiated an end run to what the Zionists perceived as British favoritism toward the Arabs and widespread discrimination against the Jews in Palestine. Initially, the new White Paper seemed to the Zionists one more obstacle to be cleared, until the German invasion of Poland a few months later and the expansion of German policies against the Jews to vast areas of occupied Europe turned the restricted immigration to Palestine into a crisis for the Jewish Agency. The issue was especially complicated because Jews inside Palestine were eager to fight against the Nazis, and could only do so within the British army. Ben-Gurion famously said: "We shall fight with Great Britain in this war as if there were no White Paper, and we shall fight the White Paper as if there were no war." He kept his word, putting the Jewish Agency in an impossible dilemma.

To distance themselves from criticism about who received the severely limited immigration permits to Palestine, the British agreed that the Jewish Agency, rather than British consulates, would distribute the permits issued in Europe. The policy allowed the Jewish Agency to exercise the authority of a shadow government, but also put them in the unenviable role of choosing which of the many Jews clamoring for certificates could come to safety in Palestine and which would be left behind to face deportation and death at the hand of the Nazis. Those who were denied permits often aimed their harsh criticisms not at the British but at the Jewish Agency.

The criteria the agency used in distributing the certificates were a balancing act between mercy and Zionist ideals that defined the sort of individuals needed to build a future Jewish state. For sixty years, since the first *aliya* of the 1880s, Jewish settlers in Palestine had battled to build a home on the harsh land, fighting the challenges of stony soils, malarial marshes, harsh climate, locusts, unfriendly or misunderstood neighbors, and hostile Ottoman and British regulations and bureaucrats. The demands of establishing settlements, a flourishing agricultural and commercial economy, cultural institutions, and a shadow bureaucracy and government required increasing numbers of strong, self-supporting, committed, and mostly young individuals, educated or trained well enough to participate in the economy, healthy and self-sufficient enough to be productive and not be a drain on the settlements or on a future Jewish state, and young enough to have children who would add to the critical population needed for a future new state. A series of incidents, from Tel Hai in 1920 through the Hebron massacres of 1929 and the open rioting and battles with Arabs in 1933 and 1936, persuaded many Zionists that the official policy of *havlagah* needed to be bolstered by defense preparations. Some Zionists talked of an eventual war with the Arabs. Self-defense measures, from watchtowers and guards at kibbutzim to paramilitary organizations like the Hagana, Palmach, and Irgun, needed strong young men and women. Many in the *yishuv* urged and participated in illegal immigration, smuggling individuals on ships and across borders, and even the emphatically legalistic Jewish Agency, accustomed to constantly demonstrating its compliance to the British, looked away when immigration regulations were circumvented. The regulations required those who received permits to bring capital with them as one of their qualifications for immigration. When they landed in Haifa or Jaffa, many would engage someone to smuggle the funds back to Poland, Slovakia, or Hungary where the same capital would be used by a *landsman* who would follow on the path to Palestine. But even with the Jewish Agency sometimes looking the other way, those who sneaked through the cracks in the British regulations were a tiny number, dwarfed by the vast numbers in occupied Europe who were denied certificates.

The allowed quotas were small, and the need for new *qualified* immigrants was great. To make places, the Jewish Agency declared some immigrants unwanted, and the Mandate government used the same policy to bolster their own restrictions. Henrietta Szold—the founder of Hadassah in the United States; a strong supporter of early Jewish settlements in Palestine; the secretary of Aaron Aaronsohn's Jewish Agricultural Research Station, which developed many of the agricultural techniques for the settlements; and later a tireless worker for medical and social service reforms in Palestine—elected to settle in Palestine. Because of her age she was declared a "burden" on the *yishuv*. In 1939, when the *St. Louis* steamed from port to port with a manifest of Jewish refugees to whom neither the United States nor any country in Europe would grant landing rights, the Jewish Agency was asked for immigration certificates lest the refugees be returned to Germany. The agency refused. Two years later, when the *Struma* was drifting in Istanbul harbor, desperate for a port of refuge that would allow them to dock, the British high commissioner in Palestine wrote his superiors that under no circumstances should the ship be allowed to anchor in Palestine because there might be enemy agents among the passengers and because Palestine could not possibly absorb "unproductive" immigrants like the Jewish professionals on the ship.

Because of these policy decisions, and because the Jewish Agency representatives were often seen as agents of the Mandate government and gatekeepers of the White Paper permits, they were frequently accused of being dupes of the British, deliberately ignoring the desperation of Jewish life under the Nazis. In reality, as the pace of Nazi measures against the Jews of Europe accelerated, the Jewish Agency kept close tabs, and they were willing to acknowledge and even publish information that remained secret or officially denied among the western Allies. In June 1942, *Davar*, a Hebrew-language daily associated with the Histadrut labor union, reported in a front-page story that one million Jews had already been murdered in Europe. Months later, in November 1942, Moshe Shertok and the Jewish Agency executive discussed intelligence reports about the Nazi Final Solution policy. Jewish Agency officials wrung their hands with each piece of news, and no doubt their concerns were heartfelt and sincere, but the fundamental priorities for Jewish immigration into Palestine, what a Zionist activist named Apolinari Hartglass called "The Zionist solution to the Jewish problem,"[11] remained intact.

"What this committee can do," Hartglass wrote, "is only a drop in the sea; it is self-delusion or conscience-salving and not real action. We must hope that despite all the atrocities, a large part of European Jewry, many more than the committee is able to save, will be saved by the force of the will to live." He concluded, in words that many others would have echoed, that if the efforts of the committee would have only the most minimal of results, the Zionists should at least achieve political gain by letting the "whole world" know that the initiative to save the Jews of Europe came from the Zionists, that the only country that wants to receive the rescued Jews is Palestine, that the only committee that wants to absorb them is the *yishuv*, and by making sure that the Jews who were saved from extermination know, during the war and after, that it was the Zionist movement and the *yishuv* that tried to save them. To that end, he said, non-Zionist Jews who arrived in Palestine should be treated generously, even when it was clear that they would leave after the war. His reason was not because the treasured notion of *tzedaka,* or justice, required that they be so treated, but so they would carry away positive feelings toward the *yishuv.* Eventually, those positive feelings would result in assistance from Diaspora Jews toward building a Jewish state, and the return to Palestine of the exodus of Jews who survived the worldwide massacre outside Palestine.

"Whom to save?" Hartglass asked poignantly. "Should we help everyone in need without regard to the quality of the people? Should we not give this activity a Zionist-national character and try foremost to save those who can be of use to the Land of Israel and to Jewry?" Acknowledging that "it seems cruel to put the question in this form," he concluded that if they could save only ten thousand "who can contribute to building the country and to the national revival of the people, as against saving a million Jews who will be a burden, or at best an apathetic element," the Zionists had no choice but to save the ten thousand and ignore the pleas of the million. That conclusion set the priorities for immigration: children first, followed by pioneer youth who had received training and were spiritually able to perform Zionist labor, and Zionist leaders from abroad who deserve something in return for their work. The priorities left no places for what he called "purely philanthropic rescue."

The executive of the Jewish Agency debated the dilemma Hartglass posed again and again, trying to balance cold calculations of the future needs of a state against the pull of calls for mercy. They reviewed sophisticated arguments that not trying to rescue everyone would tag the Zionists forever with charges of self-interest, favoritism, and callousness toward the most helpless. They worried that they would be seen as calculating, balancing politics against mercy. Golda Meir argued that in the face of the Holocaust there was no Zionism except rescuing Jews. Others argued that even funds that had been set aside for development and expansion of settlements should be committed to rescue efforts, citing Talmudic arguments that justified selling valuables or a newly built synagogue to ransom Jews in need. In the end, the needs of a future state won. The

Jewish Agency would spend several million dollars, a quarter of their entire budget, saving Jews from the Holocaust. They spent much more buying land and establishing new settlements in Palestine.

In early August, a British officer told Joel Brand that he had good news. It had been decided to let Brand travel back to Hungary. He thanked Brand "for all the information you have given us. We have found it very useful. I wish you luck, and I hope you will have been able to complete your mission successfully."

"What instructions have I been given and what am I to say to Eichmann?" Brand asked. "Is his offer accepted in principle?"

The officer said he could not answer the questions, but that Brand was taking the Istanbul plane, which would stop in Jerusalem en route. A delegate from the Jewish Agency would join them there and give Brand his exact instructions. "The Germans will have to arrange for your journey from Istanbul to Budapest," the officer explained. "My role in this matter is now finished."[12]

Brand, flushed with excitement, was taken to a round of parties in the Cairo hotels and clubs. British officers drank to his health, paid him extravagant compliments, and wished him luck. His willingness to return to the lion's den had made him a hero.

On the day before he was to leave his suitcase was returned to him with his clothes cleaned and pressed. He was handed the money he had with him when he arrived in Aleppo, and was allowed a shopping trip to buy a Turkish coffee machine for Hansi and toys for his children. That evening, at a farewell party in his honor in the British officers' mess, he passed out the books he had brought from Istanbul as gifts. His departure was scheduled for 5:30 AM.

Too excited to sleep, he got himself ready by 3:00 AM. At 5:30, no one came for him. He listened to a clock strike every hour until 9:30 when an officer came to his room to announce that they had received a cable from Jerusalem: the Jewish Authority wanted them to postpone his departure.

Brand was furious. The British officers feared he might commit suicide and put him in a cell where he was not left alone for more than a few minutes at a time. He went on a new hunger strike and refused all food. After a few days of the new strike the commanding officer told Brand that he had been invited to have lunch with representatives of the Jewish Agency. "They are your own people," he said, "and will explain everything. You will be able to arrange about your journey with them."

Brand went to the meeting at the famed Shepherd's Hotel, where he was greeted by Teddy Kollek, a close associate of Ben-Gurion and his point man for troubleshooting. Kollek had been the station chief for the Jewish Agency in Istanbul before Chaim Barlas took over that role. Kollek told Brand's British escort to come back later that afternoon, and when they were alone, he and his colleagues praised Brand. "You have undertaken a great task," Kollek said. "And we are with you to the very end. The deportations have been stopped and negotiations are under way. The Hungarian Jews will be saved."

If he was happy at the news, Brand did not show it. It was clear from Kollek's confident tone that the Jewish Agency was calling the shots and that he had been ignored. He protested: Why had he been held captive? Why had they postponed his departure?

Kollek said it was Brand's colleagues in Istanbul who had postponed the departure, and they had probably done so on the basis of messages from Budapest.

"What has been going on here?" Brand shouted. "Why haven't I been kept informed? Why am I not allowed to go back?" He had stopped believing the Jewish Agency, just as he had lost his idealistic faith in the British. They did not understand the situation. He had been convinced from the beginning that he had been chosen for the mission because of his skill at negotiations and his experience bargaining with the German agents in Budapest cafés. Now, instead of leading the negotiations as the *shaliach*, the savior of the Jews, he found himself a prisoner in Cairo, kept in the dark while someone else—who did not know or understand the Germans or the complexity of the situation—stole his calling. "I am not saying that I am the best person to undertake these negotiations," he told

Kollek. "But I wanted at least to take a hand in them. . . . I don't care about myself, but I know that while I am sitting around here, our one big chance may be lost. I am convinced that thousands are being deported and gassed each day, and I simply do not believe that without me you would be able to take the extreme measures that are necessary to stop these murderers."[13]

Kollek assured him that "your arrival here with these German proposals, and your counterproposals, have at last forced the Allies to face the question squarely. Thanks to you we have succeeded in accomplishing what we were unable to do before. The conscience of the world has been aroused. . . . You have embarked on a noble undertaking."

Over the next weeks, Brand met many times with Kollek and other Jewish Agency officials, always at Shepherd's or the Metropole, another luxury hotel. He was still on a hunger strike in his cell, showing his defiance of the British, but at the meetings with Jewish Agency representatives he ate whatever was on the table, confident the British would not find out. His departure for Budapest was repeatedly rescheduled and delayed, and as the days of postponements turned into weeks, he dropped his hunger strike. At one point the Jewish Agency officials mentioned the possibility of parachuting agents into Hungary. Brand asked if he could be parachuted with them. They discussed details of the mission with him, whether the parachutists should dress in British uniforms or civilian clothing and the choice of landing sites. When they had the information they needed they stopped talking about the mission. It was easy for Brand to conclude that these Jewish Agency officials were no different from the British, who had also only used him.

Brand was offered the opportunity to meet with Bandi Grosz, with the suggestion that perhaps he could get Grosz to tell "the truth." Grosz had been arrested when he arrived at Aleppo, then brought to Cairo for interrogation and temporarily interned on the island of Samos off the coast of Turkey. The charges against him were unclear: finding him inscrutable, unreliable, and untrustworthy, the British had concluded he was a Nazi agent and detained him until he was no longer a threat. Brand was taken to see him at a military prison in Cairo, where Grosz had a wooden pallet for a bed and not even a proper chair in his cell. He was ill, weak, and broken. Brand felt almost ashamed when he realized how much better he had been treated. He had never trusted Grosz and learned nothing from the interview.

At the beginning of September, the British officer in charge of Brand told him that the British were no longer interested in holding him and that any future arrangements would have to be made with the Jewish Agency. They transferred him to a British army camp in Gisa, near the Great Pyramids, and supplied him with a new identity as Lieutenant Jacobsen. Thirty British agents of various nationalities—French, Germans, Indians, and English—were in the camp with him, all awaiting new assignments. They had to promise not to go to Cairo, but were otherwise free to roam. Guards were posted only to keep strangers out. The agents ate well, and alcoholic beverages were officially forbidden but readily available. For ten days Joel Brand waited at the new camp, expecting any day to hear from the Jewish Agency that his travel to Budapest had been arranged. He finally wrote a letter to the Jewish Agency, informing them that he "no longer felt bound by the obligations imposed upon [him] by Moshe Shertok in Aleppo" and threatening that if he was not set free within eight days, he would "regard himself as an enemy of the British and act accordingly," which came down to a combination of a threat to commit suicide or to "seek all possible means to escape and by illegal means . . . return to my comrades in Budapest." The officers at the camp refused to forward the letter to the Jewish Agency.[14]

What Brand did not know was that the British and the Americans had already discussed his fate. "The Gestapo are very angry about the failure of Brand and Gyorgy [Grosz] to return to German territory," Secretary of State Hull wrote to the American embassy in Moscow. "Fresh evidence," the British ambassador in Moscow wrote to Molotov, the Soviet foreign minister, compels the view that the Brand proposals "constituted a political warfare trap set up by the Gestapo," hence he must not be allowed to return or to indicate any response to the Gestapo by the Allies.[15]

By mid-July, Kasztner and his colleagues realized that "the dream of the big plan"—Brand's hope of negotiating a grand exodus of Jews from Hungary—was finished. "Hundreds of thousands," Kasztner reported, "went to Auschwitz in such a way that they were not conscious until the last moment what it was all about and what was happening. We who did know tried to act against it, but after three and a half months of bitter fighting I must state that it was more like watching the unfolding of a tragedy and its unstoppable progress, without our being able to do anything of importance to prevent it. . . . The thing that happened here between May 15 and July 9 is like the burial of the last scion of an aristocratic family as they lower him into the grave and turn the face of his ancestors' shield to the wall."[16]

It was time, he argued, to revive old negotiations.

At the earliest meeting of Vaada officials with Wisliceny, even before the German invasion, there had been some discussion of permitting as many as six hundred people to leave Hungary for Constanța in Romania, so they could board a ship for Palestine. At the time, Wisliceny had demanded outrageous sums and presented obstacles to justify his harsh terms, claiming that the Jewish refugees would have to go first to German soil because the Germans could not deport them from a sovereign nation like Hungary. Later he discounted the initial negotiations and said the Germans were interested only in large-scale emigration of Jews. When Joel Brand dropped out of the negotiations with Wisliceny to accept his mission from Eichmann, Kasztner continued to talk to Wisliceny about the possibility of a group of Jews being saved from the deportations to Auschwitz in return for payments to the Nazis. Eichmann was approached for his approval, and on May 22 he authorized the emigration of between 600 and 750 Jews. The negotiations proceeded in fits and starts. On June 3, Eichmann agreed to expand the number to almost 1,700.

On June 18, Kasztner wrote, "what previously was current is today no longer the subject of negotiations; there can be no more talk of a cessation of the deportations in general. What can be negotiated is the rescue of a small part of those adults capable of labor and children." This was to be Kasztner's mission. He called it Noah's Ark.[17]

In July, Kasztner argued that the $200,000 payment in pengős the Hungarian Jewish community had given Wisliceny in April should now be considered a down payment for Noah's Ark. Despite their perilous position on the battlefronts, the Nazis knew they could demand more. Eichmann demanded $200 per released deportee, then upped the price to $500. Kurt Becher joined the negotiations, applied his horse-trading and extortion skills, and upped the demand to $2,000 per released deportee, before settling for $1,000 each. By summer 1944, the escape route via the Black Sea from ports in Romania had been overrun by the Soviet armies. The new Noah's Ark would be a train that would carry a select number of Jews from Hungary to a neutral country. The Nazi price to allow 1,684 Jews to leave by train came to SFr 7 million—almost $1.7 million.[18]

Some Budapest Jews were able to pay their share of the extortionist ransom on their own. Few from the provinces, where the Jews had experienced the full efficiency of the Nazi and Hungarian extortions and confiscations, could. The report of a gendarme commandant of the Debrecen ghetto was typical. He proudly declared that after five days of beatings and torture with electrical wires, his men had extracted the last wealth from the area's Jews: "7.5 kilos of gold, 45.67 kilos of silver, a fine selection of women's dresses and men's suits, plus 70,000 pengős."[19]

A special committee drawn from members of Vaada and the remnants of the Jewish Community Council decided to raise money to pay for those selected for the train who could not afford Becher's $1,000 per person ransom. Wealthy Jews in Budapest and a few who had survived the deportations in the provinces agreed to contribute cash, gold, and jewelry that they had somehow concealed from the Nazis. Between June 15 and June 20, Hansi Brand and Andreas Biss collected and handed over three suitcases of cash, gold, shares of stocks, and jewelry—worth SFr 11 million—to Gerhard Clages, who would give them to Kurt Becher. Kasztner later said that he asked Becher to consider the funds "as a kind of deposit, not . . . to be used for German war-purposes, and to restore them after the end of the War, if possible" and that "Becher promised me to do so."[20] The heads of fifty families independently paid Becher to assure themselves a place on the lists. Becher took their money, but insisted that their names also be included in the list of 1,684, so their ransoms were actually paid twice.

In their hiding places and heavily restricted apartment blocks, the Jews of Budapest and the surviving Jews of the provinces whispered about the new rescue effort. Kasztner's name of Noah's Ark was all too appropriate—a boat so small that someone had to choose who would go and who would be left behind. A committee of Otto Komoly, Kasztner, and Hansi Brand began drawing up lists. Kasztner seemed to relish the challenge of choosing who would be allowed on the train. "Once again we were confronted with the most serious dilemma, the dilemma which we had been faced with throughout our work," he wrote.

> Should we leave the selection to blind fate or should we try to influence it? . . . We convinced ourselves that—as sacred as every human being has always been to the Jews—we nevertheless had to strive to save at least those who all their lives had labored for the Community. . . . In brief: truly holy principles had to be employed to sustain and guide the frail human hand which, by writing down on paper the name of an unknown person, decided his life or death. Was it the gift of fate if, under these circumstances, we were not always able to prevail in these endeavors?[21]

Kasztner traveled to Cluj, an important provincial center of Jewish life and his hometown, where he selected 388 individuals for the train, including members of his own family, friends, and colleagues. His reason for choosing his family and friends, he said later, was that he knew many Jews would be afraid to join the rescue effort, fearing that it was another Nazi trick. By putting his own family and friends on the train, it would persuade others to join the enterprise.

The group from Cluj came to Budapest on July 10, where they joined others who had been selected by Kasztner and his Vaada colleagues or by leaders of the Orthodox community. They met at the camp Eichmann had authorized on the grounds of the Israelite School for the Blind, Deaf and Dumb on Columbus Street. Five temporary wooden barracks and some makeshift sanitation facilities had been quickly erected on a crowded lot. Zsigmond Léb, the president of the Orthodox community in Cluj, organized life inside the camp and learned that the five SS guards who had been assigned to guard the camp had been given orders to treat the inmates humanely. The furnishings in the camp were bunk beds and simple tables; men and women slept separately but ate together. Vaada members who would later participate in the rescue did not immediately move into the camp but stayed in the Vaada apartment on Semsey Andor Street so they could continue to organize the effort. As news of the rescue effort circulated, people who had not been on the initial lists bribed or talked their way into being included, until the group at the makeshift camp included fervent anti-Zionists like the Hasidic Satmar rabbi Joel Teitelbaum and his court (who ironically had been added to the group by the Zionist Kasztner), leaders of the Orthodox and Neologue communities in Budapest, active Zionists and Zionist youth leaders, refugees from Poland and Slovakia who had found their way to Hungary, and Jews of no special political or sect orientation who managed to bribe or persuade Kasztner and his Vaada colleagues to allow them to join the rescue group.[22]

Conditions at the Columbus Street camp deteriorated. The schoolyard was cramped and crowded, there was little privacy, the sanitation facilities were inadequate, and the interned Jews worried about the compromised hygiene, contagious diseases, and lice. And despite the repeated assurances they had been given by the Vaada members and Jewish community officials, they worried about where they would end up. Would the Nazis actually abide by an agreement to allow a group of Jews to emigrate to a neutral country? Or would they take the ransom, load the inmates onto a train, and take them across the Polish border to Auschwitz?

On June 30, the inmates of the camp were marched to a nearby siding and loaded onto a train. The cars were sealed and the train departed

Budapest toward the Austrian border. With the Allied beachhead at Normandy breaking out of the hedgerows and moving in a broad advance across France, it was impossible to reach Spain. No alternate destination was announced for the train, and those who recognized villages and signs along the route soon realized that they were traveling on the same route the deportation trains had taken toward Slovakia and Auschwitz. When the train slowed or stopped at a station, Rabbi Teitelbaum sent off desperate pleas for a rescue of himself and his court before the train headed on to Auschwitz. Stories circulated that Eichmann prided himself in his skills at routing trains, and that he resolutely ignored all pleas. Finally, the train crossed the Hungarian border into Austria and stopped in Linz. The passengers were ordered to leave the train, undress, and proceed to showers.[23]

Many of the passengers were hysterical. Although Kasztner and his colleagues had suppressed the Auschwitz Protocols in Hungary, the Jews knew about the trains that had carried twelve thousand Jews daily from the Hungarian provinces to Auschwitz. They had heard that the deportees were taken from the trains directly to the gas chambers and crematoria.[24] Were these showers gas chambers?

This time the alarms were false. The showers were what the German guards said they were: measures against lice. After the showers the Hungarian Jews were loaded back onto a train for a journey north, into Germany. On July 8 the train reached Bergen-Belsen, where a transit camp for Jews had been established by an order signed by Himmler in December 1942. The Jews from Kasztner's train were taken to a special section of the facility called the Hungarian Camp.[25]

No one made a detailed inventory of the jewelry, gold, and cash that had bought places on the train. Even before the train left Budapest, accusations broke out about the process that had gotten some chosen and others left behind. Young interlopers had snuck onto the train and were ignored by the SS guards. Kasztner's wife and Joel Brand's family found places. Those who were left behind did not blame Eichmann: what could they say about a man who called them "sample goods" and called the train the "sample train"? Instead, they blamed the Jewish leaders, asking who gave them the right to play God.

It fell to Rezső Kasztner to answer. "Do you really think we could just stand up and leave the Gestapo's table any time we want to?" he said. "So why didn't you put your heads into the lion's mouth yourself?"[26]

---

# The Bridge at
# Sankt Margrethen

*The hand of fate shall also seize Hungarian Jewry. And the later this occurs, and the stronger this Jewry becomes, the more cruel and hard shall be the blow, which shall be delivered with greater savagery. There is no escape.*

—Theodore Herzl[1]

*In the 8 and ½ weeks since I last wrote, the tragedy of Hungarian Jewry has played out. As these lines are being written, the entire land—except only for Budapest—is already without Jews. "The dream of the great plan" has become a nightmare.*

—Rezső Kasztner[2]

As many as three hundred thousand Jews were still in and around Budapest in July 1944. A month after Horthy asked the Germans to discontinue the deportations, the Jews of Budapest were still confined to apartment blocks, restricted by a curfew, required to wear a prominent yellow star on their outer clothing when they appeared in public, subject to harassment on the streets and in shops by both the occupying Germans and the resentful Hungarians, and in constant terror of deportation to Auschwitz. All of Budapest was suffering shortages of food and fuel. The laughter, music, bright lights, and easy conversation that had once animated the cafés and the Corso were only a memory. The Jews, who got last or no access to the rationed food and fuel, seemed to survive on little more than rumors. Fortunately, even after the Jews were no longer allowed in the cafés, when their only bread was in short rations and mostly sawdust, and the only coffee was a bitter, murky brown liquid that the café philosophers described with scatological quips, rumors remained plentiful in Budapest.

Pius XII's message to Horthy urging an end to the deportations had persuaded some Christian clergy in Budapest to aid the Jews by offering them the opportunity to convert. "We have to confess," the secretary of state in the Ministry of the Interior wrote to Horthy in late June 1944, "that unfortunately it is Christian clergymen of all sorts who play the primary role in saving the Jews." He complained that the priests and pastors were signing false baptismal certificates, baptizing Jews only in order to save them from deportation. To limit the abuse, the authorities prescribed a waiting period and a longer period of learning before a conversion could take place: conversion to Catholicism would now require three months, to Calvinism six months. The new measures did not deter the Jews from flocking to the parish churches in such numbers that a special office had to be set up to organize conversions. "In these difficult times," a Jewish community record noted in late July 1944, "thousands and thousands of Jews rush to get baptized." The Hungarian rabbinate protested when it was suggested that the new office for conversions be located at 12 Sip Street, the headquarters of the Jewish community organizations.[3]

On the streets and in the cafés, stories of the Allied advances across France and up the Italian peninsula and the Soviet offensives into Poland played against German reports of trumped-up victories and announcements of new weapons. Hungarians debated the tangled mixes of rumors and propaganda, but the German officer corps, and especially the SS officials, had heard enough suppressed information to recognize that with fuel supplies diminishing, manpower reserves exhausted, and the steady toll of the Allied bombing campaign on industry and transport, Germany was losing its ability to hold the fronts. The Soviets from the east and the Allied forces in the west were closing a gigantic pincer. The time to deal with unsettled matters like the Jews of Budapest was rapidly expiring.

Their reasons differed, but by late July a wide range of SS officials were eager to accelerate the deportation of the Jews. For Kurt Becher and the hundreds of officers and soldiers who saw the Final Solution as an opportunity for riches, the faster the Jews could be deported, the more quickly their property would be available. Becher was already living in the most luxurious residence in Budapest, Ferenc Chorin's fabulous Andrássy Avenue mansion, an expropriated spoil from the negotiations at the beginning of the German occupation. Becher and the corrupt and venal officials in his command did not question Hitler's leadership, were loyal to Himmler (Becher signed his letters to Himmler "*gehorsamster* [your most obedient] Becher"), and when called upon could exhibit the proper Nazi contempt toward the Jews, but they seemed oblivious to the reality of mass murder. When they saw rosters of deportees and the tallies of cattle cars leaving for Auschwitz, they saw not human beings destined for annihilation, but only opportunities for extortion and corruption. The Nazis had already declared the Jews nonhuman; hence Jewish property was up for grabs. An American assessment of a Gestapo official put it succinctly: "It was his desire to pump out the necessary labor from the Jewry of Hungary and sell the balance of valueless human material against goods with value."[4]

To pocket or abscond with property for themselves the SS officials had to skirt German and Nazi regulations, but seeing others enjoy the fruits of the campaign against the Jews inspired lesser officials to grab what they saw as their own share. Most seem to have had few qualms of conscience then or later. After the war Becher became one of the richest men in Germany. When his wartime activities were investigated, he claimed he had saved many Jews.[5]

Eichmann too was eager to accelerate the deportation of the remaining Hungarian Jews. As chief engineer of the Final Solution he was intensely proud of the smooth-running machine he had developed for transporting Jews to the killing centers, and harshly intolerant of anyone who would disrupt the operation. For diplomatic and logistical reasons Hungary, and especially Budapest, had been saved for last. With the end of the war in sight, Eichmann was determined to see the job finished.

Hitler, Ribbentrop, and Himmler also favored an accelerated

deportation. For Hitler, the destruction of Hungarian Jewry was historical necessity, an essential step in what he saw as Germany's mission: only in a Europe free of the Jews, he and his ideological henchmen believed, could Germany and German culture survive. By 1942, he had abandoned other options in favor of the Final Solution, and was unwilling to weigh the consequences of that decision on the conduct or outcome of the war. Even late in the summer of 1944 Hitler would not admit the possibility of losing the war, but Himmler, adept at playing the possibilities, considered that eventuality too, reasoning that even if the war was lost, if the Jews had first been deported to Allied countries or colonies the "burden" of the Jews would be shifted to the Allies, which ultimately would enhance the possibility of Germany surviving the end of the war and rising from the ashes.

Beyond their ideological or personal reasons, for any high-level Nazi who thought about the consequences of Germany losing the war, finishing the deportation and annihilation of the Jews also meant that the foremost witnesses to the destruction of the Jews would not be able to testify or propagandize in any postwar review of the actions of the leaders of the Third Reich.

The eagerness of the Nazis to complete the deportation of the Jews ran smack against the realization in Hungarian government circles that the war was in its final act. Enough solid news about the steady advances of the Allies in the west and the Soviet offensives in the east filtered in over the din of German propaganda for Horthy and his senior officials to realize what the ending would be, and to begin to speculate on the timetable for the German defeat. Like the Nazis, and to some degree the members of Vaada, they assumed the western Allies would be eager to help the Jews of Hungary. It was a belief without evidence. Indeed, by the late summer of 1944, press interest in the fate of the Hungarian Jews faded in the United States. Reporters, editors, and the American public seemed to have grown weary of the horrible news.[6]

The only American action in response to the plight of the Jews had been threats from high officials. "The entire Jewish community in Hungary, which numbered nearly 1,000,000 souls is threatened with extermination," said Secretary of State Hull. "The horror and indignation felt by the American people at these cold-blooded tortures and massacres has been voiced by the President, by the Congress and by hundreds of private organizations throughout the country. . . . The government will not slacken its efforts to rescue as many of these unfortunate people as can be saved from persecution and death."[7] Winston Churchill and Franklin Roosevelt had made dramatic statements about the atrocities against the Hungarian Jews, and warned about the justice that would be meted out to those who had perpetrated and assisted in the horrors of the deportations. Despite the lack of Allied action to back up the threats, these warnings were enough to persuade Admiral Horthy of the immediate and long-term consequences of not mending Hungary's image as a collaborator with the Germans before the Allies reached central Europe.

Two weeks after the departure of Kasztner's train, on July 17, the Horthy government announced that they would be willing to let certain categories of Jews leave Hungary, including Palestinian certificate holders. In reality, there were few of the prized Palestinian certificates available in Hungary, but Rezső Kasztner had learned that as many as seven thousand certificates *could* be made available by the British, and declared that the Palestinian certificates were actually for heads of families, so each certificate was valid for five individuals. This was not true, and even if it were, Kasztner was talking about certificates he did not have and to which he had no access, but the number forty thousand was soon bandied about. The Hungarians agreed to allow forty thousand Jews to depart for Palestine and asked the Germans to grant exit visas. The British angrily tried to explain that under any circumstances no more than seven thousand could possibly be admitted to Palestine. Even that number was raising eyebrows in the high commissioner's office in Jerusalem and in the British Colonial Office, where the pressure to reduce or stop Jewish immigration to Palestine had increased. The closer they got to the end of the war in Europe, the more the British worried about the postwar situation in Palestine, the renewal of Arab-Jewish disputes that had been held in check by demands for wartime tranquillity, and the beginnings of direct agitation and actions against the British Mandate.

The Nazis in Hungary also resisted the Hungarian effort. Himmler announced on August 4 that he would oppose the emigration of any Jews to Palestine, and Foreign Minister Ribbentrop ordered plenipotentiary Veesenmayer to disallow the exit of any Jews except under German auspices, which meant via train to Auschwitz. Even as Admiral Horthy was issuing orders halting the deportation of Jews, and making sure the Allies were aware of his orders, Ribbentrop and Veesenmayer were coordinating with Hungarian interior minister Andor Jaross and other Hungarian fascist sympathizers to prepare for the deportation of the Jews still in Budapest. Horthy was trapped between the Nazi demands for speedy deportation of the Budapest Jews and Allied warnings about continued deportations. He had already experienced the consequences of betraying the Führer. He could imagine the price the German forces could exact in Hungary if Hitler were provoked, and proposed a compromise. He approached Veesenmayer with the promise that if the Germans would allow a small number of Jews to emigrate, the Hungarians would deport the rest of the Budapest Jews beginning on August 25.[8]

After hasty negotiations assisted by the Swedish ambassador, Swiss vice consul Charles Lutz, and other foreign diplomats, the Germans agreed to the Hungarian requests for transit visas for a limited number of Jews in addition to those who had already departed on Kasztner's train—eighty-seven to leave for Sweden, nine to Portugal, five to Switzerland, and three to Spain—on the condition that the Hungarians agreed to deport the rest of the Budapest Jews. It was a horrifying trade: Horthy and the Hungarians had agreed that the freedom of a symbolic few would be paid for by the lives of the rest of the Jews of Budapest. Lest Horthy forget the terms, Hitler weighed in on the issue, taking time from desperate strategic decisions to write a note for Veesenmayer to deliver to Horthy: "The Führer expects that measures will now be taken against the Budapest Jews, with those exceptions that the Reich government has conceded to the Hungarian government. . . . No delay in the general Jewish measures will be allowed to take place; otherwise, the exceptions agreed to by the Führer will be revoked."[9]

Eichmann was determined that no one escape his final action. He ordered the large brickworks at Békásmegyer be prepared as a depot, and on July 24, he asked for a Security Police declaration that no emigration to Palestine would be permitted, announced that he had persuaded the German embassy to procrastinate in issuing the transit visas that had been promised earlier, and warned that if any of those scheduled for deportation managed to escape toward neutral Spain, they would be stopped in France by "appropriate measures." When Horthy tried to stall the deportation date, Eichmann protested, demanding that the operation begin sooner. He planned for six trains carrying twenty thousand Jews to depart for Auschwitz on August 27, followed by daily trains carrying three thousand Jews each. He did nothing to squelch rumors that the deportations from Budapest would be very "sudden" and that on a certain day all tram and bus traffic in the city would suddenly stop, every vehicle would be requisitioned, and gendarmes recruited from the provinces along with everyone in uniform—police, even mailmen and chimney sweeps—would round up the Jews and take them to one of the islands in the Danube before they were loaded onto the trains for deportation. The rumor was remarkably similar to Haman's plan to massacre the Jews in the book of Esther.[10]

As news and rumors about the planned operation circulated, waves of panic swept through the Jewish neighborhoods. The Budapest Jews had only sporadically known the violence and harsh anti-Semitism of the Hungarian gendarmes, whose authority was generally exercised in the provinces, but almost everyone had relatives or friends outside of Budapest or had heard stories of gratuitous cruelty and humiliation of Jews by the gendarmes. Many had tried to track down missing relatives and heard the German answer that the person was "already integrated into German economic life in a manner which made their withdrawal completely impracticable," or that "their return would present insurmountable problems."[11] The gendarmes were only their first fear. By late August, the revelations of the Auschwitz Protocols had circulated in Budapest, and it was no longer possible to pretend about the fate that awaited those who boarded the trains. The Hungarian and German troops, police, and gendarmes in the city had been reinforced, another sign that something was happening soon, and another reminder that the Jews were helpless against the German and Hungarian authorities. Even those who had talked of resistance, like the Vaada members who had once assembled a motley collection of revolvers and rifles, knew an armed uprising was suicidal. At the Sip Street offices of the Jewish community organizations, panicked Jews jostled one another as they waited for news, hoping that someone, somewhere, would come to their rescue.

While Eichmann readied his plans to deport the Jews from Budapest, Becher and Himmler exchanged notes about the progress of negotiations with the Allies. Rezső Kasztner was comfortable negotiating with Becher, but too much had happened for either man to return to the relatively easy meetings before Joel Brand left Budapest. When they met on July 15 on what Becher called "neutral ground," probably his office rather than Eichmann's offices on the Swabenberg, Kasztner said that for him there was no neutral ground, that as far as he was concerned, all German-occupied territory was hostile. He cataloged German deceptions starting with their earliest negotiations with Wisliceny, said that at least three hundred thousand Hungarian Jews had already been murdered at Auschwitz, and that the Germans surely could not have expected the trucks for use on the Eastern Front to suddenly arrive two weeks after Brand left for Istanbul. In response, Becher called Kasztner an "uppity dog" and pointed out that it was not two weeks but six weeks since Brand had left, and still no trucks or even a trustworthy confirmation of serious negotiations had arrived.[12] It wasn't the friendliest reopening of negotiations.

Becher, eager for more funds than the Budapest Jews could raise on their own, suggested arranging meetings with the western aid and relief organizations to explore what ransom they could pay. Kasztner answered that no one had told those on the special train he had already arranged their ultimate fate because the Jews hoped the negotiations with the Nazis would prove fruitful (which wasn't quite true), and insisted on the release of the train passengers interned at Bergen-Belsen as a precondition to further financial negotiations.

Becher had his own agenda. The Germans were aware of the financial resources available to the American Joint Distribution Committee, and were eager to meet with Joseph Schwartz, the European representative of the JDC. In return they were willing to discuss the release to Spain of 17,290 Hungarian Jews. They had originally proposed negotiations in Lisbon, then after the assassination attempt on the Führer changed their proposal to specify negotiations at Irun, on the French-Spanish border. Kasztner argued that a journey to Spain or Portugal for negotiations with Joseph Schwartz made no sense without preconditions: the Germans would have to agree to stop the deportations and gassing at Auschwitz, report how many had survived the deportations, and give a price for returning them to Hungary. Becher disdained any discussion of details and told Kasztner to look to Eichmann for the answers to his questions.[13]

Before he could look for a response to his proposal, Kasztner was arrested and interrogated by the Hungarian secret police, who had not been involved in any of the negotiations and were still suspicious of both the Germans and Vaada. While Kasztner was under arrest, Andreas Biss, whose apartment had been a secret headquarters for Vaada, and whose Aryan ID provided a good cover, held his own meeting with Becher and wrote a memorandum arguing that stopping the deportation and murder of Hungarian Jews—he left out any mention of other Jews under German occupation—was in the Germans' own interest. He gave the memo to Clages to deliver to Himmler, and later claimed that it had been influential in ending the deportations in Hungary.[14] No one else seems to have shared his high opinion of his efforts.

It took the intervention of the Nazis, who were still eager to keep the Hungarian secret police out of their negotiations with the Jews, to get Kasztner released from custody. Kasztner, who was eager to continue the talks with the Germans at the highest possible level, proposed that talks take place in Switzerland and that Saly Mayer, the European representative of the JDC, represent the Jews. Mayer, a retired lace manufacturer, an observant Orthodox Jew who followed the dietary and Sabbath laws, and the former head of the Union of Swiss Jewish Communities, had worked with the Swiss government, despite their harsh policies toward Jewish refugees, until he was forced to resign in 1942 in the face of fierce criticism of what some saw as his collaborationist policies. After 1940 he became the Swiss representative of the JDC. By 1944, when revelations about Auschwitz and other death camps reached the United States, Mayer controlled almost $6.5 million in JDC relief funds. A portion of those funds was earmarked for the upkeep of Jewish refugees in Switzerland and for pledged obligations to Jews in Romania and France, but $2.7 million was unrestricted aid for the Jews of Europe and Shanghai, subject only to American policies on the use of funds abroad.

Mayer was short and balding, conservative in his views, unhappy in his family life, and formal in his dress and manner. His Orthodoxy, three-piece suits, and stiff, businesslike manner were a stark contrast to the frank manner and outspoken secularism of the Zionists. He was not liked by the Allies. His overweening secrecy about the funds he controlled and the status of various negotiations infuriated the representatives of organizations that tried to cooperate with the JDC. The Americans and British opposed involvement with Mayer because of his occasional grandiose proposals, like moving Jews from occupied Europe temporarily to Spain. Cordell Hull, the American secretary of state, worried about Mayer committing the American government and ordered that he make "no (repeat no) reference to the United States Government or any interest in the matter on its part" in his negotiations.[15] The one group that trusted Mayer was the JDC, which relied on him because as a Swiss citizen he was exempt from the American restrictions on direct negotiations with the Germans.

When Kasztner suggested using Mayer to pursue negotiations, Joseph Schwartz of the JDC agreed. Schwartz had long advocated keeping negotiations open by any means possible but as an American had been denied permission to negotiate with the Nazis. Roswell D. McClelland, the head of the WRB office in Berne, also supported the idea, as long as the Swiss government agreed.[16] McClelland was almost alone among the Allied government representatives in understanding and agreeing with the goal Brand had tried to pursue: "to draw out the negotiations and gain as much time as possible without, if feasible, making any commitments." In McClelland's view, Mayer could negotiate and drag out any talks, but could not offer a ransom for Jewish lives, "especially in exchange for goods which might enable the enemy to prolong the war."[17] Despite McClelland's strictly limited goal for any negotiations, the U.S. State Department and especially the British Foreign Office remained skeptical and actively opposed negotiations. "Discussions with Brand already seem to have gone much further than I said they would in my letter of June 14th to Mr. Vyshinski," the British ambassador wrote to the Foreign Office, "While we cannot expect the Soviet government's reaction to be anything but unfavorable (and it would probably be violent)."[18] The Home Secretary wrote to Anthony Eden: "Read your Paper about overtures proposing an evacuation of Jews in return for supplies of war material. . . . While I recognize that your scheme does not involve the sending of any refugees to this country, I look upon it as essential that we should do nothing at all which involves the risk that the further reception of refugees here might be the ultimate outcome."[19] And a Foreign Office memo to the British ambassador in Washington warned: "We have had fresh evidence . . . political warfare trap set by the Gestapo . . . retain Brand . . . inform Moscow that there is nothing to take seriously."[20]

It was August 12 when Kasztner finally made contact by phone or in person with Eichmann, Veesenmayer, Becher, Krumey, Grüson, and Laufer (under his pseudonym Schroeder), to propose that he would arrange a journey to the Swiss border, where a German delegation could meet with a representative of the JDC. The Germans, especially Becher and Eichmann, were eager for a meeting if it promised results, and Becher, at least, saw Kasztner as someone from whom they could extort something worthwhile. With the situation on the fronts deteriorating and rumors of Eichmann's plans buzzing in Budapest, Kasztner asked Becher whether the Budapest Jews were safe from deportation. "Until we finish our talks, there will be peace in the city," Becher answered. "If the talks have a negative outcome, the situation in the city could turn critical."

On August 18 Kasztner met with Wisliceny and suggested that more trains of Jews should leave German-occupied territory for a neutral country. Both men knew that the Allied advances in France precluded rail transport to neutral Spain, the route they had discussed from the beginning of negotiations. Kasztner suggested that trains could instead be routed to Constanţa in Romania, the longtime embarkation port for ships to Palestine. He also told Wisliceny that he hoped the continuing negotiations with Becher would prevent the deportations of the Jews from Budapest. The only assurance Wisliceny would give him was that if Becher got a direct order from Himmler, Eichmann would have to obey. It was a lot to hope for.

Saint Margaret, actually the name of several saints from Hungary and ancient Antioch, is a popular place name in Central Europe. Margreten is the fifth district in Vienna, along the Gürtel, or ring road, that was built to separate the inner city from the feared worker neighborhoods outside. Budapest has an iron Margareten Bridge spanning the Danube, with access to Margareten Island. The German invasion of Hungary was code-named Operation Margarethe. And in the lush country along the upper reaches of the Rhine River, the attractive Swiss village of Sankt Margrethen sits alongside the river, connected by steel bridge to Austria. Saly Mayer chose Sankt Margrethen for his meeting with the Germans.

Instinctively cautious, Saly Mayer played by the book. Before he would meet with the Germans, he sought permission for the Hungarian Jews on the Kasztner train and the Hungarian Jews who had been deported for labor to Vienna to enter Switzerland as refugees, despite the opposition of the chief of the Swiss Alien Police, Heinrich Rothmund, who told Mayer in August 1944 that only children and adults with relatives already in Switzerland would be permitted to enter the country, and that Mayer was specifically forbidden to offer ransom funds in any negotiations.[21] Mayer also requested a clarification of his authority from the WRB, which he recognized as the overseeing and controlling agency for funds from American relief organizations. Even with all of the i's dotted and t's crossed, he was reluctant to cross into German-occupied territory and equally reluctant to invite Nazi emissaries into Swiss territory. The two sides agreed to meet on August 21, 1944, at the bridge that spanned the Rhine Canal between Sankt Margrethen and the village of Höchst in Austria. To satisfy Mayer's insistence that he would not travel into the German Reich and that the Germans must not enter Switzerland, they brought chairs to the middle of the steel bridge and talked there.

The German delegation was made up of Kurt Becher, SS officers Max Grüson and Hermann Krumey, and Rezső Kasztner. Becher spoke first, presenting a catalog of Nazi demands that sounded like a rehash of Eichmann's offer of four months before. Emigration to Palestine was off the table. Becher gave the usual excuse of the continued demands of the Germans' ally, the grand mufti. In return for allowing Jews to leave Hungary for the United States, Becher wanted ten thousand heavy-duty all-weather trucks, supplemented by agricultural equipment. He proposed that each ship that brought trucks could carry twenty-five hundred Jews from Europe back to the United States on its return voyage. To demonstrate the seriousness of their proposal, on the day of the meeting the Germans released 318 Jews from the Hungarian camp at Bergen-Belsen and brought them to the Swiss border. Eichmann and several of the other Nazis prided themselves on their knowledge of Jewish history and pretended to study the Torah and Talmud, but it is not clear that the number 318 was based on Abram in the book of Genesis, who when he heard that his "kinsman had been captured, he mustered his retainers, born into his household, numbering three hundred and eighteen, and went in pursuit as far as Dan."[22]

Saly Mayer, wearing a sports jacket with a neat white handkerchief in his pocket, responded by lecturing the Germans on the moral issues raised by their demands. Cautious not to overtly overstep his limited mandate, he turned away the demand for trucks, knowing that after what had happened to Joel Brand's mission any mention of trucks was doomed. He instead suggested that he would seek American approval for transfers of industrial goods and minerals to Germany. The latter was a timely offer: the Germans feared that the Turks might defect from their declared neutrality to seek an alliance with the Allies, which would mean that Germany would lose its main source of the chromium they needed for the production of high-grade steel. Mayer carefully side-stepped any commitment, but promised a list of available materials and funds at the next meeting. For the cautious Mayer, even that tentative offer was a daring effort: the mention of funds and industrial goods went well beyond the mandate he had gotten from the Swiss and American authorities. The two sides agreed to meet again. Saly Mayer requested a "breathing spell" of ten days.[23]

As the Germans promised, a train from Bergen-Belsen arrived at the Swiss border with 318 former passengers from the Kasztner train. The disputes in the camp when the 318 were selected were acrimonious, mirroring the conflicts within the Hungarian Jewish community, but those who were not chosen, including Joel Brand's mother and sisters, sang the Zionist hymn "Hatikva" as the train carrying the lucky few departed.[24] At the Swiss border, the Hungarian Jews on the train were greeted considerably more hospitably than the German negotiators at the bridge. As soon as the train crossed into Switzerland, the Jews were given chocolate, warm milk, and showers. They were then examined by doctors and given a sumptuous meal, which most of them, no longer used to real food, could not hold down. They were then moved to hotels overlooking Lake Geneva, and allowed to make plans to return to Hungary or to emigrate to Palestine. Allowed to read newspapers and listen to broadcasts for the first time in many months, they learned of the liberation of Paris and the now confirmed fate of the 435,000 Hungarian Jews who had been sent to certain death at Auschwitz. They also learned of the undetermined fate of the Jews who waited in Budapest.[25]

When he got back to his office in Bern, Saly Mayer found a cable from the WRB, signed by the U.S. secretary of state, Cordell Hull, instructing him in no uncertain terms that in any meeting with the Germans he was not to offer ransom or goods and reminding him that he could not negotiate in the name of the American JDC, but only as a Swiss citizen and representative of the Swiss Jewish community. In effect, he had no authority to offer American funds in return for Jewish lives. The only action he was allowed was to try to continue talks with the goal of delaying Nazi actions against the Jews in Budapest. Mayer cautiously did not mention his tentative offer of goods and money to Becher in his report on the meeting to McClelland of the WRB. He insisted that he had negotiated only with Kasztner and not with the Nazis, emphasized that "political aspects rather than goods are the main motive" for the Germans, that the Roman Catholic Church had done nothing to aid the Jews, that the deportations had stopped only because "Germans said don't send any more—can't handle them," and that Eichmann and Krumey could not be bribed: "they want goods and rescue [of] SS men after the war." Mayer also warned that they had reached the point in the negotiations "where it is no longer possible to gain time."[26]

On the German side, Kurt Becher waited three days before sending his report on the negotiations to Himmler, probably because he feared Himmler's reaction.[27] Knowing what Himmler wanted to hear, Becher reported that Mayer had been impressed by the delivery of three hundred "pieces," his term for the Jews from the Kasztner train who had been brought from Bergen-Belsen to the Swiss border, and that Mayer had promised a list of materials for their next meeting. Himmler could no doubt read between the lines of Becher's report and conclude that Mayer was stalling for time and was either not authorized or not disposed to make concrete offers that would lead to more substantive negotiations. Becher later claimed that he had gotten information from Himmler he could use to "bluff World Jewry," but the symbolic gesture of the meeting on the bridge seemed a long way from Himmler's goal of a separate peace with the western Allies. Time was running out on Himmler's great scheme.[28]

Time had also run out for the three intrepid Palestinian parachutists. Emil Nussbacher and Peretz Goldstein, turned away by Kasztner and Hansi Brand with the draconian choice of surrendering to the Nazis or taking their chances on the streets, were arrested by the Gestapo, interrogated, tortured, and deported from Hungary. Nussbacher managed to escape from the train carrying him to a concentration camp. Goldstein was taken to the Oranienburg concentration camp, and died there or at another camp. Hannah Senesh, who had been arrested as soon as she crossed the border into Hungary, was held in a series of Budapest prisons, where she was interrogated and tortured. She steadfastly refused to provide details about her mission. To persuade her to confess and identify others, the Gestapo had her mother arrested, and brought Hannah into a room where her mother was waiting. By then Hannah's blond hair was crudely shorn; the beatings and torture had left her face swollen and bruised, her eyes blackened, and one of her front teeth missing. She wept when she saw her mother and lied about the beatings. Despite the presence of her mother and the implied threat, she still refused to tell the interrogators what they wanted to hear. For weeks she and her mother were kept in the same prison, but apart and forbidden to communicate, while the guards tortured prisoners near their cells so Hannah and her mother could hear the screams. Still Hannah refused to disclose any information about her mission or her colleagues. Her mother was finally released and sought help, hiring a lawyer and trying to raise money for her daughter's defense. She went to see Rezső Kasztner to explain that Hannah had made *aliya* to Palestine and then had bravely returned to help the Jews of Hungary, hoping he and the Zionists would help. Kasztner refused to speak with her.

In early November 1944, Hannah Senesh was tried by the puppet Hungarian government as a spy, convicted, and sentenced to death. She was offered the opportunity to beg for clemency, but to accept the offer she would have had to acknowledge the authority of the Germans and the Arrow Cross fascists. She refused and was executed in secrecy, lest her martyrdom inspire others. The story of her defiance and bravery, and her simple but moving last poems, at a time when many thought the Jews of Europe had been led to their slaughter like lambs, made her a heroine.[29] Many who heard or read about the deaths of Hannah Senesh and the other brave young parachutists would later blame Kasztner.

There was one benefit Himmler could hope for from the stalemated negotiations. If progress toward a separate peace with the Allies was not a possibility, an appropriate gesture by the Nazis might at least mitigate the wholesale condemnation of Germany and especially of individual Nazis after the war. It was even possible that a truly surprising gesture, like Ribbentrop's astonishing suggestion that the Führer could present the Jews to Roosevelt and Churchill as a gift,[30] might so flummox the Allies that they would have no appropriate response. On the evening of August 24, after Becher made his report on the negotiations on the Sankt Margrethen Bridge, Himmler, without warning, sent orders to Budapest to cancel the deportation of the remaining Jews. An incredulous Veesenmayer reported the order to Ribbentrop, who confirmed that Himmler had indeed sent the order. In Budapest that night, the Hungarian Ministry of the Interior informed Eichmann that any relocation of the Jews would not begin until August 28, and that the Jews would at most be sent to five large camps set up for the purpose. They would not be sent out of Hungary to German-controlled territory. Eichmann angrily wrote that since he was no longer needed in Hungary he would ask the Security Police to recall him. That same night Himmler cabled that all preparations for the deportation of the Jews should be halted immediately.[31]

Many Jews in Budapest, expecting a roundup into detention camps momentarily, could not bring themselves to believe the newest rumors. There had been too many rumors and too many changing stories, most of them based on frail hopes rather than facts. But this time the rumors were true: the remaining Jews of Budapest had gotten a temporary reprieve.

# 12

# Endgame

*We will all go, young and old: we will go with our sons and daughters, our flocks and herds . . .*

—Exodus 10:9

*The assimilated Jew was of course very unhappy about being moved to a ghetto. But the Orthodox were pleased with the arrangement, as were the Zionists.*

—Adolf Eichmann[1]

The British detention camp near the Gisa pyramids wasn't a real prison—there were no walls or guards—but there was nowhere Joel Brand could go and no one to talk to except former British agents who for reasons as strange as his own story were being kept virtually incommunicado in the desert south of Cairo, served decent food and allowed to ward off boredom with smuggled wine and liquor, but forbidden to return to their own countries. Brand argued incessantly that they had to let him return to Budapest and his mission, but the British were adamant and would not discuss his release. Even the Jewish Agency representatives in Cairo stopped meeting with him. Then, without warning, in early October 1944 he was taken to the same house in Cairo he had waited outside when he first arrived from Aleppo four months before, and told that he would be leaving, not to Budapest as he had long demanded, but by the night train to Jerusalem. He left Cairo on October 5, 1944.

Ira Hirschmann saw him two days after he arrived in Jerusalem, at the apartment of Eliezer Kaplan, the Jewish Agency official in charge of immigration. For privacy, they went to Hirschmann's suite in the King David Hotel to talk. Brand still called himself the *shaliach* and claimed that he still spoke for the Hungarian Jews who had been murdered at Auschwitz and for those in Budapest who awaited an uncertain future. He told Hirschmann that he had not returned to Istanbul, because it would have been seen by the Nazis as a definite refusal of his proposal, and he feared reprisals if the entire proposal were refused outright. He was still intent on breaking "the ring around Hungary for refugee release" and had plans to contact Marshal Tito to arrange rescue missions through Yugoslavia. When Hirschmann told him about Saly Mayer's negotiations with the Germans, including the role of his former colleague Rezső Kasztner, Brand exploded in anger. "Mayer is an old man," he said, not the man for the kind of negotiations needed. "Unorthodox methods are needed in dealing with these bandits." Hirschmann was convinced of Brand's "frankness and integrity; that he was an impassioned young man, ready to risk his life for the sake of his people." But he was not persuaded that as a marked man Brand was "of any use now." After his visit with Brand, Hirschmann returned to the United States. His own mission was finished.[2]

Brand had long had suspicions about his colleague Kasztner and Hansi. The political betrayal—Kasztner and Mayer usurping his role as the emissary of the Hungarian Jews—was as galling as the adultery. He reserved his greatest anger for the Jewish Agency and Shertok. They, he believed, even more than his colleagues, the British, and the Americans, had betrayed him and his mission. Jerusalem swirled with rumors. Anonymous informants said that Shertok could have come to Istanbul to talk, that he actually had a place on a plane and had given it up to a businessman. Brand put the rumors and his own accusations together in a harsh memo that attacked the lackadaisical actions of the Jewish Agency and especially Shertok for their lack of aid to the entire rescue effort. "As I have been the official representative of all of these Jews," Brand wrote,

"I feel personally responsible for these matters." "These traitors of the J.A.," he wrote, should be personally as well as collectively accountable for their handling of him.[3]

He told his story to anyone who would give him a few minutes, even imitating Eichmann's barking voice as he said, "A million Jews for ten thousand trucks is cheap!"[4] He was still on his mission, still the Emissary of the Doomed. But no one was listening anymore.

Joel Brand wasn't the only one still eager to aid the Jews of Hungary in the fall of 1944.

In 1938, the brothers Isaac and Elias Sternbuch, European representatives of Hasidic groups in the United States, established the Aid Association for Jewish Refugees Abroad, usually called the Montreux Committee after the Swiss city where Isaac Sternbuch's wife Rachel, the daughter of the illustrious Rabbi Rottenberg of Antwerp, ran their modest office. Not long after the German invasion of Hungary, the Sternbuchs proposed a forced exchange of Jews in Hungary for German populations in Africa or other territory occupied by the Allies, to be facilitated by Vatican-issued certificates and as many as ten thousand South American passports. The proposal fell on deaf ears at the Vatican and among the Nazis, but Nazi supporters in Switzerland introduced Isaac Sternbuch to Carl Truempy, the Swiss representative of the German Messerschmitt works, who in mid-July 1944 met with SS officers in Vienna to propose the rescue of twenty thousand Hungarian Jews via Romania. When that proposal failed, Sternbuch and Truempy concentrated their efforts on liberating Joel Teitelbaum, the Satmar Hasidic rabbi who had escaped Hungary on the Kasztner train and was being held with the other passengers in the Hungarian camp at Bergen-Belsen. This time their efforts were narrowly focused. "The aid organization to which I belong is not interested in the [other] people who came with the Hungarian transport to Bergen-Belsen," a Hasidic representative said. The Sternbuchs also sent a steady stream of pleas and demands to the War Refugee Board on behalf of Hasidic organizations. An American station chief scribbled on one of their telegrams: "Pressure from the Holy Men! . . . Old pressure game!"[5]

Sternbuch was quick to accuse Saly Mayer and the American diplomats in Switzerland of waylaying rescue efforts for the Jews. For his part, Saly Meyer detested Sternbuch, a legacy of conservative Orthodox versus Hasidic values. As the situation for the Jews in Hungary became more desperate in the late summer and fall of 1944, the two enemies became strange bedfellows. Saly Mayer's instructions from the Swiss and U.S. governments prohibited him from offering the American funds under his control as ransom for Jews held or threatened by the Germans; to explore other options he asked Sternbuch's contact, Truempy, whether Becher could be trusted and gave Truempy a memo to be delivered to Himmler asking for a declaration of the current Nazi policy toward the Jews.[6]

Sternbuch was also in contact with Philip von Freudiger, the head of the Orthodox community in Budapest, and proposed that Freudiger help with an arrangement to send tractors to the Nazis in exchange for the release of some Jews. Despite reminders from the WRB that no ransom could be paid from funds originating in the United States, Saly Mayer, desperate for any scheme with promise, offered to commit SFr692,000 of the funds he controlled to the project. The discussions also involved Rezső Kasztner and lists of other goods—textiles, sheepskins, gold, jewelry, and watches—"which had been stolen or otherwise sequestered with or from the Hungarian Jews." Mayer paid out close to SFr70,000 for forty tractors that were shipped to Germany. Twelve hundred Jews were supposed to be sent to Spain in return, but in the end no Jews were freed as a result of the tractor plan.[7] When the project collapsed, Freudiger and his family were granted permission to leave Hungary in exchange for "bonbons"—a box of candies with diamonds inside—surrendered to the Nazis. He and his family left for Romania on August 9 and 10 and got passports there to emigrate. Freudiger sacrificed his beard for the journey.

Around the time the tractor proposal failed, Saly Mayer learned that at least $2 million in credits from the JDC and other private American relief agencies was available in the United States for rescue and relief operations, but that "there are no materials of military value available," and while he was encouraged to "gain time by referring to this amount," no arrangement could be entered into for any payment from the fund without approval from the United States (specifically, the WRB), and that the United States did "not believe that under the present circumstances monetary payments are practical, and no approval can be given for such payments."[8] In other words, the $2 million credit was strictly show money, worth no more to the Germans than the paper on which the numbers were written.

The news about the American funds came just as Mayer was about to resume his meetings with Nazi officials on the Sankt Margrethen Bridge. Becher had withdrawn from the negotiations. The German side was now Grüson and Krumey, who had been present at one of Eichmann's earliest meetings with Joel Brand, along with Wilhelm Billitz, a baptized Jew and the new director of the huge Manfred-Weiss industrial group, and Kasztner. Mayer met the German delegation on the bridge on September 3, 4, and 5 and promised access to a credit of $5 million in Switzerland if the Germans would keep all of the Jews in occupied Europe alive. He did not have the funds he was promising even if the Americans released the $2 million they had restricted as show money, but he was hoping the Germans would delay their response while they decided what goods they wanted to purchase with the credits. Grüson, frustrated by Mayer's evasiveness, asked for a concrete offer that he could relay to Becher. Mayer answered: "A citizen of Switzerland only gives promises that he knows he can keep."[9]

Grüson was following Himmler's orders, or at least what he and his colleagues assumed were Himmler's orders: cautious about leaving records that could later be used against him, Himmler seems not to have left written evidence of his involvement in the negotiations after April 1944. Grüson knew that only an immediate and significant transfer of goods to Germany would result in the release of Jews, and that any liberation would be *some* Jews, not the guarantee for *all* the Jews in occupied Europe Mayer sought. At the same time, Grüson and his colleagues assumed that an exchange of goods for Jewish lives, even on the smallest level, would validate the seriousness of the talks, and hence could lead to serious peace negotiations with the West. After three days of talks on the bridge, when it became clear that Mayer could not or would not actually transfer credits in exchange for a release of Jews, Grüson demanded that someone with *plein pouvoir*, full authority to negotiate, join Mayer's side of the negotiations.

The rest of the world did not wait for the negotiations on the bridge.

On August 23, 1944, King Michael of Romania had the leaders of the Iron Guard fascist movement arrested and surrendered Romania unconditionally to the Allies. Three weeks later Romania committed nineteen divisions to fighting against the Germans. Around the same time Turkey announced that it was breaking relations with Germany, which meant a crucial loss of the chromium the Nazis needed for war production; if Turkey took the next step it would mean potentially hostile forces in the southeast, completing the encirclement of German-occupied Europe. Germany threatened to attack Turkey, and four British minesweepers arrived in Turkish waters. The British crews donned Turkish navy caps, like the crews of the German battleships *Goeben* and *Breslau* at the start of World War I who put on Ottoman uniforms and tarbushes to preserve Turkish neutrality.

Horthy and the exhausted population of Hungary watched another ally of Germany and a neutral neighbor switch sides. They were also subjected to barrages of propaganda from the western Allies and neutral governments. The British government was not willing to use British military assets or government authority to rescue the Jews of Europe, but they were eager to exploit the situation of the Jews in propaganda schemes. Sir C. Heathcote-Smith suggested directing broadcasts and dropping leaflets into occupied Europe that would portray the Nazis as war criminals and Germany as a pariah nation, describing the Nazi regime as a total break with the traditions of Goethe and Beethoven.[10] Swiss newspapers carried regular reports on the fate of the Hungarian Jews. The American press and Secretary of State Hull threatened that Regent Horthy and Hungarian society would be judged guilty of complicity in the crimes against the Jews and that those who participated in crimes against the Jews would be dealt with as criminals after the war. In a BBC broadcast, which despite the German ban was heard in Budapest, William Temple, the primate of the Church of England, and Francis Cardinal Spellman of New York appealed to Roman Catholics to rise up against the evil of racial persecution. Max Huber of the International Red Cross offered to send a mission to Hungary.

Now eager to curry favor with the Allies, the Horthy government sent the Germans a note requesting withdrawal of the *Judenkommando* units that were in Hungary to coordinate the deportation of the remaining Jews. Eichmann protested, but with the Carpathian front in the east collapsing in the face of the continuing Soviet attacks, the Germans had little leverage. Hoping to at least postpone a Hungarian break with the Axis, Himmler ordered the withdrawal of the *Judenkommando* units and the evacuation of the German security service offices in the Swabenberg, including Eichmann's office. "There was hardly any work left," Eichmann recalled years later. "I myself had wanted to get out of there for a long time, because, well . . . there was practically nothing left to do. . . . I wasn't used to sitting around wasting my time."[11] He moved to an estate outside Budapest.

The Gestapo remained in Budapest. A draconian new law on November 4, 1944, ordered the confiscation of all Jewish property except two weeks of food and fuel, minimal personal items, and a small amount of cash. Hungarian colonel Árpád Toldi was authorized to remove property from Jewish houses, to take over frozen Jewish bank accounts, and to distribute Jewish assets that had been sequestered by previous governments. Much of the loot he and his agents collected was loaded on a guarded train for removal from Budapest for safekeeping. Toldi and his assistants put elaborate seals on the doors of the train, and generated a flood of receipts and other documents to legitimize their thefts, claiming that they were protecting the national interest by keeping these goods from the Russians.[12] The goods would find their way to the infamous Gold Train that left Hungary for the west.

Kurt Becher was named head of a German evacuation staff in Budapest. Becher's evacuation plan also focused on the wholesale theft of Jewish property, on the basis of an understanding with the Hungarians that the Germans would concentrate on the wealthy Jewish families and enterprises and leave the property of the majority of the Hungarian Jews to the Hungarian fascist organizations and representatives. He set up a dummy company for the SS called Omnipol, which evacuated entire factories and the contents of warehouses to Germany. Under Becher's direction twenty-five thousand wagons and trucks carried away private, industrial, and Hungarian state property. In addition to taking the deposits of the National Bank, the Germans demanded 3 billion pengős (approximately $840 million) from the Hungarian government as payment for the removal of the Jews from the Hungarian provinces.[13] Some of Becher's transactions were arranged to route funds directly to Himmler. He also set aside choice treasures for himself—suitcases packed with cash that had been paid for places on the Kasztner train and caches of paper shares, jewelry, gold, and platinum. When American counterintelligence agents reached Hungary at the end of the war they booked recovered treasure from his Budapest home and other hiding places in their records as Becher Treasure I and Becher Treasure II; the latter contained 8.5 kilograms of gold and 2 kilograms of platinum. When Becher was arrested on May 24, 1945, he explained that he was keeping the goods for the Jewish Agency.[14]

With so many laden trucks and wagons leaving Budapest, it was impossible to conceal the looting or the withdrawal of the *Judenkommando*. Wisliceny telephoned Kasztner. "You have won, Herr Kasztner," he said. "Our staff is leaving." He asked Kasztner for Jewish contacts with whom he could discuss further delaying tactics in order to continue the negotiations with the Jews.[15]

In their shuttered apartment blocks the Jews balanced the good news of the departure of the *Judenkommando* against the expropriation of what little funds and property they still had, wondering if they were possibly safe and could somehow stay alive until the Allies arrived. Many knew that elsewhere in Europe large-scale expropriations had been the harbinger of deportations. Would the Germans send new units to deport them? Or would marauding Hungarian fascists murder them in the streets and throw their bodies into the Danube? In the Budapest of late summer 1944, no speculation was too bizarre to turn into a persistent rumor.

News of the new developments in Hungary spread quickly. In neighboring Slovakia, partisans who had been organizing resistance in the hills and mountains revolted against the authority of Monsignor Tiso's regime. Slovakian Jews who had fled to Hungary tried to return to Slovakia to join Jewish partisan units in taking up long-concealed arms.[16] Rudolf Vrba left his hiding place to join the rebellion and afterward remembered his joy at finally hearing a German scream in pain. Adolf Eichmann, remembering the Warsaw ghetto uprising, pointed out that Auschwitz was nearby and requested permission to have the remaining Jewish population of Slovakia liquidated. He sent Captain Alois Brunner, who had proved his efficiency as Eichmann's secretary at the Central Office for Jewish Emigration in Austria, to supervise the operation. Gizi Fleischmann and her colleagues in Slovakia desperately cabled friends in Switzerland, reporting that ten thousand Slovakian Jews were being deported each day. They sent an urgent request for help to Kasztner in Budapest, hoping he could use his relationship with Kurt Becher to halt the new deportations.

The rescue committee in Bratislava, which had been so instrumental in distributing the Auschwitz Protocols, desperately tried to collect goods and funds in the hope of negotiating a bribe to persuade Becher or another Nazi official to stop the deportations. It was too late for more private deals. "I achieved absolutely nothing when I went to the Swiss frontier," Becher answered. "Now I have no influence with Himmler."[17] He told the Slovakian Jews that he could not accept their offer until he received a telegram from Saly Mayer confirming a serious broader offer, meaning one that would lead to direct negotiations with the Allies. When no telegram arrived with an offer from the Allies, the Slovak Jews were annihilated.

Kasztner turned temporarily from the stillborn negotiations on the Sankt Margrethen Bridge to focus on the fate of the remaining passengers on his train, most of them still interned in the Hungarian camp at Bergen-Belsen. Eichmann had originally demanded a ransom of $200 per person to release the internees. Becher, as Himmler's expert on financial negotiations with the Jews, had upped the bounty to $2,000 per person. With the widespread predictions of an Allied victory in the war, and the possibility of a Hungarian defection from the Axis to the Allies in the air, Kasztner and the Vaada counteroffered $100 per person. Then they waited.

For three weeks there was no word from either side clarifying the terms of an exchange of goods or funds for the release of the Jews. Kasztner sent frantic messages to Saly Mayer in Switzerland, who answered with the same offer he had made to the Germans on the bridge at Sankt Margrethen: he would deposit funds in a Swiss account which the Nazis could draw down. Andreas Biss and Kasztner brought Mayer's answer to Becher and Clages, who promised to convey the terms to Himmler.[18] Kasztner and his Vaada colleagues hoped that the situation in Hungary had changed enough to make the stale offer appealing.

On September 29, the meetings on the bridge resumed. This time Mayer was accompanied by his lawyer, Dr. Marcus Wyler-Schmidt, who kept detailed notes on the meetings. Wyler was candid about the limits on their negotiating ability. "We have nothing positive to say to you," he told the Germans. "We have only been authorized by the American authorities to not say no." Kasztner wrote later that Mayer promised the Germans $15 million in three monthly installments. Wyler's memory of the session was that Mayer offered $2 million if the Germans stopped all their anti-Jewish policies, improved the conditions of foreign slave workers, and stopped the deportation of Jews from Slovakia. Wyler, a lawyer whose reports were written shortly after the meetings, and who was not writing for future historians, journalists, and the postwar courts, is the more credible source.[19] He claims he told Kasztner that they only had $5 million as their total budget, had spent $100,000, and that $2 million of their funds were still in the United States. Saly Mayer had once bluffed with an offer of $5 million, but promising $15 million he didn't have would have been out of the question for the sanctimonious and strict Swiss. Wyler also noted that they had strict orders from Cordell Hull: "No goods, no ransom money, but keep negotiations going."[20] Mayer was diligent about following orders.

While Mayer procrastinated, and the Germans impatiently waited, others started their own initiatives, sometimes for reasons that had less to do with the fate of the Jews of Budapest than with their own reputations. Jean-Marie Musy, a former Swiss president, conservative Catholic, and Nazi sympathizer, decided to improve his public image by arranging a meeting with Himmler in early November 1944. Musy reported that Himmler told him he could release six hundred thousand Jews without the permission of the Führer if he received adequate trucks and other goods in exchange. Musy claimed that Himmler had listened to him attentively and tried to understand his point of view, so "remote" from his own. Himmler told Becher he had broken into "compulsive laughter" at the offer and thought Musy a total fool when he talked about pharmaceutical supplies instead of trucks.[21] With Himmler determined to have his heavy-duty, all-weather trucks for the Eastern Front (to Himmler the essential symbol of separate negotiations with the West), and the American authorities behind the WRB determined not to yield goods or ransom money to the Germans, Musy's negotiations—made with the approval of Sternbuch and with hints that the Hasidic organizations would fund his proposals—were as stillborn as Brand's.

Efforts by Peter Bruno Kleist to urge good treatment of the Jews by the Germans in return for money, which he thought more likely than any release of Jews, also failed because the WRB refused to authorize negotiations in Sweden.[22] When the WRB reported the negotiations to Ambassador Averell Harriman in Moscow, the American officials wrote: "The Swiss citizens involved in these discussions have acted in the belief that lives can be saved and precious time gained by prolonging discussion pending the solution of the problem by military action. No commitments or agreements have been made or authorized." A similar cable was sent to the American embassy in London.[23]

Saly Mayer watched every effort fail. He decided to try again by renewing direct negotiations with Becher, persuaded McClelland that procrastination would no longer work, and resumed the meetings with the Germans on the bridge on October 29, November 2, and November 4. Becher knew he would not get the trucks Himmler had long sought and was prepared to take the position with Himmler that other goods or money would save German "blood" and hence could justify the release of Jewish "blood" in return. Mayer and Becher discussed the release of hundreds of thousands of Jews in exchange for a payment of SFr20 million made in two to three weeks, but Becher and his delegation again insisted that the Jews could not emigrate to Palestine. There was no other country willing to accept Jewish refugees in those numbers, and no indication that the British would change their policy and allow the Jews into Palestine, which made the entire negotiations a sham. With conditions on the Western Front improving, the Americans, who ultimately pulled Mayer's strings, were determined to procrastinate. Edward Stettinius, who a month later would become secretary of state, cabled the WRB: "because of recent military developments each day that can be gained is of increasing importance."[24]

Desperate to get the talks moving, Mayer got a Swiss visa for Becher and arranged a direct meeting between Becher and Roswell McClelland. This remarkable meeting would be the first instance of ranking American and Nazi officials meeting to discuss anything but unconditional surrender. The arrangements were made quietly, and on November 5, the two men, each in his midthirties and a passionate advocate for his own side in the conflict, traveled incognito to the Hotel Savoy-Baur-en-Ville in Zurich. There, the Quaker McClelland lectured the Nazi Becher on the inevitability of the German defeat; showed Becher a WRB cable, signed by Secretary of State Hull promising $5 million to Mayer; and demanded the end of the murders of Jewish and non-Jewish civilians, the release of orphaned children to Switzerland, and permission for the Red Cross to visit inmates at concentration camps. (The International Red Cross had only been allowed to visit the Nazi show camp at Theresienstadt.) Becher, who at that point had as little authority to negotiate as McClelland, agreed that children and the elderly would be spared, and that the Red Cross would be allowed to visit various categories of Jews.[25] In one sense, this remarkable meeting was a victory for the Germans: Himmler had finally gotten what he had long wanted, a high-level Nazi contact with a senior Allied official. But Becher realized what McClelland cautiously did not reveal, that the funds he had dangled before Becher could be used only with the specific permission of the U.S. government, which would in no circumstances allow paying ransom or purchasing goods for the Germans. The anticipated total Allied victory would not be jeopardized by humanitarian gestures.

By November 1944, when Becher and McClelland met, Saly Mayer, the JDC, and the WRB had already shifted their goals from the hope of arranging mass emigration to preventing the slaughter of the Jews before they were liberated by Allied armies. The Red Cross was probably the only organization with a chance of being admitted to the detention camps in Budapest as neutral observers, and while the $5 million that Mayer was offering was not sufficient to feed and clothe Jewish refugees in the camps and the slave laborers that Mayer wanted to include in his proposal, it was enough to serve as seed money to get a Red Cross intervention started and possibly preempt further actions against the Jews. But even that proposal was never fully put forward. Mayer was still hoping he and Becher could advance their talks when the WRB withdrew the offer of funds on November 17, and announced that no further direct talks with the Nazis would be allowed. For the United States, the reactions of the Soviets and British still mattered more than Jewish lives.

On his drive back from the meeting in Switzerland, Becher watched columns of bedraggled Jews being marched along the road from Budapest toward Vienna, thousands of ill-dressed Jewish women, children, and old men, most of them in rags, without food, proper footwear, or shelter. A cold rain was falling, and the roadsides were littered with the corpses of those who could not go on. Asked who had ordered such an atrocity in full view of the civilian population, Becher said: "It's Eichmann's regiment. They are marching at Eichmann's orders."[26]

With the Allies advancing on every front, the wily Admiral Horthy impatiently awaited the arrival of British and American forces, hoping liberation from the west would come to Hungary before Soviet occupation from the east. He finally decided he could no longer pretend loyalty to the Germans, and on October 15 announced that Hungary, like

Romania six weeks earlier, was leaving the alliance with Germany. He dismissed Prime Minister Döme Sztójay, a former ambassador to Berlin who had vacillated between placating the occupying Germans and addressing the increasingly vociferous impatience of the Hungarian fascists, and in his place appointed a liberal, General Géza Lakatos. A new acting interior minister, Béla Horváth, ordered Hungarian gendarmes to prevent the deportation of any Hungarian citizens. Horthy invited delegations from the left-wing parties to the castle in Budapest to discuss a coalition government and dispatched General Faragó, the head of the Hungarian police and a former military attaché in Moscow, to offer peace to the Russians. Hungarians watched it all happen and talked about every move.

Despite the horrors just over the border in Slovakia and the uncertainty of the future, for the hundreds of thousands of Jews crowded into the horrifyingly deteriorating new ghettos of Budapest the cool fall suddenly felt like spring. Samu Stern, the president of the Jewish Association of Communes, was invited to the Buda castle for an audience with Horthy. Otto Komoly, the engineer who had long been active in Vaada, also met with Horthy, who admitted: "I have been an anti-Semite since I was born, by virtue of my education. This is how it was, how Jews were spoken of in our house. For instance, I found it completely impossible to marry a Jewish woman lest my children be of Jewish blood."[27] Komoly was invited to accompany a Russian-speaking Hungarian Communist across the Russian lines under a white flag to discuss peace. The Vaada began cooperating with the Hungarian Communists, supplying them with money and false documents in preparation for an uprising in Hungary. Horthy sent emissaries to the Allies and to the Russians; the western Allies refused to deal with him except on terms of unconditional surrender, and the Russians demanded that he give up everything Hungary had gained since the beginning of the war. Nazi-occupied Hungary was falling apart.

The Germans watched with apprehension. They had already seen Bulgaria and Romania desert the Axis. The Hungarian moves were out in the open, and the Germans had time to react. While the Jews celebrated the sudden friendly actions of the Horthy government, Veesenmayer, the German plenipotentiary, decided to overthrow Horthy and replace the unreliable sometime ally with someone the Germans could trust. His choice was Ferenc Szálasi, the leader of the Arrow Cross fascist party. To make the situation all too clear to Horthy, Veesenmayer had the Gestapo take Horthy's son hostage and threatened to execute him. Horthy, who had already lost another son in a plane crash, agreed to resign and handed the government over to Szálasi. In the brief street violence that broke out, Gerhard Clages, who had worked closely with Eichmann and Krumey, was killed. But the sporadic resistance was quickly broken, and armed Hungarian fascist gangs began to roam the city, terrorizing the Jews. Arrow Cross thugs took six hundred Jews to the Danube and shot them on the riverbank, letting the wounded fall into the river to drown. An eloquent and moving memorial of bronzed shoes on the river embankment near the parliament building marks the spot where it happened.

Eichmann had stayed out of the negotiations in Switzerland, and had criticized the Security Police over what he saw as their cowardice and loss of commitment to the mission of annihilating the Jews of Hungary. After the German-assisted fascist coup, he reappeared in Budapest, got the backing he sought from the new Szálasi government, and on November 8 ordered the deportation of Budapest Jews to the Austrian border, where they were supposed to work on a line of fortifications to resist the Soviets. The Germans had requested as many as fifty thousand slave laborers to build fortifications for the final defense of the Reich, but Jewish men of working age were already in labor brigades, so Eichmann sent women, children, and the elderly. With no rail or truck transport available, more than twenty thousand Jews were rounded up in courtyards and on the streets. While they stood in the cold rain, gentile neighbors watched, waiting for the Jewish apartments to be emptied so they could take them for themselves. The assembled Jews were then marched out of the city and toward the Austrian border, escorted by Hungarian gendarmes and Arrow Cross paramilitary thugs. The deportees were given little or no food or water and slept in open fields under the cold November rains. Many died before reaching the border.[28]

Kasztner frantically asked Saly Mayer for funds for bribes to resist the new deportations. Mayer stalled, reluctant to admit that he had no authority to commit the funds he had tentatively offered in the negotiations on the bridge at Sankt Margrethen. From Switzerland, Ambassador Harrison and McClelland begged Washington for permission to utilize American credits to continue the negotiations with the Germans. The State Department cabled back a definitive answer: "The transaction outlined in your cable cannot (repeat not) be supported by the [War Refugee] Board in any way and further it is the Board's opinion that no (repeat no) funds from any source can be used to carry out such proposal."[29]

Kasztner tried a bluff, cabling Becher that SFr20 million was available and that Mayer only had some technical problems to work through. The Germans saw through the bluff, realizing that Mayer could or would not release the funds, and turned to Sternbuch, who asked the Hasidic organizations in the United States for a credit of $2.5 million to $5 million. The Hasidic organizations also needed American clearance to transfer the funds. Becher, frustrated by the delaying tactics and false promises, announced that he didn't want to hear any more "fairy tales" from Kasztner.[30]

Wisliceny was ordered to the Austrian-Hungarian border to supervise the entry of the Jews on the march from Budapest. Survivors of the forced march staggered to the fortification sites outside Vienna, where German engineers responsible for the construction of the fortifications rejected most them as unfit for labor. Rudolf Höss, the former commandant of Auschwitz and the recently appointed officer in charge of the construction, had come to Budapest on November 16 in anticipation of the project, but when he saw the Jews from Hungary, he announced that he would not accept any Jews over forty years of age or women for his labor brigades. Himmler, perhaps worrying that negative news about the slave labor would jeopardize the last chance for contacts and possible peace negotiations with the Allies, also intervened to stop the forced marches, and on November 27, the deportation of Budapest Jews to Vienna was canceled. For many who had survived the march to the Austrian border, the new order came too late, as they succumbed in the freezing rains on the forced march back to Budapest. Over five thousand Hungarian Jews died in the senseless six weeks of back-and-forth marches. When the survivors trudged through the villages of Wiener Neustadt, Wilhelmsburg, and Amstetten, they had the opportunity to see a sealed and heavily guarded train go by, heading west. It was the famous Gold Train, carrying the property—their life savings—that had been confiscated from them in Budapest.[31]

Eichmann was furious. "I saw it coming," he said. "I warned Becher time and time again not to let himself be led around by the nose. Now I have just this to say: Cable Switzerland that they had better get things in order. Unless I hear a positive answer in forty-eight hours, I will have the whole Jewish pile of filth in Budapest done in."[32]

The Nazis and the Jews were playing a desperate endgame. For Kasztner, Sternbuch, Saly Mayer, and the other committed individuals on rescue committees and agencies, it was too late in the war to worry about relief efforts. The Soviet troops crossing the eastern border and the American and British forces sweeping across France and into Germany would reach Hungary and the other occupied territories before the International Red Cross or any other agency could provide meaningful assistance and relief to the interned, ghettoized, and slave laborer Jews. The end of the war would end the perils of the Jews, but only if it came before a last-minute Nazi effort to annihilate the surviving pockets of Jews, like the hundreds of thousands still alive in Budapest. For the Germans too, especially Heinrich Himmler and his henchmen and close followers, the fragile negotiations of ransom to spare the Jews were too late to affect the outcome of the war. The negotiations now mattered to Himmler and his followers because they remained the last chance to open separate peace negotiations with Britain and the United States, the last chance to spare Germany and themselves the full brunt of the now inevitable collapse of the Nazi Reich.

Neither side had much to offer. Becher tried an ultimatum: if Mayer did not come up with ransom money by December 2 (postponed from November 24), Becher said the Jews would suffer, beginning with the

Chaim Barlas, Jewish Agency executive in Istanbul and friend of Angelo Roncalli (later Pope John XXIII), but not the Chaim that Joel Brand expected.

The lobby of the Pera Palas Hotel, Istanbul.

Laborers from the Kanada section of Auschwitz sorting shoes taken from
the arriving Hungarian Jews, 1944.

Edmund Veesenmayer, German
plenipotentiary in Hungary.

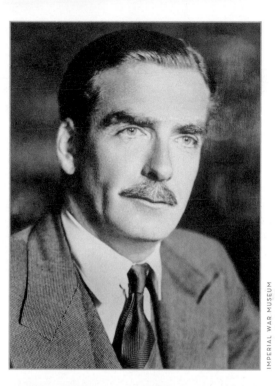

Anthony Eden, British foreign secretary.

*From left to right:* Moshe Shertok (Sharett), secretary of the political department of the Jewish Agency, with Chaim Weizmann and David Ben-Gurion.

Lord Moyne, confidant of Churchill and resident minister in Cairo.

Ira Hirschmann, 1946.

Saly Mayer.

Crowds gathered in front of the Glass House, Budapest, hoping to get *Schutzpässe*, October 1944.

Ferenc Szálasi being sworn in as head of the Hungarian government before the Crown of St. Stephen, October 1944.

Ferenc Szálasi, hanged after being turned over to the Hungarians for trial by the People's Tribunal, March 1946.

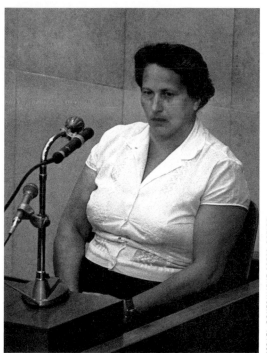

Hansi Brand testifying at the trial of Adolf Eichmann, 1961.

Joel Brand testifying at the trial of Adolf Eichmann, 1961.

Bronzed shoes on the banks of the Danube in Budapest, a memorial to Jews killed by the Arrow Cross in 1944. Buda and the seat of government are in the background.

Budapest Jews. Knowing he could not meet the deadline, Saly Mayer announced that he would resign his post. He told Kasztner on December 1, at their only private meeting, that the most he could come up with was SFr4 million ($1 million) that he might be able to raise from Swiss Jews, but even using those funds would be in defiance of the explicit Swiss and American instructions to pay no ransom. Kasztner persuaded Mayer not to resign. He convinced Mayer, Kettlitz, and another Nazi officer to send a cable to Becher stating that SFr5 million ($1,250,000) was immediately available and that the hitches in their negotiations would all iron themselves out if the rest of the Jews who had left Hungary on Kasztner's special train were released from the Hungarian camp at Bergen-Belsen. Becher answered on December 4 that the Budapest Jews could be spared, but he demanded the balance of the sum he had been promised earlier: SFr15 million ($3,750,000).

As a gesture of goodwill, the Germans allowed 1,378 Jews from Kasztner's train who were still at Bergen-Belsen to cross the border into Switzerland on the night of December 6. Joel Brand's family—his mother, sisters, and a niece—were again not included on the transport. His eighty-year-old mother had knelt in the mud in front of *Obersturmbannführer* Krumey, who was in charge of the selection at Bergen-Belsen, and begged that at least her granddaughter Margit be allowed to leave. "We are very sorry," said Krumey, as he turned his back on the weeping woman.[33]

The fitful negotiations sputtered on. McClelland intervened on behalf of the WRB and got $5 million (one-third of their total 1944 income) released by the JDC to Mayer. Even these funds were still restricted by the unyielding American policy: "This transfer has been approved solely in order that Saly Mayer may have something tangible with which to hold open the negotiations and for the gaining of more precious time."[34] Any use other than as show money required the specific approval of the WRB, which held firm to their policy of no ransom payments to the Nazis. Mayer piggybacked on negotiations the World Jewish Congress had begun with the International Red Cross to get them to agree to supply food and clothing to Jews interned in concentration camps.

Sternbuch and Musy also resumed negotiations with the Nazis, promising funds raised by the Hasidic organizations in the United States, demanding special attention for Sternbuch's brother, and suggesting as a way to get around the WRB restrictions on the use of American funds that any transfers to the Germans would be for "transport costs."[35] Musy again met with Himmler on January 1 and January 15, 1945, to discuss the intervention of the Red Cross, including provisions for the Red Cross to also support the German population. At one meeting Himmler told Musy that Jews had been involved in heavy labor that led to loss of lives, but were now being employed only in ordinary labor, a message which was no doubt intended to reach the western Allies as a mitigation of the possible future charges against the Nazis.[36] Himmler and Musy met again on January 21, and on February 7, 1,210 Jews from the Theresienstadt camp were released to Switzerland. Musy and Sternbuch asked McClelland for permission to use $1 million as a payment for the liberation of the remaining Jews of Germany. The WRB reacted by releasing $1 million to Sternbuch, but with the restriction against ransom payments still in place, the money effectively could not be used to help the Jews.

Himmler was as single-minded as the Americans. Despite the crumbling borders of the Reich, Himmler held out hope for his desperate endgame, hoping that the $6 million he had been promised from the two sets of negotiations maybe meant his leads with Jewish pawns would ultimately result in the wartime diplomatic equivalent of castling, a sudden shift of the United States and Britain toward a separate peace treaty with Germany. He remained puzzled by the American restrictions on the use of funds. "Who is really the one with whom the American government actually maintains contact?" he asked in a note to himself in mid-January, after he met with Musy at Wildbad. "Is it a rabbinical Jew or indeed the Joint? . . . If America wishes to receive Jews, we willingly take note of this. The possibility of being transferred to Palestine must not be allowed to the Jews we let go to Switzerland. Guarantees must be given on this point." Germany, he insisted, would never do such an "indecent" deed to "those poor people [the Arabs], tortured by the Jews."[37]

While intermediaries played the wary endgame of proxy negotiations between the Nazis and the Allies, on November 13 the Szálasi government issued orders requiring all Jews in Budapest to move into two ghettos in the seventh (Elizabeth) district, a neighborhood long inhabited by poorer Jews near the center of the city and bordered by the great Dohány Street synagogue. There were 293 houses in the prescribed ghetto area, close to 4,500 apartments, but the restrictions left many families crowded fourteen to a room. Few toilets worked, latrines were few and ill-kept, there was little food, water was sporadic and mostly carried by hand from questionable sources. Corpses piled up in the streets and squares. Otto Komoly, who had been running the Red Cross services for children, took charge of delivering food to the ghetto in a van, paid for by JDC funds through the Red Cross. Arrow Cross thugs routinely robbed the van before it reached the ghetto. "Inadvertently," Komoly said, "we are feeding the Arrow Cross mobs with subsistence suppers, courtesy of the Joint."[38]

A seven-foot-high fence was built around the ghetto, using horizontal wooden planks because the Arrow Cross discovered that Jews could remove a single vertical plank and escape. The new ghetto was convenient for the rampaging gangs of Arrow Cross thugs who systematically harassed Jews, seizing wedding rings, money, and clothing, and torturing suspected wealthy Jews to make them reveal where they had hidden their valuables. Women were reportedly "regularly raped."[39] The ghetto policy was meant to enable a quick final action against the Jews if the Soviet armies completed their encirclement of the city. In desperation, the Jews of Budapest turned to whatever succor and escape they could find. Those who still had money or connections turned to the diplomatic corps in Budapest.

By late 1944 men and women of remarkable goodwill, energy, and determination had come to Budapest as representatives of neutral governments; they did what they could for the beleaguered Jews, despite the changing political landscape, a fascist government in Hungary that was recognized by few other governments, the formidable German military and Gestapo bureaucracies, and the continual reassertion of Hungarian sovereignty in the form of additional restrictions and legal restraints on the Jews. Neutral Switzerland was the protecting power of Britain in Hungary, and Charles Lutz, the Swiss vice consul, whose duties included representing British interests, teamed up with Moshe Krausz, who was in charge of the Palestine Office in Budapest, and with help from the Swiss ambassador, Maximilian Jäger, tried to assist the emigration of Budapest Jews.[40] Lutz, a tall, thin, dapper man, had previously negotiated with the Germans when they agreed to allow a limited number of Hungarian Jews to emigrate in return for the freedom to deport the balance of the Jews to Auschwitz. He was officially in charge of issuing Palestine entry certificates and set up an office in the Glass House, an extension of the Swiss legation donated by a Jewish glass manufacturer. Taking advantage of his connections and knowledge of the Hungarian and German bureaucracies, Lutz began issuing papers and facilitating the recognition of emigration papers that Jews had obtained from other agencies or from forgers. In August 1944 the International Red Cross established a mission in the Glass House to provide aid to children, with Otto Komoly of the Hungarian Vaada in charge. Representatives of the Zionist youth movement also moved into the Glass House, taking advantage of Swiss extraterritoriality to organize resistance efforts. Each day thousands would line up in front of the Glass House, seeking documents and a place of refuge. The line moved slowly. Day after day, they waited. And waited. Some made makeshift sleeping quarters in corners. A group of Orthodox Jews from the eastern provinces started a kosher kitchen in the basement of the building.

Moshe Krausz had contacted the Swedish government earlier in the summer, asking the Swedish Red Cross to send someone of the stature of Count Folke Bernadotte, the nephew of the king of Sweden, to Budapest to provide protection for the Jews. After negotiations with the WRB and the JDC, the diplomat Raoul Wallenberg had arrived in Budapest on July 9, the day deportations to Auschwitz from the Hungarian provinces ended, as a special consular representative from Sweden. He joined the diplomatic representatives of Switzerland, Spain, Portugal, and the Vatican in issuing papers promising entry for Budapest Jews to their own territories. Earlier, George Mantello of the Geneva consulate of San Salvador had issued hundreds of passports, until the San Salvadoran "colony" in Budapest was as numerous as all other foreigners. The so-called *Schutzpässe* (protection papers) issued by the neutral diplomats carried no legal status, and the Hungarian authorities often ignored them—non-Jewish Hungarian lawyers actively took advantage of the circumstances to methodically transfer the clients of Jewish lawyers to themselves[41]—but sometimes the papers sufficed to get Jews exempted from forced marches or train deportations. Wallenberg was especially successful in issuing protective papers because he used contacts with Hungarian politicians to gain access to German and Arrow Cross officials and was willing to confront the officials with an astonishing boldness, leaving the officials sufficiently speechless, bewildered, or awed to cave in to his demands. Lutz, the quieter and more anonymous Swiss official, signed far more protective papers and ultimately saved more Jews than the celebrated Wallenberg.

The foreign diplomats depended in large measure on forged documents produced by the Vaada and members of the Zionist youth groups, who had been forging papers for Poles, Slovaks, and others before the German invasion had put Hungarian Jews in peril. In addition to *Schutzpässe*, the Vaada forgers generated military documents for those passing as Aryans, domicile and work documents, food coupons, and specialized documents in multiple languages. Over one hundred thousand false documents were produced in tiny shops where artists like Shraga Weil, who later became a well-known painter in Israel, applied their talents. Young women in the Zionist youth groups contributed to the effort by going into police stations in pairs. While one engaged the desk officer in conversation, the other stole copies of blanks and seals that could be used for forged documents.[42] Until late November, when the Arrow Cross officials started demanding personal verification of the validity of documents by foreign diplomats and finally refused to accept any papers for Jewish adults or children, these forgeries were lifelines for Jews with the funds and daring to try to leave Budapest.

After the Arrow Cross came to power, members of the Zionist youth groups, led and trained by the some of the same Vaada supporters who had advocated armed resistance to the Germans in March 1944, concluded that despite the paucity and poor quality of their arms and their lack of training and preparation, they had no choice but to prepare to fight against the Arrow Cross thugs and their spontaneous acts of violence against Jews. Zionist youth sought by the roving thugs hid in bunkers and fought back with smuggled arms until they were forced out with tear gas. They sabotaged train tracks to prevent the Arrow Cross or the Nazis from restarting deportations. There were sporadic street fights, despite the Vaada leaders and others urging that the resistance efforts be limited lest they provoke the Arrow Cross fascists into wholesale actions against the ghetto. Children were hidden in houses donated by supporters of the Jews: some were protected by the International Red Cross or other neutral relief agencies, others were kept safe by subterfuges, including Zionist youth organization members dressed in Arrow Cross uniforms rounding up children and bringing them to the relative safety of the concealed houses. The Zionist youth scrounged food and fuel for the rescue houses and moved children to new houses when the hiding places were discovered. When the Spanish ambassador left Budapest, an enterprising Italian, Jorge Perlasca, took over the Spanish embassy, pretended to be the representative of Spain, and sheltered Jewish children in the embassy building.

In November 1944 Soviet troops tightened their encirclement of Hungary. The Soviets had plentiful arms, clothing, equipment, and trained soldiers when Marshal Malinovsky began his direct attack on Budapest on October 29. The outsupplied and outnumbered German and Hungarian units held against the initial bombardments, but Malinovsky began a sustained assault on November 11 that lasted sixteen days. Five German and eight Hungarian divisions were available to defend the city: the Hungarians resented the Germans, and the Germans assumed the ill-equipped and unmotivated Hungarian troops would defect to the Allies at the earliest opportunity. Szálasi asked plenipotentiary Veesenmayer whether

Budapest could be declared a free city, as Paris had been, sparing it the block-by-block street fighting that would surely destroy the city. Veesenmayer answered that the Germans did not care whether Budapest was destroyed; their sole goal was to tie up Russian forces in the east. Like many German officers, he still believed that the Führer would launch an effective counteroffensive, stop the British and Americans in the west, persuade them that their true enemy was the Soviet Union, and reach a separate peace. And even if the peace could not be arranged, Veesenmayer knew that the last-stand defense against the Soviets would not be in foreign Budapest, but someplace like Vienna, the capital of Hitler's Austrian homeland.

By December the Soviet encirclement of Budapest was nearly complete. The concerted efforts of agencies in neutral countries, foreign diplomats in Budapest, individuals from Jewish organizations like Vaada, and the intrepid Zionist youth had saved thousands of Jews, but tens of thousands of Jews were still confined in overcrowded apartments in the downtown ghetto, with little food and fuel and rapidly deteriorating health conditions. Rumors floated that if the Szálasi government was threatened by the encircling Soviet armies, they had contingency plans to murder the Jews of Budapest before the government forces were defeated. Andreas Biss, on behalf of Vaada, asked Kurt Becher to intervene. Becher said he needed to show something to his superiors in Berlin to justify any intervention. He asked for thirty trucks, actually German trucks that had been supplied to Slovakia, which he wanted the Budapest Jews to purchase back and deliver to the SS. A merchant named Alois Steiger asked for SFr700,000 to deliver the trucks. Biss paid SFr188,000 and promised in the name of the JDC to pay the balance from their accounts in Switzerland, a promise he had no authority to make and which he never communicated to the JDC. According to Biss, Steiger told Becher the trucks were available, and Becher intervened with the German and Hungarian authorities on December 9, 1944, to spare the Budapest Jews.[43] There is no evidence beyond Biss's account that the story was true.

The German forces held out until December 24, when the first Soviet units reached the outskirts of Buda. Verdi's *Aida* was playing to a packed house at the opera that evening, and families in the city were preparing for their Christmas dinner, ready to splurge on the treats they had saved up for the special holiday, somehow ignoring the bombs falling on Pest and the steady ack-ack of the antiaircraft guns. Arrow Cross newspapers accused the Jews of signaling from rooftops to direct the bombs to their targets. One fascist newspaper reported that the American planes had dropped booby-trapped dolls, printed what they claimed were photographs of mutilated children holding the dolls, and bizarrely claimed that their investigations revealed that Jews in Budapest had made the dolls. Even when the city was encircled by Soviet forces and some salients had broken through into outlying districts of Buda and Pest, the Arrow Cross found time to plaster up posters warning that the punishment for helping Jews was summary execution. Roving thugs shot a few nuns in Swabenberg and building superintendents who had not reported Jews in hiding as examples.

The Budapest Jews huddled in whatever shelter they could find, including the American embassy and the Glass House annex to the Swiss legation. Andreas Biss left his apartment, once the Vaada headquarters, for a hotel, taking advantage of the German nationality on his papers. Hansi Brand also had the special papers she had gotten as a privileged Jew, which allowed her to travel outside the ghetto. She taught her children to pretend they were gentiles, and the three of them shared a cot in the basement of a Christian woman's apartment building until one night an older man demanded their place and blanket. "Why should the Jews get the comfort?" he said. That night a bomb fell through the house and landed on the very spot where their cot had been, killing the older man and his wife.[44]

After weeks of bombardment, artillery shelling, and street fighting, the streets of the city were strewn with broken glass and masonry. Horses wandered the streets until they collapsed or were brought down and slaughtered for food. Corpses stripped by scavengers were left in the streets and courtyards, spared decomposition by the December cold. When authorities sporadically intervened, bodies were collected and stacked like piles of firewood. The Jewish ghetto was still locked, but now without deliveries of food. A few working bakeries tried to produce loaves from remnants of flour mixed with sawdust.

On January 18, after a fresh snow that blanketed the horrors of the bodies in the streets, Soviet forces liberated the ghetto in Pest. Hotels and restaurants and the Corso along the Danube were on fire. The retreating Germans blew up the bridges over the Danube, cutting Buda off from Pest. Everyone in uniform, from firemen and policemen to postal workers, was taken prisoner by the Soviets and shipped off to labor camps.

By the time the Russian army liberated Buda on February 13, Raoul Wallenberg had saved 4,500 Hungarian Jews by offering them Swedish papers (far less than the one hundred thousand lives credited to him, but still a substantial number). Charles Lutz and the Swiss had saved another twenty-one thousand, and had facilitated the safety of forty-one thousand more Jews by vouching for their papers and brokering connections to other neutral legations. There is no way to calculate how many were saved through the forged papers and brave efforts of Jews who worked behind the scenes, bringing food and fuel, hiding children, and delivering documents and bribes to officials.

In the last days of the German occupation and the Arrow Cross government, forty thouand Jews were deported on the forced marches to slave labor operations, and another ten thousand to twenty thousand were killed in random street violence. The leaders and agents who kept trying to negotiate—Kasztner, Saly Mayer, Sternbuch—and those who facilitated their negotiations—Musy, Becher, even Himmler with his frail hopes that talks would lead to a separate peace with the West— had slowed the killing of Jews. We can only speculate on how many lives might have been saved if Britain and the United States had been willing to pursue serious negotiations, paying part or all of the modest sums the Germans were demanding. Even the repeated and documented reports of Nazi atrocities, widespread evidence that the revelations of the Auschwitz Protocols were true, was not enough to persuade them to modify the unyielding policy of no ransom payments.

# 13

## Aftermath

*If, instead of Jews, thousands of English, American or Russian women, children and aged had been tortured every day, burnt to death, asphyxiated in gas chambers—would you have acted in the same way?*

—David Ben-Gurion[1]

*Rightly or wrongly, for better or worse, I have cursed Jewry's official leaders ever since. All these things shall haunt me until my dying day. It is much more than a man can bear.*

—Joel Brand[2]

Budapest was left a shambles, assaulted for weeks by Soviet artillery and infantry, American bombing, the rampages of the Arrow Cross, systematic looting, and the last-minute destruction of the Danube bridges by the retreating Germans. Vicious hostility in the streets, the legacy of centuries of unresolved jealousies and resentments, was exacerbated by widespread starvation and shortages of shelter, fuel, and medical care. In the anarchy, those who had long coveted property seized what they could take, even as Jews and others who had been forced from their homes tried to repossess them. The occupation forces and the remnants of the Hungarian police were powerless to stop the disorganized redistribution of property and wealth.

Desperate Jews in the Budapest ghetto still hoped for help, relief from the unimaginable conditions. Outside Budapest some Jews had fallen between the cracks of the deportations. Some had miraculously hidden from the gendarmes and the German deportation apparatus. Others had been deported and shuttled to and fro as part of German schemes they never understood. With the end of the war they found themselves at Ravensbrück, Bergen-Belsen, or survivors at Auschwitz, lucky to have escaped the gas chambers and crematoria but not lucky enough to be free. Despite all that had happened, some still trusted that Hungarian exceptionalism would spare them the fate of the rest of the Jews of Europe, that they would somehow be identified and returned to the life that now seemed idyllic by comparison to what they had endured. But neither the Germans nor the Allies were listening.

The British and Americans remained adamant to the end about their no-ransom policy. Two months after the liberation of Budapest, Undersecretary of State Grew was still instructing McClelland at the WRB: "No repeat no part of the one million Swiss francs is used as ransom. As you were advised on March 2, the members of the board unanimously decided that no payments for ransom will be authorized."[3] Their reasons hadn't changed. George Kennan, who would later become famous for his policy of containment of the Soviet Union, predicted the Soviet reaction to any dealings with the Nazis: "The Soviet Government apparently does not believe, as a matter of principle, in dickering with bandits, and has generally taken the position with regard to its own people that the interests of the Soviet State and of the Allied powers in general override the interests of those groups who are unfortunate enough to fall into the hands of the enemy."[4]

Rezső Kasztner was in Vienna during the Soviet siege of Budapest. On February 13, with Soviet troops securing the hills of Buda, he and Becher's adjutant, Erich Krell, were again at the Sankt Margrethen Bridge, meeting with Saly Mayer and Mayer's lawyer. Power had shifted from one side of the bridge to the other. Mayer demanded a German accounting of the number of Jews alive in German hands, and on the orders of McClelland insisted that the SFr20 million that had been transferred to him as "show money" could not be transferred into an account in Becher's name. Krell asked for another direct meeting of Becher with McClelland, then acceded to Mayer's request that the Red Cross be allowed to deliver food and medications to the concentration camps. Again, the negotiations were too late to help the Jews of Hungary.

The people of Budapest quickly learned how difficult the peace that they had yearned and prayed for would be. There were others too—in the German ranks, especially the SS; in American government agencies like the WRB; in British, American, and Zionist diplomatic circles and private agencies; and in the remnants of the Jewish communities of Hungary—who had grown accustomed to war and an all-consuming enterprise of bargaining for human lives, and now faced the consequences and personal price of the peace they had claimed to yearn for.

Himmler had been careful to distance himself from the negotiations from the beginning, and had covered his tracks, and Eichmann had been a reluctant participant, but a host of SS lieutenant colonels and captains, like Becher, Wisliceny, Krumey, Grüson, and Laufer, had focused their military careers on the systematic extortion of Jewish property in exchange for offers and promises to spare Jews from deportation and annihilation. From the other side, organizations and individuals in Hungary, Slovakia, Switzerland, Portugal, Sweden, Turkey, and Palestine, including representatives of American and Britain nongovernmental agencies, had spent the better part of a year negotiating, pleading, bargaining, debating, avoiding pressing reality, and as one official wrote of Joel Brand, "playing for time," in the hopes that their efforts might spare the lives of some of the 850,000 Jews of Hungary. Whether from belief in their cause, loyalty to a government or movement, eagerness to best the Germans in the negotiations, a claim to glory in the ranks of those who resisted the Nazis, or a commitment to the Jewish concept of *tzedaka*, they defied authorities and put their own safety and sometimes the safety of their families aside. When they determined they had to, they lied to the Germans and even to their own side, misused funds, and acted without authority, convinced that what they did was justified because of the nobility of their goals. They were trapped in the most exciting of worlds, operating on the edges of legality, for high stakes and a true cause.

After the deportation of the Budapest Jews was canceled, Eichmann was without a mission. He had never favored random violence against the Jews and was an unwilling witness to the crude attacks, taunting, and sporadic executions by the Arrow Cross thugs who rampaged through Budapest and taunted Jews in the ghetto. His own carefully developed specialty had been methodic deportations, quiet and efficient transport to camps like Auschwitz. He had succeeded in deporting close to 450,000 Jews from the Hungarian provinces to Auschwitz, but Budapest was to have been the crowning jewel of his career, the achievement that would have catapulted him from *Obersturmbannführer* to *Standartenführer*, to the extraordinary prestige and perquisites of that quasi-general rank in the SS. Perhaps even more important than a promotion, his lonely skill at moving "merchandise" and his crucial role in the Final Solution would finally have been fully recognized. But that would never happen now. Budapest was the last great population of Jews in Europe. The plans he had so carefully prepared from the earliest days of the occupation of Hungary had been hopelessly compromised by political interference.

He had been a quiet and private man, but in the wake of the implosion of his plans Eichmann had a messy affair with Ingrid von Ihne, a wealthy and attractive divorcée. Even that wasn't enough to distract him from the frustrations of his thwarted effort to complete the destruction of the Jews of Hungary. By late fall 1944 he had turned into a debauched sensual-ist, a habitué of bordellos and seedy cabarets. Dieter Wisliceny, himself no slouch at spending and eating what he extorted from Jewish victims, found the extremes of Eichmann's behavior troubling. Eichmann spent his days riding his horse, hunting, pursuing women, and being chauf-feured over the Hungarian countryside in the noisy amphibious *Schwimm-wagen* Becher had given him. In the evenings he urged wife swapping and sex orgies among the SS officers. It may have all been a cover for his personal fears. A year before, Eichmann had been appointed a reserve officer in the Waffen-SS and he knew he could be appointed to active duty in the last-ditch defense of the Reich. On December 17 or 18, with the Soviet noose tightening around the city, he left Budapest, met up with his former colleague Ernst Kaltenbrunner, the head of the Security Police and, after the attempt on Hitler's life, a rival of Himmler.

Eichmann discovered that even Kaltenbrunner wanted nothing to do with someone who would surely be pursued by the Allies.

With the end of the war, Eichmann disappeared in Germany, hiding as Luftwaffe Corporal Barth and then as SS Lieutenant Otto Eckmann until he was captured by the U.S. Army. The Americans did not suspect his role in Budapest and elsewhere, and he escaped custody and hid again until he fled via Italy to Argentina, the beginning of a long journey that would ultimately bring him back to Israel.

Like Becher and some of the other high-level Nazis who had participated in the negotiations, Dieter Wisliceny, whose final job had been supervising the importation of Jewish slave laborers to build fortifications in Vienna, liked to think of himself as a savior of the Jews. His cozy apartment on the lower floor of a building in Vienna miraculously survived the bombing and fighting, and his library there included volumes by Jewish writers like Stefan and Arnold Zweig, Emil Ludwig, Karl Kraus, Arthur Ruppin, and Lion Feuchtwanger. He liked to talk about his library, spoke graciously of Gizi Fleischmann in Slovakia and the evenings he spent in cafés with Kasztner and Brand, and told whoever would listen that it was fortunate that he had been on the receiving end of the forced marches from Budapest to Vienna, because he sent the poor and sick to the Jewish hospital for treatment.[5] Despite his protestations of his role as a savior of the Jews, survivors of the brutal deportations he had directed in Greece and Slovakia, including Athenian Jews who had been hidden in country houses and monasteries by Rabbi Eliyahu Barzilai, testified about Wisliceny's introduction of the yellow star to isolate the Jews and his role in the ghettoizations and brutal deportations from Thessalonica and other Greek cities. After the Nuremberg trials Wisliceny was extradited to Czechoslovakia, where he was tried, convicted of war crimes and crimes against humanity, and hanged in 1948.

By early 1945 Heinrich Himmler had lost hope and faith in a German victory. As the fronts began to collapse, Hitler gave Himmler command of Waffen-SS units on two fronts, then replaced him. When the Soviets and western Allies closed their huge pincer on the Reich, Himmler, still convinced that the only hope for Germany was in a separate peace with

Britain and the United States, contacted Count Folke Bernadotte of Sweden and arranged a meeting with him at Lübeck, near the Danish border, to discuss a peace with the Allies. Hitler learned of Himmler's treason and, the day before he committed suicide in his Berlin bunker, declared Himmler a traitor and stripped the man who had been his heir of his ranks and titles as Reichsführer-SS, chief of the German police, Reich commissioner of German nationhood, Reich Minister of the Interior, and supreme commander of the *Volkssturm* (home army). In desperation Himmler tried to join up with Admiral Karl Dönitz, who had become the head of state after Hitler's death, but Dönitz rejected Himmler as having no place in the new German government. Himmler then contacted General Eisenhower's headquarters, offering to surrender Germany if he was spared prosecution and if Eisenhower named him minister of police in a postwar Germany. In anticipation of his meeting with Eisenhower Himmler worried whether he should give the Nazi salute or offer to shake hands. Eisenhower spared him the decision by refusing to meet or have anything to do with him. The Allies declared Himmler a war criminal, and despite shaving his mustache, wearing an eye patch, and dressing in a ludicrous costume as a sergeant major of the military secret police, he was captured. Before he could be questioned, he committed suicide with a cyanide capsule. His last words were, "I am Heinrich Himmler."

Edmund Veesenmayer, the German plenipotentiary in Hungary, was arrested by the Allies, tried in the ministries trials in Nuremberg, sentenced to twenty-five years, and released in 1951 after serving only six years. He later appeared as a defense witness at a West German trial of SS men associated with Auschwitz, where one of the Nuremberg prosecutors, at the trial as an observer, asked why Veesenmayer was "running around." A West German judge answered: "This is a very nice acquaintance of mine, he was only responsible for 400,000 Jews."[6] Veesenmayer's experience was not unusual. Although Germany opened more than thirty-six thousand criminal investigations against one hundred seventy-two thousand suspected Nazi war criminals, only one in ten investigations resulted in indictments, fewer than ten percent of those charged were found guilty, and most were given light sentences.

In January 1945, Kurt Becher, who had always stressed his background as a horseman and presented himself as a suave and worldly gentleman in Budapest, was named special Reich commissar for all concentration camps by Himmler. By then many of the camps were overrun or collapsing, and Becher could exercise little authority. He was arrested and imprisoned in May 1945, and would have been tried at Nuremberg if Rezső Kasztner had not testified on his behalf. "To the best of my knowledge," wrote Lieutenant Colonel Walter H. Rapp, evidence counsel and deputy chief to Nuremberg prosecutor Brigadier General Telford Taylor, "Kasztner arrived in Nuremberg as a voluntary witness on behalf of SS Colonel Kurt Becher . . . and I gained a definite impression that his visit was aimed solely to assist Becher. Until the arrival of Kasztner, it was hugely probable that Becher would be tried by us." After Kasztner's testimony, the Americans "came to regard Becher with increasing sympathy, and personally went out of their way to assist him in every possible manner."[7] Becher's self-serving testimony as a witness at Nuremberg claimed that between September and October 1944 he caused Himmler to issue an order that "forbid any liquidation of Jews and [to] order that on the contrary, care should be given to weak and sick persons."[8]

In a sworn affidavit Kasztner backed up Becher's claims: "Standartenführer of the Waffen-SS, Kurt Becher . . . has prevented the execution of almost 100,000 Hungarian Jews in the Budapest ghetto." The affidavit acknowledged that Kasztner took over SFr11 million in valuables "of Hungarian Jews who placed them at the disposal of the Rescue and Relief Committee of the Jewish Agency for Palestine" and delivered them to Becher "as a kind of ransom for concession made by the Germans in their anti-Jewish policy," and that he asked Becher to consider the valuables as a deposit, not to be used for German war purposes, and to restore them after the end of the war, "if possible." He swore that "Becher promised me to do so."[9]

Informally, Kasztner told everyone at Nuremberg that he was an official representative of the Jewish Agency. The Jewish Agency had not been invited to send representatives to Nuremberg but had paid his expenses there. Observers who assumed a representative of the Jewish Agency would testify for the prosecution at Nuremberg did not realize that Kasztner had frequently been treated to afternoons on the blue-and-pink silk-covered couches of the elegant Chorin House on Andrássy Avenue, hobnobbing with Becher and his beautiful German mistress, Countess Hermine von Platen, who called Kasztner "Rudolf." They may not have known that Becher entertained Kasztner at evenings of Vienna platters and piano music at the Gellért Hotel, or late nights at the Budapest Casino, nor that in return for Becher's support for his train project Kasztner had handed over to Becher the hard-earned funds the Jews on the train had entrusted to him.[10]

The funds from Kasztner were a tiny portion of the funds Becher hid during the war. Even after his enormous caches of cash, gold, platinum, and jewelry were discovered and sequestered by the U.S. Army, Becher returned to Germany with enough money and valuables from the Hungarian Jews to establish himself as a prosperous businessman in Bremen. By 1960, he was one of the wealthiest men in West Germany, with estimated assets of $30 million. He was proud that he sometimes did business with the Israeli government.

There was little afterstory for the British and Americans involved in the negotiations. For McClelland, Pehle, and the other War Refugee Board members, the negotiations had been one more problem, an interim crisis that arose soon after the establishment of the board and by the end of 1944 was supplanted by the crisis of getting supplies to relieved concentration and displaced-persons camps. Like Secretary of State Hull and Undersecretary of State Stettinius, Anthony Eden and the British Foreign Office staff, the American General Staff, and the British and American bomber command authorities, the WRB had been forced into an inflexible position. They were not allowed to put the lives of Hungarian Jews ahead of the adamant American and British policy of victory first. Even Ira Hirschmann, who had been sympathetic to Joel Brand and his mission, and had promised to do what he could to support the objectives of Brand's mission, quickly stepped back from his temporary service on behalf of the WRB to a whirl of board activities in New York.

He became the first chairman of the board of trustees of the University in Exile of the New School for Social Research, and as a board member of the Mannes College of Music and a founder of the New Friends of Music, became an effective supporter of chamber music and lieder concerts at Town Hall and other New York locales. He wrote two books about his wartime experiences.

Saly Mayer, who had dutifully walked out to the middle of the bridge at Sankt Margrethen again and again to meet the German delegations, knowing he did not enjoy enough support from the Americans and British to negotiate for anything but time, remained the European representative of the JDC after the war and handled the payments from the American organization to displaced-persons camps. He died in 1950, a loyal Swiss. The Swiss had publicized the revelations of the Auschwitz Protocols when they were first revealed during the war, but as investigations of German atrocities drew closer to the Swiss borders and began to reveal secret Swiss collaborations with the Nazis and the practices of companies that traded with or supported the Nazis from the safety of Switzerland, the Swiss press devoted less attention to the Holocaust or the role of the Swiss in negotiations between the two sides.

In Israel, too, from the turbulent years of United Nations partition, the *Exodus* affair, the birth of the new state, into the years after the War of Independence against Israel's Arab neighbors, the Holocaust was deliberately played down as a subject of public or press discourse. Many Zionist leaders had been obsessed with the task of building a new state to a point that some called callous. "The disaster facing European Jews is not directly my business," Ben-Gurion once said, and a Jewish Agency executive once told a representative of the journalists union that they did not want reporters to exaggerate the numbers of Jewish victims of the Holocaust, "because if we begin declaring that millions of Jews were murdered by the Nazis, they will ask us, rightly, where the millions of Jews are for whom, according to us, we need to find a new home in Palestine after the war."[11]

The Holocaust was a serious image problem for the new state of Israel. In 1941, the poet Abba Kovner had called upon his comrades in the

Vilna ghetto not to go to their deaths like "lambs to the slaughter." The phrase from Isaiah 53:7 stuck, and the association became a psychological trauma for the Zionists, a memory to be expunged. Building a new Jewish state required an image and a national memory of Jews not as weak and willing lambs who had been lead to slaughter without resisting but as warriors—against enemies on the battlefields and in the press; against the coastal swamps that were heroically turned into farmland; and against the skepticism that Jews, who had long been pictured as effete, intellectual, urban, and capitalist, could become socialist tillers of the soil, soldiers, and fighter pilots. To build the new national memory the Zionists appropriated the Warsaw ghetto uprising, tying it to Masada and the Maccabees.[12] They transformed the courageous but mostly unsuccessful stories of Palestinian parachutists into heroic tales, and appropriated the resistance efforts of the rescue groups in Slovakia and Hungary as actions of the Jewish Agency. "The initiative for active self-defense came from our movement," proclaimed Moshe Sharett,[13] who had changed his name from Shertok. In 1950, Israel passed a Nazi and Nazi Collaborators (Punishment) Law, intended as a basis to identify, try, and punish those whose collaboration with the Nazis had blighted the history of the Jews. The law was used to try minor collaborators, like concentration camp kapos who had slapped fellow prisoners or forced them to kneel as punishments. Mostly the new state of Israel avoided talking about the Holocaust. They were too busy building a new nation to dwell on the past.

Luck ran out for some veterans of the rescue efforts. After the British released him, Bandi Grosz was tried for espionage in Turkey and incarcerated there from 1946 until 1953. He showed up in Israel after his release, a broken man. The new country was looking for men and women with skills and polish. No one wanted to do business with the former Smuggler King.

By contrast, Rezső Kasztner, who shortened his surname to drop the Hungarian-sounding "z" and began using Israel as his first name, fit in quickly in Palestine and in the new Israeli state. Although he had not been in regular contact with the Jewish Agency during the war—their nearest offices were in Istanbul and Switzerland—he had called himself the leader of the Zionist efforts in Hungary and cultivated relationships with the Zionist leaders. On May 8, 1945, the day after the German surrender, he sent a telegram to the Jewish Agency headquarters in Tel Aviv: "Mission accomplished." It was close to an echo of General Eisenhower's famously eloquent brevity the day before: "The mission of this Allied Force was fulfilled at 0241 local time, May 7th, 1945."[14]

Kasztner and his wife were estranged while he and Hansi Brand were engaged with one another and with the leadership of Vaada. At the end of the war they reconciled and moved to Tel Aviv, where he joined Mapai, the labor party headed by David Ben-Gurion. Kasztner's skills and style fit well with the party's ambitious agenda. He looked up old acquaintances, told everyone how Brand had failed at the mission of trying to save the Hungarian Jews, and what he would have said to Chaim Barlas, the British, and the Americans. People were impressed with his skills on his feet, and he rose through a series of party positions, was asked to stand for election to the Knesset, and became a spokesman for the Ministry of Trade and Industry. He preferred his elegant suits and fancy cigarettes to the open-neck short-sleeve shirts that were a socialist identity badge for Mapai, but he was aggressive, outspoken, articulate, and relentless—qualities highly prized in Tel Aviv. Others in the Mapai party, and in the opposition parties, assumed he would go far in Israel.

While Kasztner ingratiated himself into the ruling circles of Mapai and the political-social-intellectual circles of Tel Aviv, Joel Brand remained in the wilderness. He had been a fervent Zionist since his youth, but he abandoned Mapai and joined up with Lehi, the radical group the British called the Stern Gang. It was a dramatic shift. In 1941, in an effort to save the Jews of Europe, Lehi had tried to form an alliance with the Nazis against the British. They were later responsible for the assassinations of Lord Moyne and the UN mediator Count Bernadotte, and had become pariahs in Israeli politics. It was an odd affiliation for a man who had always seen himself as a negotiator.

Joel Brand was already a forgotten man. Still convinced that his mission could have succeeded, the Emissary of the Doomed cursed that no one had listened to him. He tried to see David Ben-Gurion, to tell him the full story of his mission, but was rebuffed. From his rented room in Tel Aviv Brand sent letters, hundreds of letters. He wrote officials he had met on his mission—Shertok, Bader, Avriel, Chaim Barlas—pleading that they intervene so he would be allowed to return to Hungary. He wrote to officials he had never met, to any name he could remember or find in the newspapers. He asked Ira Hirschmann and the WRB for help in locating his mother, sisters, and niece, explaining that they had not been permitted to leave Bergen-Belsen, "on special orders of Eichmann," and that they might be alive somewhere. He asked for help for Hansi and his sons, and wired Ira Hirschmann for help with a visa so he could come to the United States to "continue work helping [the] surviving Hungarian Jews and raising money [for] their resettlement."[15] The few who answered his letters sent cursory replies. The Americans assured him that everything that could be done had been done.

He sent a copy of his memorandum castigating the Jewish Agency to Chaim Weizmann, who remained a respected name and would be elected the first president of Israel. Weizmann, whom he had once expected to find waiting for him in Istanbul, answered Brand this time. "As you may have seen from the Press," Weizmann wrote, "I have been traveling a good deal and generally did not have a free moment since my arrival here. I have read both your letter and your memorandum and shall be happy to see you sometime the week after next—about the tenth of January. . . . Miss Itin—my secretary—will get in touch with you to fix up the appointment."[16] The meeting never happened.

Teddy Kollek, who had been in Istanbul from early 1943 to establish contact with the Americans and British for the Jewish Agency, and had subsequently become a troubleshooter for Ben-Gurion and the Jewish Agency, came to see Brand in his hotel room and remembered Brand's round, red face.[17] Kollek's autobiography doesn't mention that he had been sent to silence Brand, or at least limit the damage Brand's criticism of the Jewish Agency might do in Israel and abroad. It took little effort on Kollek's part: no one was listening to Joel Brand.

Hansi Brand moved to Israel, though she and Joel remained estranged.

A few months after the end of the war she met Moshe Sharett and told him the Jewish Agency still owed her money she had spent to finance Jewish Agency activities in Budapest. Sharett asked if she had saved receipts, explaining that the Jewish Agency treasurer would not be able to pay without proper receipts. She moved to Kibbutz Givat Chaim near Haifa, where everyone was kind and welcoming, but no one wanted to hear her story. They wanted to tell their own stories, about Arab artillery shells that had landed near their chicken coop. They were ashamed of the Holocaust and talked about their own war against the Arabs to avoid hearing about hers. She told an Israeli journalist that no one in Israel seemed to care what she and others had done during the war. "If you had arrived in a coffin," the journalist told her, "we would have given you a reception worthy of a heroine."[18] It became one of her favorite stories.

Hansi was not as bitter as Joel. She recognized that Ben-Gurion and Sharett had made efforts to get the British to accept Brand's plan, but she remained adamant that they could have done much more: they could have established direct contact with the Nazis, they could have sent a tentative response and pretended they were willing to negotiate. Eichmann, who believed that Elders of Zion ruled the world, would have believed them. At the very least, the Jewish Agency could have played for time. She remembered the sound of the Russian artillery in Budapest and the horrors of the ghetto, even though she had escaped at least some of the privations when she was negotiating, alongside Rezső Kasztner, with Eichmann. If the Jewish Agency and the Allies could have stalled for only a few months they could have saved tens of thousands, maybe hundreds of thousands, of lives—but, she rued, it was obvious that Zionists were more interested in a Jewish state than in the Jews of Europe. After years on the kibbutz she moved to Tel Aviv and started a glove factory, hiring women to knit piecework. It was a return to the shop on Rozsa Street in Budapest, back in the days when Joel Brand waited in front of the Opera Café.

She and Joel eventually got past Hansi's affair with Kasztner— she had always admired him as a father to their children, and like many couples they were willing to paper over trespasses with wartime exigencies and the excuse of loneliness—but they had grown too far apart to live together. Enough ties remained for a friendship, and he visited his children regularly at the kibbutz where they lived with Hansi. Joel and Hansi both repudiated Kasztner, Hansi because she heard what happened in Bergen-Belsen, where Joel Brand's mother and sisters had been left to die by Kasztner's Nazi friends. Joel Brand had been willing to embrace Kasztner immediately after the war, two old warriors who had long fought on the same side, but the accumulated baggage of Kasztner's long affair with Hansi, his grab for credit from Joel Brand's efforts, and his own role in the negotiations with Saly Mayer, playing the role that was meant to be Brand's and doing so on behalf of the Nazis, left a gap too wide to bridge. While Kasztner hobnobbed with government officials, Joel Brand drank at cheap cafés and railed against the world, especially against the Jewish Agency officials who had let the Hungarian Jews die. Unemployed and destitute, he sent articles to the newspapers, imploring anyone to read or listen to his story. He remained gregarious, and around the card tables in Tel Aviv parks he was nicknamed "Fox" because of his red hair and cunning skills at poker. But no one read his articles and no one listened to his stories.

Joel Brand wasn't the only angry Hungarian in the new state of Israel. In the Rehavia neighborhood of Jerusalem, within walking distance of Zion Square, a seventy-two-year-old Hungarian-born stamp collector named Malchiel Gruenwald owned a ten-room hotel. Gruenwald had lost fifty members of his family in the Holocaust. After he lost his son in the War of Independence he changed the name of his hotel from the Austria to the Mount Zion, but kept the name of the Café Vienna on the ground floor, where Gruenwald liked to pass out the newsletters he wrote. His *Letters to Friends in the Mizrahi* were filled with angry essays he would write in German and find a friend to translate to Hebrew. He would run off a few hundred or sometimes a thousand copies of the three-page newsletters and stuff, address, and stamp the envelopes himself. The recipients weren't really subscribers: they paid nothing and most probably threw away the sporadic issues unread. But enough copies were read that Gruenwald had been threatened with libel suits for his vitriolic attacks on Israeli politicians and policies. A begrudging public apology was usually enough to quench the threats.

In his fifty-first newsletter, which came off the mimeograph in August 1952, Gruenwald accused Rezső Kasztner, or as he had begun calling himself, Israel Kastner, of a long list of wartime crimes: collaboration with the Nazis, testifying on behalf of Kurt Becher at Nuremberg, rescuing his own family and friends on his special train while abandoning others to their fate, pocketing funds that had been paid as bribes for the Nazis, and cruelly and deliberately deceiving Hungarian Jews about their impending fate. Gruenwald's language was harsh even by Israeli standards, as he lambasted Kasztner's political connections, Mapai membership, and Knesset candidacies. "I have waited a long time to expose this careerist whom I consider, because of his collaboration with the Nazis, an indirect murderer of my people," Gruenwald wrote, accusing Kasztner of "a sickly megalomania. . . . The smell of a corpse is tingling in my nostrils! It will be a funeral of the very best kind! Dr. Rudolf Kasztner must be liquidated!"

For Hungarians in Israel, who had brought their café tradition of exempting nothing and no one from analysis, sarcasm, and humor, the accusations were familiar. In 1948, at a celebration by former passengers on the Kasztner train, Levi Blum, a Zionist party member and workman, had jumped up and shouted: "You people are making a big mistake about Kasztner. He was the only Jew who was a close friend of the Nazis and Eichmann." Blum yelled at Kasztner: "You were a Quisling! You were a murderer! You can sue me for what I say! I'm too poor to take you into court. But I *dare* you . . . I know that you, Kasztner, are to blame for the Jews of Hungary going to Auschwitz. You knew what the Germans were doing to them. And you kept your mouth shut."[19] The incident created a brief stir in the Hungarian community in Israel, but quickly faded. Mapai officials may have squelched news reports of the incident. To those who knew Kasztner as a polished, educated, self-assured, successful journalist, who had experienced his personal charm and aplomb and assumed he would go far with his confident political connections,

the grave charges and coarse language of Malchiel Gruenwald's mimeo-
graphed newsletter were equally ridiculous.

Kasztner had brushed off criticism in the past, but Gruenwald's broad
brush also blackened the Mapai party, and by implication Ben-Gurion,
the Israeli government, and the idealistic young state. "We cannot remain
silent in the face of this publication," Chaim Cohen, then acting minister of justice and Ben-Gurion's right-hand man, wrote in a confidential
memorandum. "If, as I presume, there is no truth in the accusations, the
man who published them must be brought to trial." Cohen, on behalf
of Kasztner, the government, and Mapai, brought libel charges against
Gruenwald. In the occasional earlier trials about the Nazi era in Israel,
charges had been brought by the government under the 1950 Nazis and
Nazi Collaborators (Punishment) Law. The new trial would reverse
roles: instead of prosecuting, the state of Israel would be defending an
accused collaborator. Kasztner opposed bringing the action, but Cohen
was adamant: "I simply could not conceive that somebody tainted by the
grave suspicion of 'Nazi collaborator' could serve in a senior position in
our new, pure, ideal state."[20]

The trial was scheduled for the Jerusalem District Court in the Russian quarter. The courtroom was small, sixteen feet square, with a single
judge, no jury box, and seats for only twenty-five people. The sole judge,
Benjamin Halevi, like many in the early Israeli judiciary a German,
served as his own court stenographer. He and the prosecutor wore black
robes. The judge also wore a *kippa*.

Kasztner was the first witness for the prosecution. The prosecutor
wore yellow socks with his black robe, but Kasztner dressed elegantly,
and his eloquence matched his attire as he testified about the many meetings he had with Becher, Eichmann, Krumey, Clages, and Wisliceny.
He spoke about seeing Himmler, about the elegant offices of the Germans, described how the Nazis smoked, drank, played cards, listened to
phonograph records, went horseback riding, and made love to girls and
to each other. He described his shock "the first time I stood face to face
with this monster [Eichmann]," and their many meetings, how he had
been able to submit lists of Jews who would be allowed to leave Hungary,

and how when Eichmann refused his demands he had been able to get Krumey or Clages either to reason with Eichmann or to surreptitiously countermand Eichmann's orders: "I informed both of them I would stop all my negotiations and inform Istanbul to this effect. I pressed Clages and Krumey to reason with Eichmann. They did, and Eichmann agreed to receive me again that same day . . . capitulated and agreed to bring from Cluj a group of two hundred families."[21] Kasztner spoke carefully and confidently. He had every reason to be self-satisfied when he stepped down: he had testified convincingly on his prominence and connections with the Nazis, his importance in Vaada, and his effectiveness in rescuing his family and friends from his hometown of Cluj, and other prominent Jews. At the end of Kasztner's testimony Judge Halevi suggested that Gruenwald retract his accusations. Gruenwald refused.

The defense counsel was Shmuel Tamir, a native-born Israeli who had long opposed the governing Mapai party and had been involved in several sensational trials. His real name was Katznelson; Tamir ("tall and straight") was his nickname from his days in the Irgun, the revisionist defense organization that had bombed the King David Hotel in Jerusalem in 1946 as part of its struggle against the British. Tamir approached the trial with the same tactics. His first bomb was a question about Kasztner's testimony at Nuremberg. When Kasztner adamantly denied defending Becher, Tamir produced documentation of Kasztner's outspoken defense, calling it a "national crime." The evidence was incontrovertible, and the sensational accusation turned the trial on its head: it was no longer about Gruenwald's alleged libel, but about Kasztner's actions. Tamir relentlessly tossed bombshell after bombshell. He asked Kasztner why he was allowed to live alone in an unmarked house while the Jews of Budapest were crowded into a ghetto and required to wear prominent yellow stars on their clothing and display yellow stars on their houses. Why did he have constant access to a telephone when the phones of other Jews had been ripped out of their apartments and homes? Why was he allowed a car and unhindered travel to Vienna, Bratislava, Berlin? The revelation of the privileges and close association with the Nazis that Kasztner had enjoyed were not only damning, but invited comparisons to the privileges Mapai members enjoyed in the new Israel. Tamir asked Kasztner what happened to the Jews deported from Hungary: What did the Germans do with their clothing, their eyeglasses, their shoes, their gold teeth? What about the funds that had been collected from Jews, the blood money they had paid in the hopes of being spared deportation and annihilation? And why, Tamir demanded, did Kasztner *not* tell the Jews of Cluj that those he did not select for his train were headed to the gas chambers of Auschwitz? He had read the Auschwitz Protocols. Why did he conceal the truth about the deportations? If the Jews had known, they might have rebelled, or rioted, or tried to escape their inevitable fate. Why did he withhold this important information? In a withering cross-examination Tamir said: "I put it to you that you specifically requested favoritism for your people in Cluj from Eichmann."

"Yes," Kasztner said. "I asked it specifically." Kasztner admitted that he did not recruit anyone for his train from towns other than his hometown, and that he had "heard" about the gas chambers but couldn't "check all the rumors." Tamir would not let up, pointing out that Joel Brand had told people in Istanbul as early as May 1944 that twelve thousand Jews a day were being gassed in Auschwitz. If Brand was certain enough to share the information, surely Kasztner, who had so deftly presented himself as the head of the rescue efforts, knew the truth of what was happening to the Jews. *Why* he demanded, did Kasztner refuse to tell the Jews of Hungary? Tamir called to the stand a steel mill owner from Cluj who testified that after the war if Kasztner "had showed himself in the street he would have been killed."

Why? asked Judge Halevi.

"Because he was the man who misled the Jews to believe in the good intentions of the Germans."[22]

Tamir's cross-examination was an indictment not only of Kasztner but of Mapai. The revelations of the financial transactions, the sheer horror of the atrocities and systematic appropriation of Jewish property in Hungary and at Auschwitz, were a first in Israel. Even more, those who followed the trial were appalled by the godlike arrogance of Kasztner's assumption that he had the right to choose who would go on his train and who would stay behind. He had appointed himself the one to decide who would live and who would die.

The trial that Mapai had thought would be over quickly with a judgment against the upstart Gruenwald instead became a major cultural shock for Israelis and a scandal for the ruling party. But as the trial testimony dragged on, many, including the newspaper editors, lost interest. By March 1954, when Joel Brand was called to testify, the headlines in the newspaper were taken up by stories about a basketball game between the Israeli army and the French all-stars, and by detailed reports of the arrangements to bring the remains of Baron Edmond de Rothschild and his wife from France on an Israeli warship for reburial at Ramat Hanadiv near Zichron Ya'aqov. The report on the testimony of Joel Brand was a two-column item on the back page of *Haaretz*.[23]

Before Brand testified, Tamir met with him seven or eight times, explaining later that he worried about Brand's safety, since he "carries within him one of the greatest secrets of Jewish history."[24] The advance preparation wasn't necessary: although no one had been listening, Joel Brand had been preparing, rehearsing, and telling his story for a decade. No longer bound by Zionist discipline, and finally face-to-face with an audience, he told his story from the first meeting with Eichmann at the villa in Swabenberg and his mission as the Emissary of the Doomed to what most mattered to him, what he had always seen as the betrayal of his mission, especially by Shertok and the Jewish Agency. He recounted his astonishment when the Jewish Agency officials in Istanbul and Aleppo still had doubts about what the Germans were doing to the Jews in occupied Europe: "To a man like myself, who had just arrived from hell, it was bitter to hear that a Jewish Agency official could still have doubts on the subject. We had informed them constantly about what was going on. We knew our letters had reached them. Everything was known to them, as more or less a regular correspondence had been going on between us for some time."[25] Moshe Sharett had become prime minister late in 1953, following Ben-Gurion, and feared the testimony of Joel Brand more than the revelations from Kasztner and others. "If he [Brand] appears as a witness," Sharett wrote, "the whole thing will get very complicated because in the period after the failure of his mission he went into a frenzy of sending accusatory memoranda to the leaders of the Jewish Agency, blaming them for the slaughter in Hungary."[26] Sharett refused to testify at the trial and tried to deflect the impact of Brand's testimony with a press conference and a presentation of his version of events at an induction of new parachutists into the Israeli Defense Forces that had been set up as a memorial for the parachutists who had landed behind enemy lines in Europe. Emil Nussbacher, who now called himself Yoel Palgi, and Catharina Senesh were to be there as a hero and the mother of a heroine of the heroic Zionist efforts against the Holocaust. The ceremony turned into a public relations disaster when the light plane that was to symbolically drop the prime minister's speech to him crashed into the audience. Four veteran paratroopers of the wartime missions were among the seventeen casualties.

It took Judge Halevi nine months to write his decision in the Kasztner trial. Citing both Israeli and Jewish law ("it is forbidden to save one man by spilling the blood of another innocent man"), he ruled that Kasztner had "sold his soul to the devil," and that there was sufficient truth in Gruenwald's accusations to find Gruenwald innocent of libel, with the exception of one unproved accusation, that Kasztner had collected money from his Nazi "partners" for his aid in their program of extermination.[27] Gruenwald was fined one Israeli pound (50 cents) for that technical libel. Halevi ordered the government to pay Gruenwald 200 Israeli pounds ($100) as court costs.

Sharett and Mapai were the bigger losers. Sharett's government fell, at a time when Israel was secretly dealing with Britain and France in the planning that would lead to the Suez War. The unpredicted and overwhelming outcome of the trial was that the Holocaust, which had long been squelched as a topic of public discussion in the interest of forging a new national identity and memory, was rediscovered by the Israeli public and politicians. Soon after the verdict, a Holocaust and Heroism Remembrance Law emerged from committees and debates in the Knesset, establishing Yad Vashem as a memorial to the victims of the Holocaust, a study center, archive, and official ledger of genocidal crimes. Kasztner's trial had brought the Holocaust home to Israel.

Judge Halevi ruled Joel Brand's testimony irrelevant to the libel charges that had been brought in the trial, but after Brand's testimony, there was sudden interest in the story he had been trying to tell. When Brand first arrived in Jerusalem from Cairo, Yitzhak Jezernitzky of the Lehi group, who refused to forgive the Allies for their refusal to aid the Jews of Europe during the war and later became prime minister as Yitzhak Shamir, had urged him to publish his story. The Kasztner trial created an audience for Brand's book. Teddy Kollek urged Brand not to publish his autobiography, arguing that much of the world support for Israel was based on the failure of the Allies to help Jews during the Holocaust, and that revealing (or *claiming*, as Kollek probably said) that the Jewish Agency had also passed up a chance to help the Jews would destroy that argument and undermine support for Israel. Privately, Kollek worried what a Brand book would do to Ben-Gurion's reputation. Kollek, Ben-Gurion's most effective "fixer" before he acquired a different and more kindly persona as longtime mayor of Jerusalem, offered Brand both money and threats to stop the book; he finally persuaded Brand to let the Mapai publishing house issue the book. Brand agreed, only to discover that his manuscript was unrecognizable in the page proofs, and that Moshe Sharett—the one character Brand had most excoriated in his manuscript—had written an afterward. Furious, Brand published the original in Germany. He and Hansi collaborated on a second book that quoted Kollek's letters to demonstrate the anxiety of Mapai and the government officials about Brand's story.[28]

Three years after the court handed down its decision on the Kasztner case, in March 1957, Kasztner was assassinated outside his home in Tel Aviv. There were immediate suggestions that the lifting of Kasztner's police protection shortly before the assassination was no accident, and that the killer was a Shin Bet agent who silenced Kasztner lest he reveal secrets about contacts between Mapai and the Nazis. The government promptly denied any involvement. Ben-Gurion had returned to power after the original trial, and the consequences of the Suez War were still at the top of his agenda. Less than a year after Kasztner's death, the Supreme Court of Israel handed down its ruling on the government's appeal of Judge Halevi's decision in the libel trial. One justice voted to uphold the original decision in favor of Gruenwald; the other four voted to reverse the decision, officially exonerating Kasztner for his wartime actions.

On May 23, 1960, Ben-Gurion made the bombshell announcement that Adolf Eichmann had been captured, was imprisoned in Israel, and would be tried under the Nazis and Nazi Collaborators (Punishment) Law. The unexpected announcement was sensational because the Israelis had never engaged in Nazi hunting until Ben-Gurion secretly authorized Mossad to pursue Eichmann in Argentina. The entire process, from the identification of Eichmann in Buenos Aires and the bold kidnapping and flight across the South Atlantic to the Jerusalem trial, would be Ben-Gurion's answer to those who had criticized the government and the labor party for neglecting the Holocaust. Ben-Gurion had returned to the prime minister's job after Moshe Sharett's government fell, was near his final retirement, and also had other agendas that the celebrated trial was meant to serve. It would provide and publicize a narrative on which to base a reform of the historical curriculum in Israeli schools, which as late as 1948 used textbooks with ten pages on Napoleon and one page on the Holocaust. The trial would also serve public relations and foreign policy objectives by presenting evidence of the wartime alliance of the grand mufti of Jerusalem with the Germans and an accusation that their alliance may have prompted the Holocaust. The evidence for this latter charge was desperately slim and coincidental—the grand mufti visited Berlin in November 1941, and the Final Solution began at the end of the year—but the government was determined to link the Arabs with the Nazis. That linkage was key to Ben-Gurion's new foreign policy of a strong Israeli military and an aggressive defense policy as the only protection against a new Holocaust by Israel's Arab neighbors.

To make sure a guilty plea by Eichmann would not preempt the presentation of an exhaustive narrative of the Holocaust in the trial, the Knesset passed a special law that allowed a trial to proceed even if the defendant pleaded guilty. Even so, the trial required extraordinary leniency on the part of the judges. To condemn Eichmann, it was only necessary to prove that he had ordered a single deportation to a death camp. But the Ben-Gurion government's larger agenda required that the trial expose the full range of Nazi crimes against the Jews and the sins of the Allies who stood by and let it happen. The pretrial preparations and testimony deposed witnesses from every continent—in Israel, at consulates abroad, or in a few instances (like Kurt Becher, who refused to risk a trip to Israel) by telephone.

When the trial opened in 1961, the dramatic glass booth, the Nuremberg-like spectacle of simultaneous translations of the testimony, and the unprecedented circus of reporters drew the attention of the world. Inside the courtroom, the carefully orchestrated parade of witnesses revealed a narrative of the Holocaust that had never been presented in its entirety to the Israeli public or to the world. Within the building crescendo of testimony, Hansi Brand's testimony about Eichmann's drinking and rages, his pleasure when Brand's mission failed, and his determination to carry out the destruction of Hungarian Jewry added to the argument of the "banality of evil" that Hannah Arendt wrote about in her *New Yorker* reports. Joel Brand's now practiced testimony about his mission as Emissary of the Doomed was not the sensation his story had been at the earlier Kasztner trial, and the skilled prosecutors deflected much of the antigovernment thrust of his testimony.

In his own preparations for the trial, Eichmann focused on the negotiations and Joel Brand's mission as evidence of his efforts to help the Jews. "They even approved of the 10 percent condition, which I stipulated," Eichmann testified. This was the one hundred thousand Jews who would be allowed to leave Hungary as soon as Brand returned from his mission with a favorable reply. It hadn't been a sincere offer in 1944, and only Eichmann's desperation and self-delusion could have brought up that detail seventeen years later. In the futile hope of inspiring pity or favor from the judges, Eichmann said, "I think I can fairly claim to be one of the few who could understand Joel Brand's fury and anguish. And in reverse, I believe that Joel Brand, now he knows from these documents that I had nothing to do with the annihilation, can also, for his part, understand my anger about this affair, about this matter going wrong." Joel Brand had been calm and collected in the courtroom, raising his voice and becoming excitable only when the questions of the lawyers seemed to skip what he considered the important details of his mission. He had a fit when he heard Eichmann's pseudo-plea for his understanding.[29]

The three judges at the Eichmann trial—Benjamin Halevi, who had presided over the Kasztner trial was one—had little sympathy for Eichmann's effort to portray himself as trying to save Jewish lives. "We are of the opinion," wrote Chief Judge Moshe Landau,

> that this whole effort to appear now before this court as the initiator of the above transaction is nothing but a lie. There is no doubt that the order to begin negotiations about the exchange of Jews came from Himmler himself. What caused Himmler to make this proposal, we do not know. Possibly all this was nothing but a maneuver, or he was seeking to prepare an alibi for himself or wanted to show what he could achieve by obtaining essential goods for the Reich. In any case, all these were matters of general high policy, entirely beyond the sphere of activity of the accused, who concentrated all his efforts on the implementation of the Final Solution. On receiving the order to conduct negotiations with the Jews, he carried it out. There is proof that when Brand did not return and the whole matter collapsed, the accused expressed satisfaction. . . . But it is sheer hypocrisy to come now and testify that his reactions to the failure of the negotiations were sorrow, fury, and anger, like the feelings of Joel Brand. The entire version was invented by the accused only after he had read Joel Brand's book, from which he thought he could find something to hold on to, in order to show himself in a more favorable light.[30]

If the Kasztner trial brought the Holocaust home to Israel, the Eichmann trial brought the horrifying details of the Holocaust, and the sad story of the unsuccessful effort to bargain for Jewish lives, to a wider world. Joel Brand, who had tried so long to find an audience for his story, was now sought out by reporters for his comments. His autobiography was translated into English and other western languages. He became a regular witness in trials of accused Nazis in West Germany.

Ben-Gurion's strategy of using the trial of Eichmann to link the horrors of the Holocaust to Israel's Arab neighbors worked. The revelations of the horrors and the catalog of the failures of the Allies to come to the rescue of the Jews of Europe, including the failure to respond to Joel Brand's mission to save the Jews of Hungary, became an indelible part of the collective memory of Israel. *Never again!* became the slogan of Israeli defense and foreign policy, as Arab attacks on kibbutzim and moshavim were equated with the extermination policies of the Nazis, and any attack on the state of Israel was seen as a renewed effort to destroy the Jewish people. Amid that fervor, Joel Brand remained an outsider in Israel, a lonely man who demanded only to set the historical record straight. He died in Israel in 1964, probably from liver disease brought on by alcoholism, shortly after traveling to Frankfurt to testify in the trial of Eichmann's aide Krumey. Teddy Kollek, who became mayor of Jerusalem in 1965, offered to memorialize Brand, but it never happened.

In 1968, not long after the Six Days' War that changed the trajectory of Israeli history irrevocably, a retired David Ben-Gurion eagerly told a historical anecdote to visitors at his modest home in Kibbutz Sde Boker. During World War II, he related, a Jewish man, whose name he could not remember, arrived with a proposal to free a million Jews in exchange for ten thousand trucks. "Where could we find 10,000 trucks?" Ben-Gurion said.[31]

He said it as if he were hearing the idea of rescuing Jews from the Holocaust for the first time.

# ACKNOWLEDGMENTS

Authors write alone, but a book like this one would be stillborn without the wisdom, counsel, encouragement, and contributions of others. Ilan Diner provided invaluable help with materials in Israeli archives. Lawrence McDonald of the National Archives in College Park, Tricia Boyd of the Special Collections at the Edinburgh University Library, Virginia Lewick at the Franklin D. Roosevelt Library archives, and Amalia Levi and Nisya İşman Allovi at the Jewish Museum of Turkey provided counsel and assistance. Caroline Waddell at the U.S. Holocaust Memorial Museum, Lisa Nugent at the University of New Hampshire, Stephanie Stefka of Süddeutsche Zeitung Photo, Paul Friedman at the music division of the New York Public Library, László Csősz of the Holocaust Memorial Center in Budapest, Ron Lustig at the Memorial Museum of Hungarian Speaking Jewry in Safed, Dani Brand and Yaalah Cohen in Israel, and Agnes Borhegyi identified, located, and graciously granted permissions for the use of photographs. Jeffrey Lesser offered wisdom and help in Israel. Hasia Diner graciously allowed me to quote from an unpublished paper. Bob Lunnon of the UK Met Office and Joel Tenenbaum of Purchase College offered suggestions for historical climate research. Judith Romney Wegner provided fine points of German grammar. Maud Mandel and the late Alan Zuckerman offered nuanced suggestions and comments on the manuscript. I was again blessed with the wise enthusiasm and encouragement of Wendy Strothman and Wendy Wolf as agent and editor.

Many strangers in Budapest, some old enough to find reminders of the wartime era painful, were generous with directions and helpful comments about a long-changed landscape and cityscape. Others, in Istanbul, Aleppo, Samos, Cairo, and on the *Taurus Express,* made it possible to trace long-ago journeys by the characters in this story. My wife, Heather, cheerfully accompanied me to strange places, put up with a long obsession with another time and place, and provided gracious and wise insights and unstinting support.

To all who helped, encouraged, cautioned, and shared, I am grateful.

# NOTES

*Abbreviations*

AKA   Arthur Koestler Archive, University of Edinburgh Library, Edinburgh
CZA   Central Zionist Archive, Jerusalem
ETT   Eichmann Trial Transcripts, http://www.nizkor.org/hweb/people/e/
      eichmann-adolf/transcripts/
HA    Hagana Archive, Tel Aviv
IHP   Ira Hirschmann Papers, Franklin D. Roosevelt Library, Hyde Park,
      New York
ILP   Isador Lubin Papers, Franklin D. Roosevelt Library, Hyde Park, New
      York
LSP   Laurence A. Steinhardt Papers, Manuscript Division, Library of Con-
      gress
MA    Moreshet Archive, Giv'at Haviva, Israel
NA    National Archives, College Park, Maryland
TNA   The National Archive (formerly Public Records Office), Kew, UK
WRB   War Refugee Board Archives, Franklin D. Roosevelt Library, Hyde
      Park, New York
YV    Yad Vashem Archives, Jerusalem

The WRB archives were reboxed in 2004. References to WRB papers in studies researched before that year may use box numbers and/or folder descriptions different from those now in use. Some archives at Yad Vashem have also been issued new identification numbers. I have used the new box references and identification numbers throughout.

Hungarians can be creative in their spelling of German and other non-Magyar names; Americans, British, and Germans were equally creative in their spelling of Hungarian names; and many Jews who immigrated to Israel changed their names to favor Hebrew over German or other European origins. In the text, including quotations, I have conformed proper names to the most commonly used form, and have used "Joel Brand" instead of the Hungarian "BRAND Joel." Except in the titles of documents and other bibliographic data, I have corrected minor typographical,

293

syntax, and spelling errors in translating and quoting from letters, cables, and memoranda when conforming the language did not change the meaning.

## Epigraphs

Arthur Koestler: Diary-Notebook, March 22, 1944, AKA: MS 2305. A shorter version of this quotation appears in David Cesarani, *Genocide and Rescue: The Holocaust in Hungary* 1944 (Oxford: Berg, 1997), 1.

## 1. Budapest, April 1944

1. Fülöp Freudiger, "Five Months," in Randolph L. Braham, *The Tragedy of Hungarian Jewry: Essays, Documents, Depositions* (Boulder, CO: Institute for Holocaust Studies of the City University of New York, 1986), 249.

2. In his interrogation in Cairo during the war, Brand said his first meeting with Eichmann was April 16. Interrogation of Brand, Cairo, June 16–30, 1944. TNA: FO-371/42811. In his Eichmann trial testimony and his autobiographies, when he seems to have had a copy of his Cairo interrogation and other testimony may have inspired his memory or his imagination, he gave April 25.

3. *Va'adat Ezrah Vehatzalah* in Hebrew, shortened here to Vaada.

4. Brand testimony, ETT: Session 56-02; Joel Brand and Alex Weissberg, *Desperate Mission: Joel Brand's Story* (New York: Criterion Books, 1958), 34. Brand wrote several versions of his autobiography. *Bi-Shelihut nidonim la-mavet* [A mission on behalf of the sentenced to death] (Tel Aviv: 'Ayanot, 1956) was heavily censored before publication by Teddy Kollek and Mapai. The German original, written with Alex Weissberg, was published as *Die Geschichte von Joel Brand* (Cologue: Kiepenheuer & Witsch, 1956), and later translated as *Desperate Mission: Joel Brand's Story*. Brand then wrote *Ha-Satan Veha-Nefesh* [The devil and the soul] (Tel Aviv: Ladori, 1960) with Hansi Brand, quoting some of the letters from Kollek. The books were written more than a decade after the events, and Alex Weissberg acknowledges in a foreword: "It may be objected that it is impossible to reconstruct a conversation word for word that took place ten years ago. This objection is, of course, valid, but it would also apply to conversations ten days ago. The dialogue in the book does not pretend to be a verbatim reproduction of the words spoken. It is simply a form chosen for the sake of brevity." I have quoted Brand's remembered or reconstructed dialogues only when they seemed reasonably likely for the characters and situation.

5. Thomas Keneally, *Schindler's List* (New York: Simon & Schuster, 1982), 146f; David Crowe, *Oskar Schindler: The Untold Account of His Life, Wartime Activities, and the True Story Behind the List* (Boulder, CO: Westview Press, 2004), 292f.

6. Brand and Weissberg, *Desperate Mission*, 91.

7. Brand testimony, ETT: Session 56-01.

8. András Juhász Gyula-Szántó, *A Svábhegyi Üdülöszállók Története* [History of the Svábhegy Resort Hotels] (Városháza kiadása, 1999), 48–50, cited in Szabolcs Szita and Sean Lambert, *Trading in Lives? Operations of the Jewish Relief and Rescue Committee in Budapest, 1944–1945* (Budapest: Central European University Press, 2005), 33.

9. Hansi Brand testimony, ETT: Session 58-02; Brand testimony, ETT: Session 56-03.

10. Rudolf Vrba and Alan Bestic, *I Cannot Forgive* (New York: Grove Press, 1964), 248. Vrba has published the story of his escape from Auschwitz in many editions. See Rudolf Vrba and Alan Bestic, *44070: The Conspiracy of the Twentieth Century* (Bellingham, WA: Star and Cross, 1989); Rudolf Vrba, *I Escaped from Auschwitz* (Fort Lee, NJ: Barricade Books, 2002). Vrba later corrected some details of his story in a private letter to Martin Gilbert, July 30, 1980; see Martin Gilbert, *Auschwitz and the Allies* (New York: Holt Rinehart and Winston, 1981), 202–204.

11. The ledgers, along with lists of Hebrew texts and torahs appropriated by the Nazis, are mentioned in [Ludwig Kastner,] "Allgemeiner Bericht an Agudas Israel," August 1, 1944. YV: 033/3311/a, 9–10. This is not the Rezső Kasztner of Vaada, but an Orthodox staff member of the Bratislava Social Institute for Emigrants and Refugees in Istanbul.

12. Gizi Fleischmann wrote to both the Jewish Agency in Istanbul and the Joint Distribution Committee office in Geneva, reporting that a million Jews had been deported from Poland and that Sobibór, Treblinka, Belzec, and Auschwitz were "annihilation camps." By August 1943, rumors about the gas chambers at Auschwitz were rife in some Jewish ghettos. See, for example, the deposition of Yechiel De-Nur, given to Inspector Michael Goldman-Gilad of the 06 division of the Israeli police before the Eichmann trial, http://yiddish.haifa.ac.il/tmr/tmr11/tmr11012.htm.

13. Yehuda Bauer, *Jews for Sale? Nazi-Jewish Negotiations, 1933–1945* (New Haven, CT: Yale University Press, 1994), 72.

14. Ibid., 86.

15. Vrba and Bestic, *I Cannot Forgive*, 201–202; Rudolf Vrba, "The Preparations for the Holocaust in Hungary: An Eyewitness Account," appendix V of Vrba, *I Escaped from Auschwitz*, 394–395.

16. Deposition for the Eichmann trial, London, July 16, 1961, in Vrba, *I Escaped from Auschwitz*, 367.

17. Vrba and Bestic, *I Cannot Forgive*, 248f.

18. Ibid., 251. I have taken the liberty of changing Rudolf Vrba, the nom de guerre Rosenberg later took, to the name by which he was then known.

19. The phrase is from Clive James, "Lewis Namier: The Eccentric Historian

Who Changed British Postwar Culture," *Slate*, March 8, 2007, http://www.slate.com/id/2161403.

20. "The Preparations for the Holocaust in Hungary: An Eyewitness Account," appendix V of Vrba, *I Escaped from Auschwitz*, 402–403; Randolph L. Braham, *The Politics of Genocide: The Holocaust in Hungary* (New York: Columbia University Press, 1981), 691–731.

21. John S. Conway, "The Significance of the Vrba-Wetzler Report on Auschwitz-Birkenau," appendix I of Vrba, *I Escaped from Auschwitz*, 394n; Gilbert, *Auschwitz and the Allies*, 204, 209.

22. Rudolf Vrba, "The Preparations for the Holocaust in Hungary: an Eyewitness Account," appendix V in Vrba, *I Escaped from Auschwitz*, 375–376, 385–387. Yehuda Bauer and others have argued that Vrba embellished his story years after the fact to include warnings about the Jews in Hungary. See http://en.wikipedia.org/wiki/Rudolf_Vrba. Whether or not this is true, it would have been difficult for him not to notice the construction of the new ramp and crematoria at Birkenau.

23. Vrba and Bestic, *I Cannot Forgive*, 251; Gilbert, *Auschwitz and the Allies*, 204.

24. John S. Conway, "The Significance of the Vrba-Wetzler Report on Auschwitz-Birkenau," 301.

25. Eichmann was not well known even after the war. When Justice Francis Biddle, a senior member of the Nuremburg tribunal, saw Eichmann's name in an early draft of the judgment, he scribbled next to it, "Who was he?" None of the Nazi hunters, including Simon Wiesenthal, initially set out to find Eichmann. David Cesarani, *Becoming Eichmann: Rethinking the Life, Crimes, and Trial of a "Desk Murderer"* (Cambridge, MA: Da Capo Press, 2006), 1.

26. Brand testimony, ETT: Session 56-03; Brand and Weissberg, *Desperate Mission*, 91–92. Terezin was the Theresienstadt model concentration camp; Oswiecim is the Polish town where the Aushwitz-Birkenau camp was built.

27 Ibid., 92–93.

28. Interrogation of Brand, Cairo, June 16–30, 1944. TNA: FO-371/42811. The dialogue Brand gives in his autobiography is similar but not identical.

## 2. *When the Germans Came*

1. Curzio Malaparte, *Kaputt* (New York: New York Review of Books, 2005), 94.

2. Interrogation of Brand by Ira Hirschmann, Cairo, June 22, 1944. TNA: FO 371/42807.

3. Quoted in Randolph L. Braham, *The Politics of Genocide: The Holocaust in Hungary* (New York: Columbia University Press, 1981), 1:468.

4. Miklós Horthy, *Memoirs* (New York: R. Speller, 1957), 162, 181.

5. Pál Teleki to Horthy, April 3, 1941, in Miklós Szinai and László Szücs, *The Confidential Papers of Admiral Horthy* (Budapest: Corvina, 1965), 175.

6. Saul Friedländer, *The Years of Extermination: Nazi Germany and the Jews, 1939–1945* (New York: HarperCollins, 2007), 603–604.

7. Barry Rubin, *Istanbul Intrigues* (New York: McGraw-Hill, 1989), 143–144.

8. "Whether or not there will be an invasion from the West is hard to predict; on the other hand, I definitely anticipate an attack against Northern Transylvania." February 12, 1944. Szinai and Szücs, *The Confidential Papers of Admiral Horthy*, 267–269.

9. John Toland, *Adolf Hitler* (Garden City, NY: Doubleday, 1976), 781; Horthy, *Memoirs*, 215–216; Ian Kershaw, *Hitler, 1936–45: Nemesis* (New York: W. W. Norton, 2000), 627–628.

10. Kinga Frojimovics and Géza Komoróczy, *Jewish Budapest: Monuments, Rites, History* (Budapest: Central European University Press, 1999), 360.

11. Ibid., 369.

12. Yitzhak Arad, Israel Gutman, and Abraham Margaliot, *Documents on the Holocaust: Selected Sources on the Destruction of the Jews of Germany and Austria, Poland, and the Soviet Union* (New York: Ktav Pub. House in association with Yad Vashem [and the] Anti Defamation League, 1981), 173–178; Braham, *Politics of Genocide*, 1:447.

13. Fülöp Freudiger, "Five Months," in Randolph L. Braham, *The Tragedy of Hungarian Jewry: Essays, Documents, Depositions* (Boulder, CO: Institute for Holocaust Studies of the City University of New York, 1986), 238; Ben Hecht, *Perfidy* (New York: Messner, 1961), 97.

14. Braham, *Politics of Genocide*, 1:475–476.

15. Quoted in Ibid., 1:451.

16. McClelland to WRB, August 17, 1944, No. 5343. WRB: Box-66/Jews in Hungary; Washington to Algiers, March 24, 1944 and Washington to Berne, February 20, 1944. NA: RG-226/E-190/B-76/Sparrow.

17. Yoel Palgi, "The Mission: How She Fell" in Hannah Senesh, *Hannah Senesh: Her Life and Diary* (Woodstock, VT: Jewish Lights, 2004), 236. This may have been an after-the-war thought; there is no mention of the plight of the Jews of Hungary in Hannah Senesh's diary or letters before her mission.

18. Szabolcs Szita and Sean Lambert, *Trading in Lives? Operations of the Jewish Relief and Rescue Committee in Budapest, 1944–1945* (Budapest: Central European University Press, 2005), 21.

19. The pengő was worth approximately US$0.28 in 1944. The pengő later suffered the worst hyperinflation ever recorded for a currency; when the forint was introduced on July 23, 1946, the exchange rate was 1 forint = 400,000,000,000,000,000,000 pengős = US$0.085.

20. Götz Aly, *Hitler's Beneficiaries: Plunder, Racial War, and the Nazi Welfare State* (New York: Metropolitan, 2007), 191–193.

21. "Interrogation of Kurt Becher," March 2, 1948, Nuremberg, in John Mendelsohn and Donald S. Detwiler, *The Holocaust: Selected Documents in Eighteen Volumes* (New York: Garland, 1982), 15:51–55.

22. Ribbentrop telegram, July 19, 1944. NA: T-120/1757/E025079; Chorin to Horthy, May 17, 1944, in Szinai and Szücs, *The Confidential Papers of Admiral Horthy*, 293; Interrogation of Kurt Becher, July 19, 1947, Nuremberg War Crimes Trial Interrogations. NA: M-1019/R-5/F-534; on Becher's biography and the expropriation of the Chorin house see Gábor Kádár and Zoltán Vági, *Self-Financing Genocide: The Gold Train, the Becher Case and the Wealth of Hungarian Jews* (Budapest: Central European University Press, 2004), 179f, 195–205.

23. Braham, *Politics of Genocide*, 1:516.

24. "Notes of a Conversation between M. Shertok and Joel Brandt [*sic*]," Aleppo, June 11, 1944. AKA: MS-2403/1–2; Brand testimony. ETT: Session 56-01; Fülöp Freudiger, "Five Months," in Braham, *The Tragedy of Hungarian Jewry*, 246; Yehuda Bauer, *The Holocaust in Historical Perspective* (Seattle: University of Washington Press, 1978), 101. Other sources have listed the bribe as $20,000, SFr12,000, and fifty to sixty $20 gold coins.

25. Interrogation of Brand, Cairo, June 16–30, 1944. TNA: FO 371/42811.

26. Rezső Kasztner, *Der Kasztner-Bericht über Eichmanns Menschenhandel in Ungarn* (Munich: Kindler, 1961), 98.

27. Dr. Karl von Kleczkowski to Henderson, Cairo, March 12, 1944. NA: RG-226/E-190/B-76/F-200/11. See also David Crowe, *Oskar Schindler: The Untold Account of His Life, Wartime Activities, and the True Story Behind the List* (Boulder, CO: Westview Press, 2004), 292–295.

28. Fülöp Freudiger, "Five Months," in Braham, *The Tragedy of Hungarian Jewry*, 266; Braham, *Politics of Genocide*, 1:455.

29. Brand testimony, ETT: Session 56-02; Szita and Lambert, *Trading in Lives*, 62; Kasztner, *Kasztner-Bericht*, 72.

30. "Notes of a Conversation between M. Shertok and Joel Brandt [*sic*]," Aleppo, June 11, 1944. AKA: MS-2403/2–5; Brand testimony, ETT: Session 56-02; Joel Brand and Alex Weissberg, *Desperate Mission: Joel Brand's Story* (New York: Criterion Books, 1958), 66. The Eichmann pretrial testimony and Brand's autobiography were many years after the events of March 1944, and after some of this history had been publicized at the Kasztner trial; I have only relied on portions of his later accounts that are not contradicted by 1944 accounts or testimony.

31. Brand testimony, ETT: Session 56-02.

32. Wisliceny and Krumey to Brand, in Interrogation of Brand, Cairo, June 16–30, 1944. TNA: FO 371/42811.

33. Freudiger, "Five Months," in Braham, *The Tragedy of Hungarian Jewry*, 245.

34. Ibid., 247.

35. Braham, *Politics of Genocide*, 1: chap. 16.

36. Simon Kemény, *Napló* [Diary], March 21, 1942, quoted in Frojimovics and Komoróczy, *Jewish Budapest*, 363.

## 3. Negotiations

1. Interrogation of Mr. Joel Brandt [*sic*] by Mr. Ira Hirschmann, June 22, 1944. TNA: FO 371/42807.

2. Hannah Arendt, *Eichmann in Jerusalem: A Report on the Banality of Evil* (New York: Viking, 1963), 178.

3. The English translations of the ranks, and the Wehrmacht equivalents of *Oberstleutnant* and *Oberst*, make the ranks seem closer than they were in general perception or in insignia. The SS *Obersturmbannführer*'s four diamonds and a bar on the collar was closer to a *Sturmbannführer* or major's four diamonds or even a *Hauptsturmführer* or captain's three diamonds and a double bar than to the exalted SS *Standartenführer*'s collar leaf, which resembled the insignia of a general officer.

4. Interrogation of Brand, Cairo, June 16–30, 1944. TNA: FO 371/42811.

5. Brand gave different references to his birthplace in his various interrogations. In Cairo, he said he was born in Nazgod, the shorthand name of a province of Greater Hungary; in his autobiographies he gave Mukachevo, in Transcarpathia. They are not contradictory; he may have been asserting his Hungarian roots in the Cairo interview. Joel Brand and Alex Weissberg, *Desperate Mission: Joel Brand's Story* (New York: Criterion Books, 1958), 3.

6. Andreas Biss, *A Million Jews to Save: Check to the Final Solution* (London: Hutchinson, 1973), 38–39.

7. Brand and Weissberg, *Desperate Mission*, 12. Details from this period, like the meeting with Krem, are documented in other sources, like Biss, *A Million Jews to Save*, 40.

8. Brand testimony, ETT: Session 56-01; Biss, *A Million Jews to Save*, 41.

9. Brand and Weissberg, *Desperate Mission*, 37–38.

10. Robert Rozett, "Jewish Armed Resistance in Hungary: A Comparative View," in David Cesarani, *Genocide and Rescue: The Holocaust in Hungary 1944* (Oxford: Berg, 1997), 135–136.

11. John S. Conway, "The Significance of the Vrba-Wetzler Report on Auschwitz-Birkenau," in Rudolf Vrba, *I Escaped from Auschwitz* (Fort Lee, NJ: Barricade Books, 2002), 302. The date that Kasztner and Brand first saw the

Auschwitz Protocols has been controversial, because they were later accused of withholding information from the Jews of Hungary. See Randolph L. Braham, *The Politics of Genocide: The Holocaust in Hungary* (New York: Columbia University Press, 1981), 2:705; Yehuda Bauer, *Jews for Sale? Nazi-Jewish Negotiations, 1933–1945* (New Haven, CT: Yale University Press, 1994), 157; Fülöp Freudiger, "Five Months," in Randolph L. Braham, *The Tragedy of Hungarian Jewry: Essays, Documents, Depositions* (Boulder, CO: Institute for Holocaust Studies of the City University of New York, 1986), 262.

12. Fleischmann and Weissmandel to Hechalutz, Geneva, May 22, 1944, trans. from Hebrew as "re: Extmn. Camps for Jews in Poland." WRB: Box-60/Correspondence of Roswell McClelland/Misc. Docs.

13. Braham, *Politics of Genocide*, vol. 2, chap. 27; Biss, *A Million Jews to Save*.

14. Anna Porter, *Kasztner's Train: The True Story of an Unknown Hero of the Holocaust* (New York: Walker, 2008), 137.

15. "Summary Report of the Activities of the War Refugee Board with Respect to the Jews in Hungary," Oct. 9, 1944 (WRB), in John Mendelsohn and Donald S. Detwiler, *The Holocaust: Selected Documents in Eighteen Volumes* (New York: Garland, 1982), 15:22.

16. Brand and Weissberg, *Desperate Mission*, 123.

17. Quoted in Szabolcs Szita and Sean Lambert, *Trading in Lives? Operations of the Jewish Relief and Rescue Committee in Budapest, 1944–1945* (Budapest: Central European University Press, 2005), 36.

18. In his autobiographies Brand is imprecise about the dates of the follow-up meetings. In his Cairo interrogation, he said the second meeting was on April 25, after an initial meeting on April 16. The latter schedule does not seem likely, given the gap between the first and second meetings, the short period after April 5 for the meetings with Wisliceny, and Freudiger's detailed account that the funds paid to Wisliceny were not put together until the last day of Passover, April 15. See Fülöp Freudiger, "Five Months," in Braham, *The Tragedy of Hungarian Jewry*, 247. For the details of the meetings I have relied primarily on the account Brand gave British interrogators in Cairo. Interrogation of Brand, Cairo, June 16–30, 1944. TNA: FO-371/42811.

19. Gábor Kádár and Zoltán Vági, *Self-Financing Genocide: The Gold Train, the Becher Case and the Wealth of Hungarian Jews* (Budapest: Central European University Press, 2004), 100–108.

20. Interrogation of Brand, Cairo, June 16–30, 1944.

21. Interrogation of Mr. Joel Brandt [*sic*] by Mr. Ira Hirschmann, June 22, 1944.

22. Brand testimony, ETT: Session 56-02.

23. Moshe Shertok's Preliminary Report, June 27, 1944. CZA: z4/14870; Report prepared for Laurence Steinhardt, Ambassador of the U.S. to Turkey, June 4,

1944. MA: D.1.721. The Jewish Agency used Grosz as a courier for funds and messages, knowing he was an agent of the Hungarian police and the Gestapo.

24. Brand testimony, ETT: Session 56-03; Memo to Czech Desk, S-I Branch, from X-2 Branch, June 9, 1944, and "German Espionage Activities Hungary," May 23, 1944. NA: RG-226/E-190/B-76/Hungarian Desk.

25. "Notes of a Conversation between M. Shertok and Joel Brandt [*sic*]," Aleppo, June 11, 1944. AKA: MS-2401/1.

26. Biss, *A Million Jews to Save*, 55.

27. Brand interrogation, Cairo, June 16–30, 1944; Brand testimony, ETT: Session 56-03.

28. "Memorandum on the situation of Hungarian Jewry," May 25, 1944, Miklós Szinai and László Szücs, *The Confidential Papers of Admiral Horthy* (Budapest: Corvina, 1965), 296. "Report of a Hungarian deported woman from the extermination camp," September 11, 1944, Exhibit M, Part III. IHP: Box-2/Preliminary Report re Activities in Turkey, 7/18/44–8/19/44; Norton (Berne) to Foreign Office, July 27, 1944. TNA: FO-371/42811/p. 200; "Summary of a Report sent by the General Federation of Jewish Labor, Tel Aviv," received in Istanbul July 1, 1944, sent to Shertok, September 8, 1944. NA: RG-226/E-1/B-1; "Plight of Jews: March–August 1944" [notes from a Hungarian Army reserve officer]. NA: RG-226/E-191/B-1; Szita and Lambert, *Trading in Lives*, 40; Braham, *Politics of Genocide*, 2:781; Translated memo to the file, May 22, 1944. WRB: Box-66/Jews in Hungary. The latter memo mentions but does not quote a "detailed report of twenty-nine pages which has been prepared by the individuals who were in Auschwitz in February."

29. Abraham's servant in Genesis 24:2–60 is generally assumed to be the Eliezer of Damascus in Genesis 15:2, "the one in charge of my household."

## 4. Dissembling

1. "Report of Leslie A. Squires, American Vice Consul, Istanbul," June 8, 1944 (WRB), in John Mendelsohn and Donald S. Detwiler, *The Holocaust: Selected Documents in Eighteen Volumes* (New York: Garland Pub., 1982), 15:99–110.

2. "The Confessions of Adolf Eichmann," *Life* 49, no. 22 (Nov. 28, 1960): 110.

3. FDR to Marshal Stalin, with a note added by General George Marshall, Dec. 7, 1943. http://www.eisenhower.archives.gov/dl/dday/Dec743RooselvelttoStalin.pdf.

4. "Report by the Supreme Commander to the Combined Chiefs of Staff on the Operations in Europe of the AEF, June 6, 1944–May 8, 1945," vi, vii, quoted in Dwight D. Eisenhower, *Crusade in Europe* (New York: Doubleday, 1948), 225.

5. Yehuda Bauer, *Jews for Sale? Nazi-Jewish Negotiations, 1933–1945* (New Haven, CT: Yale University Press, 1994), 256.

6. John Toland, *Adolf Hitler* (Garden City, New York: Doubleday, 1976), 780.

7. Saul Friedländer, *The Years of Extermination: Nazi Germany and the Jews, 1939–1945* (New York: HarperCollins, 2007), 473; Toland, *Adolf Hitler*, 735.

8. Friedländer, *The Years of Extermination*, 604.

9. Quoted in Toland, *Adolf Hitler*, 778.

10. Himmler claimed that the annihilation of the Jews was legal "because the Führer decided . . . that the Jews should be annihilated. And the order of the Führer is the highest law in Germany." Felix Kersten, *Totenkopf und Treue: Heinrich Himmler ohne Uniform: Aus den Tagebuchblättern des Finnischen Medizinalrats* (Hamburg: R. Mölich, 1952), 149. See also Felix Kersten, *The Memoirs of Doctor Felix Kersten* (Garden City, New York: Doubleday, 1947), 41. "The Führer's will is supreme law. He knows why he gives a command: all I have to do is carry it out in detail."

11. See http://www.holocaust-history.org/himmler-poznan/.

12. Bauer, *Jews for Sale*, 102–103.

13. Kersten, *The Memoirs of Doctor Felix Kersten*, 212.

14. Felix Kersten, *The Kersten Memoirs, 1940–1945* (London: Hutchinson, 1956), 119–120, 160–162.

15. "Ich habe den Führer wegen der Loslösung von Juden gegen Devisen gefragt. Er hat mir Vollmacht gegeben, derartige Fälle zu genehmigen, wenn sie wirklich im namhaften Umfang Devisen von auswärts hereinbringen." Himmler note to file, December 10, 1942. MA: D.I.5753. [copy of the original in the Bundesarchiv, Koblenz: Bestand Alg. Schumacher 240 I]

16. Report of Dr. Karl von Kleczkowski to Henderson, Cairo, 12 Mar. 1944. NA: RG-226/E-190/B-78/folder 200-11.

17. Bauer, *Jews for Sale*, 113.

18. Friedländer, *The Years of Extermination*, 621–622.

19. Eichmann also liked to brag that he knew Hebrew. "The Confessions of Adolf Eichmann," *Life* 49, no. 2 (Nov. 28, 1960): 21–22. In 1937 he did set out for Palestine, but the British gave him a transit visa for only one night, which he spent in Haifa. When he went on to Cairo, he summoned a Jew from Jerusalem named Feibl Folkes, who was his source on Palestine. Folkes was a member of the Hagana, the clandestine Jewish defense force, and a Nazi agent.

20. Adolf Eichmann, Jochen von Lang, and Claus Sibyll, *Eichmann Interrogated: Transcripts from the Archives of the Israeli Police* (New York: Farrar Straus & Giroux, 1983), 24.

21. Becher claimed that he "never met a man that could lie so much." "Interrogation of Kurt Becher," July 7, 1947, Nuremberg, in Mendelsohn and Detwiler, *The Holocaust*, 15:76.

22. Joel Brand and Alex Weissberg, *Desperate Mission: Joel Brand's Story* (New York: Criterion Books, 1958), 104.

23. David Cesarani, *Becoming Eichmann: Rethinking the Life, Crimes, and Trial of a "Desk Murderer"* (Cambridge, MA: Da Capo Press, 2006), 176.

24. Brand and Weissberg, *Desperate Mission*, 119–120.

25. Brand testimony, ETT: Session 56-04.

26. Quoted in Dina Porat, *The Blue and the Yellow Stars of David: The Zionist Leadership in Palestine and the Holocaust, 1939–1945* (Cambridge, MA: Harvard University Press, 1990), 210.

27. Brand and Weissberg, *Desperate Mission*, 115.

## 5. Bandi

1. Memorandum to John Pehle, March 13, 1944. LSP: Box 45.

2. Cable to Abdul [MacFarland], Istanbul, July 7, 1944, NA: RG-226/E-88/B-609/Wash-Commo-R&C/Istanbul/Sibex Kandy/Jerusalem. See also OSS to Ustravic, London, July 7, 1944. NA: RG-226/E-121/B-12/WASH-X-2-R&C-2/. The OSS officials often butchered their spelling of Grosz's and Brand's names and aliases.

3. Interrogation of Andor Grosz, Cairo, June 6–22, 1944. TNA: FO-371/42811, p. 1, 48–49.

4. [Ludwig Kastner,] "Allgemeiner Bericht an Agudas Israel, Jerusalem und New York," August 1, 1944. YV: 033/3311/b, p 29; Interrogation of Andor Grosz, Cairo, June 6–22, 1944.

5. "Allgemeiner Bericht an Agudas Israel, Jerusalem und New York," August 1, 1944, 36.

6. Ibid., 39.

7. Brand and Weissberg, *Desperate Mission*, 21.

8. Anna Porter, *Kasztner's Train: The True Story of an Unknown Hero of the Holocaust* (New York: Walker, 2008), 119, 135.

9. Interview with László Devecseri, a Holocaust survivor from Leányfalu, quoted in Szabolcs Szita and Sean Lambert, *Trading in Lives? Operations of the Jewish Relief and Rescue Committee in Budapest, 1944–1945* (Budapest: Central European University Press, 2005), 79.

10. Hansi Brand testimony, ETT: Session 58-02 and 58-03.

11. Brand and Weissberg, *Desperate Mission*, 27.

12. Harrison telegram, No. 3506, June 2, 1944. WRB: Box-70/UOR/Sternbuch; Anti-Semitic flyer, May 1944. WRB: Box-66/Jews in Hungary/May 1944.

13. Fülöp Freudiger, "Five Months," in Randolph L. Braham, *The Tragedy of*

*Hungarian Jewry: Essays, Documents, Depositions* (Boulder, CO: Institute for Holocaust Studies of the City University of New York, 1986), 250–251.

14. Nuremberg prosecution exhibit 1116-5, and Eichmann to Sassen, quoted in Gideon Hausner, *Justice in Jerusalem* (New York: Harper & Row, 1966), 148–149; Rezső Kasztner, *Der Kasztner-Bericht über Eichmanns Menschenhandel in Ungarn* (Munich: Kindler, 1961), 273.

15. Yehuda Bauer, *Jews for Sale? Nazi-Jewish Negotiations, 1933–1945* (New Haven, CT: Yale University Press, 1994), 167–168.

16. The German version of his name was Wenja Pomeranz; when he later settled in Israel, he adopted a Hebrew name, Ze'ev Hadari.

17. [Ludwig Kastner,] "Allgemeiner Bericht an Agudas Israel, Jerusalem und New York," August 1, 1944. YV: 033/3311/a, 25–27; Brand and Weissberg, *Desperate Mission*, 130; Stanford J. Shaw, *Turkey and the Holocaust: Turkey's Role in Rescuing Turkish and European Jewry from Nazi Persecution, 1933–1945* (New York: New York University Press, 1993), 257.

18. L. Kastner, "Aktennotitz," May 26, 1944. YV: 033/3311/b; Dina Porat, *The Blue and the Yellow Stars of David: The Zionist Leadership in Palestine and the Holocaust, 1939–1945* (Cambridge, MA: Harvard University Press, 1990), 188–189.

19. Brand and Weissberg, *Desperate Mission*, 131.

20. L. Kastner, "Aktennotiz," May 26, 1944.

21. "Allgemeiner Bericht an Agudas Israel," August 1, 1944, 29.

22. Brand and Weissberg, *Desperate Mission*, 132–134.

23. Barry Rubin, *Istanbul Intrigues* (New York: McGraw-Hill, 1989), 120. Steinhardt to John Pehle [executive director, WRB], July 26, 1944. LSP: Box-44.

24. Barlas to Steinhardt, April 2, 1944. LSP: Box-45; Barlas to Shertok, May 21, 1944. TNA: WO-208/685a/91B (MI5 Files).

25. Brand and Weissberg, *Desperate Mission*, 135.

26. Brand was aware that the deportations from Nyiregyháza had started as early as May 15. "Allgemeiner Bericht an Agudas Israel," August 1, 1944, 28.

27. Thomas Keneally, *Schindler's List* (New York: Simon & Schuster, 1982), 145.

28. "Allgemeiner Bericht an Agudas Israel," August 1, 1944, 40.

29. Only recently have the Russians admitted what they long denied—that a Soviet submarine sank the *Struma* with a torpedo.

30. Summary on Struma sinking prepared for Hirschmann, November 3, 1944. IHP: Box-1. Also unsigned letter to Hirschmann, March 17, 1944. IHP: Box-2. Correspondence, 1943–1955.

31. Steinhardt to Secretary of State, February 20, 1944. LSP: Box-45.

32. Quoted in Porat, *Blue and Yellow Stars of David*, 192.

33. Memorandum to Laurence A. Steinhardt, June 4, 1944. MA: d.1.721; Stein-

hardt to Secretary of State, May 25, 1944 (WRB), in John Mendelsohn and Donald S. Detwiler, *The Holocaust: Selected Documents in Eighteen Volumes* (New York: Garland, 1982), 15:83–84. "Memo by Reuben B. Resnik, representative of the Joint in Istanbul, on Brand and György," June 5, 1944 (WRB), in Mendelsohn and Detwiler, *The Holocaust*, 15:85–91.

34. This dramatic story of a delegation showing up at the railway station may not be true. Ludwig Kastner wrote that he told Brand on the day he was supposed to go to Ankara that he could not go because he lacked a proper visa and was being watched by a detective. "Allgemeiner Bericht an Agudas Israel," August 1, 1944, 30.

35. Menachem Bader to Venia Pomerany, May 27, 1944, MA: D.1.719; Interrogation of Andor Grosz, 45.

36. Brand and Weissberg, *Desperate Mission*, 140.

37. Ibid., 141. See also Bader to Pomerany, May 27, 1944.

38. Hansi Brand testimony, ETT: Session 58-03; Kasztner, *Kasztner-Bericht*, 98–99.

39. Hansi Brand testimony, ETT: Session 58-02.

40. Interrogation of Joel Brand, Cairo, June 16–30, 1944. TNA: FO-371/42811, 30; Brand and Weissberg, *Desperate Mission*, 143.

41. Brand and Weissberg, *Desperate Mission*, 144.

42. Ibid., 147.

43. Protokoll, May 29, 1944. MA: d.1.720; see also Ibid., 149–151. Brand quotes the proposed interim agreement as if it were a verbatim transcription, but allows that it is "the sense" of the document and not the actual words.

44. Martin Gilbert, *Auschwitz and the Allies* (New York: Holt Rinehart and Winston, 1981), 216–217; Interrogation of Andor Grosz, Cairo, June 6–22, 1944, 45.

45. Hirschmann, speech to American Friends of Hebrew University, May 4, 1944. LSP: Box-44.

46. Brand and Weissberg, *Desperate Mission*, 154.

47. Menachem Bader to Pomerany, June 10, 1944, and Bader to Pomerany, May 27, 1944. MA: d.1.720.

48. Lord Moyne to Foreign Office, July 8, 1944. TNA: FO-371/42808.

49. Interrogation of Brand, Cairo, June 16–30, 1944, 30–31, 31A; Interrogation of Andor Grosz, Cairo, June 6-22, 1944, 47.


## 6. Playing for Time

1. Quoted in David S. Wyman, *The Abandonment of the Jews: America and the Holocaust, 1941–1945* (New York: New Press, 1998), 291.

2. Jewish Agency Executive, July 23 1944, and September 3, 1944, quoted in Dina Porat, *The Blue and the Yellow Stars of David: The Zionist Leadership in*

*Palestine and the Holocaust, 1939–1945* (Cambridge, MA: Harvard University Press, 1990), 211.

3. See http://www.eisenhower.archives.gov/dl/dday/InCaseofFailureMessage .pdf; Dwight D. Eisenhower, *Crusade in Europe* (New York: Doubleday, 1948), chap. 13 "Planning Overlord."

4. [Ludwig Kastner] "Allgemeiner Bericht an Agudas Israel," August 1, 1944. YV: 033/3311/a, p. 32; Joel Brand and Alex Weissberg, *Desperate Mission: Joel Brand's Story* (New York: Criterion Books, 1958), 152.

5. Hirschmann diary, July 31, 1944. IHP: Box-1/Diary Feb.-Oct. 1944; Stanford J. Shaw, *Turkey and the Holocaust: Turkey's Role in Rescuing Turkish and European Jewry from Nazi Persecution, 1933–1945* (New York: New York University Press, 1993), 276–277, 297; Dina Porat, "Tears, Protocols and Actions in a Wartime Triangle: Pius XII, Roncalli and Barlas," *Cristianesimo nella storia* 27, no. 2 (2007): 599–632; Alex Holt, *Pope's Secret Role in Saving Transnistria Jews* (2007); available from http://www.tiraspoltimes.com/node/869; Ira Arthur Hirschmann, *Life Line to a Promised Land* (New York: Vanguard 1946), 181–182.

6. Barry Rubin, *Istanbul Intrigues* (New York: McGraw-Hill, 1989), 41, 213–214.

7. "Report of Leslie A. Squires, American Vice Consul, Istanbul," June 8, 1944 (WRB), in John Mendelsohn and Donald S. Detwiler, *The Holocaust: Selected Documents in Eighteen Volumes* (New York: Garland, 1982), 15:99–110.

8. Interrogation of Brand, Cairo, June 16–30, 1944. TNA: FO-371/42811, 31–32.

9. "Aide-Mémoire from British Embassy, Washington to State Department," June 5, 1944, and "Cypher Telegram No. 683 to Foreign Office from High Commissioner, Jerusalem," [June 4, 1944?] (WRB), in Mendelsohn and Detwiler, *The Holocaust*, 15:92–97; Michael Makovsky, *Churchill's Promised Land: Zionism and Statecraft* (New Haven, CT: Yale University Press, 2007), 181.

10. Brand and Weissberg, *Desperate Mission*, 155.

11. "Allgemeiner Bericht an Agudas Israel," 37.

12. Menachem Bader testimony at the Kasztner Trial in Jerusalem, quoted in Ben Hecht, *Perfidy* (New York: Messner, 1961), 215.

13. The *Taurus Express* no longer runs through Ankara, and instead follows a route from Istanbul to Konya and Adana before crossing into Syria at Meydanekbez. What was once an international train comparable to the fabled *Orient Express* is now a single Syrian sleeping car hooked onto the regular Turkish Railway Istanbul-Gaziantep train.

14. Brand and Weissberg, *Desperate Mission*, 157; Yehuda Bauer, *The Holocaust in Historical Perspective* (Seattle: University of Washington Press, 1978), 121.

15. Hugo Will memorandum, June 15, 1944. NA: RG-226/E-154/B-35; Rubin, *Istanbul Intrigues*, 163.

16. There are heavily censored lists of the Dogwood agents in Harry S. Harper, "The Dogwood Organization" [July 1944] and in the Memo to the file, August 24, 1944. NA: RG-226/E-148/B-34/Istanbul OSS OP-1

17. OSS Report, December 30, 1943, quoted in Yehuda Bauer, *Jews for Sale? Nazi-Jewish Negotiations, 1933–1945* (New Haven, CT: Yale University Press, 1994), 123.

18. Harry H. Harper Jr., "The Dogwood Organization" [July 1944]. NA: RG-2 26/E-148/B-34/Istanbul-OSS-OP-1, 4, 8.

19. Ibid., 2. Harper's report dismisses the idea as "never more than a wild dream." Bauer, *Jews for Sale*, 130, cites this passage as evidence that Laufer had proposed a trade even before Joel Brand's mission, but Harper's report was written in midsummer 1944 or later, after Grosz was in British custody; Laufer's leak was probably about the Brand mission.

20. Director OSS to Abdul [MacFarland], May 31, 1944, and July 7, 1944. "Besides Hatz, Brand and Georgy known to you already, persons corresponding to following numbers in flower list: nine, seventeen, one, eighteen, twenty-three, four, twenty-two and three listed here in order of importance, range from extremely dangerous to dangerous." OSS to Abdul, July 17, 1944. All three cables are in NA: RG-226/E-88/B-609/Wash-Commo-R&C/Istanbul/Sibex Kandy/Jerusalem.

21. According to Carl Schorske, who was in the OSS before his careers at Berkeley and Princeton. Shlomo Aronson, "The 'Quadruple Trap' and the Holocaust in Hungary," in David Cesarani, *Genocide and Rescue: The Holocaust in Hungary 1944* (Oxford: Berg, 1997), 106.

22. Rubin, *Istanbul Intrigues*, 159. Copies of the *Donauzeitung*, August 2, 1943, and the *Berliner Börsu. Zeitung*, August 27, 1943, are saved in NA: RG-226/E-148/ B-34/Istanbul-OSS-OP-1.

23. See http://www.eisenhower.utexas.edu/dl/DDay/ssa.jpg.

24. Brand and Weissberg, *Desperate Mission*, 158–160.


## 7. *Aleppo*

1. [Ludwig Kastner,] Memo to the file, Agudas Israel, May 26, 1944. YV: 033/3311/b.

2. JAE Executive meeting, July 23, 1944. CZA: JAE-25/544.

3. Shertok's Preliminary Report, June 27, 1944, CZA: z4/14870,1. Shertok reported that his first phone call from Jerusalem was on May 24; his dates seem about one week off. Brand did not leave for Istanbul until May 25, and it was several days later that the Jewish Agency there decided to send Pomerany to Jerusalem.

4. "Nazis Planned Holocaust for Palestine: Historians," *Boston Globe*, April 7, 2006, cited in Robert Satloff, *Among the Righteous: Lost Stories from the Holocaust's Long Reach into Arab Lands* (New York: Public Affairs, 2006), 211.

5. Dina Porat, *The Blue and the Yellow Stars of David: The Zionist Leadership in Palestine and the Holocaust, 1939–1945* (Cambridge, MA: Harvard University Press, 1990), 191.

6. Eastwood to Henderson, July 28, 1944. TNA: FO-371/42811/p. 204f.

7. OSS memo, "Allied Interrogation Office in Aleppo," August 10, 1943; Victor Cordovi to Steve Penrose, September 1, 1944, both in NA: RG-226/E-190/B-76/F-400.

8. Travel details from Shertok's Preliminary Report, 2–3; Shertok to Linton, June 15, 1944 (WRB), in John Mendelsohn and Donald S. Detwiler, *The Holocaust: Selected Documents in Eighteen Volumes* (New York: Garland, 1982), 15:181.

9. Shertok's Preliminary Report, June 27, 1944, 7. No verbatim transcript was made of their conversation, only notes that Shertok wrote up in reports to the Jewish Agency. Several versions of Shertok's report have survived. See "Notes of a Conversation between M. Shertok and Joel Brandt [*sic*], Aleppo, June 11, 1944," AKA: MS-2403/1 and "Brand-Shertok, Interrogation," June 12, 1944, TNA: FO-371/42759.

10. Joel Brand and Alex Weissberg, *Desperate Mission: Joel Brand's Story* (New York: Criterion Books, 1958), 160–163.

11. Shertok's Preliminary Report, June 27, 1944, 5.

12. Brand's memoirs may not be trustworthy on this dialogue: the number "six million" was often used after the war, but not in the summer of 1944.

13. Ibid., 6; see also "Notes of a Conversation between M. Shertok and Joel Brandt [*sic*], Aleppo, June 11, 1944," p. 5–6.

14. Brand and Weissberg, *Desperate Mission*, 162–163.

15. Ibid., 163–165.

16. Reuven Dafne, "The Mission: The Last Border," in Hannah Senesh, *Hannah Senesh: Her Life and Diary* (Woodstock, VT: Jewish Lights, 2004), 239; Gabriel Barshaked's taped interview of Hansi Brand (YV), quoted in Anna Porter, *Kasztner's Train: The True Story of an Unknown Hero of the Holocaust* (New York: Walker, 2008), 185, 187.

17. Hansi Brand testimony, ETT: Session 58-03.

18. Ben Hecht, *Perfidy* (New York: Messner, 1961), endnote 187.

19. Shertok to Linton [JA London Executive], June 15, 1944. TNA: WO-208/685a/91B (MI5 Files); Hecht, *Perfidy*, 7.

20. Shertok's Preliminary Report, June 27, 1944, 7–8.

21. Brand and Weissberg, *Desperate Mission*, 165–166.

22. Hirschmann to Lubin, telegram, June 6, 1944. ILP: Box-52/Ira A. Hirschmann; Hirschmann to Pehle, May 11, 1944; Hirschmann to Lubin, May 24, 1944. IHP: Box-2/Correspondence 1943–1955.

23. Hirschmann, *Life Line*, 7–8.

24. Hirschmann diary, March 21, 1944, June 16, 1944, and *passim*. IHP: Box-1/ Diary Feb.–Oct. 1944.

25. Hirschmann, *Life Line*, 81, 87; Stanford J. Shaw, *Turkey and the Holocaust: Turkey's Role in Rescuing Turkish and European Jewry from Nazi Persecution, 1933–1945* (New York: New York University Press, 1993), 259–261; Ira Arthur Hirschmann, *Caution to the Winds* (New York: McKay, 1962), 141–142.

26. Telegram #953 to Foreign Office, June 22, 1944. TNA: FO-371/42759/ W-10023.

27. Hirschmann to Pehle, June 9, 1944. IHP: Box-2/Correspondence, 1943– 1955.

28. Undated memo, possibly a draft for *Life Line to a Promised Land.* IHP: Box-1/ Miscellaneous Office Memoranda and Working Papers, 1944; Hull to American Embassy, Ankara, June 9, 1944 (WRB), in Mendelsohn and Detwiler, *The Holocaust*, 15:111–115.

29. FDR to Hirschmann, June 8, 1944. IHP: Box-2/Correspondence, 1943–1955; Hirschmann, *Caution to the Winds*, 172.

30. Robin W. Winks, *Cloak & Gown: Scholars in the Secret War, 1939–1961* (New York: William Morrow, 1987), 129–130.

31. "Report of Leslie A. Squires, American Vice Consul, Istanbul," June 8, 1944 (WRB), in Mendelsohn and Detwiler, *The Holocaust*, 15:99–110.

32. Hirschmann, *Life Line*, 109.

33. *The Times*, Feb. 13, 1919.

34. Hirschmann diary, June 23, 1944. IHP: Box-1/Diary Feb.–Oct. 1944; Hirschmann memo to Steinhardt, "Interview with Joel Brand, Observations and Recommendations," June 22, 1944. ILP: Box 52/Ira A. Hirschmann; Hirschmann, *Life Line*, 112–116. The Hirschmann papers on his dealings with Brand are also collected in IHP: Box-3/Joel Brandt [*sic*].

## 8. Brand's Last Stand

1. "Note by the Secretary of State for Foreign Affairs," June 26, 1944. TNA: CAB-95/15/F-176.

2. Diary, July 25, 1944. IHP: Box-1/Diary Feb.–Oct. 1944.

3. Randolph L. Braham, *The Politics of Genocide: The Holocaust in Hungary* (New York: Columbia University Press, 1981), 2:831; Asher Cohen, "Resistance

and Rescue in Hungary," in David Cesarani, *Genocide and Rescue: The Holocaust in Hungary 1944* (Oxford: Berg, 1997), 131; Martin Gilbert, *Auschwitz and the Allies* (New York: Holt Rinehart and Winston, 1981), 244–245.

4. Rudolf Vrba, "Footnote to Auschwitz Report," *Jewish Currents* (March, 1966); Gilbert, *Auschwitz and the Allies*, 215.

5. John S. Conway, "The Significance of the Vrba-Wetzler Report on Auschwitz-Birkenau," appendix I of Rudolf Vrba, *I Escaped from Auschwitz* (Fort Lee, NJ: Barricade Books, 2002), 294n.

6. March 9, 1942, quoted in Saul Friedländer, *The Years of Extermination: Nazi Germany and the Jews, 1939–1945* (New York: HarperCollins, 2007), 463.

7. "Le Saint Siège et les victimes de la guerre, Janvier 1944–Juillet 1945," in *Actes et documents du Saint Siège relatifs à la seconde guerre mondiale* (Vatican City, 1980), 10:281.

8. As late as the fall of 2008, when the Vatican's efforts to canonize Pius XII are questioned by many, some Vatican archives on Pius XII's papacy remain closed, and Benedict XVI has spoken about his "venerable predecessor, who immediately ran to help and comfort the stricken population in the smoldering rubble" of the Holocaust, http://www.haaretz.com/hasen/spages/1042282.html.

9. Joel Brand and Alex Weissberg, *Desperate Mission: Joel Brand's Story* (New York: Criterion Books, 1958), 170–171.

10. Interrogation of Brand, Cairo, June 16–30, 1944. TNA: FO-371/42811.

11. Brand and Weissberg, *Desperate Mission*, 173–174.

12. Ibid., 174–175.

13. Jewish law agrees with Brand's interpretation. Maimonides bases the argument in his *Code* on Leviticus 19:16, "Do not profit by the blood of your neighbor." The Talmud (Sanhedrin 73a) goes a step further and argues from Deuteronomy 22:2, "and you shall give it back to him," that a bystander must go to extraordinary lengths to rescue someone in peril.

14. TNA: CAB-95/15, frames 152–153.

15. By mid-June messages from Budapest to friends in Switzerland were reporting that the Hungarian provinces were now "Jew free." Kasztner to Nathan [Schwalbe], June 14, 1944 and June 24, 1944, WRB: Box-66/Jews in Hungary.

16. Shlomo Aronson, "The 'Quadruple Trap' and the Holocaust in Hungary," in Cesarani, *Genocide and Rescue*, 106.

17. The British perception is especially clear in Interrogation of Andor Grosz, Cairo, June 6–22, 1944. TNA: FO-371/42811.

18. Deborah E. Lipstadt, *Beyond Belief: The American Press and the Coming of the Holocaust, 1933–1945* (New York: Free Press, 1986), 220–223.

19. Ben Hecht, *Perfidy* (New York: Messner, 1961), 191.

20. Ira Arthur Hirschmann, *Life Line to a Promised Land* (New York: Vanguard 1946), xv.

21. Tony Kushner, "The Meaning of Auschwitz: Anglo-American Responses to the Hungarian Jewish Tragedy," in Cesarani, *Genocide and Rescue*, 163; Yehuda Bauer and Nili Keren, *A History of the Holocaust* (New York: F. Watts, 1982), 317.

22. Draft telegram, May 30, 1944, TNA: CAB-95/Frames 169–171.

23. "State and WRB to Harriman," Moscow, July 5, 1944 (WRB), in John Mendelsohn and Donald S. Detwiler, *The Holocaust: Selected Documents in Eighteen Volumes* (New York: Garland, 1982), 15:186–191.

24. Viscount Halifax, War Cabinet Distribution from Washington to Foreign Office, June 22, 1944, TNA: CAB-95/15/F-180.

25. Hirschmann, *Life Line*, chap. 11; Brand and Weissberg, *Desperate Mission*, 181–184; "Interrogation of Mr. Joel Brandt [*sic*] by Mr. Ira Hirschmann, June 22, 1944," TNA: FO-371/42807.

26. "Interrogation of Mr. Joel Brandt [*sic*] by Mr. Ira Hirschmann, June 22, 1944." Hirschmann's account of the interview in Hirschmann, *Life Line*, seems to be based at least in part on information from the British interrogation of Brand, which Hirschmann would not have seen at the time of his own interview.

27. Brand and Weissberg, *Desperate Mission*, 184.

28. Hirschmann memo to Steinhardt, "Interview with Joel Brand, Observations and Recommendations," June 22, 1944. IHP: Box-3/Joel Brandt [*sic*]; Hirschmann diary, August 15, 1944. IHP: Box-1/Diary Feb.–Oct. 1944.

29. Shertok to Dr. Weismann, June 19, 1944. ILP: Box-52/Ira A. Hirschmann; Shertok to Ben-Gurion, June 30, 1944, CZA: z4/14870; Kasztner to Nathan [Schwalbe], June 26, 1944, and "Note by the Secretary of State for Foreign Affairs," June 26, 1944. WRB: Box-66.

30. Shertok memo, June 30, 1944. CZA: z4/14870; Pinkerton [American Consul-General, Jerusalem] to Secretary of State, July 11, 1944 (WRB), in Mendelsohn and Detwiler, *The Holocaust*, 15:203–204.

31. A. W. G. Randall [head of the Foreign Office Refugee Board] to Chaim Weizmann, June 24, 1944. CZA: z4/14870-1.

32 Eden memo, June 29, 1944, TNA: FO-371/42807; Cf. Tuvia Friling, *Ben Gurion Vehasho'ah* (Ph.D. dissertation, Hebrew University, Jerusalem, 1990), 299–307, quoted in Yehuda Bauer, *Jews for Sale? Nazi-Jewish Negotiations, 1933–1945* (New Haven, CT: Yale University Press, 1994), 187–188.

33. Embassy Moscow to Secretary of State, June 19, 1944, no. 2184. WRB: Box-79/Negotiations in Switzerland.

34. Lipstadt, *Beyond Belief,* 228.

35. Archbishop of Canterbury to Prime Minister, June 28, 1944. TNA: FO-371/42807.

36. Churchill to Anthony Eden, July 11, 1944; to Archbishop of Canterbury, July 13, 1944; to Lord Melchett, July 13, 1944. TNA: FO-371/42809.

37. Draft memo for interview granted by the Secretary of State to Deputation of National Committee for Rescue from Nazi Terror [archbishops of Canterbury, York, Westminster, moderator of the Church of Scotland, chief rabbi, MPs], July 26, 1944. TNA: FO-371/42811; Archbishop of Canterbury to BBC, June 28, 1944. TNA: FO-371/42807; Eden, March 10, 1944, JF (44). TNA: CAB-95/15.

38. Draft minute to the Prime Minister, July 16, 1944. TNA: FO-371/42809.

39. Full-page advertisement, *New York Times,* February 8, 1943, quoted in Tony Kushner, "The Meaning of Auschwitz: Anglo-American Responses to the Hungarian Jewish Tragedy," in Cesarani, *Genocide and Rescue,* 160.

40. Lipstadt, *Beyond Belief,* 225.

41. *Congressional Record,* June 19, 1944.

42. Martin [PM's office] to P. J. Dixon [FO], July 26, 1944, quoting Lord Halifax's telegram no. 2717 of May 24, 1944, TNA: FO-371/42811, 307.

43. Department of State Visa Department, confidential memorandum, May 7, 1943, quoted in Tony Kushner, "The Meaning of Auschwitz," in Cesarani, *Genocide and Rescue,* 161.

44. Brand and Weissberg, *Desperate Mission,* 188–191. The alleged remark was widely repeated in Palestine, and cited as motivation for the assassination of Lord Moyne by the Lehi group in November 1944. Brand later admitted that he learned that the man he spoke to was not Lord Moyne, but "another British statesman," and that Lord Moyne may have "paid with his life for the guilt of others." The entire story may be apocryphal, but the sentiments Brand attributed to Moyne reflect a viewpoint common in the British government at the time.

## 9. *The Lull*

1. Joel Brand and Alex Weissberg, *Desperate Mission: Joel Brand's Story* (New York: Criterion Books, 1958), 190.

2. [to Nathan Schwalbe], May 16, 1944. HA: 187/0032p/090/160544.

3. Quoted in Kurt Emenegger, "Reichsführer's Gehorsamster Becher," *Sie und Er,* January 17, 1963.

4. Rezső Kasztner, *Der Kasztner-Bericht über Eichmanns Menschenhandel in Ungarn* (Munich: Kindler, 1961), 96, 109–110. At Kasztner's trial in Jerusalem (1953) he testified that when he told Eichmann that a hundred human beings were

jammed into a single train compartment under unbearable conditions, Eichmann answered, "In the Karpato Ukraine, the Jews have innumerable little children. It will be possible there to jam even larger numbers into the compartments." Ben Hecht, *Perfidy* (New York: Messner, 1961), 60; Adolf Eichmann, Jochen von Lang, and Claus Sibyll, *Eichmann Interrogated: Transcripts from the Archives of the Israeli Police* (New York: Farrar Straus & Giroux, 1983), 208.

5. Hansi Brand testimony, ETT: Session 58-05; Becher confirmed Eichmann's fondness for liquor. "Interrogation of Kurt Becher," July 7, 1947, Nuremberg, in John Mendelsohn and Donald S. Detwiler, *The Holocaust: Selected Documents in Eighteen Volumes* (New York: Garland, 1982), 15:76; Kasztner, *Kasztner-Bericht*, 110, 127.

6. Eichmann, Lang, and Sibyll, *Eichmann Interrogated*, 260.

7. "Confessions of Adolf Eichmann," *Life* 49, no. 23 (Dec. 5, 1960): 146.

8. Kasztner to Schwalbe, June 12 and 13, 1944. HA: 187/0032p/090; Kasztner to Schwalbe, June 14, 1944, and June 24, 1944. WRB: Box-66/Jews in Hungary; Kasztner [postscript from Hansi Brand] to Wenja, August 15, 1944. HA: 187/0032p/090/150844; David Cesarani, *Becoming Eichmann: Rethinking the Life, Crimes, and Trial of a "Desk Murderer"* (Cambridge, MA: Da Capo Press, 2006), 179–180.

9. Cesarani, *Becoming Eichmann*, 182.

10. There are multiple copies of the report in different subfolders of WRB: Box-66/Jews in Hungary.

11. Yitzhak Gruenbaum to the Rescue Committee, June 29, 1944. CZA: s/26/1327.

12. Sternbuch to Union of Orthodox Rabbis, May 25, 1944. WRB: Box-70/UOR; G. Farley to Ben Gurion, July 11, 1944. CZA: s25/5206/48; Martin Gilbert, *Auschwitz and the Allies* (New York: Holt Rinehart and Winston, 1981), 190–191, 222.

13. August 25, 1944. WRB: Box-66/Jews in Hungary/August 1944; Michael Mockford, http://news.bbc.co.uk/2/hi/uk_news/7457795.stm; Richard Foregger "Two Sketch Maps of the Auschwitz-Birkenau Extermination Camps," *Journal of Military History* 59, no. 4 (Oct. 1995): 687–696.

14. Michael Makovsky, *Churchill's Promised Land: Zionism and Statecraft* (New Haven, CT: Yale University Press, 2007), 181–182.

15. Foreign Office to Prime Minister, July 6, 1944, and Air Ministry to Eden, July 15, 1944. TNA: FO-371/42809. Bombing proposals were turned down as early as June 1944; on July 3, Eden dismissively declared that the argument was over, that they were already bombing Budapest. Berne to FO, June 26, 1944, and Eden to Churchill, July 3, 1944. TNA: FO-371/42807.

16. David S. Wyman, *The Abandonment of the Jews: America and the Holocaust, 1941–1945* (New York: New Press, 1998), 297–306.

17. Shertok to Kaplan [Jewish Agency, Jerusalem], July 29, 1944. HA: 187/0032p/090/290744.

18. Kasztner to Schwalbe, June 14, 1944. WRB: Box-66/Jews in Hungary.

19. Itzhak Gruenbaum to Shertok, June 29, 1944. CZA: z4/14879; McClelland to Saly Mayer, June 28, 1944. WRB: Box-66/Jews in Hungary; Kinga Frojimovics and Géza Komoróczy, *Jewish Budapest: Monuments, Rites, History* (Budapest: Central European University Press, 1999), 382–383.

20. Hansi Brand testimony, ETT: Session 58-05; McClelland memo, June 30, 1944. No. 4170. WRB: Box-66/Jews in Hungary.

21. Randolph L. Braham, "The Holocaust in Hungary: A Retrospective Analysis," in David Cesarani, *Genocide and Rescue: The Holocaust in Hungary 1944* (Oxford: Berg, 1997), 31.

22. Ribbentrop to Veesenmayer, July 17, 1944. NA: T120/1757/E025082–5.

23. Felix Kersten, *The Kersten Memoirs, 1940–1945* (London: Hutchinson, 1956), 162–163.

24. Peter Padfield, *Himmler: Reichsführer-SS* (New York: Holt, 1991), 419–424.

25. NA: RG-242/T-175/R-94/F-2615074; Richard Breitman, "Nazi Jewish Policy in 1944," in Cesarani, *Genocide and Rescue*, 76.

26. Ibid., 79.

## 10. Revelation

1. JAE Executive meeting, July 23, 1944. CZA: JAE-25/544.

2. Quoted in Idith Zertal, *Israel's Holocaust and the Politics of Nationhood*, trans. Chaya Galai, *Cambridge Middle East Studies 21* (Cambridge & New York: Cambridge University Press, 2005), 51, fn. 127.

3. Catherine Senesh, "The Mission: Meeting in Budapest," Hannah Senesh, *Hannah Senesh: Her Life and Diary* (Woodstock, VT: Jewish Lights, 2004), 277.

4. [London] *Times*, July 20, 1944; Winant [U.S. Embassy, London] to Secretary of State, July 20, 1944 (WRB). in John Mendelsohn and Donald S. Detwiler, *The Holocaust: Selected Documents in Eighteen Volumes* (New York: Garland, 1982), 15:221–222.

5. Quoted in Ben Hecht, *Perfidy* (New York: Messner, 1961), 209.

6. Altenburg to Veesenmayer, July 20, 1944, nr. 1557. NA: T-120/4203/E025305; Veesenmayer to Ribbentrop, July 22, 1944, nr. 2055. NA: T-120/4203/E025306; Weber to Steengracht, July 26, 1944; Veesenmayer to German F.O., July 28, 1944, in Randolph L. Braham and World Federation of Hungarian Jews, *The Destruction of Hungarian Jewry: A Documentary Account* (New York: Pro Arte for the World Federation of Hungarian Jews, 1963), 2:629.

7. See Harrison to McClelland, July 20, 1944. WRB: Box-66/Jews in Hungary.

8. A. Brodie to Eden, July 20, 1944. TNA: FO-371/42811, 145.

9. Joel Brand and Alex Weissberg, *Desperate Mission: Joel Brand's Story* (New York: Criterion Books, 1958), 187.

10. Michael Makovsky, *Churchill's Promised Land: Zionism and Statecraft* (New Haven, CT: Yale University Press, 2007), 184. Lord Moyne to Foreign Office [copies to Washington, Jerusalem, Ankara], July 29, 1944. TNA: FO-371/42811, 265.

11. Apolinari Hartglass, "Comments on Aid and Rescue," [undated, ca. 1943], CZA: S/26 1306. Portions of this memo (cited to a different folder in the CZA) are quoted in Segev, *The Seventh Million: The Israelis and the Holocaust* (New York: Henry Holt, 1991), 99–100.

12. Brand and Weissberg, *Desperate Mission*, 191.

13. Ibid., 194–195.

14. Hirschmann, "Memorandum of Conversation with Mr. Joel Brand in Jerusalem on October 7, 1944," October 10, 1944 (WRB), in Mendelsohn and Detwiler, *The Holocaust*, 15:247–249.

15. Secretary of State to Am. Embassy, Moscow, July 7, 1944 and HM Ambassador, Moscow to M. Molotov, July 18, 1944 (WRB), in Ibid., 15:195–199, 206–208.

16. Kasztner to Nathan Schwalbe, July 12, 1944. HA: 187/0032p/090/120744.

17. Kasztner to [Nathan Schwalbe, Geneva], June 18, 1944. HA: Brand/Kasztner; Rezső Kasztner, *Der Kasztner-Bericht über Eichmanns Menschenhandel in Ungarn* (Munich: Kindler, 1961), 130.

18. Yehuda Bauer, *Jews for Sale? Nazi-Jewish Negotiations, 1933–1945* (New Haven, CT: Yale University Press, 1994), 198.

19. Quoted in Anna Porter, *Kasztner's Train: The True Story of an Unknown Hero of the Holocaust* (New York: Walker, 2008), 184.

20. Kasztner affidavit [n.d.]. HA: 187/0032p/090.

21. Quoted in Randolph L. Braham, *The Politics of Genocide: The Holocaust in Hungary* (New York: Columbia University Press, 1981), 2:838.

22. Kasztner, *Kasztner-Bericht*, 130–131.

23. Ibid., 134.

24. "Summary of a Report sent by the General Federation of Jewish Labor, Tel Aviv," received in Istanbul July 1, 1944, sent to Shertok, September 8, 1944. NA: RG-226/E-1/B-1.

25. See Nathan Schwalbe's translation into German of a Hebrew letter sent from Bratislava, July 6, 1944. WRB: Box-66/Jews in Hungary.

26. Quoted in Szabolcs Szita and Sean Lambert, *Trading in Lives? Operations of the Jewish Relief and Rescue Committee in Budapest, 1944–1945* (Budapest: Central European University Press, 2005), 90.

## 11. The Bridge at Sankt Margrethen

1. In a 1903 letter to Ernö Mezei, a respected Hungarian Jewish politician.

2. To Nathan Schwalbe, July 12, 1944. HA: 187/0032p/090/120744.

3. Kinga Frojimovics and Géza Komoróczy, *Jewish Budapest: Monuments, Rites, History* (Budapest: Central European University Press, 1999), 386.

4. McClelland memo, August 11, 1944, No. 5197. WRB: Box-66/Jews in Hungary.

5. Interrogation of Kurt Becher, July 19, 1947, Nuremberg War Crimes Trial Interrogations. NA: M-1019/R-5/F-534

6. Deborah E. Lipstadt, *Beyond Belief: The American Press and the Coming of the Holocaust, 1933–1945* (New York: Free Press, 1986), 237.

7. WRB daily report, July 10–15, 1944, in David S. Wyman, *America and the Holocaust* (New York: Garland, 1989), 11:247–248.

8. Eichmann to RSHA, July 24, 1944. Hermann Göring and International Military Tribunal, *Trial of the Major War Criminals Before the International Military Tribunal, Nuremberg, 14 November 1945–1 October 1946* (Nuremberg, Germany: [s.n.], 1947), NG series, 1806; Ribbentrop to Veesenmayer, July 7, 1944. NA: T120/4203/E420969; Veesenmayer to Ribbentrop, July 9, 1944. NA: T120/1757/E025088-9. I'm indebted for the last two references to Yehuda Bauer, *Jews for Sale? Nazi-Jewish Negotiations, 1933–1945* (New Haven, CT: Yale University Press, 1994).

9. Veesenmayer to Foreign Office, August 14, 1944. NA: T120/4355/E422278–9; Veesenmayer to Foreign Office, July 25, 1944. NA: T120/4355/E4221778-9; Ribbentrop to Veesenmayer, July 17, 1944. NA: T120/1757/E025082-5;

10. Esther 3:13; Frojimovics and Komoróczy, *Jewish Budapest*, 383.

11. Gideon Hausner, *Justice in Jerusalem* (New York: Harper & Row, 1966), 150.

12. Becher to Himmler and Telegram, Himmler to Becher, both August 25, 1944, in Randolph L. Braham and World Federation of Hungarian Jews, *The Destruction of Hungarian Jewry: A Documentary Account* (New York: Pro Arte for the World Federation of Hungarian Jews, 1963), 2:635–637; Kasztner and Komoly to Schwalbe, July 28, 1944. WRB: Box-66/Jews in Hungary; Kasztner's notes of the meetings, translated from Hungarian to Hebrew by Dov Dinur, in Bauer, *Jews for Sale*, 216–218.

13. "Special Negotiations with the Gestapo and SS for Saving the Jews of Europe," January 17, 1945. WRB: Box-78/Saly Mayer Negotiations.

14. Andreas Biss, *A Million Jews to Save: Check to the Final Solution* (London: Hutchinson, 1973), 47.

15. Hull to McClelland, July 10, 1944. WRB: Box-66/Jews in Hungary.

16. McClelland memo, August 11, 1944, No. 5197; Schwartz memo, August 7, 1944. WRB: Box-66/Jews in Hungary.

17. McClelland to Mayer, July 12, 194; McClelland to Washington, August 1,

1944, no. 4197. WRB Box-66/Jews in Hungary. In handwritten notes on a June 1944 conversation with Saly Mayer in the same folder, an American official in Switzerland wrote the word "ransom" in oversized letters and underlined it.

18. June 30, 1944. TNA: FO-371/42807.

19. July 1, 1944. TNA: FO-371/42808.

20. July 18, 1944. TNA: FO-371/42809; British Embassy, Washington to G. Warren, Department of State, July 18, 1944 (WRB) in John Mendelsohn and Donald S. Detwiler, *The Holocaust: Selected Documents in Eighteen Volumes* (New York: Garland, 1982), 15:206–208.

21. In 1938 Rothmund persuaded the Germans to issue passports with a red letter *J* for German Jews to distinguish them from other Germans; he favored the new passports because it enabled the Swiss to identify (and discriminate against) German Jewish refugees.

22. Genesis 14:14. Kasztner claimed that the release of the 318 from Bergen-Belsen was the first time the Third Reich had allowed an organized group to depart to a neutral country. Rezső Kasztner, *Der Kasztner-Bericht über Eichmanns Menschenhandel in Ungarn* (Munich: Kindler, 1961), 13.

23. McClelland to WRB, August 25, 1944, No. 5588, and "Conversation with SM" [handwritten], August 27, 1944. WRB: Box-66/Jews of Hungary.

24. Kasztner claimed that Brand's relatives were excluded from the 318 on Eichmann's explicit orders. Kasztner, *Kasztner-Bericht*, 173.

25. Marcus Wyler to Saly Mayer, August 14, 1944 and August 23, 1944, WRB: Box-66/Jews in Hungary. A handwritten note in the WRB archives says there were 320 on the train, ranging in age from 2 to 82, including two distinguished rabbis.

26. "Notes on conversations with SM," August 23, 1944, and August 27, 1944. WRB: Box-66/Jews in Hungary.

27. Becher later claimed that he reported to Himmler in person on August 24, and confirmed his report with a written memo the next day. YV: Becher Testimony/9104, xiv; Braham and World Federation of Hungarian Jews, *Destruction*, 2:481, 635–637; Kasztner, *Kasztner-Bericht*, 173. Bauer argues that it was unlikely that Becher waited a full four days, and that he may have telephoned earlier. Bauer, *Jews for Sale*, 221, 287.

28. Kasztner, *Kasztner-Bericht*, 217.

29. Hannah Senesh's poetry, coupled with her martyrdom, has had a long-standing impact, especially in the United States. The Reconstructionist high holiday prayer book, first published in 1948, substitutes a poem by Hannah Senesh for the *Eleh Ezkerah*, the long paean in the Yom Kippur liturgy to rabbis tortured and executed by the Romans. Hasia Diner, "Before 'the Holocaust': American Jews Confront Catastrophe, 1945–1962" (unpub., 2006, courtesy of the author).

30. Veesenmayer to Ribbentrop and Ritter, April 3, 1944. IMT: NG/2234 cited in Bauer, *Jews for Sale*, 222.

31. Werner Grothmann, Himmler's adjutant, later testified at Nuremberg that Himmler ordered the end of deportations from Budapest because of Becher's report. Ibid., 287; Veesenmayer to Wagner, August 24, 1944; Veesenmayer to Ribbentrop, August 25, 1944. NA: T120/4355/E422180–1.

## 12. Endgame

1. "Confessions of Adolf Eichmann," *Life* 49, no. 22 (Nov. 28, 1960): 106.

2. Hirschmann diary, October 10, 1944. IHP: Box-1/Diary Feb.-Oct. 1944; Hirschmann, "Memorandum of Conversation with Mr. Joel Brand in Jerusalem on October 7, 1944," October 10, 1944 (WRB), in John Mendelsohn and Donald S. Detwiler, *The Holocaust: Selected Documents in Eighteen Volumes* (New York: Garland, 1982), 15:247–249.

3. Joel Brand, "Dringende Vorschläge betr. Hazallah," November 19, 1944. CZA: s25/5206/248–249; [Ludwig Kastner,] "Allgemeiner Bericht an Agudas Israel," August 1, 1944. YV: 033/3311/a, 36.

4. Brand would later do that same imitation at the Eichmann trial. ETT, Session 56-03.

5. [Isaac] Sternbuch to Union of Orthodox Rabbis of the USA, April 1944. WRB: Box-70/UOR; *Sie und Er*, Oct. 5, 1961, cited in Yehuda Bauer, *Jews for Sale? Nazi-Jewish Negotiations, 1933–1945* (New Haven, CT: Yale University Press, 1994), 287. Sternbuch to McClelland, July 20, 1944. WRB: Box-66/Jews in Hungary/July 1944/2.

6. McClelland memo, August 5, 1944. No. 5023. WRB: Box-66/Jews in Hungary. Saly Mayer also had a stormy relationship with Truempy. See the handwritten memo to the file after a conversation with Saly Mayer, August 30, 1944. WRB: Box-66/Jews in Hungary.

7. Marcus Wyler to Saly Mayer, August 24, 1944, and "Memo on Whole Tractor Affair," July 21–22, 1944. WRB: Box-66/Jews of Hungary; McClelland to Sternbuch, August 18, 1944, and Harrison telegrams, July 26 and 29, 1944. WRB: Box-70/UOR.

8. "Marcus Wyler's Note re Negotiations with Becher," August 1, 1944, and WRB [signed by Hull] to McClelland & Harrison, August 30, 1944, No. 2990. WRB: Box-66/Jews in Hungary.

9. Judah Magnes to [Eliezer] Kaplan, September 8, 1944. HA: 187/0032p/090/080944; Joel Brand and Alex Weissberg, *Desperate Mission: Joel Brand's Story* (New York: Criterion Books, 1958), 259–260.

10. P. Mason to P. Malin, December 7, 1944. TNA: FO-371/42897.

11. Adolf Eichmann, Jochen von Lang, and Claus Sibyll, *Eichmann Interrogated. Transcripts from the Archives of the Israeli Police* (New York: Farrar Straus & Giroux, 1983), 241.

12. Ronald W. Zweig, *The Gold Train: The Destruction of the Jews and the Second World War's Most Terrible Robbery* (London: Allen Lane, 2002), 68, 73, 85, 89.

13. István Deák and others have challenged the validity of this figure. On Becher's evacuation of property from Hungary see Gábor Kádár and Zoltán Vági, *Self-Financing Genocide: the Gold Train, the Becher Case and the Wealth of Hungarian Jews* (Budapest: Central European University Press, 2004), 244–249.

14. See, for example, the anonymous memo to file ["Jews in Europe: Musy Affair, inter alia"], January 26, 1945. WRB: Box 70/UOR/Becher.

15. Rezső Kasztner, *Der Kasztner-Bericht über Eichmanns Menschenhandel in Ungarn* (Munich: Kindler, 1961), 176.

16. "Preliminary Report re Activities in Turkey, 7/18/44–8/19/44," September 11, 1944. IHP: Box-2.

17. On the annihilation of the Slovakian Jews, see the handwritten memo to the file after a conversation with Saly Mayer, August 30, 1944. WRB: Box-66/Jews in Hungary; Brand and Weissberg, *Desperate Mission*, 261.

18. Andreas Biss, *A Million Jews to Save: Check to the Final Solution* (London: Hutchinson, 1973), 127–130.

19. Marcus Wyler did not trust Kasztner and thought him a hothead. Wyler to Mayer, August 24, 1944. WRB: Box-66/Jews in Hungary.

20. Kasztner, *Kasztner-Bericht*, 178; "Dr. Marcus Wyler's Note re Negotiations with Becher," August 8, 1944. WRB: Box-66/Jews in Hungary/General Correspondence/McClelland's File; JDC documents, cited in Bauer, *Jews for Sale*, 224.

21. McClelland to Bigelow, March 23, 1945. WRB: Box-70/UOR/McClelland-Musy; Alain Dieckhoff, "Une action de sauvetage des Juifs européens en 1944–1945: 'L'Affaire Musy,'" *Revue d'Histoire Moderne et Contemporaine* (1989), 2: 291; Becher testimony, June 22, 1948, Nuremberg Testimonies. YV: 2710-c/062248.

22. "Special Negotiations with the Gestapo and SS for Saving the Jews of Europe," January 17, 1945. WRB: Box-78/Saly Mayer's Negotiations in Switzerland; "Jews in Europe: Musy Affair, inter alia," January 26, 1945. WRB: Box 70/UOR/Becher.

23. "Special Negotiations with the Gestapo and SS for Saving the Jews of Europe," January 17, 1945. WRB: Box-78/Saly Mayer's Negotiations in Switzerland.

24. Stettinius to WRB, November 18, 1944. WRB: Box-78/Saly Mayer's Negotiations in Switzerland.

25. Bauer, *Jews for Sale*, 226; Biss, *A Million Jews to Save*, 159.

26. Juettner testimony, ETT: Testimony-Abroad/Hans-Juettner-01 and Session 85-05; see also Kasztner, *Kasztner-Bericht*, 274.

27. Quoted in Kinga Frojimovics and Géza Komoróczy, *Jewish Budapest: Monuments, Rites, History* (Budapest: Central European University Press, 1999), 371.

28. Harrison to Secretary of State, October 23, 1944. NA: RG-226/E-191/B-1; Hansi Brand testimony, ETT: Session 58-05.

29. Stettinius to Harrison and McClelland, November 18, 1944. WRB: Box-78/Saly Mayer's Negotiations.

30. McClelland to WRB, December 9, 1944. WRB: No. 8045; WRB to McClelland, November 28, 1944. WRB: No. 4014; Bauer, *Jews for Sale*, 228.

31. Veesenmayer to Berlin, November 20, 1944, nr 3353. NA: T120/3237/E548787; Becher testimony. YV: (1945) 9104, p. xvii; Zweig, *The Gold Train*, 97-98; Kasztner, *Kasztner-Bericht*, 223, 233; Kádár and Vági, *Self-Financing Genocide*, 221-223.

32. Kasztner, *Kasztner-Bericht*, 244; Eichmann, Lang, and Sibyll, *Eichmann Interrogated*, 254.

33. Brand's mother died. The granddaughter remembered being transferred into a neighboring Dutch enclosure where she met a young girl about her own age—Anne Frank. Anna Porter, *Kasztner's Train: The True Story of an Unknown Hero of the Holocaust* (New York: Walker, 2008), 268–269.

34. "Special Negotiations with the Gestapo and SS for Saving the Jews of Europe," January 17, 1945. WRB: Box-78/Saly Mayer's Negotiations in Switzerland.

35. WRB to McClellan, December 19, 1944; McClelland to WRB, December 28, 1944, No. 4273. WRB: Box-66/Jews in Hungary.

36. "Report of an Interview with Mr. Sternbuch on Friday, January 19th 1945," WRB: Box-79/UOR/Musy Affair.

37. Himmler note, January 18, 1945, YV: 0-51/DN-39/2119; Biss, *A Million Jews to Save*, 255.

38. Quoted in Porter, *Kasztner's Train*, 271.

39. Interrogation Reports from the Palestinian Camp at Athlit [undated, but probably 1946–47]. NA: RG-226/E-190/B-76/Hungarian Desk.

40. McClelland memo, August 11, 1944, No. 5197. WRB: Box-66/Jews in Hungary.

41. See http://www.haaretz.com/hasen/pages/ShArt.jhtml?itemNo=789726.

42. Interrogation Reports from the Palestinian Camp at Athlit [Joseph Martin, an American CIC agent in plainclothes was at the camp]. NA: RG-226/E-190/Box-76/Hungarian Desk.

43. Bauer, *Jews for Sale*, 236–237; Biss, *A Million Jews to Save*, 255. Like many

of Biss's stories, this one is uncorroborated. Steiger demanded the balance of the promised money from the JDC after the war and did not get it.

44. Porter, *Kasztner's Train*, 281–282.

## 13. Aftermath

1. *Zionist Review*, Sept. 22, 1944, quoted in Yehuda Bauer, *The Holocaust in Historical Perspective* (Seattle: University of Washington Press, 1978), 28–29.

2. Concluding remarks at the Kasztner trial, quoted in Ben Hecht, *Perfidy* (New York: Messner, 1961), 229.

3. Grew to McClelland, March 23, 1945. WRB: Box-70/UOR

4. Kennan to State Department, January 29, 1945. WRB: Box-79/Negotiations in Switzerland.

5. "Affidavit of Dieter Wisliceny," United States. Office of Chief of Counsel for the Prosecution of Axis Criminality. et al., *Nazi Conspiracy and Aggression . . . Office of United States Chief of Counsel for Prosecution of Axis Criminality* (Washington, DC: U.S. Government Printing Office, 1946), 8:606–607.

6. Peter Maguire, *Law and War: An American Story* (New York: Columbia University Press, 2000), 285.

7. Becher and Kasztner testimony, July 10, 1947. YV: Nuremberg testimony, No. 929 Becher 070747, 19–23; Affidavit, Tel Aviv, February 6, 1957, quoted in Hecht, *Perfidy*, 81.

8. Becher testimony, Nuremberg, April 12, 1946, http://www.nizkor.org/hweb/imt/tgmwc/tgmwc-11/tgmwc-11-106-08.shtml.

9. Kasztner affidavit, n.d. HA: 187-0032p-090; Gábor Kádár and Zoltán Vági, *Self-Financing Genocide: The Gold Train, the Becher Case and the Wealth of Hungarian Jews* (Budapest: Central European University Press, 2004), 235f.

10. Anna Porter, *Kasztner's Train: The True Story of an Unknown Hero of the Holocaust* (New York: Walker, 2008), 159, 226.

11. Quoted in Tom Segev, *The Seventh Million: The Israelis and the Holocaust*, 1st ed. (New York: Hill and Wang, 1993), 98–99.

12. Idith Zertal, *Israel's Holocaust and the Politics of Nationhood*, trans. Chaya Galai, *Cambridge Middle East Studies* 21 (Cambridge & New York: Cambridge University Press, 2005), 28–36.

13. Quoted in Segev, *The Seventh Million*, 184.

14. According to Susan Hibbert, who typed the message, Eisenhower's staff "groped for resounding phrases as fitting accolades to the Great Crusade and indicative of our dedication to the great task just completed." Eisenhower insisted on keeping it simple. http://news.bbc.co.uk/2/hi/europe/4497947.stm.

15. Brand to Hirschmann, May 2, 1945. IHP: Box-2/Correspondence, 1943–1955; Telegram, May 12, 1945 and Hodel [WRB] to Leavitt [American JDC], May 19, 1945, and Brand to Hirschmann, October 3, 1950. WRB: Box-26/Joel Brand.

16. Dec. 29, 1944. Quoted in Hecht, *Perfidy*, 229.

17. Teddy Kollek and Amos Kollek, *For Jerusalem: A Life* (London: Weidenfeld and Nicolson, 1978), 52.

18. Porter, *Kasztner's Train*, 317; Segev, *The Seventh Million*, 473.

19. Quoted in Hecht, *Perfidy*, 109–110.

20. Segev, *The Seventh Million*, 257; Zertal, *Israel's Holocaust and the Politics of Nationhood*, 81–82.

21. Hecht, *Perfidy*, 60–61.

22. Ibid., 109.

23. Segev, *The Seventh Million*, 265n.

24. Hecht, *Perfidy*, 219.

25. Ibid., 221.

26. Segev, *The Seventh Million*, 280.

27. In *Pesachim* 25b, a man tells Rabbi Rava the governor of his town has ordered him to murder an innocent man, and has warned that if he does not do so he will be killed. "Let yourself be killed but do not kill him," rules Rava. "Who says your blood is redder? Perhaps the blood of that man is redder."

28. *Bi-Shelihut nidonim la-mavet* [A mission on behalf of the sentenced to death] (Tel Aviv: 'Ayanot, 1956); Joel Brand and Alex Weissberg, *Die Geschichte von Joel Brand* (Köln: Kiepenheuer & Witsch, 1956); Joel Brand and Hansi Brand, *Ha-Satan Veha-Nefesh* [The devil and the soul] (Tel Aviv: Ladori, 1960); Segev, *The Seventh Million*, 473.

29. ETT: Session-086-03; Gideon Hausner, *Justice in Jerusalem* (New York: Harper & Row, 1966), 358.

30. ETT: Judgement-036.

31. Ben-Gurion to Tom Segev and two friends, April 1968. Segev, *The Seventh Million*, 467–469

# INDEX